LIBRARY OF .... OF ....

VOLUME I

The History of Ideas:
Canon and Variations

LIBRARY OF THE HISTORY OF IDEAS

ISSN 1050–1053

Series Editor: JOHN W. YOLTON

THE
HISTORY OF IDEAS
CANON AND VARIATIONS

Edited by
DONALD R. KELLEY

UNIVERSITY OF ROCHESTER PRESS

This collection first published 1990
Reissued in hardback and paperback 1994

University of Rochester Press
34-36 Administration Building, University of Rochester
Rochester, New York 14627, USA
and at PO Box 9, Woodbridge, Suffolk IP12 3DF, UK

ISBN   1 878822 00 4 Hardback
ISBN   1 878822 40 3 Paperback

Library of Congress Catalog Card Number 91-190844

This publication is printed on acid-free paper

Printed in the United States of America

TABLE OF CONTENTS

PART THREE: QUESTIONS

ACKNOWLEDGEMENTS

The articles in this volume first appeared in the *Journal of the History of Ideas* as indicated below, by volume, year and pages, in order.

Crocker, Lester G., "Interpreting the Enlightenment: A Political Approach", 46 (1985) 211–230.

Duffin, Kathleen E., "Arthur O. Lovejoy and the Emergence of Novelty", 41 (1980) 267–281.

Edel, Abraham, "Levels of Meaning and the History of Ideas", 7 (1946) 355–360.

Huizinga, Johann, "History Changing Form", 4 (1943) 217–223.

Hutton, Patrick H., "The Art of Memory Reconceived: From Rhetoric to Psychoanalysis", 48 (1987) 371–392.

Katz, Joseph, "A Reply to J. Huizinga on the Form and Function of History", 5 (1944) 369–373.

Kelly, Donald R., "Horizons of Intellectual History: Retrospect, Circumspect, Prospect", 48 (1987) 143–169.

Krieger, Leonard, "The Autonomy of Intellectual History", 34 (1973) 499–516.

Kristeller, Paul O., "The Philosophical Significance of the History of Thought", 7 (1946) 360–366.

Kristeller, Paul O., " 'Creativity' and 'Tradition' ", 44 (1983) 105–113.

Kvastad, Nils B., "Semantics in the Methodology of the History of Ideas", 38 (1977) 157–174.

Lovejoy, Arthur O., "Reflections on the History of Ideas", 1 (1940) 3–23.

Lovejoy, Arthur O., "Reply to Professor Spitzer", 5 (1944) 204–219.

Lovejoy, Arthur O., "Historiography and Evaluation: A Disclaimer", 10 (1949) 141–142.

Mahoney, Edward P., "Lovejoy and the Hierarchy of Being", 48 (1987) 211–230.

Mazzeo, Joseph Anthony, "Some Interpretations of the History of Ideas", 33 (1972) 379–394.

Oakley, Francis, "Lovejoy's Unexplored Option", 48 (1987) 231–245.

Rand, Calvin G., "Two Meanings of Historicism in the Writings of Dilthey, Troeltsch, and Meinecke", 25 (1964) 503–518.

Spencer, Theodore, "Lovejoy's 'Essays in the History of Ideas' ", 9 (1948) 439–446.

Spitzer, Leo, "Geistesgeschichte vs. History of Ideas as applied to Hitlerism", 5 (1944) 191–203.

Teggart, Frederick J., "A Problem in the History of Ideas", 1 (1940) 494–503.

Wiener, Philip P., "Logical Significance of the History of Thought", 7 (1946) 366–373.

Wilson, Daniel J., "Arthur O. Lovejoy and the Moral of 'The Great Chain of Being' ", 41 (1980) 249–265.

Wilson, Daniel J., "Lovejoy's 'The Great Chain of Being' after Fifty Years", 48 (1987) 187–206.

Chapter I

INTRODUCTION: REFLECTIONS ON A CANON

By Donald R. Kelley

"The history of ideas itself has a history," Joseph Mazzeo remarked, and indeed its canon, bound up as it has been with the history of philosophy, may be traced back at least as far as Plato and Aristotle's critique of their predecessors. In this country, however, the history of ideas is associated above all with the work of Arthur O. Lovejoy, his colleagues, his epigones, and his constructive critics, and with the *Journal of the History of Ideas*, which (just now entering its second half-century) is largely his creation. The centerpiece of the canon and the manifesto of this movement, which in recent years has become virtually a sub-discipline, is Lovejoy's own masterpiece, *The Great Chain of Being* (published in 1936), which has not only illuminated one of the major ideas of western thought but also has cast a very long shadow over the practice of intellectual history in the past two generations far beyond the confines of the *Journal* itself.

According to Lovejoy's original conception, the history of ideas was an interdisciplinary undertaking, designed to encompass a variety of fields of study. In one moment of intellectual euphoria he listed twelve such areas ready for settlement: the history of philosophy, the history of science, folklore and ethnography, some parts of the history of language, the history of religious beliefs, literary history, "what is unhappily called comparative literature," the history of the arts, economic history, the history of education, political and social history, and the historical part of sociology. Yet despite this extraordinarily eclectic agenda, Lovejoy remained a philosopher, convinced of the "existence," the persistence, and the temporal mobility of ideas; and indeed much of the later criticism of his methods centered on his ill-concealed (though allegedly "critical") idealism, which is to say his notion of "unit-ideas" as the common currency of these areas of study and the vehicles of intellectual historiography. In historical perspective Lovejoy's position resembled nothing so much as the early nineteenth-century Eclectic school of Victor Cousin, a philosopher who was likewise endebted to German conceptions, was attached to an interdisciplinary and historical approach, and was enamored of neo- or crypto-Platonic "ideas."

In the first issue of the *Journal* Lovejoy issued another manifesto (ch. IIa, continuing the discussion begun in the first chapter of his *Great Chain*), again protesting the excesses of specialization, calling for the interdisciplinary study of culture as a means of achieving historical self-knowledge (the "Delphian imperative"), designating "ideas" as the defining characteristic of humanity, and offering the new *JHI* as a "liaison" between particular humanistic fields of research and writing. Among the areas especially deserving of examination in such historical terms he pointed to the influence of the classical tradition; of philosophy on literature, arts, religion, and social thought; of science on thought and culture; and of particular doctrines, including evolution, progress, primitivism, and various notions of the individual and society. From the study of human efforts in these areas one may find an answer to the question not only of what humanity has accomplished but also (recalling especially the cultural mood and ideological threats of the late 1930s, when Lovejoy was writing) of "What's the matter with man?"

In this "rethinking of intellectual history" Lovejoy distinguished the history of ideas from the history of literature (which has figured so importantly in his own publications), but he acknowledged the significance of problems of value, especially of aesthetic value—questions that lay at the heart of the debates over the "new criticism" and the role of history (if any) in the understanding of literature and, inversely, the role of a literary creation in understanding an author. Lovejoy's own characteristically eclectic view was that aesthetic experience and knowledge of historical context were reconcilable and indeed interdependent. History was not "value-free," and literature and art have social as well as psychological and aesthetic functions. He repeated this point in a response to the reservations expressed by Theodore Spencer (ch. IVa) about what he regarded as Lovejoy's undervaluation of—or rather historicist conception of—the aesthetic dimension.

Lovejoy acknowledged, too, the existence of non-rational and "extra-logical" forces, social (and *wissensoziologisch*) and cultural as well as psychological and affective, and he posited a sort of periodic "oscillation" between intellectualist and anti-intellectualist tendencies—between classicism and romanticism, for example— a suggestion to which at least one more rationalist critic took exception. For Frederick Teggart (ch. IIb) "oscillation" suggested old theories of cycles and "recurrences"; and he reminded Lovejoy of alternative views, especially that of Progress, of "advancement," which have also been employed to give "meaning" to the history of ideas—and which likewise need critical examination. In response Lovejoy denied commitment to any particular doctrine (and the openness of the *Journal* to a variety of "opinions" on the matter), and he reaffirmed his faith in the primacy of reason (and in effect of his own field, philosophy), in the independent life of ideas, and in the study of history, if not in history itself.

A more serious challenge was mounted by the philologist and literary historian Leo Spitzer (ch. IIIa), who questioned the historical validity of Lovejoy's conception of "unit-ideas." Spitzer rejected the notion of "unemotional" and unchanging ideas, which he attributed to Lovejoy, and especially the logical, algebraic, or even "chemical" methods (and units of particular "-isms") which they implied. Employing the hard test case of Nazism and the allegedly contributory ideas produced in earlier German history (especially the Romantic School), Spitzer rejected naturalistic models of interpretation and argued that ideas were transformed with passing time and changing cultural climates. In a longer view this appeared to be another skirmish in the long war between philology, or rhetoric, and philosophy. Spitzer's critique opposed his own "historical semantics" to Lovejoy's "philosophical semantics"; and though fashioned in terms of an incendiary ideological issue, Spitzer's protest was very much like the "meta-critique" brought by Herder (and before him Hamann) against Kant. According to Spitzer, Lovejoy, for all his concern with literature and language, had missed the linguistic turn, and his idealism, according to Spitzer, was inappropriate for perceiving and appreciating the configurations of cultural change. In his response (ch. IIIb) Lovejoy recognized this as a fundamental difference of methodology but reaffirmed the validity of his "analytical" method.

A new generation of historians of ideas has made Lovejoy himself, as well as his view of ideas, the object of critical and historical study. Daniel Wilson (ch. VIIIa), commenting on the "moral" of Lovejoy's great study of the great chain of being, showed the tension between Lovejoy's roles as historian and as philosopher—between his dualistic conception of temporal change and his search for rational intelligibility. In contrast to Hegel, Lovejoy regarded the process of Becoming not only as the fulfillment but also as the undoing of Being, as a source not only of pluralistic hope but also of metaphysical tragedy. Kathleen Duffin (ch. VIIIb), emphasizing the importance of Lovejoy's philosophical premises, his own "endemic assumptions," in his conception of intellectual history, pointed out the ways in which Lovejoy's evolutionary perspective, much like that of Henri Bergson, accommodated and even promoted ideas of "novelty," while rejecting vulgar and deterministic notions of "causality" which would "explain" the future.

In an issue of the *Journal* reviewing the fortunes of *The Great Chain of Being* a half-century after its appearance, Wilson, Edward P. Mahoney, and Francis Oakley (ch. IX) summarized various criticisms of the book, the method it illustrated, scholarly advances made in its wake, and the contemporary state of the question. Wilson surveys some of the small-scale attacks by specialists (medievalists, historians of ancient philosophy, of Romanticism, and of political theory, and philosophical critics), showing how Lovejoy's program has continued to figure centrally in discussions of methodology, as a target of if not always as an inspiration for, intellectual historians. Mahoney provides a critical analysis of later scholarship concerning the "hierarchy of being" in the middle ages, the overemphasis on Platonic origins, the neglect of major figures such as Proclus, and the revisionist implications which more recent investigations have for the story that Lovejoy told. Oakley, while pursuing such revisionism into the tradition of conventional conceptions of order, reasserts the essential validity of Lovejoy's methods.

As "the history of ideas" gained a disciplinary (or at least paradisciplinary) status, in Europe as well as in this country, questions of methodology and interpretation became popular topics of discussion (although the *Journal* itself has always been concerned with the practice more than the theory of intellectual history). In this connection Abraham Edel (ch. Va) distinguished several "levels of meaning," political and sociohistorical as well as philosophical, which are essential to the understanding of significance as well as explanation in terms of historical causation. Paul Kristeller (ch. Vb) commented on the relation between the history of ideas and the history of philosophy, reaffirming the centrality (and in effect priority) of the latter and the "auxiliary" status of the general history of thought, while Philip Wiener (ch. Vc), also a philosopher and executive editor of the *Journal* through its first forty-five years) distinguished between "external" and "internal" approaches to "intellectual development" and defended the role of logic in the history of thought.

The hegemony of philosophy over the field of the history of ideas has not gone unexamined or unchallenged, and indeed the adoption of the *Journal's* subtitle ("an international journal devoted to intellectual history") testifies to the desire to mitigate the controversial idealism suggested by the term "ideas." In a more historical or doxographical mode Joseph Mazzeo (ch. VI) examined various interpretations of the history of ideas, including the Hegelian view and the reactions to it by Jacob Burckhardt, Wilhelm Dilthey, and others, as well as the work of Ernst Cassirer (who had been an early contributor to the journal) and the philological approach of Spitzer, Karl Vossler, and other critics of Lovejoy.

Leonard Krieger (ch. VII) shifted the emphasis from "ideas" to "history" and expanded the canon of Lovejoy's field to include Marx as well as Hegel and the likes of William Lecky, William Draper, Lucien Febvre, and James Harvey Robinson as well as Dilthey and Cassirer. Krieger complained about the plurality of "methods" derived from philosophy, literature, and other disciplines; and he called in effect for the adoption of a broad historical perspective which, though maintaining an "internal" approach, would accommodate linguistic, social, and aesthetic dimensions and form the basis for the "integrity" and the "autonomy" of intellectual history. In effect Krieger's essay called for a return to the eclectic values of Lovejoy, though centered more on historical perspective than on philosophical analysis.

The nature of the historical process remained a central methodological question for the history of ideas, and then exchange between Johann Huizinga and Joseph Katz (ch. X) returned to the old issue of aesthetic value. Preserving his belief in the "classic" status of history as an independent "intellectual form," Huizinga argued that the associations between "history" and "story" were more than etymological, that history necessarily remained a kind of literary recreation invoking Michelet's "resurrection") and that economic, quantitative, or other sort of explanatory reductionism destroyed this essential story-telling function, which alone can give human meaning. Katz protested both Huizinga's dramatic (and dramatizing) view of contemporary history and his apparently contradictory recourse to eternal values in the face of "irreversible change." Like Lovejoy, Huizinga seemed to be trapped, philosophically, by the conceptual contradictions of evolutionism as a philosophy of history.

Calvin Rand (ch. XI) confronted what has been a crucial issue of both history and philosophy in recent times—"historicism," which has lain at the heart of the cultural "crisis" of the early part of this century and of the interpretation of intellectual history (and indeed which has been criticized as one of the fallacies of Lovejoy's historical method). Yet, despite the misconceptions of Popper and other philosophers, historicism has promoted a specifically humanistic and consciously anti-positivist (and even anti-evolutionist) approach to historical understanding, as a study of the work of Dilthey, Troeltsch, and Meinecke (who was a distinguished practitioner of German-style "history of ideas" [*Ideengeschichte*]) makes clear. Philosophical misconceptions and misapplications aside, "historicism" has been a positive factor in the theory and practice of intellectual history.

Many other problems have been discussed in the pages of the *Journal of the History of Ideas*. In a technical and textualist way that Lovejoy (despite his approval of "analysis") might not have appreciated Nils B. Kvastad (ch. XII) discussed the question of semantics, beginning with the key concept of "ideas" itself and focussing in general on questions of linguistic propriety and consistency. Paul Kristeller (ch. XIII) took up the old problem of creativity in history—"tradition and the individual talent," in the famous phrase of Eliot—and concluded with an effort of reconciliation similar to Lovejoy's own assumptions that human achievement, literary and artistic as well as philosophical, was necessarily a product of a cultural heritage. Lester Crocker (ch. XIV) reviewed recent interpretations of that central and seminal topic of the history of ideas, the continental Enlightenment (from Cassirer's work down to his own), recommending an emphasis on the practical and "political" rather than the philosophical and intellectual dimensions. And in a less conventional mode Patrick Hutton (ch. XV) has reinterpreted the "art of memory"—from Renaissance mnemonics through Vico's new science down to psychoanalysis—as a many-formed but recurrent effort to achieve historical and even archeological understanding of lost or forgotten aspects of experience.

The history of ideas began as an interdisciplinary enterprise, and so it remains, at least in the work of its best practitioners. Some of the same premises, problems, and aspirations of intellectual history in its classic Lovejovian form have also been preserved. Of these I would emphasize in particular the attribution to history of a role not only in science and philosophy but also in cultural self-understanding more generally speaking; the awareness of social context and the extra-rational forces of ideology and the unconscious; the appreciation of the "linguistic turn" in philosophy and of the role of rhetoric in the study of history; the acknowledgement of questions of value, aesthetic and moral, in historical research and writing; and the hermeneutical need to distinguish "levels of meaning" in the investigation of texts and the past more generally.

Yet this is by no means to deny the emergence—whether evolutionary or revolutionary, whether terminological or methodological—of novelty, especially with the introduction of ideas from modern—or "post-modern"— philosophy, science, and literary theory. The last essay in this collection (ch. XVI), which begins by looking back over that earlier history of intellectual history referred to by Mazzeo and ends by surveying some of these new approaches and their implications for the prospects of a field that, after some difficult times, survives and is even prospering in the second half-century of its modern American career—and the last decade of our millenium.

PART ONE

FOUNDERS

Chapter II.a

REFLECTIONS ON THE HISTORY OF IDEAS[1]

By Arthur O. Lovejoy

I

Whatever other definitions of man be true or false, it is generally admitted that he is distinguished among the creatures by the habit of entertaining general ideas. Like Br'er Rabbit he has always kept up a heap o' thinking; and it has usually been assumed—though the assumption has been nominally disputed by some schools of philosophers—that his thoughts have at all times had a good deal to do with his behavior, his institutions, his material achievements in technology and the arts, and his fortunes. Every branch of historical inquiry, consequently, may be said to include within its scope some portion of the history of ideas. But as a result of the subdivision and specialization increasingly characteristic of historical as of other studies during the last two centuries, the portions of that history which are pertinent to separate historical disciplines came to be treated usually in relative, though seldom in complete, isolation. The history of political events and social movements, of economic changes, of religion, of philosophy, of science, of literature and the other arts, of education, have been investigated by distinct groups of specialists, many of them little acquainted with the subjects and the researches of the others. The specialization which—the limitations of the individual mind being what they are—had this as its natural consequence was indispensable for the progress of historical knowledge; yet the consequence proved also, in the end,

---

[1] It has been thought desirable by the Board of Editors that the first number of this journal should contain some prefatory observations on the nature and aims of the studies which the journal is designed to promote, and for some of the fruits of which it may provide a suitable vehicle of publication. The Editor to whom the task has been assigned has, however, already written somewhat lengthily elsewhere on the general subject (in *The Great Chain of Being*, 1936, Lecture I and in *Proc. of the Amer. Philos. Soc.*, vol. 78, pp. 529–543), and some repetition, in substance if not in phraseology, of these previous disquisitions on the same topic has been unavoidable. Some aspects of it, on the other hand, which have been there dealt with, have been here passed over, in order to have space for comments on certain relevant but currently controverted questions. For the opinions expressed on these questions the writer alone is responsible.

an impediment to such progress. For the departmentalization—whether by subjects, periods, nationalities, or languages—of the study of the history of thought corresponds, for the most part, to no real cleavages among the phenomena studied. The processes of the human mind, in the individual or the group, which manifest themselves in history, do not run in enclosed channels corresponding to the officially established divisions of university faculties; even where these processes, or their modes of expression, or the objects to which they are applied, are logically discriminable into fairly distinct types, they are in perpetual interplay. And ideas are the most migratory things in the world. A preconception, category, postulate, dialectical motive, pregnant metaphor or analogy, ''sacred word,'' mood of thought, or explicit doctrine, which makes its first appearance upon the scene in one of the conventionally distinguished provinces of history (most often, perhaps, in philosophy) may, and frequently does, cross over into a dozen others. To be acquainted only with its manifestation in one of these is, in many cases, to understand its nature and affinities, its inner logic and psychological operation, so inadequately that even *that* manifestation remains opaque and unintelligible. All historians—even, in their actual practice, those who in theory disclaim any such pretension—seek in some sense and to some degree to discern causal relations between events; but there is, unhappily, no law of nature which specifies that all, or even the most important, antecedents of a given historic effect, or all or the most important consequents of a given cause, will lie within any one of the accepted subdivisions of history. In so far as the endeavor to trace such relations stops at the boundaries of one or another of these divisions, there is always a high probability that some of the most significant—that is, the most illuminating and explanatory—relations will be missed. It has even sometimes happened that a conception of major historic influence and importance has long gone unrecognized, because its various manifestations, the parts which make up the whole story, are so widely dispersed among different fields of historical study, that no specialist in any one of these fields became distinctly aware of it at all. Historiography, in short, for excellent practical reasons, is divided, but the historic process is not; and this discrepancy between the procedure and the subject-matter has tended, at best, to produce serious lacunae in the study of the history of man, and at worst, sheer errors and distortions.

Of such considerations as these, scholars in many branches of historical inquiry have in recent years become increasingly sensible. None, certainly, questions the indispensability of specialization; but more and more have come to see that specialization is not enough. In practice this sometimes manifests itself in a crossing-over of individual specialists into other fields than those to which they had originally devoted themselves and for which they have been trained. Administrative officers of educational institutions have sometimes been known to complain, with a certain puzzlement, of teachers and investigators who will not "stick to their subjects." But in most cases this propensity to disregard academic fences is not to be attributed to a wandering disposition or a coveting of neighbors' vineyards; it is, on the contrary, usually the inevitable consequence of tenacity and thoroughness in the cultivation of one's own. For— to repeat an observation which the present writer has already made elsewhere, with primary reference to literary history—"the quest of a historical understanding even of single passages in literature often drives the student into fields which at first seem remote enough from his original topic of investigation. The more you press in towards the heart of a narrowly bounded historical problem, the more likely you are to encounter in the problem itself a pressure which drives you outward beyond those bounds." To give specific illustrations of this fact would unduly lengthen these prelusive remarks;[2] examples will doubtless appear in abundance in subsequent pages of this journal. It is sufficient here to note, as a highly characteristic feature of contemporary work in many of the branches of historiography that are in any way concerned with the thoughts of men (and their related emotions, modes of expression, and actions), that the fences are—not, indeed, generally breaking down— but, at a hundred specific points, being broken through; and that the reason for this is that, at least at those points, the fences have been found to be obstacles to the proper comprehension of what lies on either side of them.

There is, unquestionably, some danger to historical scholarship in this newer tendency. It is the danger already intimated, that scholars soundly trained in the methods and widely acquainted with the literature of one limited—even though it be an arbitrarily limited—field may prove inadequately equipped for exploring other

[2] Some have been adduced by the writer in a paper above mentioned, *Proc. of the Amer. Philos. Soc.*, Vol. 78, pp. 532–535.

provinces into which they have, nevertheless, been naturally and legitimately led by the intrinsic connections of the subjects that they are investigating. Most contemporary historians of any national literature, for example, or of science or a particular science, recognize in principle—though many still recognize too little—that ideas derived from philosophical systems have had a wide, and sometimes a profound and decisive, influence upon the minds and the writings of the authors whose works they study; and they are constrained, therefore, to deal with these systems and to expound these ideas for their readers. But they do not—it is perhaps not too unmannerly to say—always do it very well. When this is the case, the fault, no doubt, often lies partly with the existing histories of philosophy, which frequently fail to give the non-philosopher what he most needs for his special historical inquiry; but they are, in any case, unsatisfying to the scholar who has learned from experience in his own specialty the risks of too implicit reliance upon secondary or tertiary sources. Even more, however, than an extensive reading of philosophical texts is needed for the accurate and sufficient understanding of the working of philosophical ideas in literature or in science—a certain aptitude for the discrimination and analysis of concepts, and an eye for not immediately obvious logical relations or quasi-logical affinities between ideas. These powers are, by a happy gift of nature, sometimes found in historical writers who would deprecate the title of "philosophers"; but in most cases, when they are attained at all, they owe much, also, to a persistent cultivation and training, of which the student of philosophy naturally gets more than specialists in the history of literature or science—and for lack of which the latter sometimes seem to the philosopher to go more or less widely astray in their necessary divagations into philosophy. They, in turn—especially the historian of science—could doubtless not infrequently respond with a *tu quoque* to the historian of philosophy; if so, the present point is the better illustrated; and many other illustrations of it might all too easily be found.

The remedy for the effects defective of specialization in historical inquiry, then, does not lie in a general practice, on the part of specialists, of simply invading one another's territories or taking over one another's jobs. It lies in closer coöperation among them at all those points where their provinces overlap, the establishment of more and better facilities for communication, mutual criticism and mutual aid—the focussing upon what are, in their nature, common problems, of all the special knowledges that are pertinent to them. It is one of the purposes of this journal to contribute, so far as its resources permit, towards such a more effective *liaison* among those whose studies have to do with the diverse but interrelated parts of history, in so far as history is concerned with the activities of man's mind and the effects of these upon what he has been and has done—or (to change the metaphor) to assist towards more cross-fertilization among the several fields of intellectual historiography. It is hoped that the journal will serve—among other things—as a useful medium for the publication of researches which traverse the customary boundary-lines, or are likely to be of interest and value to students in other fields than those in which they primarily lie. Its prospectus has already indicated, by way of illustration, some topics concerning which its editors believe further investigation to be potentially profitable, and on which contributions will be especially welcome:

1. The influence of classical on modern thought, and of European traditions and writings on American literature, arts, philosophy, and social movements.
2. The influence of philosophical ideas in literature, the arts, religion, and social thought, including the impact of pervasive general conceptions upon standards of taste and morality and educational theories and methods.
3. The influence of scientific discoveries and theories in the same provinces of thought, and in philosophy; the cultural effects of the applications of science.
4. The history of the development and the effects of individual pervasive and widely ramifying ideas or doctrines, such as evolution, progress, primitivism, diverse theories of human motivation and appraisals of human nature, mechanismic and organismic conceptions of nature and society, metaphysical and historical determinism and indeterminism, individualism and collectivism, nationalism and racialism.

But the function of this journal is not solely to help to bring about a fruitful correlation between older and more specialized disciplines. For the study of the history of ideas does not need to justify itself by its potential services—however great—to historical studies bearing other names. It has its own reason for being. It is not merely ancillary to the others; it is rather they that are, in great part, ancillary to it. To know, so far as may be known, the thoughts that have been widely held among men on matters of common human concernment, to determine how these thoughts have arisen, combined, interacted with, or counteracted, one another, and how they have severally been related to the imagination and emotions and behavior of those who have held them—this, though not, indeed, the whole of that branch of knowledge which we call history, is a distinct and essential part of it, and its central and most vital part. For, while the fixed or changing environmental conditions of human life, individual and collective, and conjunctions of circumstance which arise from no man's thinking or premeditation, are factors in the historic process never to be disregarded, the actor in the piece, its hero—some would in these days say, its villain—is still *homo sapiens;* and the general task of intellectual historiography is to exhibit, so far as may be, the thinking animal engaged—sometimes fortunately, sometimes disastrously—in his most characteristic occupation. If—as some would be content to say—the justification of *any* study of history is simply the human interestingness both of its episodes and of the moving drama of the life of our race as a whole, then this study has that justification in the highest degree. Or if historical inquiry in general is defended on the ground—which some contemporary historians appear to reject— that the knowledge which it yields is "instructive," that it provides material towards possible general conclusions—conclusions which do not relate merely to the occurrence and successions of past and particular events—then no part of historiography seems to offer a better promise of this sort of serviceableness than a duly analytical and critical inquiry into the nature, genesis, development, diffusion, interplay and effects of the ideas which the generations of men have cherished, quarreled over, and apparently been moved by. That the knowledge which man needs most is knowledge of himself is a sufficiently old and respectable opinion; and intellectual history manifestly constitutes an indispensable, and the most considerable, part of such knowledge, in so far as any study of the past may contribute to it. At no moment, indeed, in the life of the race has the pertinency of the Delphian imperative been more tragically apparent; for it must now be plain to everyone that the problem of human nature is the gravest and most fundamental of our problems, that the question which more than any others demands answer is the question, "What's the matter with man?"

II

The general observation that knowledge concerning the history of ideas has an independent value, and is not merely instrumental to other studies, might well seem too obvious to require emphasis, were it not that it has consequences, not always clearly realized, with respect to the methods and aims of literary history. The thoughts of men of past generations have had their most extensive, and often their most adequate and psychologically illuminating, expression in those writings which are commonly differentiated from other writings—though by criteria not usually very clear—as "literature." Wherever the line of division be drawn, it would generally be agreed that literature is, at least among other things, an art. Since there is no universal consensus as to the meaning of "art," this classification does not, of itself, greatly clarify the subject; but one may perhaps say, without too much risk of dissent, that a work of "art" is such by virtue of its relation either to an artist who produces it or to a potential reader, hearer or beholder of it (or to both). And, considered solely in the second relation, the work of art may be said to be differentiated from other visible or audible artificial objects by its capacity to produce in the perceiver a distinctive something called an "aesthetic enjoyment," or at least an "aesthetic experience," which (though definition of it is here judiciously avoided) is at all events not simply identical either with cognitive experience or with a recognition of a possible ulterior utility which the object may serve. Works of art, further, are usually held to differ widely in respect of their aesthetic values—however these are to be measured. Now it has, especially by some recent writers, been maintained that a work of art, so conceived, must contain its aesthetic value, that is, the sources of the aesthetic experience it evokes, in itself, and not in anything extraneous to itself. It makes no difference, so far as the aesthetic quality and efficacy of a poem are concerned, who wrote it, or when, or what sort of person he was, or from what motive he wrote it, or even what he meant to convey by it; and if the reader permits his mind to be occupied with such questions as these, he weakens or wholly loses the experience which it is the function of the poem, as a work of art, to afford. And it is consequently argued, by some who are preoccupied with this aspect of literature, that the study of literary history results chiefly in the accumulation of collateral information *about,* *e.g.,* poems, which adds nothing to the aesthetic experience as such, but, on the contrary, impedes or annuls it, by interposing what is aesthetically irrelevant between the poem and the reader. Thus Mr. C. S. Lewis observes that "any and every result which may follow from my reading of a poem cannot be included in my poetical apprehension of it, and cannot, therefore, belong to the poem as a poem," and, starting from this (in itself undisputable) premise, he attacks, with an argumentative verve and skill which has itself a good deal of art in it, the notion that "poetry is to be regarded as an 'expression of personality,' " and laments "the steadily increasing role of biography in our literary studies." "When we read poetry as it ought to be read, we have before us no representation which claims to be the poet, and frequently no representation of a *man,* a *character,* or a *personality* at all." There can, in fact, be "poems without a poet"—*i.e.,* writings which (like passages in the English Bible) have in the course of time acquired a poetic value which is not due to anything that anyone ever *put* into them.[3] (Any essential distinction between the experience of beauty in natural objects and in works of art is here apparently obliterated.) If knowledge about the poet's "personality" is thus foreign to the "poetical apprehension" of the poem, still more foreign must be the other sorts of knowledge which the literary historians so busily pursue, about his experiences, education, associations, "background," sources, philosophical opinions, contemporary reputation, later influence, and the like.

These views are not cited here principally for the purpose of discussing the issues of aesthetic theory which they raise; yet one of these issues has some pertinency to the present subject, and is worth brief consideration before passing to the main point. It is the general question whether information about, say, a poem, not contained in it, is necessarily incapable of enhancing the aesthetic experience, or "poetical apprehension," of the reader; and I suggest that the answer must be in the negative. One may, of course, so *define* the terms "aesthetic" or "poetical apprehension" that an affirmative answer to the question necessarily follows; but the con-

[3] *The Personal Heresy: A Controversy.* By E. M. W. Tillyard and C. S. Lewis, 1939, pp. 1, 4, 5, 16.

sequence is then a purely verbal one, having nothing to do with any matter of psychological fact. But it is hard to see how anyone can, except through such verbal inference, find plausibility in the thesis that the sources of what would commonly be recognized as the aesthetic enjoyment of a poem, or of any work of art, must consist wholly in its own literal and explicit content.[4] For—upon the very view which has been illustrated by some sentences of Mr. Lewis's—the aesthetic value of the poem depends upon its effect on the reader; and this in turn, surely, depends much upon the reader—upon what the psychologists once liked to call "the mass of apperception" which he brings to the reading. The external stimulus giving rise to the experience consists, it is true, in the actual words of the poem; but the capacity, even of the separate words, to suggest imagery or to arouse emotion, not to say to convey ideas, is due to the associations which they already possess in the reader's mind, and these may be, and often are, the products of other reading. Any allusive word or passage illustrates this.

> Perhaps the self-same song that found a path
> Through the sad heart of Ruth, when, sick for home,
> She stood in tears amid the alien corn.

The poem does not tell you who Ruth was, nor where she is elsewhere mentioned in literature; *that* is a piece of extraneous historical information—though one, fortunately, familiar to all Occidental readers. Will anyone venture to assert that, for most of them, the aesthetic enjoyment of the lines is diminished, and not, rather, heightened, by their possession of this knowledge? And is there any reason to suppose that knowledge of a similar kind, even though less generally possessed, may not similarly enrich—for those who have it—the aesthetic value of many other passages? Instances in which it quite certainly does so might be adduced by the hundred, if there were space for them. The historical perspectives which a word or a poem may bring, clearly or dimly, to mind are often (given the necessary acquaintance with history) a great part of the aesthetic experience which it evokes—an augmentation of its imaginative voluminosity. Nor are the possible contributions of the his-

---

[4] The subject has been dealt with illuminatingly, and more adequately than is possible here, by Louis Teeter in an essay ("Scholarship and the Art of Criticism," *ELH* September, 1938) which should be required reading for any who concern themselves with this question.

torian to the "poetical apprehension" of the reader limited to obviously allusive or evocative single passages. It is he, often, who enables the reader to recapture, in writings of earlier times, aesthetic values which had been lost because the frame of reference, the preconceptions, the mood, which once gave them such value for their contemporaries were no longer current. How meager would be the aesthetic content of the *Divine Comedy* as a whole, or of most of its parts, to a modern reader—especially a non-Catholic reader—wholly ignorant of medieval ideas and feelings and pieties, or incapable, while reading it, of making these in some degree his own, by an effort of the imagination! Indeed, the exercise of the historical imagination, even apart from its function in the revitalizing of this or other masterpieces, has itself been, since Western men became historically-minded, one of the chief sources of aesthetic experience—though that is another story. Obviously, not all historical or other knowledge pertinent to, but derived from sources extrinsic to, a given work of art thus adds to its potency. Some does and some does not; no general rule can be laid down on the subject in advance. But it is by no means evident that even knowledge from external sources about the *artist,* his "personality" or his life, is one of the sorts of collateral information which necessarily do *not* have this effect, and that biographical studies consequently cannot contribute to the enjoyment of literature. The aesthetic irrelevance of a considerable part of the chronicles, scandalous or edifying, of the lives of authors, can hardly be denied. Whether any of the discoveries about Shakespeare heighten the effect of the plays is at least debatable; and it is more than dubious whether an acquaintance with the private life of the Reverend C. L. Dodgson makes *Alice in Wonderland* more enjoyable. But there are many instances on the other side of the account. Doubtless there would be a touching pathos in "All, all are gone, the old familiar faces," if the poem were anonymous, but there is much more when I know that it was written by Charles Lamb—a fact which is no part of the poem—and know something of the tragic circumstances in his life. Or consider Coleridge's "Dejection, an Ode": our present knowledge (which we owe to his biographers and the collectors of his letters) of the experiences out of which it arose, and of the fact that it marked the end of his great creative period as a poet, makes the poem far more moving than it can have been to the generality of the readers of the *Morning Post* in 1802. Such knowledge adds what may be called a new dimension to a work of art, the dramatic dimension—as, in a play, a single poetic passage, though it may have beauty in isolation, owes its full effect to the reader's knowledge of the fictitious personality of the speaker and of the situation which evokes it and makes it dramatically apposite.

> For God's sake, let us sit upon the ground
> And tell sad stories of the death of kings. . . .

The whole passage might be taken out of its context and given a place in an anthology; but would one who had known it only as a detached fragment find his "imaginative apprehension" of it diminished upon learning that it is, in the play, spoken by a king, and that king, Richard II, and at a crisis in his fortunes calling for resolute action rather than self-pitying musings on the ironies of royal state? The increment of aesthetic content which the lines gain from such knowledge of their dramatic setting is essentially similar to that which a poem or other writing may sometimes gain from the reader's knowledge of its authorship, its place in the author's life and its relation to his character. This is not, to be sure, an element in the art, *i.e.*, the design, of the creator of the work; but it is not the less on that account an enrichment of aesthetic experience on the side of the reader—which is presumably one of the purposes of the "teaching of literature."[5] And if the work be considered with respect to the skill, or "artistry," of its creator, the "aesthetic appreciation" of this is least of all possible without going beyond the work itself. For it is dependent upon a knowledge—or an assumption—about what he was trying to do,

[5] In the debate of Lewis and Tillyard, to which reference has been made, two "personal heresies," not sufficiently discriminated, seem to be at issue. One is the assumption that a poem (and a single poem is usually meant) *necessarily* tells us anything about the "personality" of the poet. In maintaining the negative on this issue, Mr. Lewis seems to me to have the better of the argument. But the correct answer, I suggest, is that no generalization on the point is legitimate; some poems do, and some don't. The more serious question concerns Mr. Lewis's view that, when "we read a poem as it ought to be read," we *ought not* to know, or want to know, anything about the poet, since this interferes with the "imaginative experience." And this is a part of the larger question, above discussed, whether *any* extrinsic knowledge about a poem can contribute to the aesthetic experience generated by reading it. This more general and fundamental issue, however, is not very definitely considered by either contributor to this, in many respects, brilliant example of the gentle art of controversy.

which can by no means always be safely or fully inferred from the obvious content of the work; and it is also dependent upon an acquaintance with other extrinsic matters, such as his subject (if or in so far as his purpose is assumed to be descriptive or realistic), the limitations of his medium, other examples of the treatment of the same subject or of essays in the same *genre,* and (when they can be certainly determined) the sources of which he made use. This element in the appreciation of (for example) "Kubla Khan" has, surely, not been decreased by the publication of *The Road to Xanadu.*

The very notion, then, of a work of art as a self-contained kind of thing is a psychological absurdity. It *functions* as art through what it does for the experiencer of it; nothing in it has aesthetic efficacy except through its power to evoke certain responses in him; so that one may say that, except in a physical sense, its content is as much in him as in itself. And this general consideration alone, even apart from the citation of particular examples, seems to establish a sufficient presumption against the doctrine, now somewhat fashionable in various quarters, that, in the reading of literature, ignorance is always bliss, that the best reader is the one who has least in his mind, and that, consequently, the sort of knowledge which may result from the historical study of literature is never serviceable to the aesthetic purposes of that art. But though many and notable services of this kind can be and have been rendered by such study, it is still needful to insist—and this is the point chiefly pertinent to the present theme—that that is not its only, or even its principal, function. "Literary history," as the late Edwin Greenlaw wrote, "looks on literature as one phase of that history of the human spirit which is one of the chief learnings, is humanism itself."[6] It is, in short, a part, and a major part, of the quest of that knowledge of the workings of man's mind in history which, having its own excuse for being, is not subservient even to ends so valuable as the aesthetic appreciation or the criticism of individual works of art. But so conceived, the province and the methods of literary history must be determined by its own historical-psychological purpose, and not by contemporary critical appraisals either of the aesthetic excellence or the philosophical validity of the writings of men of former times. Evident as this may appear, some confusion of ideas with respect to the matter still seems common, not only in

[6] *The Province of Literary History,* 1931, p. 38.

the public mind, and among literary critics, but also among students and teachers of literature. Because, *as* an art, it exists to be "enjoyed" (in the wider sense of the term), it is sometimes, tacitly if not explicitly, assumed that the purpose of studying or teaching it is exclusively to increase or communicate that enjoyment; and, in so far as this assumption prevails, the natural result is the limitation of the study to what is now regarded as "good" literature—the writings which still have (or are, often somewhat naïvely, taken by academic teachers to have) a high aesthetic value for most readers of our own time. Thus a distinguished English scholar who has recently rediscovered an almost forgotten but admirable English prose writer of the seventeenth century (Peter Sterry), and has edited selections from his works, explains that his (the editor's) "aim has been to exhibit not so much those aspects of Sterry's work that probably made the greatest impression on his contemporaries as those elements which appear to me to have the universal and enduring qualities of great literature." Here, obviously, the part of the contents of this author's writings which is of greater historical value—the part which throws most light upon what was distinctive of the thoughts, the moods, the taste, of his age and group—is treated as more or less negligible, because it has (or, *for that very reason,* is presumed to have) less "literary" value. Now, to make available to the contemporary reader a forgotten piece of "great"— or at all events, still enjoyable—literature, is assuredly a laudable thing. But it is a strange thing to disregard, in such a writing, what is most pertinent to that "one of the chief learnings"—that essential portion of the "history of the human spirit"—to which it is the prime office of the literary historian, *quâ* historian, to contribute. It is not now in general true that those who devote themselves to this study neglect their function as historians of ideas (including artistic methods and aesthetic valuations and tastes); but, because of the confusion of the two aims, they are sometimes subject to reproach for occupying themselves so much with what is *not* "good literature," perhaps not even "literature" at all; and they themselves often seem a little apologetic about it. Something like a declaration of independence for the genuinely historical study of literature, in itself and in its relations to other phases of the history of man thinking, feeling, imagining and evaluating, is even now not wholly superfluous. In this journal, the independence (which does not imply the indifference) of the historiography of literature with respect to all non-historical criteria of relevance and importance, and also its inseparable connection with most of the other parts of that total history, are assumed *ab initio*. As a source of delight and a means to the widening and deepening of inner experience, literature has one value; as "criticism of life" it has another (for the appraisal of which a knowledge of its history is one of the necessary means); and it has a third as an indispensable body of documents for the study of man and of what he has done with ideas and what diverse ideas have done for and to him.

III

To avert possible misunderstanding, let it be said that the terms "ideas" and "intellectual" are not here used in a sense implying any assumption of the solely or chiefly logical determination of opinions and behavior and of the historical movement of thought. There is now widely current even among the general public a doctrine that the beliefs, and professed grounds of belief, as well as the acts, of individuals and of social groups are not shaped by "intellectual" processes, but by unavowed or "subconscious" non-rational desires, passions or interests. This "discovery of the irrational," a recent writer has declared, "makes the genius of our age. . . . The intellectual revolution of the twentieth century is likely to prove the charting of the *terra incognita* of the irrational and the extraction of its implications for every area of human thought." It is "nothing short of a Copernican revolution in ideas," since it means that "the rational, right-thinking man has as surely ceased to be considered the center of our intellectual system as the earth has ceased to be the center of our planetary system."[7] The discovery is not so new as it is commonly supposed to be, and it is questionable whether exploration of the *"terra incognita* of the irrational" was not attempted with as much diligence and subtlety in the seventeenth century as in the twentieth. But at all events it is little likely to be unduly neglected by contemporary students of the history of thought. Few of them are accustomed to look upon man as a highly rational animal, in the laudatory sense, or to deny that alogical factors play a great part in most of the phenomena which they investigate; and it would be a misconception to suppose

---

[7] Max Lerner in *The Nation*, Oct. 21, 1939. The term "rational," of course, needs definition, and the assumption of the equivalence of "non-rational" and "irrational" requires examination; but into these topics it is impossible to enter here.

that the intellectual historian is concerned solely with the history of intellection.

Perhaps the greater danger at present lies upon the other side. One of the safest (and most useful) generalizations resulting from a study of the history of ideas is that every age tends to exaggerate the scope or finality of its own discoveries, or re-discoveries, to be so dazzled by them that it fails to discern clearly their limitations and forgets aspects of truth against prior exaggerations of which it has revolted. Now, that the doctrine of the non-rational determination of men's judgments and ideologies is not true without exceptions is the obvious assumption of all who enunciate opinions and publish ostensibly reasoned arguments for them—and therefore, the assumption of the authors of the doctrine, and of all who seek to justify by evidence any historical proposition whatever. It is true that some representatives of the theory known as "the sociology of knowledge" (*Wissenssoziologie*), holding that the "modes of thought" of all individuals are determined by, and therefore relative to, the nature of the social groups to which the individuals belong—not merely economic classes but also "generations, status groups, sects, occupational groups, schools, etc."—deduce from this psychological hypothesis a sort of generalized relativistic (or, as they prefer to call it, "relational") logic or epistemology. Upon the set of presuppositions characteristic of a given group, some conclusions are valid, some invalid—but (apparently) each group has its own "thought-model," its distinctive standards of what is true or false, which do not hold good for others. And certain adherents of this form of the general doctrine seem willing to have this relativism applied to their own contentions; thus Mr. Karl Mannheim writes that "even one's own point of view may always be expected to be peculiar to one's [social] position."[8] Yet the ingenious and often suggestive interpretations of history put forth by members of this school do not, in fact, have the air of being presented as valid for the reader in one of his capacities, say that of a professor of sociology, and invalid for him in another capacity, say that of a man over forty years of age, or an income-tax payer in one of the lower brackets; nor are these reasonings presented (as might

[8] Karl Mannheim: *Ideology and Utopia*, 1936, p. 269; *cf.* the whole section "The Sociology of Knowledge," pp. 236–280. See also Robert K. Merton's excellent brief review of this movement, "The Sociology of Knowledge," in *Isis*, XXVII, 3, November, 1937, pp. 493–503.

be expected) as valid only for readers belonging to precisely the same economic class and generation and status-group and occupational group and sect as their authors. If they were so presented, their claims to consideration would obviously be extremely restricted. The spokesmen of this sort of sociological relativism, in short, patently give *some* place to common criteria of factual truth and of legitimacy in inference, which their theory, in its extreme interpretation, would exclude. They do not, it is clear, really believe that the proposition that George Washington was a great landed proprietor is true for a Virginia Episcopalian but false for a Chicago Baptist—nor that their own thesis that opinions and "thought-models," outside of pure science, are shown by historical evidence to be correlated with social status or position, ought to be accepted only by persons of a particular status or position. Even they, then, necessarily presuppose possible limitations or exceptions to their generalization, in the act of defending it.

But if there *are* limitations or exceptions to the truth of the doctrine of the non-rational determination of men's judgments, it follows that two types of factor are at work in the history of thought; and it is the business of the historian—if he can—at once to discriminate and to correlate them, and perhaps, in the long run, to arrive at some rough quantitative estimate of the relative part played by each. But to make this discrimination in particular instances—which must be done *before* any general conclusions can be regarded as established—is unquestionably a hazardous and uncertain business; and the more weight you initially give to the rôle of the non-rational in these matters, the more hazardous and uncertain the appraisal of that rôle must itself appear. It is perilously easy to find more or less plausible explanations, in terms of non-rational motives, for other mens' reasonings, opinions or tastes—to "unmask ideologies" which you happen to dislike—and, in the nature of the case, it is exceedingly difficult to demonstrate the correctness or adequacy of such specific explanations, unless by deduction from *a priori* general premises dogmatically assumed at the outset—a type of question-begging exemplified in our own time on a huge scale. Nevertheless, given a sufficient degree of caution as well as of acumen on the part of the historian (including the biographer), some success in this delicate task of distinguishing the two components in the formation of men's judgments is, doubtless, not past hoping for.

Meanwhile, the usual ambition of the contemporary histori-ographer to find conjectural "affective" or "sociological" explana-tions for the explicit facts of the history of ideas obviously cannot justify—though it sometimes tends to result in—a neglect to ob-serve with as much adequacy, accuracy and judicial-mindedness as may be, the facts to be explained—to investigate widely and to analyze searchingly, through their expression in words, the kinds of ideas that have actually appealed to men, to note upon what grounds beliefs have seemed to those who held them to have been based, how they have changed from generation to generation, and under what conditions these changes have taken place. Even if most or all expressed judgments and reasonings were but "rationa-lizations" of blind emotions or cravings, the nature of the cravings must be chiefly inferred from the content of the rationalizations; the need to rationalize is, upon the same hypothesis, not less imperative than the cravings; and once a rationalization has been formed, it is antecedently improbable—and could be shown by historical evidence to be untrue—that it will remain otiose and inert, having no reper-cussions upon the affective side of consciousness out of which it may have arisen. When a man has given a reason for his belief, his moral approbation or disapprobation, his aesthetic preference, he is—happily or otherwise—caught in a trap; for the reason is likely to entail, or to seem to entail, consequences far beyond and, it may be, contrary to, the desire which generated it, or, not less awkwardly, contrary to undeniable matters of fact; even if he seeks to evade those consequences, he will suffer the embarrassment of appearing to his fellows irrational because arbitrary and incon-sistent; and an aversion from manifest and admitted irrationality is, after all, by no means the least pervasive or least powerful of emotions in the creature that has long, and with evident gratifica-tion, been accustomed to define himself as the rational animal. Man, moreover, is not only an incurably inquisitive but an incurably ratiocinative being, and the exercise of this function, as of others, carries its own pleasure with it. To recognize a nice distinction, to discover a new truth, or what appears to be such, to feel that one is reasoning well and coercively, to triumph over an at first baffling problem—these are all accompanied by a sense of power and there-fore by lively satisfactions. And the satisfactions cannot be en-joyed without the presupposition of rules of procedure and of

criteria of success not peculiar to oneself, but inherent in the nature
of the subject-matter.

For these reasons, if there were no others, the intellectual
historiographer will still do well to entertain the hypothesis that
logic is one of the important operative factors in the history of
thought, even though he cannot accept this assumption in the extreme form in which it was once widely held. According to that
older but now evanescent view, what we chiefly witness, in the temporal sequence of beliefs, doctrines and reasonings, is the working of
an immanent dialectic whereby ideas are progressively clarified and
problems consecutively get themselves solved, or at least advanced
towards less erroneous or inadequate "solutions." Perhaps the
strongest reason why we no longer find this picture of a majestic
logical forward movement in history convincing is that we have
become increasingly aware of the oscillatory character of much of the
history of thought, at least of Western thought, outside the domain of
strictly experimental science. On any intelligibly formulable general question, there are usually two not entirely unplausible extreme positions, with a number of intermediate ones; and much of
the historic spectacle, so far as the dominant tendencies of successive periods are concerned, seems to consist in alternate shifts from
one extreme to the other, either abruptly or gradually through the
intermediate stages. This phenomenon is, of course, especially conspicuous in political and social history, and in the history of taste
and of the arts. A tendency to radical innovation flourishes for a
time and perhaps eventuates in a revolution, which is followed by
a reaction, more or less extreme, and a period of dominant conser-
vatism. Democracy, or some measure of it, through a long struggle,
replaces absolute monarchy, to be succeeded suddenly by dictatorship. This seems to be the all-but universal pattern of the sequences of politico-social history—excepting those contemporary
revolutions of which the end is not yet. There is little in such
history thus far to encourage the belief that it moves continuously
in any particular direction; it has, in the long view, as Polybius long
since observed, much more the look of a series of periodic recurrences, though the periods are of very unequal length. So in
matters of taste and aesthetic fashions: the majority of connois-
seurs in one period care, for example, only for Gothic architecture,
then they despise it, then they admire it again, then they once more
revolt against it; now fixed "form" is the criterion of excellence,

now "irregularity" and freedom of expression; once the "picturesque" was all the go, now it is belittled. "Romanticism," in some sense of the vague term, displaces "classicism" in literature, and gives place to it again. If you wish to prophesy about the future, in any of these matters, the actuarially safest working rule would seem to be to take what are now venerated idols and predict that they will sooner or later become hobgoblins—and still later, idols once more.

And no honest observer even of the history of philosophical opinion can deny that a similar phenomenon of oscillation is to be found in it. Moods of radical intellectualism are followed by anti-intellectualisms, of one or another variety. In recent American and British philosophy, after the dominance of idealism for a generation, realism, as we all know, came flooding back—and there are now some indications that its tide is receding. (These oscillations, it should hardly need saying, have no relevance to the question of the validity of any of the views which succeed one another; there is nothing more naïve, or more indicative of a failure to learn one of the real lessons of the history of thought, than the tendency of some, even among philosophers, to take the bare fact that a way of thinking is now *démodé* as indicative either that it is false or that it will not come back.) The history of philosophy assuredly is not, in the successions of the ideas and systems which it presents, an exclusively logical process, in which objective truth progressively unfolds itself in a rational order; its course is shaped and diverted by the intrusion of many factors which belong to the domain of the psychologist or the sociologist, and have nothing to do with philosophy as a would-be science. But since this aspect of the matter is now in so little danger of being disregarded, it is more to the purpose to dwell upon the residuum of truth in the older view. It must still be admitted that philosophers (and even plain men) *do* reason, that the temporal sequence of their reasonings, as one thinker follows another, is usually in some considerable degree a logically motivated and logically instructive sequence. For a very familiar example that will hardly be disputed, both Berkeley and Hume did, plainly, bring to notice implications of Locke's premises which Locke had not seen—implications that were actually *there,* waiting, as it were, to be brought to light. In both cases, perhaps—certainly in Berkeley's—extra-logical motives help to explain why the later philosophers *noticed* these implications; the idealism which Berkeley thought it possible to deduce, in part, by combining the simple Lockian thesis that "the mind hath no immediate objects but its own ideas" with the principle of parsimony was a consequence manifestly welcome for religious reasons: it dished the materialists completely, it provided a new argument for the existence of God, it seemed to imply a more direct and intimate relation, even in the common business of sense-perception, between the human and the divine mind. In Hume's case, at least in his non-political works, it is hard to see any extra-logical motivation, except a certain pleasure in horripilating the orthodox and an intense ambition for a reputation as an original writer; it seems questionable whether his sceptical conclusions themselves were really emotionally welcome to him. And even when alogical motives may seem to explain psychologically the readiness of one philosopher to observe a *non-sequitur,* or an unexamined presupposition, or an undeveloped implication, in a doctrine of his predecessor, it frequently, and perhaps usually, remains the case that it is such actual logical facts that he observes—as a review of the entire history of philosophy would easily show. In their criticisms of other people's ways of thinking men inevitably appeal largely to common rational principles, or what at the time are accepted as such, however partially they may follow such principles in arriving at their own beliefs or valuations. On the offensive, many a thinker little capable of self-criticism has shown himself an acute and cogent reasoner; so that, somewhat paradoxically, it is through their quarrels that philosophers have most illuminated the logic of their problems, and it is in the polemical part of the history of reflective thought that the cool white light of reason may most often be seen emerging.

The study of the history of thought, then, must still be pursued with an open and alert eye for the action of "intellectual" processes in the narrower sense, processes in which—along with all the emotive factors, the blank, quasi-aesthetic likings for one or another type of concept or imagery or "metaphysical pathos," and the biases due to personal or group interests—ideas manifest their own natural logic. By natural logic I do not mean necessarily good logic. It sometimes may and sometimes may not be that; and the question how far it can be would involve a digression into logical theory itself, which would be out of place here. But it will hardly be denied that numerous ideas have, if not necessary connections, at least elective affinities, with various other ideas, and incongruities with yet others, and that most propositions, taken in conjunction with others which are usually assumed though they may be unexpressed, have implications not always evident or welcome to those who affirm them. An idea, in short, is after all not only a potent but a stubborn thing; it commonly has its own "particular go;" and the history of thought is a bilateral affair—the story of the traffic and interaction between human nature, amid the exigencies and vicissitudes of physical experience, on the one hand, and on the other, the specific natures and pressures of the ideas which men have, from very various promptings, admitted to their minds.

Johns Hopkins University

Chapter II.b

DISCUSSION

A PROBLEM IN THE HISTORY OF IDEAS

By Frederick J. Teggart

In his prefatory "Reflections on the History of Ideas" the editor points out that one of the aims of the *Journal* is the promotion of "mutual criticism and mutual aid" among those who pursue the study of intellectual history. I accept this definition of policy as warrant for calling attention to the stress which the writer has placed upon "the oscillatory character of much of the history of thought" (20). That a particular interpretation of historical phenomena should be given prominence at the inauguration of this new enterprise, and should be further emphasized by the declaration that "no honest observer . . . can deny" its applicability to the subject under consideration, is a matter of utmost concern for the future of a highly significant branch of scholarship. When an editor speaks in an authoritative manner, it is to be anticipated that prospective contributors, seeking for guidance and looking for approval, will adopt the commended interpretation, and as a consequence will overlook the necessity of comparing it with others current at the present time.

The use of the term "oscillation" to describe the movement of change in ideas is not without support in recent literature. Bertrand Russell, for example, devotes a chapter of his *Sceptical Essays* (1928) to consideration of "the oscillation from synthesis and intolerance to analysis and tolerance, and back again," and is of opinion that "various periodic oscillations run through the history of mankind" (219). The theory has, indeed, been accorded wide recognition since Pareto published his *Sociology* in 1916. In this work the author speaks of oscillations observable during many centuries "between scepticism and faith, materialism and idealism, logico-experimental science and metaphysics" (§1680); he thinks that to write the history of oscillations in ideas would be to write the history of human thought (§2329); he asserts that the human mind oscillates between two extremes of opinion, and, being unable to halt at either, continues in movement indefinitely (§2342). The description which Professor Lovejoy gives of the view he has adopted is that "on any intelligibly formulable general question, there are usually two not entirely unplausible extreme positions, with a number of intermediate ones; and much of the historic spectacle, so far as the dominant tendencies of successive periods are concerned, seems to consist in alternate shifts from one extreme to the other, either abruptly or gradually through the intermediate stages" (20).

The general statement which has just been quoted is followed at once by the remark that "the phenomenon is, of course, especially conspicuous in political and social history." Pareto also brings changes in ideas into juxtaposition with political phenomena. Thus he observes that "in history a period of faith will be followed by a period of scepticism, which will in turn be followed by another period of faith, and this by another period of scepticism, and so on" (§2341). He then declares that oscillations in ideas are consequences of social movements, and so infers that the "alternating periods of faith and scepticism have to be correlated with other facts" (§2343). His next step—and it is to be remembered that Pareto was a professor of economics—is to say that "the oscillations we are trying to understand are like oscillations in the economic field" (§2344). If now we consider the formula in use by economists—depression followed by revival, revival by prosperity, prosperity by crisis, crisis by depression again, in continuous round—it will be recognized that the pattern underlying Pareto's argument is that of the "business cycle." So, too, the increasing awareness of oscillations in ideas which Professor Lovejoy postulates would seem to be another expression of the extent to which the imagery of economics has imposed itself on the thought of the moment.

Confidence in the graphic representation of undulations, fluctuations, and cycles is a definite phase of contemporary mentality. There will be many, therefore, to agree with Pareto that the effort required for an investigation of the history of oscillatory theories "could much more profitably be devoted to objective study of the phenomena themselves, . . . along with a search for measurable indices for the phenomena and for a classification of fluctuations in order of intensity, with the object, if possible, of determining what the major oscillations are, and of discovering a few of the very numerous correlations prevailing between oscillations in different phenomena" (§2330). The policy advocated by Pareto is, then, that we should accept his program and go to work. The plan cannot, however, be endorsed by the student of intellectual history, for the special activity to which he is committed is just that of inquiring into the history of theories and patterns of thought. He might rather be expected to wonder at the emphasis placed, in 1940, on our awareness of oscillations in thought, when Aristotle, twenty-two or three centuries ago, had remarked that "the same opinions appear in cycles among men not once or twice, but infinitely often" (*Meteorologia* I. 339b; *De Caelo* I. 270b; *Metaphysics* XII. 1074b). And he might be expected to wonder at the current interest in a type of cyclic movement for which Machiavelli, at the beginning of the sixteenth century, provided the pattern in his *Florentine History:* "States," he said, "will always be falling from prosperity to adversity, and from adversity they will ascend again to prosperity. Because valor brings peace, peace idleness, idleness disorder, and disorder ruin; once more from ruin arises good order, from order valor, and from valor success and glory."

The phenomenon of oscillation, Professor Lovejoy thinks, is especially

23

conspicuous in political and social history; in his opinion the succession of absolute monarchy, democracy, and dictatorship "seems to be the all-but universal pattern of the sequences of politico-social history," and in confirmation of this opinion he argues that political history, "as Polybius long since observed, . . . [has much] the look of a series of periodic recurrences." It would appear, therefore, that in the field of intellectual history the inquirer may, without further question, accept the views of a political historian concerning the course of change in forms of government as a standard by which to judge the course of change in ideas. Such being the case, it is essential to notice that in the opinion of Polybius "every body or state or action has its natural periods first of growth, then of prime, and finally of decay" (vi. 51. 4), and that the cycle of change in political organization is "the course appointed by nature in which constitutions change, decline, and finally return to the point from which they started" (vi. 9. 10).

Professor Lovejoy mentions the "recurrences" of Polybius with approval, but without making reference to the reliance which that writer placed upon the conception of the "life cycle." It is of interest, therefore, to notice that other writers of recent years who have accepted the theory of "recurrences" have even been at pains to disclaim any dependence upon the analogy. To take an example, Dean Inge, in the *Outspoken Essays* published in 1922, was emphatic in saying that "this doctrine of recurrence is not popular to-day; but," he continued, "whether we like it or not, no other view of the macrocosm is even tenable" (160), and he referred to Goethe, Nietzsche, Kierkegaard, and Shelley as among those who adhered to this belief. Three years later (1925), however, he found it necessary, seemingly in response to critics, to speak of "the notion that civilizations grow old and die like individuals" as untenable, and went on to say that "there is no valid analogy between the life of an organism and that of society"—yet in the same article he continued to employ the analogy in discussing the rise and fall of nations. Pareto found himself in a similar difficulty. In a particular passage (§2330) he gave it as his opinion that the theories of Dr. Draper (*History of the Intellectual Development of Europe*, 1864) "come very close to experimental realities." Draper had separated the intellectual progress of Europe, "like that of an individual," into five periods: the ages of credulity, inquiry, faith, reason, and decrepitude. In a second passage, after quoting Draper's statement about these "ages," Pareto (§2341 note) professed that the author "clearly had an intuitive perception of one of our wide oscillations," but then went on to say that he had let himself be "led astray by a mistaken analogy." The fact is, however, that Draper was a physiologist who, later in life, became interested in intellectual history; and if he arrived at one of Pareto's major oscillations, it was through "tracing analogies," as he himself says, "between the life of individuals and that of nations." Were Pareto writing now, he might with equal propriety claim the conceptions of Spengler and of Toynbee as intuitive perceptions of his larger oscillations, but he would again be met by the fact that in these instances also the patterns introduced had been derived from the biological analogy. And in this situation it is worth mentioning that, in the judgment of O. G. S. Crawford (*Antiquity*, 1931, p. 6), "no one except Spengler has brought the wave theory of civilization into relation with the organic concept of society and shown that the two are really inseparable." Pareto assumed that he might adopt the pattern which Draper utilized in his *History* and yet reject the presuppositions upon which the pattern was based. When, however, a theory formulated by an earlier writer is taken over by a later, acceptance of the conclusions reached carries with it of necessity an acceptance of and responsibility for the antecedent steps. The procedure by which a result is obtained is part and parcel of that result. One cannot admit the validity of Bury's contention (*Idea of Progress*, 110) when he speaks of "those truths which were originally established by false reasoning."

Professor Lovejoy approves of the ideas of Polybius concerning "recurrences," but does not refer to the historian's use of analogy. As a consequence he does not find occasion to comment upon the insistence of Polybius on the conception expressed in the terms "the course appointed by nature" and "the natural periods" of growth and decay. Now Polybius was entirely familiar with the idea that each and every form of life has a characteristic "life history," for then as now one recognized activity of biological inquiry was a determination of the changes which a given organism passes through in its development from its primary stage until its natural death. A "life history" is the course which an individual of a given species may be expected to follow, if nothing interferes. The term "life cycle," as distinguished from "life history," applies to the series of stages which the organism exhibits between successive recurrences of its primary stage. Interest in the way things "naturally" grow or develop was prominent in Greek thought. Thus Thucydides (i. 16) held that in all the different localities of Hellas the peoples would have had a similar development if this, in certain cases, had not been interfered with; he thought that certain of the Hellenic peoples had met with obstacles to their natural and continuous growth. The point of view is characteristic of the teaching of Hippocrates. In his judgment the first business of medical science was to determine the course which diseases normally run, so that in each particular case the physician might be in a position to make a prognosis, might be able to tell what was to be expected. In his opinion the aim of the practitioner was to protect the patient against conditions or circumstances which might interfere with the normal course of the disease and of his recovery. The conception of prognosis was adopted by Polybius, as is clear from his remark that "he alone who has seen how each form naturally arises and develops, will be able to see when, how, and where the growth, perfection, change, and end of each are likely to occur again'' (vi. 4. 12, tr. W. R. Paton). Cicero's way of thinking was not dissimilar: ''The foundation,'' he said, ''of that political wisdom which is the aim of our whole discourse is an understanding of the regular curving path through which governments travel, in order that, when you know what direction any commonwealth tends to take, you may be able to hold it back or take measures to meet the change'' (*Republic* ii. 45, tr. C. W. Keyes).

The type of argument which appears in Polybius and Cicero was made use of by Machiavelli, and at no time since the Renaissance has ceased to influence the thought of Western Europe. It lies back of the ''true history'' of Locke; the ''life of the species'' which Rousseau undertook to write ''after laying facts aside''; the ''natural order of things,'' which, in all the modern states of Europe, Adam Smith thought had been, ''in many respects, entirely inverted''; the ''hypothetical history of a single people'' which Condorcet regarded as ''the golden mean between historical detail and philosophical speculation.'' The procedure exemplified in these instances was still consciously employed in the earlier part of the nineteenth century. Comte, for example, thought that in dealing with historical information it was necessary, for scientific purposes, to strip off from it whatever is peculiar or irrelevant in order to transfer it from the concrete to the abstract. This is obviously the idea expressed by William Whewell, in his *History of the Inductive Sciences* (1837): ''Natural History, when systematically treated, excludes all that is historical, for it classes objects by their permanent and universal properties and has nothing to do with the narration of particular or casual facts.'' In the twentieth century its presence is evident in the various theories of political and cultural cycles and recurrences which are the latest developments in the long endeavor to enlist Hippocratic prognosis in the service of the State. It will, then, be apparent that ''theoretical,'' ''conjectural,'' ''abstract,'' or ''natural'' history, as it was spoken of in the eighteenth century, was arrived at by abstraction from the actual chronological history of men and countries; and, further, that ''abstract'' history is not History as the word is to be understood in the title of the *Journal*. The search for natural, normal, typical sequences of change, whether oscillations, undulations, recurrences, or cycles, is a pursuit inapplicable to the History of Ideas.

In his ''Reflections'' Professor Lovejoy introduces oscillations and recurrences, not by way of contrast to History, but as providing an alternative to the idea of progress. Thus he opposes ''the oscillatory character of much of the history of thought'' to the view that ''what we chiefly witness in the temporal sequence of beliefs . . . is the working of an immanent dialectic whereby ideas are progressively clarified'', and, again, he sets the idea that history has much the ''look of a series of periodic recurrences'' over against the notion that it moves continuously in some particular direction. The editor is not the first to place in opposition the idea of recurrences and that of a single series of changes. Aristotle, indeed, remarked that "Empedocles supposes the course of Nature to return upon itself, coming round again periodically to its starting-point; while Anaxagoras makes it move continuously without repeating itself" (*Physics* I. 187a, tr. P. H. Wicksteed). Among others, John Stuart Mill, a century ago, in his *System of Logic* (VI. x. 3) argued that, from the reciprocal action of the circumstances in which men are placed and their efforts to mould and shape these circumstances for themselves, "there must necessarily result either a cycle or a progress"; one of these, he thought, "must be the type to which human affairs must conform." He went on to say that, while Vico conceived the phenomena of human society as going through periodically the same series of changes, later writers—and he has much to say of Comte—"universally adopted the idea of a trajectory or progress in lieu of an orbit or cycle."

There were writers in Mill's period, however, who found the choice between the idea of a cycle and that of a progress less simple than it appeared to him. Not long after the publication of the *Logic* Herbert Spencer expressed the conviction that "the current conception of progress was shifting and indefinite," and set himself, in his essay on "Progress: its Law and Cause" (1857), to demonstrate "what progress was in itself." The undertaking was accorded more elaborate treatment in his *First Principles* (1862), and the point to be observed is that in this later work (ch. 23, §183) the argument led him "to the conclusion that the entire process of things, as displayed in the aggregate of the visible Universe, is analogous to the entire process of things as displayed in the smallest aggregates." In the next paragraph he states his final position, and this is that "the universally co-existent forces of attraction and repulsion . . . produce . . . alternate eras of Evolution and Dissolution. And thus," he continues, "there is suggested the conception of a past during which there have been successive Evolutions analogous to that which is now going on; and a future during which successive other such Evolutions may go on"—presumably to infinity. It is certainly a fact worthy of notice that a distinguished advocate of the idea of progress should, in the last resort, have found himself committed to a theory of recurrences. Singularly enough, the position of Dean Inge is also anomalous. In his discussion of the idea of progress, this writer began by making the emphatic statement in favor of recurrences which has already been quoted, and proceeded to denounce the idea of progress, as he himself says, "unmercifully." Nevertheless, in the course of his essay, he came to the point of saying that humanity has not advanced "except by accumulating knowledge and experience and the instruments of living" (175)—which is just what advocates of the idea take it to mean. Moreover, his conclusion, that "for individuals, the path of progress is always open," renders appropriate allegiance to the Stoic doctrine of

27

progressio. It might be added that, while Spencer was busy with his "Progress: its Law and Cause," James Martineau had occasion to declare that without a large acquaintance with the history of ideas "the utmost acuteness and depth may waste themselves in reproducing doctrines which have run their cycle, and been forgot."

The examples given, and they might readily be multiplied, suggest strongly that the ideas which Mill regarded as antithetical have displayed a marked tendency to appear in the same literary context and even to maintain themselves in the same mind. It is not remarkable, therefore, that in the published writings of a present-day statesman the thought that "there is a mysterious cycle in human events" should crop up in the midst of an ever-present appeal to the idea of progress. As long ago as the seventeenth century, however, Pascal, who contributed to the formation of the idea of progress in his "Preface to a Treatise on Vacuum," recorded thoughts of a different tenor in his *Pensées*: "Man's nature is not always to advance; it has its advances and retreats" (§354) ; "Nature acts by progress, *itus et reditus;* it goes and returns, then advances further, then twice as much backwards, then more forward than ever, and so on" (§355). In his note to this passage M. Brunschvicg refers to Herbert Spencer; he would, however, have found a closer resemblance in the writings of Madame Blavatsky.

If the difficulty presented by the association in men's minds of ideas apparently incompatible is to be resolved, this end can be attained only through recourse to the history of ideas. Should one, then, turn to Bury's history of the idea of progress, he would find that the first step in the formulation of a "complete doctrine" of progress consisted in a simple modification of the analogy between the life of mankind and that of a single individual. Pascal (in 1647) had argued that "not only does each individual man progress from day to day in knowledge, but mankind as a whole constantly progresses in proportion as the universe grows older, because the same thing happens in the succession of men in general as in the different ages of a single individual man; so the whole succession of men, throughout the centuries, should be envisaged as the life of a single man who lives forever and learns continually" (*Oeuvres*, 1908, II, 139). Fontenelle (in 1688) likewise utilized the analogy between "the men of all ages and a single man." This man, he says, who has lived from the beginning of the world up to the present, had his infancy and his youth, and is now in his prime; but at this point, Fontenelle continues, the comparison fails, for "the man in question will have no old age . . . he will be ever more and more capable of those things which are suited to his prime," in short, the writer thinks, there will be no end to the growth and development of human wisdom (*Oeuvres*, 1728, II, 134). It may be imagined that in the realm of ideas great oaks do not from trifling acorns grow. Yet even today the author of *Mysticism and Logic*, in discoursing of the idea of progress, makes the endeavor to recapture or possibly to modern-

28

ize this same mode of thought. "An extra-terrestrial philosopher," he says (106), "who had watched a single youth up to the age of twenty-one and had never come across any other human being, might conclude that it is the nature of human beings to grow continually taller and wiser in an indefinite progress towards perfection." The argument of Fontenelle, it may be added, was introduced as a weapon in a literary controversy, and in opposition to views which one may find correctly, though undesignedly, presented in Santayana's *Soliloquies*.

It appears, then, that in the attempt to arrive at a comprehension of the facts of human experience different intelligent persons at the present time represent change as a movement in a circle—a "life cycle"; in a semicircle, arc, or trajectory—a "life history"; in a series of undulations or waves— a sequence of "life histories"; and in a straight line. Further, it is now evident that these various ways of looking at the historical world issue from the same source—an analogy between the movement or motion perceptible in human affairs and the growth or development of a living being.

The theories of recurrence and progress alike have their ground in the biological analogy. Nevertheless, the influence of the theories has not been the same, for, while the one implies that the natural course of change, if not interfered with, will lead to desirable results, the other calls imperatively for action. On the one hand, as has already been pointed out, an acceptance of the concept of the "natural," held by Hippocrates and employed in the eighteenth century, found expression in the doctrine of *laissez faire*. Condorcet, on the other hand, an apostle of progress, wanted a science, not merely to foresee the future progress of mankind, but to direct and hasten it. Comte, too, based his Positive Philosophy on the idea that "from science comes prevision, from prevision comes action"; and the purpose of his new science was the creation of a new social system. In our own day, John Dewey calls for "a foreseeing and contriving intelligence" to direct our progress, and puts "primary emphasis upon responsibility for intelligence, for the power which foresees, plans and constructs in advance." It is only a step from this position to that of another contemporary who thinks "humanity must take the management of things into its own hands." Moreover, the long way that the advocates of action are prepared to go is aptly illustrated by Whitehead's declaration (*Adventures of Ideas*, 53) that "Progress consists in modifying the laws of nature," and the purpose of this dramatic measure is "that the Republic on Earth may conform to that Society to be discerned ideally by the divination of Wisdom."

It is time, however, to return to the "Reflections" which have incited this commentary, and to ask who is supposed to be referred to when the editor says that "we have become increasingly aware of the oscillatory character of much of the history of thought." The personal pronoun obviously does not apply to those confidently addressed in the words, "Most of us

29

accept the prosaic fact that the way to make progress is to build on what we have," and so forth. It cannot be intended for the present-day followers of Kant, Hegel, and Marx, of Rousseau and Comte, of Charles Darwin. It certainly does not represent those who still have faith in the Christian conception of history. The pronoun must stand, then, for some of the "intellectual elements of a population" which Pareto disparaged (§2344) rather than for the persons he grouped under "the masses at large." The historian of ideas, however, will not concern himself with either of these groups to the exclusion of the other, though he may show a predilection for the recorded views of the "intellectual elements." Hence the pronoun, far from indicating an increased unanimity of opinion on a matter of importance, actually directs attention to large classes of persons who remain unaffected by or indifferent to the ideas of oscillations, undulations, and cycles. If one were to hazard a parallel to the editor's idea of "increasing awareness," it might be suggested that in recent years popular literature in the United States gives evidence of striking differences of opinion with respect to interpretations of human experience. The fact that these differences of opinion are accentuated may be tested by a moment's reflection on the probable reception in any group should one outspokenly advocate the exact recurrence of social phenomena, the progress of mankind towards perfection, the "economic interpretation" of anything, or the view that events in the world today are in accordance with the conscious designs of Divine Providence.

Earlier in these comments I expressed the opinion that the preference shown by the editor for the theory of oscillations would lead readers and contributors to overlook the existence of other interpretations of history. The remark was not introduced for the purpose of leading up to some alternative view which might be considered preferable, but with the intent of directing attention to the diversities of opinion manifest in the writings of our contemporaries. The remark was, in fact, inspired by the observation (recorded times without number in the history of science) that all advances in knowledge since the time of Thales and Anaximander have been the outcome of inquiries set on foot by the perception of some difficulty, anomaly, or inaccuracy in accepted explanations or explications of phenomena. It had seemed, indeed, when the publication of the *Journal* was announced, that those by whom it was instituted must have been convinced that the present menacing confusion of ideas in the interpretation of human experience not only called for investigation, but created a situation in thought which, under adequate leadership, held promise of new critical and constructive efforts. With this situation and possibility in mind, it was cause for acute distress to find the editor counselling all and sundry that the history of human thought reveals a perpetual swinging of the pendulum between "two not entirely unplausible extreme positions." The motion may be doubted. Three hundred and twenty years ago it was said that "wise

30

and serious men" are wont to suppose "that in the revolution of time and of the ages of the world the sciences have their ebbs and flows; that at one season they grow and flourish, at another wither and decay, yet in such sort that when they have reached a certain point and condition they can advance no further." But the statement made then in the *Novum Organum* was not given as advice or uttered with approval—it was put forward to describe "by far the greatest obstacle to the advancement of knowledge and to the undertaking of new tasks therein."

The problem to which the title of these comments refers is set by the multitude of opinions expressed at the present time in regard to the meaning and significance of civilization and culture. The comments made have been designed to show that, without the conscious use of the history of ideas as a discipline, we go on generation after generation, not swinging between two extremes, but echoing confusedly the conflicting views which have been accumulated by our predecessors in the course of centuries.

University of California

Editorial Note

Professor Teggart's interesting and learned comment on a single page of the editor's "Reflections on the History of Ideas" in Vol. I, No. 1, is especially welcome as a contribution towards that aim of "mutual criticism and mutual aid" which is not least among the purposes of this journal. In further pursuance of this aim the editor had proposed to comment in turn, in this issue, upon some of Mr. Teggart's observations with which he finds himself in incomplete agreement. To do so adequately, however, would result in devoting too much of the space in a single number to one topic, to the exclusion of other contributions; publication of further discussion of it is therefore deferred to the next volume. But one or two apparent misconceptions of Mr. Teggart about the policy of the journal should be corrected without delay. The journal is not committed to any "particular interpretation of historical phenomena"; nor does the editor, when suggesting any such interpretation, "speak in an authoritative manner"; nor are contributors such timid folk as Mr. Teggart seems to imagine. On the other hand, the editor enjoys (though Mr. Teggart would seem to imply that he should not enjoy) the same freedom of opinion as other contributors; and in the "Reflections," after indicating in the first section the general aims and hopes inspiring the foundation of such a periodical, he proceeded (as was expressly explained) to present "opinions" on certain "currently controverted questions," for which "the writer alone [was] responsible." It is therefore difficult to understand the cause of the apprehensions which Mr. Teggart intimates in his first paragraph; at all events, he, and others, may be assured that they are groundless—and also that, where controversial questions of interpretation and theory are concerned, much is likely to appear in these pages to which no member of the Editorial Board should be presumed to subscribe.

ARTHUR O. LOVEJOY

Chapter III.a

DISCUSSION

GEISTESGESCHICHTE VS. HISTORY OF IDEAS AS APPLIED TO HITLERISM

By Leo Spitzer

"No es la idea la que apasiona, sino la pasión que idealiza" (José Bergamín)

Professor Lovejoy, in a provocative article entitled "The Meaning of Romanticism for the Historian of Ideas" (*Journal of the History of Ideas*, III, 3), considers the particular combination of three "separate," "ruling ideas" of "the Romantic period" (1780–1800) in Germany, and sees therein an important factor "in the production of the state of mind upon which the totalitarian ideologies depend for their appeal" and, consequently, of "the tragic spectacle of Europe in 1940"; these three ideas, as excogitated in the 1780's and 90's, are *Ganzheit, Streben,* and *Eigentümlichkeit* (holism or organicism, dynamism or voluntarism, diversificationism).

While recognizing the presence and the importance of these three ideas in Hitlerism, I cannot see in them, or in their "combination," an important factor in the production of this system; I do not believe in their historical continuity, nor can I accept the assumption that any historical movement may be explained by that analytical kind of "History of Ideas" of which Professor Lovejoy is the most outspoken and the most illustrious advocate. I submit that not analytical History of Ideas but only synthetic *Geistesgeschichte* (which untranslatable term I do not consider to be properly rendered by "History of Ideas," with its plural unintegrated into a unity)[1] can explain historical events. It is as a criticism of his general methodology that this paper is primarily intended; but I have chosen to concentrate on this particular article of Professor Lovejoy's because the contemporary significance of the conclusions drawn therein offers a singular opportunity to test the soundness of his method

The first step taken by Professor Lovejoy is to disavow the title of his article "The Meaning of Romanticism . . .," for to him "Romanticism" has no meaning ("signification")—that is, it defies definition. Because the term cannot be straightforwardly defined he proceeds as though the phenomenon did not exist; since the whole is ungraspable he clings to individual facts of thought; instead of considering Romanticism he chooses a side-path by considering instead certain ideas, to him distinctive of "the Romantic

[1] I do not use the English expression *"intellectual* history," because of the overintellectual connotation of this term, which does not include, as does the German word *Geist, all* the creative impulses of the human mind (e.g., feelings): the *Histoire littéraire du sentiment religieux en France* of Abbé Bremond is *Geistesgeschichte,* not intellectual history.

period." But it is just such an analytical procedure that destroys the organic entity and makes the understanding of the whole no longer possible.

"Romanticism" is of course a very complicated "thing," since it is a "thing" hypostatized by the student of history in order to represent as a unit many traits concurring in different and not always precisely measurable doses in this particular movement. But so is any other classificatory term introduced by historians, as, for example, its opposite "classicism" (Romanticism is of course *more* complicated, for a certain anarchy is an inherent feature of this phenomenon born of revolt). There is, of course, a certain violence done in cutting out of the flow of time a particular period, marked by various traits, and subsuming these under a label. But such violence is in the nature of the classifying function of language. If Professor Lovejoy's terminological punctiliousness were to be generally adopted by historians, they would be thereby deprived of the linguistic symbols which spare them the trouble of redescribing each time a given series of events which have been integrated into a unit, held together by a certain *Geist*, by the scholar who hopes to have grasped historic reality. And this would tend to encourage indulgence in the easy scepticism of that professor of history who, faced with the different conceptions of the French Revolution entertained by different historians (and by the revolutionaries themselves), asks cynically: "*Was* there ever a French Revolution?" And why stop at this stage of scepticism? Why not ask "was there any Goethe?"—since we know that no parcel of Goethe's mind or body remained the same during the whole course of his life, marked by the manifold utterances of so self-contradictory a genius. By coining nouns in *-ism* and *-ist* the historian is simply following the natural trend of any linguistic community; indeed science in general does nothing but carry forward and perfect the work of language, as Condillac and Lichtenberg have said. Thus Romanticism is an appropriate symbol, coined by language, which suggests an emphasis on emotion, on the irrational, the mysterious, the metaphysical, the Christian, the fatalistic, the historical, a reaction against classicism (that *romantisme dompté*), etc., etc.—all of which features have in reality been found together in a definite period.

But since Professor Lovejoy does not recognize the factual existence of this compound phenomenon, he eschews the term "Romanticism." He uses the adjective "Romantic," but only with strictly temporal limitations ("the Romantic decades," "the Romantic period") or else in expressions which exempt him from responsibility ("writers traditionally labelled 'Romantic'," "the German writers who . . . first introduced the term 'Romantic' "). He does not hesitate to use the personal substantive, since historians are agreed on the specific individuals to whom this term in *-ist* applies—but who can these be save the well-known representatives of German "Romanticism"? It is as if one should speak of Protestants while denying that such a thing as "Protestantism" exists (there are at least two features common to both Romanticism and Protestantism: rebellion against previous beliefs, and the supposition, for each one, of a creed of its own). Professor Lovejoy refuses to take the step which the Romanticists of whom he writes took, and which has been endorsed by common speech after them: the positing of an *-ism* as a—more or less hypothetical—unit. We may, *quâ* philosophers of language, welcome the *Sprachkritik*[2] which Lovejoy applies to language as a human institution, in regard to an *-ism*, but why should we, *quâ* historians, shun a generally accepted term—and, in fact, a generally understood term? For the cultured public reacts to this word with the correct associations of connotations; not everyone is led by "his own associations of ideas with the word": there is a *communis opinio* concerning the descriptive elements implied by "Romanticism." It is only when analysts seek to replace the synthetic and descriptive implications of such a term by clear-cut definition (an attempt in which they must inevitably fail) that anarchy results; the unity which was understood by everyone is destroyed. It is a bias to believe that understanding must always wait on definition. To define even the word *table* is more difficult than to use the word correctly. And to distinguish all the different senses of *nature*, as Lovejoy has sought to do in other papers, does not release us from the obligation to see all these senses as a unit—since common use has posited this unit. In fact, the *-ism* "Romanticism," offered to us by language, can be, *pace* Lovejoy, a proper object of scientific research.

Having renounced an investigation of the phenomenon of Romanticism (i.e., denied "signification" to the term) he turns toward the "significance," the historic results, of some Romantic ideas: he limits himself to an examination of three separate ruling ideas which he has isolated by analysis out of the bulk of the German writings of the 1780's and 90's. Professor Lovejoy outlines the next procedure incumbent upon the historian of ideas: to inquire into (1) the "logical," (2) the "psychological," (3) the "historical" relations of the ideas so discriminated. The first two inquiries the historian of ideas is admonished to carry out in his own mind "before he goes on to confront their results with the historical evidence to be found in his sources." That is, one should ask oneself: "what are the logical implications of such an idea as *streben?*," then, "what psychological relationships, what elective affinities, what emotional concomitants, are theoretically possible to such an idea?," and finally, "what actually *were* the implications of this idea, as found with a given thinker, in a given period?" According to Lovejoy the first two steps correspond to "the phase of constructing tentative hypotheses in the work of the natural scientist."

This obsession with the methods of natural science I shall discuss later; here I should like to stress the a priori approach advocated by Lovejoy as

[2] Fritz Mautner, the coiner of this term, has spoken of the *Schlangenbetrug der Sprache.*

proper for the analyst of historical events. The analyst is not to seek to understand the given historical event in its complexity; he must analyze the compound offered to him (before really having understood its entirety), then close his eyes to the real event as it has taken place in history, and proceed to the combination, in his alembic, of the supposedly "pure chemical elements"—only later to compare with the *homunculus* of his breeding what history really has done with the same elements. But this last, properly "historical" operation is the *only one* which history itself, in its concreteness, has carried out: the operations (1) and (2) are useless games *in abstracto*. It is as if before contemplating a picture called "Spring" the student of art, after having read simply the inscription, should close his eyes and attempt to figure out the various logical possibilities of depicting Spring —only later to discover that he has not reckoned with the possibility (or possibilities) actually chosen by the painter. Why not first look at the actual picture?

Underlying the whole reasoning of Professor Lovejoy's scientific program is the assumption of the possibility of an "unemotional idea": an idea detachable from the soul of the man who begot or received the idea, from the spiritual climate which nourished it; an abstract idea that survives in history from generation to generation; a separate idea, always identifiable to the eye of the historian, in whatever period. *Eigentümlichkeit, Streben, Ganzes* may be discriminated in Romanticism; *Eigentümlichkeit, Streben, Ganzes* are just as easily to be discriminated in Hitlerism. I must object to that divorce between thought and feeling which Lovejoy seems to think possible: according to his phrase "affective *concomitants*" he would imply that it is only in a secondary way, as a result of a kind of adulteration, that the abstract idea is given a new slant by emotional factors. I should say rather that important ideas are from the start a *passionate* response to problems which agitate their period. Even the rationalism of Descartes was conceived, by him and by his contemporary followers, as a passionate destruction of an ageing order (Victor Klemperer, the German philologian, has spoken of the *"heisse Vernunft,"* "rationalism hot with passion" of Corneille the Cartesian). And the three Romantic "ideas" which Professor Lovejoy has singled out, organicism, dynamism, and diversificationism, seem to me to spring from *feelings:* basically, from the bodily or vital feelings of a healthy organism which enjoys the full display of its forces, and takes pride in its individuality. Indeed it is precisely this "healthiness" of Romantic thought which distinguishes it from the unhealthy, hectic fanaticism of the Hitlerites.

The assumption that an idea in history is a completely separate element is inconceivable to me: in any movement, with any individual, one idea is ever ready to merge with another. Nor may the living idea be considered apart from the movement, from the individual. *Streben* with the Schlegels

35

cannot be the same as with Goethe or Nietzsche—and the idea of any philosopher must be *toto coelo* different from an "idea" of a Hitler.[3] Professor
Lovejoy will not permit himself the use of the "label" *Romanticism,* but he
does not hesitate to employ the three labels: *organicism, dynamism, diversificationism.* The first label, it is true, has been applied to a phenomenon
composed of elements which, taken singly, may appear disparate and even
antithetical. But surely not as disparate, not as antithetical as are the three
main tendencies of Romantic idealism to those of Hitlerian barbarism, to
which Lovejoy would apply the same labels.

To a large extent Lovejoy admits this disparity. He does not suggest
for a moment that the Nazis have an organic attitude toward life and nature
and art. Obviously, the ideal of a personal striving toward the Infinite, as
an aim for the German individual, has no place in the Nazi system. Nor
does the New Order foster that tolerance, that joy in diversificationism,
which the Romantics knew. How then, one may wonder, can he say that
the Romantic ideas of *Ganzheit, Streben ins Unendliche,* and *Eigentümlichkeit* have survived?

He is enabled to say this, without the slightest difficulty, because he is
dealing, not with the Romantic ideas themselves (i.e., *the ideas as conceived
and as applied by the Romantics*) but with three abstract entities which he
has chosen to name with the same names. As for the disparity between the
actual Romantic ideas and those of Hitlerism, this is to be explained by reference either to (1) shift of application of the abstraction, or (2) a change
in the nature of the "affective concomitants" attached thereto. *Eigentümlichkeit,* he says, has remained *Eigentümlichkeit.* It is true that, in utter
opposition to the Romantic ideal of diversification, the New Order depends
upon a system of standardization, of *Gleichschaltung,* which aims to obliterate all individuality. But this involves factor (1): shift of application:
Eigentümlichkeit has shifted from the individual to the State. Or again,
whereas to the Romantics *Eigentümlichkeit* inspired an essentially tolerant
attitude, which encouraged each thing's growing in its kind, in Hitlerism
it manifests itself in an essentially *in*tolerant insistence on one's own particular kind as supreme. To explain this we need only turn to factor (2):
there has been an alteration in the "affective concomitants." Thus we need
not be surprised that Lovejoy is able to find organicism with the Nazis: *das
Ganze* has been applied to the political sphere, emerging from this operation
as Totalitarianism, even though in this New Order the organic attitude may
not endure, and in this Whole, which is the State, the individual functions,
not organically, as a living member, but as a machine. Shift of application

[3] The great truth on this subject is implicitly stated, in the same number of this
Journal, in a quotation from Karl Mannheim, which turns up in a review: "All the
ideas that must be described as historical, change with the changing conception of
human nature, and with the ethic and psychology that goes with it."

likewise explains how *Streben ins Unendliche* may be destroyed and yet survive: now it is the State that strives. In such enormous shifts as this lies precisely the subject-matter which should properly concern the historian of ideas: which historical forces are responsible for the alterations? There is no driving force in any historical "line" *itself!*

After comparing the three Romantic ideas with their travestied counterparts in Hitlerism, one may well ask the reason why ideas potential of such good have borne such bitter fruit. This reason Lovejoy finds, not in any abrupt sociological change, not in the slow development of various trends deep-rooted in German civilization; he is able to solve the problem without stepping beyond the limits of the three ideas themselves. He insists that it is the *combination* of the three elements which is such an important factor in the establishment of Hitlerism. Any one or two of the ideas alone, he states, might have had beneficial results; it is in the compound formed by the three elements that the source of the evil must be sought. One is tempted to ask why the "culminating joint-effect" of which he speaks did not materialize until a century and a half after the teachings of the Romantic decades, and why the period immediately following upon Romanticism was attended with such a marvelous expansion in all fields of the humanities. It was then that modern philology, linguistics, history of art, folklore, etc., were brought to birth; and in these fields it is clear how the self-same "combination of elements" culminated in a quite different joint-effect. Here the diabolic trinity *Ganzheit—Streben—Eigentümlichkeit* did not work to the hurt of science and art. And, in opposition to Professor Lovejoy, I submit the thesis that it could just as well have brought about a beneficial German and international situation. It might have led to an introspective mystic way of life as advocated by Rilke after the first World War, which would have consisted in an individual striving toward the goal of developing the particular richness of the German spirit, by incorporating the whole of the world in itself. It is just such an ideal that Hitler would erase forever from the minds of his subjects.

But perhaps Professor Lovejoy does not mean to imply that his three elements must *necessarily* have combined to such a pernicious effect. At one point he indicates that it was because *das Ganze* had come to represent the State (a development apparently harmful *per se*) that *Streben* and *Eigentümlichkeit* were perforce modified and accommodated to this new nationalistic implication. But how is one entitled to assume that, within this combination, it was *das Ganze,* as the State, which represented the controlling idea, behind which the other two must needs fall in line? Moreover, the influence of the concern with the State is a variable factor, and the question of "dosage," disregarded by Professor Lovejoy, is highly important; the application of this combination of ideas to the State could, theoretically, have produced an ideal situation.

And one may even question the legitimacy of positing a combination of a, b, and c. Professor Lovejoy recognizes that other ideas are present in Hitlerism; he would probably admit the presence of an indeterminate number of ideas, d, e, f, . . . x. How then, in a discussion purporting to deal with Hitlerism, which is all of these things and all of these things at once, can one assume that any three of these elements have joined together to form a compound, and produce a joint effect? Or, even assuming such a combination, $a + b + c$, since a given idea has now this implication and now that $(a_1, a_2, a_3, . . . a_x)$, the actual number of combinations and permutations is virtually endless. Is it $a_2 + b_5 + c_{12}$ that have formed a compound? If so, the result may very well be quite different from that produced by $a_3 + b_7 + c_{16}$, etc.

The development suggested by Professor Lovejoy could perhaps be illustrated by the following diagram:

$$a\ + b\ + c\ + \ .\ .\ .\ x \qquad \text{Romanticism (``ideas of the Romantic critics}$$
$$\downarrow \quad \downarrow \quad \downarrow \qquad\qquad\qquad\qquad \text{of the 1780–90's'')}$$
$$a_1 + b_1 + c_1 + \ .\ .\ .\ x_1 \qquad \text{Hitlerism}$$

a is continued in a_1, etc.; $a + b + c$ form a compound; this compound "helps to explain" Hitlerism; therefore Romanticism helps to explain Hitlerism.

In contrast I submit a different diagram:

$$(a_{a\text{-}\rho},\ b_{a\text{-}\rho},\ c_{a\text{-}\rho},\ .\ .\ .\ x) \qquad \text{Romanticism}$$
$$(a_{\nu\text{-}\omega},\ b_{\nu\text{-}\omega},\ c_{\nu\text{-}\omega},\ .\ .\ .\ x) \qquad \text{Hitlerism}$$

I draw no lines to indicate a continuity between the separate ideas in the first and second series; such a line might suggest an identity between, for example, a_η and a_π, and would give no indication of the differences that might exist between the subscripts. There has been no continuity nor are the ideas separate entities. The subscripts α–ρ and ν–ω make allowance for the possibility of really identical variants in the two systems, although the likelihood of their occurrence is not too great; thus the "ideas" ν, ξ, o, π, ρ may be common to both. Nor are the combinations of the three ideas separate entities. The only two entities involved are Romanticism and Hitlerism, each conceived as a whole. These form "climates," here indicated, for convenience in printing, by parentheses; there should really be an ellipse enclosing each polynome. There are no connecting threads; the two entities are disparate and incommensurable.

It must be stated that at no point does Professor Lovejoy declare his belief in the inevitable efficacy of the combination he posits; nowhere does he speak in terms of rigorous laws. Indeed, he is continually introducing qualifications lest any statement seem over-bold or too rigorously scientific. But I maintain that the very appeal of his article rests precisely upon the bold *implications* of his study, upon the scientific attitude *underlying* all his propositions. A scholarly text, as well as a poem, may have overtones; and listening to them is an essential part of reading. And it is to these implications, to this underlying attitude, that I am opposed.

For I do not doubt that like most readers I should find myself mainly in agreement with Professor Lovejoy's conceptions both of Romanticism and of Hitlerism. He must feel as keenly as I the vast differences between the two climates; it is evident that he recognizes that the *Eigentümlichkeit* of Hitlerism is a far cry from the *Eigentümlichkeit* of the Schlegels. And if I have insisted so strongly upon these differences of climate it is because, in my opinion, it is the two climates which must first be grasped; it is the differences which strike me as far more significant than any single details which might be said to exist in common. If Professor Lovejoy, faced with the same two climates, chooses to emphasize continuity, to deal with separate ideas abstracted from their wholes, it is because he has adopted the analytic method of the chemist, who isolates elements from their compounds.

Now the chemist claims for each element certain constant properties, a certain determinable efficacy; he establishes rigorous laws—otherwise he could not convince. Professor Lovejoy makes no such claim for his "element-ideas." But in spite of his own caution the very method he has chosen is one which must depend for its cogency upon scientific rigor. An article entitled "The Meaning of Romanticism," which rejects the possibility of ascertaining the "signification" of this term and seeks, in its stead, the "significance" of the historical phenomenon—and finds it in Hitlerism: such an article, orientated from the start to such a goal, can reach it only by establishing clear-cut, uncontrovertible relationships. Otherwise, Hitlerism has no place in this article on Romanticism. *Tertium non datur.*

To a reader who has made up his mind to follow the scientific method in the history of ideas, it must be disappointing that Lovejoy's method, while not flexible enough to cope with the complexity of the problems envisaged, is, at the same time, not rigorous enough—not as rigorous as a "scientific" approach should be.

But now let us step beyond the limits of the narrow system of *a, b,* and *c* and examine the second "climate." As with Romanticism, Lovejoy does not discuss Hitlerism-as-a-whole or seek to define it. Nor shall I hazard a clear-cut definition or a lengthy discussion; instead I shall try to "describe" it, simply by jotting down a list of catch-words, *-isms*—a list which does not pretend to be exhaustive. This description will be as little original as any description must be of a phenomenon which has become familiar to all thinking contemporaries:

nationalism + socialism [= national socialism] in domestic as in foreign policy; collectivism (*Volksnähe*); messianism (*Führerprinzip*); anti-intellectualism; *Realpolitik* and worship of technology (the German word *Gleichschaltung,* originally applied to electrical contrivances, is significant!); paganism (this-worldliness); acceptance of death and dangerous life; racism ("diversificationism"); *étatisme* (*das Ganze*); machiavellianism (force + ruse); emphasis on a simple, austere private life (in contrast with the sumptuous "life of the State"); politicism (everything must be considered from the political angle—especially the power of words); dynamism (called *"Dezisionismus"* by Karl Schmidt, the theoretician of the Reich); an (officially stated) hierarchy of values and of individuals—subject to change.

To this list of the component parts of Hitlerism it may be objected that some are only the methods purporting to carry out the "ideas"—as, for example, machiavellianism and the worship of technology. But who could truly claim that in Hitler's system Machiavelli's story of the lion and the fox serves merely the subordinate purpose of suggesting a means for the carrying out of certain ideas, and has not itself come to represent an idea, an ideal of a new type of mankind? And as for technology, this is surely an "idea," an *idée fixe* with Hitler. Again, one may object that my descriptive terms are often contradictory: socialism of the Hitler brand is not egalitarian but tinged with diversificationism (as much so in the international as in the national field); and the anti-intellectualistic creed of "soil and blood," "back to nature and hearth" should inspire a hatred of technicism. But such is the reality of Hitlerism and to iron out contradictions would be to falsify this reality.

It is the totality of just such heterogeneous features that gives us the moral climate of Hitlerism—which tinges each of the single features. Embedded in this whole one may discern Lovejoy's three elements. But with a picture, however roughly sketched, of this whole before our eyes, how arbitrary now it seems to single out any given three component parts and marshal them into a combination! Indeed, I wonder if a study of Hitlerism would ever lead one to single out, even for emphasis, these particular three (unless, of course, one had begun his inquiry with these ideas already in mind). That Professor Lovejoy found these ideas in Romanticism is one matter, and everyone must agree that they are indeed highly characteristic of the German Romantics. But what student of Nazi philosophy, concerned immediately with the "tragic spectacle of Europe today" considered in all its complexity, would think of characterizing it in terms of *Ganzheit— Streben ins Unendliche—Eigentümlichkeit?* This is only another way of saying that the "Romantic" elements *a, b, c* found in Hitlerism occupy a different position in relation to other elements and possess a different degree of relevance for the Hitlerian system.

Now the question of the relative importance of these three ideas in the Hitlerian system has, if considered merely as a difference of opinion about the present-day political situation in Germany, no particular significance for the debate in question. But I am not objecting that Prof. Lovejoy, after studying Hitlerism, has chosen to assign more importance to certain aspects than I should. My objection is that he found these ideas first, not in Hitlerism, but in Romantic idealism, and then sought to find them in Hitlerism by the procedure of tracing the career of individual, abstract ideas as isolated units. This method seems to me erroneous, and bound to lead to erroneous conclusions; and as a corollary to my objections to his method, I must object also to its results—which consist not only of a questionable characterization of Hitlerism, but, what is far more important, of the conclusion that present events can be blamed on the great Romantic thinkers.

This is a startling opinion to ascribe to Prof. Lovejoy, and I do not make the statement lightly. I find this assumption implied throughout the article in his insistence on *continuity;* if I believed, as does Prof. Lovejoy, that the main ideas of Romanticism had survived until today and that they represented the main ideas of Hitlerism, then I should *have* to believe that Romanticism has been responsible for Hitlerism. To this argument based on his paper as a whole, it might be objected that, since Prof. Lovejoy is dealing with abstract ideas the nature of which I fail to grasp and the existence of which I doubt, it is possible that he has not drawn the logical deductions which appear to me inevitable, given, e.g., such a statement as *"Eigentümlichkeit* has survived." But how, then, is the following positive statement to be explained?

For a particular group of these [Romantic] ideas, *continuously at work on the minds of the educated and reading public,* for fifteen decades, have produced in our time a sort of culminating joint-effect, which is at least an essential and conspicuous part of the monstrous scene presented by Germany and by Europe today.

What meaning does this sentence possess, if not that Romanticism has been influential in the production of Hitlerism? For while it is one thing to say that the Nazi leaders have seized upon certain Romantic ideas, distorting them to serve their purpose, it is quite another to say that these ideas worked continuously upon the people, making it easier for them to accept Hitlerism.

But it is hardly accurate to speak of the continuous influence of these or any other Romantic ideas on the "educated and reading public." In German secondary schools and universities, the teaching of the humanities was, until the unhappy day when Hitler came to power, based upon the German *classics* of the eighteenth century: Goethe and Schiller were given three times more space and importance in the literature classes than the Romanticists, who in Germany at least produced few lasting and perfect works of art. Indeed, it was the humanistic spirit of the classics and of Kant which managed to counterbalance the strong nationalistic tendencies which betrayed themselves in the *Gymnasien.* In the second place—perhaps this is primary—it was precisely *not* the educated and reading public which had become conditioned for Nazism: it was from quite other ranks of society that Hitler recruited his followers. Thomas Mann, who is after all the typical representative of humanistic tendencies in the higher German bourgeoisie, in his *Deutsche Ansprache* called the Hitlerites "truants from school" (*entlaufene Gymnasiasten*). And this is the true analysis: Hitlerism arose not among those who formed the backbone of German culture, but from the masses of the uneducated (ever a more ready prey for slogans) who had increased in number under the impact of war and post-war conditions. Thus there is no continuity of teaching from the Schlegels to Hitler; between them there is a cultural break caused by social upheaval. To the intellectuals of the Reich, the seizure of power by the Nazis appeared, as Eric Vögelin has phrased it, "an invasion by a foreign nation" (*The Journal of Politics*, III, 164).

Hitlerism is pagano-collectivism, the German variant of a worldwide development—the ancestry of which is certainly not to be sought in the German Romantics of the eighteenth century, but, as Vögelin correctly states, in Marx and Lenin, to whom the *Führer* has avowed his debt (or rather, to the vulgarized decoctions of their philosophies, as he understood them). Naturally, if one wanted to "analyze" Hitler's "ideas" and trace them back to Marx, and from Marx to Hegel and from Hegel to the Romantics, one could say that, in a way, Hitler's thinking goes back to the Romantics; but then one would arrive at the truism that Europe in general has gone through Romanticism, a conclusion which would not lead to any specific reduction of this or that Hitlerian thought to Romantic ideas.

It is not the letter of any idea, or of any set of ideas, but the "spirit" in which the ideas are carried out and allowed to associate with each other— it is the total system of ideas charged with emotion that explains an historical movement. Professor Lovejoy's analytic "History of Ideas" fits easily into the pattern which, according to his own description, was superseded by the new scientific ideas which germinated in the 1780's and 90's:

> The whole was just the aggregate of its parts, and apart from them was nothing; and the dominant conception of scientific method . . . proceeded in its investigation of any complex thing, by an "analysis" or "resolution" of it into its ultimate component parts. To understand *it,* you had but to take it to pieces, to know the parts and *their* characteristics and the laws of their action, and how many of them there were in the given complex—and your problem was solved.

This is exactly what Professor Lovejoy is doing in his History of Ideas and what, according to my way of thinking, has made him miss the right explanation of Hitlerism. In fact, this atomistic kind of History of Ideas is derived, *via* the immediate French models (Lanson's history of the idea of progress, etc.), from the analytical philosophy of history of the French Encyclopedists, more specifically from Voltaire's *Dictionnaire philosophique,* which obviously rests on the assumption that, just as words may be listed in a dictionary detached from the whole of the linguistic system in question (and, supposedly, may exist as detached items), so ideas are detachable from their "climate" (Voltaire would say *"moeurs"*).

But we are only now beginning to realize how little justified is the linguistic analogy itself: the boundaries between words are never fixed; and it is impossible to trace the history of a single word without taking into account the whole conceptual field (*Begriffsfeld*). One cannot outline the history of *wit,* for example, without taking into account *wisdom, cleverness, intelligence, humor, sage, wizard,* etc. And it is even more true that the linear histories of ideas, in order to correspond to reality, must fit into larger histories of spiritual aggregates. Even Voltaire occasionally recognizes this; it is true of his French followers, it is especially true of Professor Lovejoy himself, whose masterpiece, *The Great Chain of Being,* the history of "three ideas which have . . . been so closely and constantly associated that they have often operated as a unit," turns out to be a kind of universal *Geistesgeschichte,* a world history of spiritual climates focused on these several ideas. The most brilliant chapters, those dealing with the cosmography of the Renaissance, the philosophy of the Enlightenment and of Romanticism, really belong to universal history—and are only incidentally connected with Plato's "chain of being." It could not happen otherwise; it happened fortunately (*felix culpa!*)—and this in spite of the program, outlined in the introduction, for an analytic history of ideas comparable to analytic chemistry: the program carried out, if somewhat hesitatingly, in the article under discussion.

I do not deny the possibility of writing a history of one idea; but in that case the idea must remain in its proper climate—that is, within the limits of one definite science or field of activity. Obviously one may write the history of the idea of evolution *in biology,* the idea of inhibitions *in psychology,* the idea of ideology *in political science.* It is also possible to study horizontally the influence of the idea of biological evolution in other fields of human thought and activity, the influence of the idea of psychic inhibitions on other fields, etc. But to reduce artificially the history of an historical event or movement, which rests on the whole human climate of an epoch, to two or three components, and to make this match a similar "reduction" of another epoch arrived at with equal artificiality, seems to me to involve an encroachment of the analytic capacities of the inquirer on the human reality that is the object of his research. Moreover, to shift continuously from an "idea" in the realm of thought to an "idea" in the realm of action, and to assume their basic identity, seems to me to be based upon an illicit generalization which in our case blurs the clear lines of demarcation between thinking and action.

In opposition to such an *histoire des idées,* with its bias for naturalistic and atomistic methods applied to the history of the human mind, I propose a *Geistesgeschichte,* in which *Geist* represents nothing ominously mystical or mythological, but simply the totality of the features of a given period or movement which the historian tries to *see as a unity*—and the impact of which, the philosophy of the Encyclopedists and positivistic mathematicians to the contrary, does in fact amount to more than that of the aggregate of the parts.   There have been, God knows, many *Fabrikate* of more or less recent German make, in which the pursuit of the integration of features of detail into one whole has served as an excuse for confusion and muddled thinking—so rightly condemned by Professor Lovejoy.   But such writings should not be allowed to discredit the legitimate endeavors of a Burckhardt, a Dilthey, a Simmel, a Max Weber, a Tröltsch.   There is nothing fraudulent or even revolutionary in a procedure which seeks to see wholes, to put one whole into relation with another, instead of making combinations of parts detached from their wholes.   This is simply the *factual,* the more accurate approach toward the historical problem in question.

And so it seems to me tragic that in inorganically detaching certain features from the whole of Romanticism in order to draw lines of continuity with our times, the historian of ideas has discarded the very method, discovered by the Romantics, which is indispensable for the understanding of the alternation of historical or cultural climates.

Johns Hopkins University.

Chapter III.b

REPLY TO PROFESSOR SPITZER

By Arthur O. Lovejoy

Professor Spitzer's animadversions upon my paper range so widely over many issues that it is impossible to deal adequately with all of them within reasonable limits of length. I shall therefore confine my reply chiefly to an examination of his views and reasonings on three topics.

I. *Methods of the study of intellectual history.*

The most general and fundamental, and at least in that sense the most important, question raised by Professor Spitzer has to do with the nature of the methods which legitimately may be used in the study of the history of thought. He contrasts two methods. One of them is "analytical" in its procedure; it regards the historic products of thought as compounds which can be better understood when they are resolved into their "elements." The other method treats all such products—including apparently every -ism and -ity for which language provides a general name—as "organic wholes," to which an "analytical procedure" cannot be applied, since such procedure "destroys the organic entity and makes the understanding of the whole no longer possible." The former method assumes that there can be such a thing as a history of "ideas," in the plural; the latter eschews the plural, and can be properly designated only by the "untranslatable" German compound *Geistesgeschichte*. The principal purpose of Mr. Spitzer's paper is to show that the second method is the only admissible one, while the first can lead only to misunderstanding of the phenomena it seeks to investigate, and should therefore never be employed.

Since the "analytical method" of which Mr. Spitzer would enjoin the use seems to be identified by him with one which I have elsewhere attempted to define, and sometimes to practise, I may perhaps be permitted to recall precisely what it is—and what it is not. However complex its procedures and results may sometimes be, it is based upon two very simple and (as I had supposed) innocent working hypotheses: (a) There are certain discriminable factors or "units," both ideational and affective, logical and alogical, which may be, and often are, recurrent or persistent in the historic manifestations of the workings of the human mind; i.e., one or another of them may be found in different writers, systems or periods, though in very diverse combinations with other factors. (b) The thought of an individual writer or of a school, or the dominant fashion of thought of a period, may, and usually does, contain a number of such distinct conceptual and affective components. To understand such a complex as a whole, it is necessary to discriminate these components and observe their relations and interplay.

How far or in what instances these hypotheses are true is a question of historical fact; they can be finally verified only by an examination of texts.

REPLY TO PROFESSOR SPITZER

But to maintain that they cannot possibly be true is equivalent to the assertion of the two following propositions: (1) that no specific concept, judgment, mode of reasoning, or belief, and no specific type of emotion, can ever occur in the consciousness of more than one individual; (2) that no historic thought-product—e.g., Platonism, Thomism, the Critical Philosophy, "Romanticism," "Protestantism"—has any discriminable parts or elements; each of them is a pure "logical simple." For it is only logical simples that are insusceptible of analysis. In short, to deny in principle the legitimacy of the analytical method is to set up two very odd premises: that no two or more writers ever have the same idea, and that no one writer ever has more than one idea.

Since Mr. Spitzer does deny in principle the legitimacy of the analytical method, it is to these two singular paradoxes that he is committed. But if an analytical procedure is applied to his article, it becomes evident that he also frequently contradicts both of them, and that, when dealing with the concrete phenomena of intellectual history, he usually employs the method which, when employed by others, he reprobates. Thus—assuming that "Romanticism" is a distinct entity already unequivocally identified by that term—he tells us what its "descriptive elements" are: there are eight of them, plus an unspecified number of others presumably referred to by "etc., etc." So with the movement "Hitlerism," in the ideology of which he finds no fewer than 15 "component parts." I am unable to imagine how these "elements" or "parts" could have been discovered except by an "analytical procedure"—though it is not always quite clear to me to precisely what the analysis has been applied. In these cases Mr. Spitzer is plainly adopting the second of the two hypotheses underlying the analytical method: that historic doctrines, -isms, etc., are compounds, of which the components can be logically distinguished and enumerated. If analysis "destroys the organic entity," Mr. Spitzer has evidently destroyed Romanticism, Hitlerism, and other such entities. It is also clear that, on occasion, he accepts the first of the two hypotheses mentioned: that the same ideas, or "descriptive elements," may be recognizably present in different complexes or "wholes." There is, he grants, "a possibility of identical variants in two systems," though he thinks the likelihood of their occurrence not great. The possibility is enough to justify the method, which primarily consists simply in carefully scrutinizing the textual evidence to see whether or not an identical component recurs in two or more contexts. The question as to the frequency with which this happens can be answered only after the method has been extensively applied. On this question Mr. Spitzer presents no evidence; but in practice, his analyses of certain particular systems, -isms, and the like, disclose a number of elements which obviously may, and historically do, repeat themselves. The "emphasis on the fatalistic" which he finds in Romanticism is presumably not wholly different from the same emphasis in

Mohammedanism.   Certain ideas which he agrees are "highly characteristic of the German Romantics" may also be found "embedded in Hitlerism," though with different concomitant ideas; Romanticism and Protestantism have "at least two features in common"; and so on.

Mr. Spitzer, then, is far from a consistent denial of the presuppositions of the analytical method, and he, happily, sometimes skillfully practises what he preaches against.   Nevertheless, he does preach against it, and insists that a method which he represents as its polar opposite must be exclusively used.   Let us, then, inquire what this alternative method is.   Mr. Spitzer's zeal for it interestingly illustrates the persisting influence of certain characteristic ideas of the Romantic period—ideas associated with the sacred term "organic whole."   All the entities with which this branch of historiography deals being assumed a priori to be "organic," its premises and procedure must be deduced from the distinctive properties of this sort of entities.[1]

What, then, does Mr. Spitzer conceive these peculiar properties to be, and what do they imply for the methodology of intellectual history?   Historically there have been a number of partially diverse ideas conveyed by the term "organic whole," but the one which evidently plays the greatest part in his reasoning is the following: in an "organic whole," though there are, indeed, discriminable parts or elements, every part is so inseparably related to all the other parts constituting that particular whole, and to the "nature of the whole," that no one of the parts could exist, or be the kind of part that it is, if dissociated from precisely those other parts, or as a member of a different whole.   Philosophers call this, for short, the conception of the internality of relations.   Now if it is assumed that all individual systems of thought, all ideologies, etc., are "organic wholes," it follows that the first of the two above-mentioned hypotheses (though not the second) underlying the analytical method must be false: the same component can never be present in more than one compound.   Wherever there are two such wholes, all the elements of each of them are eo ipso "not the same," i.e., not of the same kind, as those of the other.   It is manifestly from this a priori premise that Mr. Spitzer is arguing when he tells us, for example, that "Streben cannot be the same [not merely, 'is not the same,' which would be a question for textual analysis] with the Schlegels as with Goethe or Nietzsche," simply because they are different individuals, and "the living idea may not be considered apart from the individual."   Almost his entire argument about "Romanticism" and Hitlerism rests upon the same premise, applied to "movements."

[1] No reason is given for this assumption; it is a pure unexamined dogma. The only proof that could be given for the proposition that all thought-complexes are "organic" would consist in a complete induction showing that all of them do in fact have the properties which the term is supposed to connote.

This sort of inference from the supposedly "organic" character of all combinations of ideas which have ever entered any man's mind is, then, the route by which Mr. Spitzer arrives at the extraordinary historical generalization that no two thinkers ever have the same idea; the "organistic method" entails this consequence, even though Mr. Spitzer denies and affirms the consequence by turns.   One of the implications of the premise is the impossibility of using common nouns when referring to components of different wholes assumed to be "organic."   If every part of any such whole is a kind of thing capable of existing only *in* that whole, it is necessarily a misrepresentation to call it by the same name as a part of any other whole.   To say that any two philosophers have ever entertained any identical idea of "organic whole" itself would be false, since an individual's thought is, for Mr. Spitzer, an "organic whole."   Consequently Mr. Spitzer's own conception of what *he* calls "organic wholes" "cannot be the same" as that of anyone else.   No other mind has ever shared or ever can share it.   It is the kind of conception which implies its own incommunicability, as well as that of all other conceptions.   There would therefore seem to be some inconsistency in writing articles to persuade others to embrace it.

Though this is a premise plainly presupposed and required by Mr. Spitzer's general denunciation of the analytical method and by some of his more extreme deductions from the method of "organicism," he sometimes employs it in a considerably qualified or vestigial form.   For in some passages, as we have seen, he grants that, even in two or more "organic" wholes, there may be parts of the same sort, i.e., ideas properly describable as "the same" may be found in different systems, periods, etc.   Nevertheless, he would still insist, each of these parts must be *in some degree modified* by the constitution of the particular whole in which it has been incorporated. "The totality of heterogeneous features" which make up the whole called Hitlerism *"tinges* each of the single features"; in short, when the same idea occurs in two complexes it is also *partly* different.   On this two comments will suffice.   First, if a "feature" which is generically the same occurs in two or more contexts, the analytical method is obviously justified and indispensable; recurrent elements are admittedly there, and only analysis can discover them.   Second, the question whether a given component has been "tinged" by its presence in a particular totality is a question of fact, to be settled, if possible, by an examination of textual evidence; it may conceivably sometimes be the case and sometimes not.   But Mr. Spitzer settles the question in advance by a sweeping *a priori* generalization.   For this generalization there is no evidence, and there is plenty of evidence against it.   For example, in spite of the remarkable talent of many philosophers for misunderstanding what other philosophers are talking about, it has sometimes happened in the history of philosophical controversy that issue was really joined; one school affirmed, the other denied, precisely the same proposition.

When medieval philosophers debated the reality of universals, the specific notion "universal" appears to have been, at least for most of them, the same notion; if it had not been, they would not have been debating the same question. Again, when Leibniz and Locke—and many others—talked about "the chain (or scale) of being," it is demonstrable from their texts that the same conception of the world of creatures as characterized by plenitude, continuity and gradation was present to their minds, though Leibniz and Locke were different individuals and their systems were on certain other questions notoriously antagonistic. Scores of similar examples will readily suggest themselves. This is not to say that contrary examples may not be found, cases in which—not, strictly speaking, the same concepts, but—the meanings of the same terms are made different by their contexts. A competent analytical historian is, of course, careful to recognize such differences where they exist, but it is only by analysis that their existence can be ascertained.

It is, however, the affective elements in any mental complex that, Mr. Spitzer thinks, most indubitably determine the nature of the concepts or propositions with which they are associated, so that where the emotions are different the ideas cannot be the same. Here I must digress from the argument to repudiate a view which Mr. Spitzer ascribes to me. He assures the reader that I believe in the possibility of "a divorce between thought and feeling"—that, in fact, "underlying [my] whole program" is "the assumption of an 'unemotional' idea." If this is meant to imply that I hold that "ideas" can be present in human thought unaccompanied by emotions and unaffected by them, or that they are not frequently generated by them, it is, I need hardly say, a complete and inexplicable misapprehension of my "program"—inexplicable because I have more than once, even in contributions to this journal, expressed with considerable insistence precisely the opposite opinion.[2] Of course ideas are associated with emotions and interact with them. I should, however, equally insist that, though ideas are not "detachable" from emotions, they are not emotions, and that what may be correctly described as the same "idea"—the term including concepts and propositions—can be associated with different emotions, and different ideas with the same emotions. Some people delight in cats, others have a phobia for those animals. The emotional attitudes are precisely opposite, and what may be called the value-quality of cats is different for the two sorts of persons. Nevertheless, there is an identical factor in both complexes, namely, just cats, and to disregard it would be to miss what is psychologically most interesting in the two phenomena, and most suggestive of further questions for investigation—e.g., what are the preconditions for these opposite reactions to the same kind of object of perception or thought. So with the more

[2] E.g., in the paper on which Mr. Spitzer comments, 265–266, and in Vol. I, 1, 16–21. Cf. also *The Great Chain of Being*, 10–14.

intangible entities with which the historian of ideas is concerned. To St. Augustine, Friedrich Schlegel, and many others, the idea of the *ewige Wiederkehr* was repellent, to Nietzsche it was attractive. Both attitudes had an obvious emotional element, but they were opposite emotions directed upon the same idea; and it was not a whit less the same because the "soul" of St. Augustine and the "spiritual climate" in which he lived were about as different as can be imagined from Nietzsche's. Other instances of this sort of thing, also, could be cited to the point of tedium. It is one of the more important tasks of the analytical historian to study the diversities of men's emotional responses to the same ideas, and, if he can, to find some psychological explanation of them. But if the difference of the emotions always and necessarily made the ideas different, no such problem could arise.

Seeking, however, to make comprehensible to myself Mr. Spitzer's (intermittent) belief in this unconvincing thesis of the necessary differentness of all the components of any two different thought-complexes, I conjecture that it is partly due to a confusion of that proposition with another which it may seem to resemble: namely, that when an identical component is differently combined with other components, the *wholes* are different (which is tautological), and may also exhibit different total properties, modes of action and effects which are not simply the sum of the properties exhibited by the components in isolation. This latter proposition is both true and important. It is one which, either as a general philosophical principle or in its bearing on the history of ideas, I have never denied, nor is there anything in the analytical method which implies that it cannot be true. The wholes still contain components which must be discovered by analysis, some of the components in one whole may be the same as those in another, and to become acquainted with the potentialities and the historic rôles of any one of these recurrent components you must observe it in the different combinations into which it has entered. If, in maintaining the "organic" character of thought-complexes, Mr. Spitzer asserted no more than this proposition, there would (on this issue) be no disagreement between us.[3] A book of mine to which he generously refers is chiefly devoted to showing how various have been the effects of the acceptance of a certain idea (itself not simple) when it has been diversely combined with others, or applied in different provinces of thought, or employed by writers having different doctrinal motivations or emotional biases; nevertheless, through all this diversity of the wholes, there has been present the same "abstract idea that survives in history from

---

[3] "Organic," however, would not be an appropriate adjective; for it is true even of chemical substances that a given substance when combined with different other substances does not cease to be discoverably present, but that the several compounds as such nevertheless have different sensible, pharmacal and other properties and modes of action not wholly deducible from the properties of the components in isolation.

generation to generation, always identifiable to the eye of the historian.''
There is, in short, no inconsistency between the recognizable identity of a
given part in various combinations and the differentness—which may even
amount to opposition—of the wholes resulting from those combinations.
Mr. Spitzer's fundamental error appears to be that—being justly sensible
of the differentness of such wholes as ''Romanticism'' (in his sense) and
Hitlerism—he has quite gratuitously and mistakenly concluded that they
cannot have any identical elements—even though (when his eye as a perceptive and learned historian is on the actual facts) he is constrained to
contradict this theoretical implication of the ''organistic'' method and recognize that those wholes do have identical elements, which analysis can reveal.

This error has been facilitated by Mr. Spitzer's failure to note into *what
sort* of wholes ideas are combined in men's thinking. The wholes are in most
cases logical or would-be logical structures—in short, judgments or arguments, implicit or explicit. And it is a primary presupposition of ordinary
logic that the same concept can occur in judgments of wholly different logical import and an identical proposition serve as a premise for different conclusions, provided the other premises are not identical. Many ideas are
what logicians call propositional functions, i.e., propositions of which the
subject is indeterminate; e.g., ''x is a superior race,'' or is ''the chosen
people.'' This presupposes that there is or may be such a thing as a
superior race, or a people preferred above others by some supreme and super-
human power. Such an idea, as we know, has had wide currency and a long
history; it is a constant in a number of historic ideologies. But it may be,
and has been, combined with different assumptions as to what people x
should stand for—e.g., the Jews, or the English, or the Germans, or the
Japanese; and, obviously, the resultant determinate propositions, the
''wholes,'' will have very different practical consequences. The analytical
historian will note the recurrence of the general idea and of its accompany-
ing emotional attitudes, and also the diversity of the ''values'' assigned to x;
having thus isolated a generic type of phenomenon appearing in various
specific instances and forms, he will inquire, *inter alia*, whether there are,
in all the instances, any common antecedent conditions for the occurrence of
the phenomenon, and how far it has had similar and how far, and through
what causes, dissimilar effects; and he may be able to trace the transmission
of the general idea from an earlier to a later instance.[4] Or again, you may
find certain historic ethical creeds reducible to two different syllogisms having as their common major premise: ''The interests of the individual should
be subordinated to the good of the whole.'' But when, in the minor premise,

[4] Professor Hans Kohn has pointed out in this journal the part which ''the
three main ideas of Hebrew nationalism'' played in the minds of Cromwell and his
generation: ''the chosen-people idea, the covenant, the messianic expectancy'' (I
[1940], 1, 82).

"the whole" is in the one case identified with the national state, and in the other case with all humanity, you have two extremely dissimilar total doctrines. To recognize the identity of the major premise in both is nevertheless the first essential both for the historian and the philosopher. All this is very obvious, but it appears necessary to recall it in order to remove the supposed difficulty of understanding how the same idea can not only be present in, but be an essential of, two or more radically different "systems."

Before leaving this question of methods, however, we must consider the terms "*Geist*" and "spiritual climate," which have so large a place in Mr. Spitzer's discussion. They are apparently synonymous, and are supposed to designate an important type of factor in the history of thought which the good, or organistic or "synthetic," method recognizes, and the bad, or analytical, method not only misses but denies. It is this factor alone which enables us to "understand" and "explain" a "period" or "movement"— and apparently also "the totality of the thoughts" of any individual; through ignoring it, the analytical historian is necessarily incapable of understanding any of these things. But what do the terms mean? "*Geist*" is formally defined as "the totality of features of a given period or movement which the historian tries to *see as a unity*." Since the "totality" admittedly contains "features," in the plural, the way to discern a *Geist* is evidently not to refrain from analyzing the literature of the period in order to observe and discriminate them; Mr. Spitzer can hardly hold that you can understand a period better by *not* observing and discriminating its features (though if he does not, his antipathy to "analysis" remains incomprehensible). The essential thing is evidently "seeing the features as a unity." But what, in turn, does "unity" mean?—the term being, as philosophers are well aware, far from unequivocal. It appears to mean chiefly "organic" unity, in the sense already indicated. A "climate" or *Geist* is something by which all the elements of an aggregate of ideas are "held together" and "integrated into a unit"—*viz.*, the kind of unit whose "features" or components are so inseparably interrelated and mutually implicative that none of them can be "the same" as any component of any other unit having a different climate.

Geistesgeschichte, then, appears to be (for Mr. Spitzer) simply the history of ideas treated in accordance with the "organistic" method;[5] and the only fruit which this method has to offer the historian is, once more, so far as I can see, the proposition that no two mental complexes or "wholes" can

[5] In spite of Mr. Spitzer's aversion to plurals, I venture to suggest that—if we *must* have a German word—"*Geistergeschichte*" would be a more appropriate name. For in his use *Geist* does not mean mind or intellect; it is the somewhat that at once unifies the ideas or "features" of a period, movement, *etc.* and differentiates them from all others. But there are for him many *Geister*—as many as there are periods, movements, or even individuals; and it is with the series of these *Geister* that the sort of historiography which he desiderates would presumably deal.

have any ideas in common. The untenability—to express it moderately—
of this proposition has already been sufficiently demonstrated. If the notion
of "climate" or *Geist* has any more positive contribution to make to historiography than this negation of any possibility of either the sharing or the
communication of thoughts by different minds, Mr. Spitzer does not appear
to me to make clear what it is. And even supposing that there may be a
positive something which is the particular climate or *Geist* of, e.g., a movement, it can only be one "feature" of it, an idea or group of ideas, or an
emotional attitude, common to all who participate in the movement—a component to be discriminated by analysis from all the others, and capable of
being described or characterized. You must be able to say something about
it—for if nothing can be said about it, then, surely, the less said about it the
better. It might, indeed, have a special relation to the others; i.e., it might
be a dominant idea, a major preconception or attitude, which tended to
determine, so to say, the eligibility of other ideas for admission to membership. Those congruous, or seemingly congruous, with it would be readily
accepted, those incongruous would be rejected or disregarded. But even in
such a case, it would remain a question for factual inquiry how far the actual
components of a given "whole" *are* logically or psychologically congruous.
Most historic complexes of ideas, when analyzed, can be seen to include an
abundance of pregnant incongruities, the eventual discovery of which is one
of the frequent causes of changes or revolutions in thought. You cannot
simply say that because the complex has a climate of its own, there can't be
any incongruities in it; indeed, Mr. Spitzer himself quite correctly recognizes such incongruities in the Nazi ideology, even while insisting that its
climate "integrates" it into a "unit."

How loosely conceived Mr. Spitzer's notion of "climates" is may be
judged from a curious contradiction into which he falls in his application
of it. The sorts of "units" to which he ascribes mutually exclusive climates
include (a) the totality of the thoughts of an individual; (b) movements;
(c) periods; (d) "definite sciences or fields of activity." A period may
presumably include—and in historical fact always does include—a number
of movements, and a movement many individuals. But if nothing in the
"organic whole" which consists of the thoughts of an individual is the same
as any thought of another individual—if everybody has his own exclusive
Geist—there can be no such things as movements, since a "movement" of
thought presumably presupposes that those who adhere to it have at least
some ideas which are the same. And if there *could* be movements, there
could be no "periods," having *Geister* or climates of *their* own, since the
period as a whole would include different movements having mutually exclusive and incompatible *Geister*. If a whole has no parts which are the same
as those of any other whole, it cannot be a part of any other whole; but individuals (i.e., their thoughts) are parts of movements, and movements of

periods. But Mr. Spitzer repeatedly makes the self-contradictory assumption that there can be overlapping "organic" wholes—except when it is to his purpose to draw an inference from the assumption that there can *not* be (e.g., in "Romanticism" and Hitlerism).

One such inference is perhaps the most extraordinary of all. From the assumption (for which no reason is given) that every "definite science or field of activity" has its own "climate," he infers that, while it is "possible to trace the history of an idea" through one science, the same idea can never be discovered in any other science;[6] e.g., "the history of the idea of evolution" must be limited to biology. Comment is hardly necessary, since there is nothing more familiar or more certain about the history of the past two centuries than that the "idea of evolution" (in more than one of the several senses of the term, including its biological sense, i.e., the doctrine of the descent of species from other species) has penetrated most of the provinces of thought. A score of other ideas which have played a potent part in many fields of inquiry and reflection and practice could easily be pointed out. If the theory of the all-important rôle of mutually exclusive "climates" or *Geister* (whatever they may be) in intellectual history implies the contrary (as Mr. Spitzer tells us that it does), the theory unhappily collides with one of the most massive and conspicuous of all historical facts.

What this chiefly illustrates is the arbitrary and *a priori* character of Mr. Spitzer's whole "method." By the procedure which his article illustrates, you may attribute a "climate" to any set of ideas you like—and without any obligation to specify what in particular the climate is. When you have done this, you simply deduce that no idea in this set is the same as any idea in a set to which you have attributed a different climate. The method is the reverse of that to which the responsible investigator of intellectual history is committed. His procedure, in dealing with such a question, must always consist in *examining* the two sets—be these individual systems, movements, sciences, or "periods"—in order to determine by analysis of the relevant evidence whether or not common elements are to be found in them. He will make no *a priori* assumption either that there must be or that there cannot be such common elements.

II. *The Term "Romanticism."*

On this topic Professor Spitzer begins by attributing to me a thesis quite different from that which I had expressed. I have not said that there is a thing, "Romanticism," which "defies definition." The question does not concern the definability of an entity already identified, but the meaning, in

---

[6] While Mr. Spitzer categorically asserts this, he seems to say the opposite two sentences later. This is one among numerous examples of a propensity to affirm contradictory theses on identical questions—which makes discussion of his article somewhat difficult.

past and current usage, of a certain word. And what I have said about the word is not that it "has no meaning," but the contrary, that, in the century and a half since it was invented, it "has acquired so many—and such incongruous and opposed—meanings," that it no longer has any "*one* understood and accepted meaning," and has therefore "come to be useless as a verbal symbol." In short, when one historian or critic uses the word "Romanticism" as the name for a set of ideas or theses or "attitudes," the reader can no longer assume that he is referring to the same set as any other writer who uses the word. And from this diversity in the connotations and denotations which different writers attach to the word I observed that a deplorable amount of confusion, and even of historical error, has resulted. One writer, for example, attacks, another defends, "Romanticism"; they seem, therefore, to their readers, and even to themselves, to hold conflicting opinions on the same issue. But it may presently appear, after a certain amount of misdirected controversy, that the Romanticism which the one attacks is by no means the same as the Romanticism which the other defends, except in name; the two writers may, in fact, be in substantial agreement, except in their terminology.[7] If everyone when employing the term would append his own definition, together with a list of the authors whom he regards as the typical Romanticists; and if he would, in his actual use of the word, always keep in mind his definition; and if he would, finally, when referring to other writers on the subject, refrain from assuming that they mean by the word the same thing that he does, and take pains to ascertain (if possible) what they do mean by it—then, no doubt, much of the confusion, at least, would be avoided, though it would still be awkward to have so many current senses for a single semi-technical term in historiography. But in practice the confusion has not been avoided, and one consequence has been the raising of equivocal and misleading historical questions—as Professor Fairchild's article in the same issue of this journal pointed out. Were the leaders of the Oxford Movement "Romantics"? Yes, if you take certain ideas or sentiments—such as "responsiveness to the romantic charm of the Middle Ages"—as constituting the essence of "Romanticism"; No, if you take certain other and more important ideas, which other uses or definitions of it would include among its essentials. Until the definition is specified, the question is meaningless because the crucial term in it is multivocal.

Professor Spitzer does, however, presently join issue on this matter. He maintains that there is *no* multiplicity of current meanings of "Romanticism"; it is "in fact, a generally understood term, . . . there is a *communis opinio* concerning the descriptive elements implied" by it, and "historians are agreed on the specific individuals to whom the term ['Romanticist'] applies." His reasons for asserting this are of two sorts.

[7] Readers of this journal have had an interesting example of this since my paper was published; see Professor Barzun's review of Mr. Peter Viereck's *Metapolitics*, and Mr. Viereck's reply, III (1942) 1, 107–112.

1. The first is of an *a priori* character: it consists in a general assumption falling within his own special province of etymology and semantics. Whenever common speech has created a verbal unit—such as the word "romanticism" or "nature"—we are under the "obligation to see all its different senses as a unit." This proposition is, indeed, somewhat puzzlingly expressed. If there *are* "different senses," it would seem that they are not (*quâ* senses) the same unit. But what Mr. Spitzer would apparently have us think is that, though there are seemingly "different" senses of the word, they are all really the same sense, so that the word is always used to connote the same attributes and to denote the same subject of discourse. And for this highly improbable, not to say self-contradictory, generalization the only reason suggested is that, unless the senses *were* the same, common speech would never have employed the same word to express them.

But there is no proposition on any matter in linguistics which is more certainly false than this last. Words notoriously shift their meanings through gradual processes of association of ideas by partial qualitative similarity, or similarity of function, or contiguity, or even similarity to the sound of other words; and these shifts take place in chains or series in such a way that, between the meaning or referent of the first term in a series and that of the last there may be no significant similarity whatever. Some object having the characters *a b c* is called A; then some other object, having the characters *c d e,* is also called A, by virtue of the partial similarity; then a third object, having the characters *e f g,* is called A, not because it resembles the first object so called (which it does not), but because it partially resembles the second.

If an example is required, consider the word "table." The original sense of *tabula* was apparently "a board, plank." From this arose, in Latin or in English (and other modern languages), often in both, several divergent series of senses, of which it will suffice to mention two: (a) Any flat surface on which you could write, as on a board, became a "table"—a slate, a sheet of paper or a collection of them, e.g., a notebook; then various things written on such surfaces—accounts, records, written laws (the "Twelve Tables"); then any series of related items arranged in a systematic sequence—a multiplication table, time-table, table of contents—and so on. (b) Meanwhile, also from the sense "board," came the sense, "an article of furniture having a flat top," not necessarily of board, and the more special sense of such a piece of furniture used for serving food; then, by one metonymy, the sense "food," and by another, the sense "the company that gathers round a table"; from the latter arose the name of a fictitious order of chivalry, the Round Table, and also, later, of a group of persons gathered, not necessarily about a table, for discussion on a set topic; finally, "a round table" is now sometimes used as a synonym of "symposium," to designate this kind of discussion whether in oral or printed form. Throughout these series there

is an intelligible continuity of transition from one meaning to the next; in
no intelligible sense can all the meanings be said to be "a unit." And
what is true of "table" may obviously be equally true of "nature" or
"Romanticism." I regret to be obliged to recall considerations so elementary; but Mr. Spitzer appears to have forgotten them when he bases his
assertion of the unequivocality of "Romanticism" on the extraordinary
premise that wherever a single word is in common use there must be a corre-
spondingly single sense.

It is true that he elsewhere contradicts this and lays down the opposite
but equally odd generalization already mentioned, that when two or more
writers use the same word they never use it in the same sense: "*Streben*
with the Schlegels cannot be the same as with Goethe or Nietzsche," because
they are different individuals. It should follow that *romantisch* also not
only is not, but cannot be the same for Goethe and the Schlegels, and that
the senses of this or any other word are as numerous as the persons who have
ever used it—an embarrassing situation for the lexicographer! But with
this side of Mr. Spitzer's reasoning I have already sufficiently dealt.

2. The question whether everybody—or every "cultured" person—who
talks about "Romanticism" attaches to the word the same connotation and
denotation is, in any case, not one to be settled by *a priori* generalizations;
it is a question of fact, to be settled by evidence. That such a universal
identity of meaning is a fact Mr. Spitzer asserts; that, before making such
an assertion, it is desirable to examine the evidence has apparently not
occurred to him. In an earlier essay,[8] cited in the paper under discussion,
I have presented a large mass of evidence on the point, which it is impossible
to reproduce here; but a few samples may be given, some of them not previously adduced. The denotation of "Romanticism"—the group of thinkers
or writings that exemplify the phenomenon so designated—has been variously conceived, by different critics or historians, to include (among many
others) Nietzsche, Flaubert, Newman and the Tractarians, Hegel, Shelley,
Schopenhauer, Byron, Wordsworth, Rousseau, Joseph Warton, Kant,
Fénelon, Madame Guyon, Pascal, Bacon, the *Grand Cyrus*, St. Paul, Plato,
the *Odyssey*, and "the Serpent in Eden"; while most of these have been
declared by other learned writers *not* to be "Romantic." The connotations
of the term—what Mr. Spitzer would call the "descriptive elements implied
by Romanticism"—are, naturally, equally diverse and discrepant. For one
eminent literary historian Romanticism is simply "the fairy way of writing," for another it is the direct source of "the realistic error." For some
historians it is a sort of retrospectivism, a preoccupation with the past or
a "cult of the extinct"; for others, while "the classic temper studies the
past, the romantic neglects it," and looks forward to the future; and for
some of the French "Romantics," its motto was *il faut être de son temps*.

[8] "On the Discrimination of Romanticisms," *PMLA* (1924), 229–253.

For Mr. Paul Elmer More it was "the illusion of seeing the infinite in the stream of nature itself, instead of apart from that stream"; for a recent German author the deepest thing in Romanticism is *eine Religion, die dieses Leben hasst. . . . Romantik will die gerade Verbindung des Menschlichen mit dem Überirdischen.*[9] For Professor Spitzer himself, "healthiness" is the basic characteristic of "Roman thought"; for Goethe "the Romantic" was "the diseased." Among those for whom the word implies, *inter alia,* a social and political ideology or temper, one writer, typical of many, tells us that "Romanticism spells anarchy in every domain, . . . a systematic hostility to everyone invested with any particle of social authority—husband or *paterfamilias,* policeman or magistrate, priest or Cabinet minister";[10] but Professor Goetz Briefs finds "the climax of political and economic thought within the Romantic movement" in the doctrine of Adam Müller, which sought to vindicate the sanctity of established social authority embodied in the family and the state; "by an inescapable logic the Romanticist ideology was drawn into the camp of reaction."[11] Such examples of the diversities and contradictions in the historic and current meanings given to the term could be multiplied *ad libitum.* This is what Mr. Spitzer would describe as a *communis opinio.* To none of this evidence, however, has he troubled to attend; he is therefore able to retain a serene faith that everyone else understands by the term precisely what he understands by it. He thus affords a fresh illustration of a common but regrettable practice on which I had commented in the article under discussion—that of postulating "a determinate entity existing prior to the definition, which *must* be the thing that the word 'Romanticism' denotes"; of defining the nature or "descriptive elements" of this thing under the guidance of one's own associations of ideas with the word; and of then reading the same signification into all other people's uses of it. For many years I have collected definitions and characterizations of Romanticism as some people collect postage-stamps. Mr. Spitzer now provides a welcome addition to the collection. It is welcome because it is different from all the others.

III. *"Romanticism" and Hitlerism.*

Here also it is unfortunately necessary to point out first of all that Mr. Spitzer gives his readers a doubly erroneous account of what had been said in the article he criticizes.

(a) The reader is told that I seek to "solve the problem" (of the sinister outcome of the Hitlerian ideology) "without stepping beyond the limits of the . . . three ideas" mentioned in the second part of the article; I "arti-

[9] Julius Bab, *Fortinbras, oder der Kampf des 19. Jahrhunderts mit dem Geiste der Romantik.*

[10] G. Chatterton-Hill, *Contemporary Rev.* (1942), 720.

[11] This *Journal,* II (1941), 279 ff.

ficially *reduce* the history of an historical event or movement to two or three components'' (italics mine). What I had actually written was that the combination of these ideas was "*a* factor in the production of the state of mind upon which the totalitarian ideologies depend for their appeal,'' but that "these three are *by no means the only ones* of which the same might be said.'' I "inclined to think them the most important and most fundamental,'' but added that "this estimate is certainly debatable.'' And in the concluding summary: in these three ideas "one may discern an important part (though assuredly far from all) of the pattern of ideas'' associated with the Nazi movement; "a host of other factors between the 1790s and the present of course contributed to this outcome.'' The thesis imputed to me is thus one which I had explicitly and repeatedly repudiated.

(b) Mr. Spitzer supposes that I would make "*das Ganze* of the Romantic idealists *responsible* for the hideous growth of totalitarianism,'' and that I assume that "present events can be *blamed* on the great Romantic thinkers'' (italics mine). This is a curious misconception of the relation which I suggested between certain characteristic ideas of the Romantic period and the Nazi ideology. To say that there is some causal relation between two events, A and B, is not to say that A is "responsible'' for B, and (if B is a bad thing) that A is to be "blamed'' for B; it is only to say that A is one of the antecedent conditions without which B would not have occurred in the particular way it did. To say that the German *Blitzkrieg* of 1940 could not have occurred if the internal combustion engine had not previously been invented is not to say that that invention was "responsible'' for the *Blitzkrieg* or that its inventor is to be "blamed'' for the horrors which his device was eventually to play a part in making possible.[12] Mr. Spitzer thinks it especially incomprehensible that any one should suppose that "ideas potential of such good'' (as the three mentioned) "have borne such bitter fruit'' as Hitlerism. It is no more incomprehensible than the fact that the internal combustion engine has borne both good and bitter fruit; or that a chemical element may be an ingredient in one compound which is harmless or therapeutic, and an ingredient in another which is toxic or deadly; or that a given proposition when combined as a premise with certain other premises in an argument may yield a true and useful conclusion, and when combined with different other premises may yield a false and dangerous one.

When these two misinterpretations of my thesis are eliminated, little is left in Mr. Spitzer's observations on this third topic which seems to me to call for further comment. For the most part he argues from the *a priori* premise already discussed: no two different "systems,'' or "organic

[12] It is true that simple minds sometimes reason in this manner. It is said that the fishwives of Palos in 1898 stoned the statue of Columbus on the ground that, by discovering America, he was to blame for the defeat of Spain by the United States.

wholes," *can* have any elements in common; "Romanticism" and Hitlerism, however, are organic wholes, and are manifestly extremely different wholes; *ergo,* they cannot have any elements in common; no idea present in the one is the same as any idea present in the other. The reasons for rejecting this premise have already been set forth, and the conclusion is the less in need of refutation because Mr. Spitzer himself,—when, as a historian and not an *a priori* reasoner, he actually examines the two complexes—denies that conclusion: the three ideas in question are (to quote again his own words), "highly characteristic of the German Romantics" and are also "present and important in Hitlerism." This is precisely what, in this part of my paper, I was chiefly concerned to point out. In admitting it, Mr. Spitzer not only admits my principal contention (on this topic); he also destroys the general argument of his article. That argument was, as he explains in his second paragraph, designed to prove the unsoundness of the analytical method by showing that a certain specific proposition to which the use of that method had led me—*viz.*, that at least three ideas highly characteristic of the German Romantic period are present and important in Hitlerism— is in fact false. But since he expressly acknowledges that this proposition is in fact true, nothing is left of the argument.

There remains one further factual question, namely, whether the emergence and vogue of these ideas in the Romantic period has any causal relation to their presence in the Hitlerian ideology. This question has no bearing upon the validity of the analytical method, since it is not a presupposition of that method that the appearance of a given idea in one period or movement is *always* causally related to a later appearance of it. Mr. Spitzer apparently holds that there is no causal connection in this case; he seems to think that the ideas in question emerged and had great influence in the Romantic period, that all of them then ceased to have any considerable currency, and that they quite spontaneously sprang up afresh among the uneducated classes in Germany in the 1920s and 1930s. Such acquaintance as I have with German philosophy and literature of the nineteenth and early twentieth century appears to me to disprove the asserted discontinuity, and Mr. Spitzer presents nothing which I can regard as serious historical evidence in support of his thesis; but since adequate presentation of the evidence against it is forbidden by limitations of space, I must be content to leave this question to the judgment of the learned reader.

Johns Hopkins University.

Chapter IV.a

REVIEW

LOVEJOY'S *ESSAYS IN THE HISTORY OF IDEAS*

By Theodore Spencer

Essays in the History of Ideas. By Arthur O. Lovejoy. The Johns Hopkins Press, Baltimore, 1948. 359 + xvii pp.

1

This volume contains sixteen articles, most of them published in periodicals during the last twenty years; they include about a fifth of the articles listed in the appended bibliography of Mr. Lovejoy's writings. The occasion of their publication is the twenty-fifth anniversary of the founding of the History of Ideas Club at Johns Hopkins University, a club which Mr. Lovejoy originated, and which, through a committee consisting of Professors D. C. Allen, George Boas and Ludwig Edelstein, thus appropriately honors him by giving renewed emphasis to the important aspect of scholarly concern with which his name is chiefly associated.

The volume is both a unit in itself and a series of expansions of themes and theories which Mr. Lovejoy has developed elsewhere. Most of the articles are concerned with the eighteenth century-attitudes towards nature, primitivism and romanticism; there is an introductory general article on the "Historiography of Ideas," and the volume concludes with articles on Milton, St. Ambrose and Tertullian, the last two being sections from the uncompleted and unpublished second volume of *A Documentary History of Primitivism and Related Ideas,* by Mr. Lovejoy and Mr. George Boas.

Mr. Lovejoy's main interest, in these essays as elsewhere, is to see that we have as clear as possible a picture of our intellectual past and as full as possible an understanding of the thinkers and writers who expressed it. He has given us, as Professor Allen points out in a foreword, a new insight into our intellectual heritage; he has made us aware of past schematizations, discriminations and conflicts so that not only are we directly fascinated and illumined by the analytical pictures of the past which he has drawn with such clarity, we are also indirectly influenced as we reflect on our present situations in the light of the past he has revealed. With each generation our intellectual heritage changes; fresh analysis carves new facets, new intellectual tools reveal new articulations in its structure. Mr. Lovejoy has been for our generation one of the most adroit and penetrating of analysts, and his intellectual tools have been among the sharpest of those which have helped us to visualize the features of our intellectual ancestors. First among them has been his gift for discriminating between different meanings of crucial words; the sixty-odd definitions of Nature in the present essay on " 'Nature' as an Aesthetic Norm" form a useful parallel to the

list of different meanings of the same word which is appended to the first
volume of the *History of Primitivism*. A tool of a similar kind is that
which enables Mr. Lovejoy to take apart the large vague complexes—''romanticism,'' ''primitivism,'' etc.—which we have been accustomed to use so
loosely, and to clarify our concepts of them by determining their ''unit-
ideas''; it is hardly necessary to mention at this date that no student of
intellectual history can have read Mr. Lovejoy's major works without having his own views permanently sharpened. In the present volume this
analytical tool of Mr. Lovejoy's is to be seen (at least by the student of literature) most clearly and excitingly at work in the essay ''On the Discrimination of Romanticisms,'' where the author, after pointing out how confused is our present use of the word ''Romantic,'' suggests that we may be
able to clear the confusion by thinking not of one Romanticism but of several. He describes his analytical ideal as follows:

> Each of these Romanticisms—after they are first . . . roughly discrim-
> inated with respect to their representatives or their dates—should be re-
> solved, by a more thorough and discerning analysis than is yet customary,
> into its elements—into the several ideas and aesthetic susceptibilities of
> which it is composed. Only after these fundamental thought-factors or
> emotive strains in it are clearly discriminated and fairly exhaustively enu-
> merated, shall we be in a position to judge of the degree of its affinity with
> other complexes to which the same name has been applied, to see what tacit
> preconceptions or controlling motives or explicit contentions were common
> to any two or more of them, and wherein they manifested distinct and
> divergent tendencies.

The remainder of the essay brilliantly illustrates this ideal by showing,
among other things, that a ''Romanticism'' such as that of Joseph Warton's
Enthusiast is a very different thing from the ''Romanticism'' of the German
aesthetic theorists:

> Between the assertion of the superiority of 'nature' over conscious 'art'
> and that of the superiority of conscious art over mere 'nature'; between a
> way of thinking of which primitivism is of the essence and one of which the
> idea of perpetual self-transcendence is of the essence; between a funda-
> mental preference for simplicity—even though a 'wild' simplicity—and a
> fundamental preference for diversity and complexity; between the sort
> of ingenuous naïveté characteristic of *The Enthusiast* and the sophisticated
> subtlety of the conception of romantic irony; between these the antithesis
> is one of the most radical that modern taste and thought have to show. . . .
> One of the widest and deepest-reaching lines of cleavage in modern
> thought has been more or less effectively concealed by a word.

Mr. Lovejoy ends the essay with one of his several definitions of the
function of the historian of ideas; for the purpose of the present discussion
it is important to notice the following points; they are throughout basic
to his interpretation of recorded human expression. 1) The categories, such
as ''Romantic,'' which have previously been used to distinguish and classify

movements in literature are far too rough, crude, and undiscriminating. 2) Hence the historian should attend, not to such large *complexes* of ideas, but to their simpler, "diversely combinable, intellectual and emotional components . . . that are the true elemental and dynamic factors in the history of thought and of art." 3) Such an acquaintance is necessary as a preliminary to any judgment of value, to any decision we make as to whether the preponderant effect of the diverse and often conflicting strains on, say, a given "romanticism" is morally or aesthetically good or bad. In fact, 4) When the preliminary task of analysis and detailed comparison has been made, it is doubtful "whether the larger question [the question of value] will seem to have much importance or meaning."

2

In discussing this definition, its aim and its illustration in the present collection of essays, I write from the standpoint of the student of literature, and any apologies which Mr. Lovejoy, as a philosopher, may makè for trespassing beyond his field must be doubly echoed by me. But Mr. Lovejoy's work, to the literary student, is of such great interest and importance, both in theory and practice, that it demands a serious examination and evaluation. Hence on the present occasion I should like to discuss, however briefly: a) just how it illuminates our understanding of literature; b) where it seems either inadequate or over-emphatic on a particular side; and c) certain general questions which it raises concerning our response to literary art and literary aims.

In one of the essays in this volume Mr. Lovejoy politely suggests that the conventional discipline of literary study has to a great extent lost its validity and vitality; the suggestion has frequently been made by others with more vehemence elsewhere. The editing of texts, the study of merely literary sources, the tracing of the transmission of merely literary themes, themes of mere entertainment—all these scholarly games have seemed to have less and less importance in a world of decreasing leisure and growing individual responsibility. Furthermore the material has been giving out. The study of literature has needed new subject matter, new methods, new depth and new vitality. Most of all it has needed a recognition, on the part of its practitioners, of its relationships, especially of its relation to the history of thought. Literature has too often been studied in a vacuum, and the main relationship that has appeared to be relevant has been the dubiously important one between the work of art and the private life of its creator. Mr. Lovejoy's approach, his emphasis on the importance of ideas, the persuasiveness of his learned analyses, have helped to put that sort of thing in its place. He has opened new avenues for investigation and new possibilities of understanding. An example, on a small scale, is the present essay on "Milton and the Paradox of the Fortunate Fall," in which a pas-

63

sage in the twelfth book of *Paradise Lost* depicting the fall of Adam as the necessary preliminary to the redemption by Christ and hence as a fortunate rather than an unfortunate occurrence, is related to a long tradition of Christian thought which goes back at least to St. Ambrose. This sort of investigation is obviously much more relevant to Milton's own conscious intention than one which attempts to trace merely verbal parallels or other mnemonic phenomena. Even more important for the student of literature are such essays as those on the Schlegels and on Coleridge and Kant, for here the subject of discussion is not a single passage and the tracing of parallels, but the clarification of a central issue in the thought of the author.

But though the study of the history of ideas can give, and has given, renewed vigor to the study of literature, though it offers a wider and wiser training than a discipline that is mainly philological, it cannot do everything, and when it tries to do too much, as it sometimes does in hands less skilled than Mr. Lovejoy's, it can produce as dry a harm as philology. There are certain authors, and they are usually authors who catch experience at its liveliest, for the understanding and appreciation of whom the study of the history of ideas is irrelevant. That study does little to help us to read Chaucer correctly, for his only dealings with ideas are when he rather childishly and ineptly steals the platitudes of Boethius about fate and fortune, and it is of primary importance for only one kind of novelist, a rather rare kind. Defoe, Smollett and Dickens it leaves relatively untouched. It is useful chiefly when we are dealing with didactic and critical authors; much lyrical poetry, though not all by any means, has little to do with it.

Furthermore too much emphasis on it tends to obscure, if not to obliterate, aesthetic values. The common complaint against the historian of ideas is that he does not care whether an author is first-rate or fifth-rate so long as his work expresses characteristic or significant views. The answer to this complaint is, of course, that the historian is right not to care, since an inferior writer is valuable because he is likely to illustrate the standard opinions of his time uncontaminated by the originality of genius. But though this answer is quite valid, as far as the historian's goal is concerned, it leaves the seeker for a total view of literature dissatisfied; such a person is bound to be a little troubled, for example, by the attention which Mr. Lovejoy gives to a poem like Warton's *Enthusiast*. Important though it may be as a means for illustrating the feelings and opinions that compose one strand in the thought of its age, a poem like this seems, to the student seeking the total view, to receive more attention than its intrinsic merit as a work of art justifies, and he asks himself whether there is not an opportunity here for misconception—realizing, as he does so, that he is looking at an irreconcilable split between himself and the historian.

Mr. Lovejoy himself, of course, is thoroughly aware of these potential limitations. In his introductory essay he makes it quite clear, by describing the sort of scholarly project he has in mind as a present requirement—an edition of *Paradise Lost* annotated to reveal its intellectual background, a history of the development of the idea of evolution before Darwin—that aesthetic concerns and evaluations are not his goal, and, indirectly, that the study of the history of ideas is not an infallible or universal remedy for the difficulties facing the student anxious to achieve a total view of literature. Nevertheless the implication, unquestionably present throughout these essays, that the understanding and analysis of unit-ideas is the major task of the student of literature tends to underestimate the importance of other elements in a work of art; the same implication is likely to give a misleading impression of how the mind of the imaginative writer works. The danger of the method is its rigidity, its coldness. The unit-ideas can sometimes be too clearly separated from each other by analysis; there are times when one is led to see them, unrealistically, as independent puppets, clashing and mingling on the stage of an author's mind, moved by invisible hands not his own. And, like so much that is said about the nature of a work of art, an emphasis on the history of ideas can make the artistic process seem a much more deliberate and self-conscious matter than it often is. However revealing the sixty-odd definitions of the word "Nature" may be to a later student, their enumeration, as far as an understanding of the minds of the authors who used the word are concerned, makes their use seem too cut and dried; it suggests an assortment, like different sizes of nail in a hardware store, from which the writer deliberately chose. Actually, of course, he did nothing of the sort. The creative act is more supple than that; conception and the emotion that goes with it, tend to melt, or rather to fuse, intellectual definition into something that analysis cannot completely account for.

3

In a passage I have quoted above Mr. Lovejoy suggests that when we are dealing with the history of ideas as expressed in literature the task of analysis and detailed comparison is not only the most important but in the long run the only task it is worth while to perform; once it is performed, it is doubtful whether the larger question of the aesthetic or moral value of a given complex of ideas "will seem to have much importance or meaning."* The Present reviewer, trained in the school of Irving Babbitt, is unwilling to let such a statement pass unchallenged. Mr. Lovejoy convincingly corrects Babbitt's interpretation of Rousseau in one of the most penetrating of the essays in this volume, but to set Babbitt right in the reading of a text is not to prove, in the opinion of the present reviewer, that Babbitt's judgment of the effects of Romanticism, of the several Romanticisms he was dealing with, was wrong, or that he was wrong to include moral

* See Editor's Note on p. 446 below.

effect as one of the things to be looked for in the behavior of literature.　Is the historian of ideas to say that all complexes of unit-ideas are of equal value for expressing the truth about human experience in artistic form? Two of the great unit-ideas which Mr. Lovejoy has so brilliantly described and differentiated—the Great Chain of Being and the theory of evolution— have had to find, so opposite are they, very different artistic forms for their expression, and it could be shown (though it would need considerable space) that the different forms have a different aesthetic effect and therefore a different aesthetic value; the authors who have interpreted the human situation from one point of view or the other have interpreted it, morally as well as formally, in quite different ways.　The Great Chain of Being, a root concept in the consciousness of both Shakespeare and Pope, could give each a basis for a vision of evil; Shakespeare's portrayal of the individual villainy of Iago and Pope's general condemnation of pride, are among the results. The theory of evolution, so dramatically opposed, as Mr. Lovejoy has shown, to the concept of the Great Chain, by removing or seeming to remove a permanent standard of value and a permanent pattern of relationships from the cosmos, has helped to destroy any basis for a vision of evil, and the moral thinness of contemporary literature is one of the consequences.

In saying this I greatly oversimplify, of course, a most complicated matter.　Let us take a more concrete example from one of Mr. Lovejoy's key authors, Milton.　Partly under Mr. Lovejoy's influence, and certainly stimulated by his example, several scholars have recently described more completely and accurately than before the cosmological picture in *Paradise Lost*.　We can see as clearly as Milton allows us to see, in terms of the cosmological ideas available at the time, what his picture of the universe was.　But this admirable, and admirably performed, exercise in the history of ideas (and now I return to the point of view of our hypothetical student seeking the total view of a work of art) is not enough.　It does not explain the central fact of Milton's cosmology: the fact that it is, at bottom, an imaginative failure.　The universe of Dante is an imaginative success partly because its shape was for him inevitable; his use of it involved no doubts; his age supplied him with nothing else but the Ptolemaic image he so vividly portrayed.　But Milton had to make a choice between three universes: the Ptolemaic, the Copernican and the Tychonian; he chose the one that was theologically most convenient and apparently most easy to visualize; unfortunately, it was scientifically out of date and the choice, combined with his own peculiarities of imagination, nearly wrecked his poem.　The inconsistency between the relatively sharp picture of the universe given by Milton himself in the earlier books and the ambiguity in such matters recommended in book eight by Raphael, is a serious flaw, and the attempt Milton requires of his reader to visualize certain details—the sphere of fire and the nature of chaos for example—can result only in images that are vague and blurred, the sort of thing that never results from Dante's descriptions, just as Dante spares us Milton's embarrassing anthropomorphism.

It would seem, in other words, that our awareness of the back-ground of a unit-idea (the state of cosmological knowledge in Milton's day) here leads us inevitably to a judgment of value; or rather, what we make as a judgment of value (the clumsiness of Milton's picture) is explained by our awareness of the unit-idea. Knowledge of fact and judgment of effect are part of the same complex, and the total view should include both. We know that Milton had a choice to make; in terms of contemporary science he made it wrong. If we are not, perhaps, justified in assuming that a consequent sense of intellectual guilt made him fumble, we at least can see the unlucky results in his poem, and can have an aesthetic opinion accordingly.

We are also led by his relations with science to some interesting speculations concerning the rôle of choice in the creation of a work of art. Is the artist more likely to write a successful poem when his basic "unit-ideas" are those which every serious thinker in his time unquestioningly accepts, so that his cosmology, say, is everyone's cosmology, and his general view of man's place in the scheme of things that which everyone believes in? The comparison between Dante and Milton, if we make the violent omission of any consideration of the difference in their characters and the quality of their imaginations, would seem to make us assume so. Are we then to conclude that the greater the freedom of intellectual choice given to the artist by his age, the less likely he is to produce a major work of art? Is the spirit of unlimited enquiry, apparently so encouraging to artistic endeavor, really fatal to it? Is the final weapon of science against art the two-edged words "Be free"?

The study of the history of ideas raises (among others) a further question of a quite different kind. Why and how does our appreciation and understanding of a work of art change when we learn that one of its central ideas was an intellectual commonplace at the time it was written? When Mr. Lovejoy shows us, for example, that Milton's account of the fortunateness of Adam's fall was something that had been in the minds of theologians for centuries, why are we so interested, why does our own mind feel an extra satisfaction? Milton's meaning was clear enough already; does our knowledge that he was saying nothing new change the meaning or merely change our attitude towards it? If the latter, what does the change amount to? Mr. Lovejoy, in discussing another of Milton's ideas (p. 5), suggests that when we know that it was one of the most influential and widely-ramifying ideas in Western thought, "in this larger historical vista Milton's expression of the idea gains a great enrichment of interest—an increase, so to say, of voluminosity." But what does this really mean? Why is voluminosity more interesting and satisfying than its opposite? There are several revealing layers in the human psyche to be laid bare before we can arrive at an adequate answer to questions like these.

67

Such speculations may seem to be irrelevant to Mr. Lovejoy's subject matter, but if we think about that subject matter as something that concerns the present, the potentially creative present, as well as the past, the irrelevance disappears. It is one of the many great merits of Mr. Lovejoy's work, as I suggested at the beginning, that, though it is almost exclusively historical, the issues it raises are so fundamental and of such permanent significance, they are presented so cogently and so accurately analyzed, it is impossible for the reader who values the continuing life of art not to reflect on them in relation to immediate problems. There are times when one wishes that Mr. Lovejoy himself would do so; in the introductory essay, as in the conclusion of the *Great Chain of Being*, one would be grateful (one thinks at first) for a further kind of analysis than that which has already been given; an analysis not of past fact, but of contemporary resulting implications. But Mr. Lovejoy might reply that it is not the business of the historian of ideas to be concerned directly with the present; his concern should be wider and deeper, since its aim, like all scientific aims, is to create foundations of understanding that will make the past as permanently available as possible, unobscured by the myopia of local peering. "Today we study the day before yesterday," says F. W. Maitland, "in order that yesterday may not paralyze today and today may not paralyze tomorrow."

Harvard University.

[*Editor's Note:* Mr. Lovejoy has written a comment (which will appear in our Jan. 1949 issue) on the above review, dealing particularly with the criticism expressed in the opening paragraph of part 3 (pp. 443 ff. above). Mr. Lovejoy wishes to clear up a misunderstanding of what he meant by "the larger question." It was *not* "the question of value" put by Mr. Spencer, but (to quote a part of Mr. Lovejoy's comment) "It was the question of value *applied to large, unanalyzed, undiscriminated, historic complexes of ideas,* as distinct from their 'simpler diversely combinable, intellectual and emotional components.' It is with respect to these latter and to them only (I observed), that the question of value has much meaning or importance.' "]

Chapter IV.b

HISTORIOGRAPHY AND EVALUATION: A DISCLAIMER

By Arthur O. Lovejoy

Having read in proof the very friendly, fair-minded, and thought-provoking review with which, in the preceding number of this journal, Mr. Theodore Spencer honored my recent book of *Essays in the History of Ideas,* I hoped to take advantage of that opportunity to disclaim without delay an opinion, or set of opinions, which he had attributed to me. But as the number was already made up, there was room only for a brief footnote, not, perhaps, sufficient to clarify the point. By the courtesy of the Editors I am now afforded space to correct Mr. Spencer's misapprehension in a less syncopated manner—and to explain how it appears to have arisen.

Mr. Spencer reports me as having written that "when the preliminary task of analysis and detailed comparison" of a historic complex of ideas "is made, it is doubtful 'whether the larger question [the question of value] will seem to have much importance or meaning'," and that this task of analysis and comparison "is not only the most important but in the long run the only task which it is worth while to perform." "Such a statement" Mr. Spencer declares that he, "trained in the school of Irving Babbitt, is unwilling to let pass unchallenged." Babbitt was not wrong "to include moral effect as one of the things to be looked for in the behavior of literature. Is the historian of ideas to say that all complexes of unit-ideas are of equal value for expressing the truth about human experience in artistic form?"

Now Mr. Spencer is, in my judgment, quite right in challenging the statement which he imputes to me. But I have made no such "statement." I do not think that the task of analysis and comparison is the only one which it is in the long run worth while to perform; nor that the moral (or aesthetic) effect of a given idea is not one of the things "to be looked for"; nor that the historian of ideas should regard "all complexes of unit-ideas as of equal value." And I did not suppose that I had ever written anything which could be construed as asserting or implying these opinions. Since so careful a critic as Mr. Spencer supposes that I *have* asserted them, I must have failed to express myself with sufficient clarity.

Mr. Spencer has simply mistaken the antecedent of the phrase "the larger question," in the sentence from which he quotes. The "larger question" to which I referred was *not* "the question of value," as such, but the question of value *applied to large, unanalyzed, undiscriminated, historic complexes of ideas,* as distinct from their "simpler, diversely combinable, intellectual and emotional components." It is with respect to these latter, and to them only (I observed), that the question of value has "much meaning or importance." This last opinion is one which I do hold; and the reason for it, I should suppose, is obvious. In any complex of beliefs,

69

tendencies, valuations, some may be true, some false, some good, some bad. For example, a particular historic religion is usually a complex of discriminable beliefs, emotional attitudes, and practices. Much the same is true of the "system" of any individual philosopher. And it is (I think) a dangerously undiscriminating and relatively unprofitable question to ask whether, in its content and its historical effects, some particular form of (for example) Buddhism (say that of the Pāli Pitakas) is a "good" religion or a "bad" religion; or whether "the philosophy of Aristotle" is true or false. The really important "question of value" about any such complex, I argued, is, what specific *parts* of it are logically sound, or ethically right, or have had benign or injurious effects upon the individuals or the cultures it has influenced. For idea-complexes are usually like the curate's egg; there is likely to be, as the popular saying goes, "something bad in the best of them, and something good in the worst of them." To trace the effects of a given complex as a *whole* is, moreover, hardly possible; for it is not as a whole that it has effects. A later writer, or group, or sect, selects from it for adoption or for special emphasis one or more of its component ideas, other writers or sects select others, combine these diversely with ideas coming from other sources, and the components of the original complex thus go on divergently ramifying and forming new combinations through a long series of historical processes. The *actual* historic effects of a complex thus consist in what men subsequently do with—and add to— its several components; for though the persistence or recurrence of one or another of the components can be discerned by the historian, the whole seldom persists as initially constituted. The histories of Buddhism and of Christianity are perhaps the most glaring examples of this; but almost the entire history of ideas is a gigantic illustration of it.

I cannot, however, forbear to add that there is, I think, considerable danger to the objectivity and accuracy of the historiography of ideas in a too hasty preoccupation with the question of value—in being so eager to find matter for praise or blame—especially blame—in an author or a so-called "movement," that the prior analytical question as to what the author meant by what he wrote, or what diverse ideas and feelings the movement actually expressed, is insufficiently inquired into. And (since Mr. Spencer has introduced into his comment the honored name of Irving Babbitt) I hope it is not unbecoming to say that Mr. Babbitt—who rendered a service of inestimable importance to humanistic studies in America, by arousing students of modern literary history to a concern both about ideas in literature and about their effects—nevertheless seems to me to have often exemplified this danger. Historical analysis and moral or aesthetic evaluation are distinct processes; they should not be mixed; and the first, which demands (what is difficult) a high degree of cool detachment from the analyst's personal enthusiasms and moral or aesthetic ideals, should be in each case patiently completed before the second is attempted.

PART TWO

FOLLOWERS

Chapter V.a

A SYMPOSIUM

LEVELS OF MEANING AND THE HISTORY OF IDEAS*

The history of ideas has sometimes been written as if an idea has an initially independent meaning so that its history is its external career. Just as some have sought to describe the history of a culture trait without special reference to the history of peoples—its first appearance, its spread, its interrelation with other traits, the conditions favorable or hostile to its perpetuation, the consequences of its appearance—so attention may be focused on an idea as such. People appear on the scene, if at all, merely as vehicles for it or as necessary conditions of its existence. Some ideas appear to admit of such treatment, at least as a first step in their historical exploration.

More often in recent times history has been incorporated into the idea. The meaning of an idea is seen not as initially separable but as unfolded in a continuous development. Historical study of the idea consists in drawing a smooth curve after plotting its appearances. Thus the idea of the brotherhood of man may be seen to unfold from the Stoic conception of the divine fire in all existence through the Christian idea of the fatherhood of God, the Kantian human imperative, the Marxian idea of a classless society, to present-day conceptions of one world and a global outlook of indivisible human welfare. Where a pattern of development is found the idea is almost seen as growing. In this sense the history of an idea is not external to it but constitutive of it. Yet it remains the history of the idea, not of the human beings in whose lives the idea functions. It is an immanent development which Hegelianism made popular but which has persisted even on non-Hegelian premises.

A profounder historical sense is found in the view that the history of an idea is essentially human history; the idea itself is clarified by being set in a socio-historical matrix. This whole approach is implicit in pragmatism, with its instrumental treatment of ideas, in naturalism, which regards an idea as a quality of natural events rather than as non-natural energy, and in materialism, for example in the view that philosophical ideas reflect or express social movements. Such approaches are often hindered by a residual dualism found in our thinking. Any attempt to give the historical meaning of an idea is treated usually not as providing an important dimension of meaning, as clarifying its *content,* but as reducing it to something else in some mechanistic fashion, replacing philosophical analysis by causal descrip-

* This and the two following papers formed a symposium delivered at the meeting of the Eastern Division of the American Philosophical Association held at Sarah Lawrence College, Bronxville, New York, February 22, 1946.

tion. Studies of the social history of ideas are not rejected; they may even be welcomed, but only as purely separable scientific ventures in the search for causality. The old dualism of mind directly grasping the content of ideas and matter providing "external" causality, remains as a dualism of method.

In what follows I do not mean to deny that different categories are employed in dealing with content or meaning and with causal explanation. In any given context judgments of truth, validity, and intellectual adequacy are fundamentally different from judgments of causation, necessary conditions, natural history. I am asserting, however, that such distinctions in categories and types of inquiry do not require relegating socio-historical elements as a whole to the causal sphere, leaving more or less abstract elements in sole possession of content or meaning. There are *levels of meaning*[1] in the actual understanding of philosophic ideas, among which socio-historical meaning is far from unimportant.

That the concept of historical causation does not preclude that of historical meaning can be seen readily if we begin an analysis of the thesis that philosophical ideas "reflect" or "express" socio-historical movements. At least four senses of this relation emerge:

(a) The appearance of philosophical ideas on the historical scene is in some general sense the *effect* of social processes.

(b) The development of an idea is in some sense *isomorphic* with social development. For example, hierarchical conceptions of the cosmos might be found to parallel hierarchical economic and social structures. The reflection metaphor here has literal mirror-image components, in addition to presumed causal relations.

(c) Philosophical ideas serve *instrumental* functions for social groups. This is less a theory of causal origin than one of acquired significance. The point has been popularized in the hard-boiled political approach which sees ideas and ideals as propagandist slogans for special interests. Examples abound in writers of the Machiavellian tradition. Thus, many hallowed legal ideas treated abstractly constitute folk-lore, according to Thurman Arnold. Even from Mr. Arnold's own treatment, however, it can be seen that once these ideas are viewed in terms of the interests they support they clearly make sense. Instrumental functions can therefore constitute elements in the meaning of an idea.

[1] The term "levels" is used in the sense in which we often speak of physical, biological, or psychological levels of existence. Emphasis here is on the difference of area or dimension, not on any ascending or descending relationship. The question of primacy or priority among levels is treated below as a separate problem. Nor is there any attempt *a priori* to delimit the kinds or number of levels or the mode in which they may be distinguished. If we think of *content* instead of *meaning*, perhaps "phases of content" best expresses the intent of "levels of meaning."

(d) When the third sense is broadened, it becomes the view that an idea, abstractly stated, is a kind of incomplete symbol. It requires supplementation by socio-historical material to achieve completeness, just as the spatial location of an object requires completion by a temporal framework in a more intimate relationship than tradition imagined. An idea fully expounded thus has a *dimension of historical meaning*. Such concepts as liberty and equality simply cannot be understood by any of the traditional abstract formulae—arithmetic, geometric, or even psychological. Explication of their meaning demands reference to a given historical period and the aims of social groups within a given economic and institutional setting. Thus "freedom from want" today refers to unemployment, low production levels and recurrent crises in a capitalist framework, and to proposals of social security and full employment. To treat it abstractly results in such a travesty as Mr. Burnham's in his book *The Machiavellians,* when he argues that the idea is meaningless in terms of real politics because "men are wanting beings; they are freed from want only by death."[2]

We may illustrate the concept of historical meaning as one of a variety of levels of meaning by a brief examination of a familiar philosophical idea. Take the Aristotelian idea of the *mean*. Actually, various levels of meaning can be found for it in the Aristotelian writings. Abstractly, Aristotle describes it as a concept of measure; just as the carpenter cuts his lumber to the right size and the sculptor molds the statue to the right proportion, so in conduct the mean is selection of the right amount and rejection of excess and defect. In his treatment of the virtues and vices, where considerable cultural content is introduced, the mean appears as the path of moderation. This level of meaning is considerably deepened by a study of Greek culture in all fields; it reveals the general pattern of avoidance of extremes as *hybris,* which Spengler, following Nietzsche's suggestions, has made popular as the Apollonian outlook. In Aristotle's *Politics,* the distinct sense of "balance" replaces that of "measure"; extremes are synthesized in the resultant instead of being discarded alternatives.[3] The political balance turns out to be that of the rich and the poor, of oligarchy and democracy, to avoid faction and secure order under the mean, which is quite literally the middle class.

[2] James Burnham, *The Machiavellians* (1943), 26, 177.

[3] This shows that there may be more than one abstract meaning associated with the given term. While the failure to distinguish these senses may indicate a confusion on Aristotle's part, it is also sometimes possible to reconcile them on a given level. Thus on the ethical level "measure" may apply to the perfectly virtuous man who has no evil desires, and "balance" to the self-controlled man (ethically one step below the virtuous man) who has evil desires but habitually checks them. It may be added that many of the ideas in Aristotle—even the most apparently abstract—admit of an analysis in terms of levels similar to that offered of the mean. Even the principle of identity turns out to have a content on several levels varying from fixed species to natural slavery.

On each level of meaning we could, as a separate enterprise, look for causes. The use of the idea in its abstract meaning might be traced to the constant Socratic analogy of the arts, or, on the other hand, to the social institutions of craftsmanship, including medicine, and their impact in Aristotle's life. The causal basis of the cultural meaning could be sought in the whole social history of the Greek people. The politico-economic meaning points to a causal analysis in terms of economic conflicts in the Greek city-states. In all such analysis, however, even where the same materials provided insights into both meaning and causation, these inquiries would remain distinct in type.

The question naturally arises whether there is any unity in the various levels of meaning of a given idea to justify regarding them as all meanings of the "same" idea. Otherwise the term might simply be judged equivocal and separate terms provided to designate what we have called the various levels. This unity is not furnished by speaking of a "given idea." The analysis of an idea may start on any level and such reference to it simply indicates the point at which the inquiry happened to begin. Nor does the use of the single term (e.g., the Aristotelian idea of the mean) commit us to finding a content common to all contexts on all levels. How we look for unity varies with the context of inquiry. In the case of the mean we have a body of Aristotelian writings in different fields; the same term is used and there are probably sufficient cross-references to verify the hypothesis that Aristotle intends his discussions to be dealing with the "same" idea. In the case of freedom from want or any similar economic or political ideal, the unity may be found in the fact that abstract idea and political program are advanced by the same statesman or group, with the obvious intent of implementation. Greater difficulties are encountered where the social meaning of a philosophical idea has to be patiently determined by the historical study of a whole period with its groupings, conflicts, and instruments. In principle the problem though complicated is no different. The criteria of unity must themselves be worked out in empirical terms to suit the different types of inquiries in which the study of the history of ideas may be carried on.

Further questions arise concerning the relation of levels once they are established. The following are a few suggestions as to what some such relationships may be:

(1) The relation of levels of meaning may sometimes also represent a relation of causation. That is, an abstract or political meaning of an idea may be what it is because the socio-historical meaning has been what it is. Thus it is conceivable in the case of the mean that the political meaning in terms of class-relations historically determined the cultural meaning in terms of moderation. This would, however, require independent verification as a causal hypothesis.

(2) Is there a correlation between meanings on the various different

levels? At first glance there would appear to be different abstract meanings associated with the same social meaning and conversely. The first occurs, for example, when the same social aims are justified on different theoretical grounds, e.g., absolute monarchy on King James's divine right theory and on Hobbes's peace ethics. However, in such a case the social content may vary beyond the limits of the initial statement; James's view, regarding rebellion as parricide, has no place for accommodation, whereas Hobbes allows the breakdown of absolute obedience after successful rebellion establishes a new power. Moreover, the very quality of the subject's obedience is different even where the same act is performed; in the one case it is absolute and unquestioning, whereas in the other, resting ultimately on empirical grounds, it has a tentative potential.

Conversely, the same limited abstract or psychological meaning may be associated with different social content. This happens, for example, when the same avowed abstract end is pursued by different social policies. It is a commonplace, however, that the end acquires a different quality under different means, so that a fuller picture may again yield a more intimate relation of the different meaning levels.

It follows that the apparent correlation of different content on the various meaning levels may not ultimately disprove the possibility of discovering historically unique or one–one relations of the various meaning levels of a given idea. Decision on this question is certainly premature and can only be made on the basis of extended empirical analysis. In order to carry out such analysis it is possible that a distinction might profitably be made between a "cross-sectional" study of an idea on all levels at one time and a "transitional" study of the interrelation of levels over an extended period in which there is change of content. Some characterizations of the relations of levels—e.g., when a philosophical theory is called a "garb" for political aims—while phrased as cross-sectional relations, may really refer to dynamic properties in a transitional study; e.g., it is predicted that the garb will be shed as soon as it is politically expedient.

(3) Is any one level of meaning in some sense more primary than others? Our philosophical tradition has tended to stress the level of abstract meaning. This represents a valuation which may be spurious. The history of ideas should reveal whether this idea of the primacy of the abstract level itself has a socio-historical meaning.

In a transitional study a primacy in a different sense may be assigned to one level if it maintains a relative constancy under changing meanings in other levels. (This constancy may be only relative because, as pointed out above, it may involve qualitative changes corresponding to these other changes.) Thus in religious ideas ritual meanings may be primary in comparison with mythological meanings; and in social transformations the socio-economic meaning of an idea may prove more basic than the legal or political meaning. For example, the Marxian claim that democracy in capitalist countries is primarily bourgeois democracy is partly a cross-sectional view of the economic meaning of political democracy in action, and partly the transitional hypothesis that political democracy gives way to an opposing political form under bourgeois economic necessities. It is difficult in such an analysis to dissociate meaning elements from causal elements, but it is worth trying.

The above comments exhibit the complexity of the relationships we are examining. They establish at the very least the injustice done to the historical meaning of philosophic ideas by reducing all investigation of it to the external search for causality. This conclusion and the enlarged treatment of ideas that it envisages point in the long run to the need for reconsidering the criteria of the philosophical evaluation of ideas. Adherence to the narrow criterion of consistency alone tends to make the choice among consistent philosophic ideas purely a matter of taste or of temperament or of some "pragmatic" consideration narrowly construed. Consideration of an idea on all meaning levels should incorporate such elements within the idea fully conceived, and thereby render them more responsible to criticism. And if the refutation of a philosophic idea thereby becomes more complicated than the simple exhibition of an inconsistency, the acceptance of a philosophic idea becomes grounded in the whole character of human life and action. So construed, the history of ideas takes no ancillary place; it is rather in the forefront of the philosophical enterprise.

College of the City of New York.

THE PHILOSOPHICAL SIGNIFICANCE OF THE
HISTORY OF THOUGHT

By Paul Oskar Kristeller

Philosophy, and its history, may be understood either in a narrower or in a broader sense. In a narrower sense, philosophy is a separate field of study and teaching, which originates in a specific tradition of thought and uses an elaborate method of its own. In a broader sense, philosophy comprises any attempt, with or without method, to answer the general problems with which a human being finds himself confronted in his surrounding world. I shall speak first and at greater length of philosophy in the narrower sense of the term, and shall add at the end of this paper some remarks on the history of philosophy in the broader sense.

The purpose of this paper is to justify the study of the history of philosophy, which happens to be my special field of interest, in the eyes of contemporary philosophers. I am fully aware that this attempt may be vain since many may feel that no such justification is needed whereas others will not be convinced by my arguments.

In the first place, the history of philosophy may be considered merely as a special branch of historical studies in general, along with political and economic history, the history of literature, of the arts, of religion, and of science. In this sense, the history of philosophy participates in the significance which belongs to all historical studies: it satisfies our curiosity about the past, and it contributes to a better understanding of our present civilization which has developed on the basis of its past heritage. The history of philosophy would thus appeal to the philosopher in the same manner as would any other field of historical studies. For the facts discovered and reported by the historian thus become part of the reality accessible to us, and may stimulate the thought of the philosopher just as do the facts discovered by science or by personal experience. On the other hand, the method followed by the historian in discovering and verifying his facts may be analyzed by the philosopher just as the methods of scientific thought have been. However, in this sense the history of philosophy and history in general are merely objects of philosophical thinking. It does not follow that the study of the history of philosophy should be the business of the philosopher; it might as well be left to the general historian, or rather to the historian of literature. As a matter of fact, large areas of the history of philosophy have been cultivated only by students of literature who have wanted to explore a certain philosophical background of other writers which has not interested students of philosophy.

Without minimizing the important contributions made to the history of philosophy by students of literature, I should like to argue that the history of philosophy should be primarily the business of the student of philosophy. The understanding of philosophical texts and ideas requires a philosophical competence which the average student of literature does not possess. For this reason, the treatment of the history of philosophy becomes a kind of duty for the philosopher who happens to be interested in historical questions at all. I should like to add that to perform this duty is also rewarding, and this leads us to our main point. Philosophical knowledge is not only needed for the study of the history of philosophy, but vice versa, the study of the history of philosophy makes a significant contribution to philosophical thought.

Above all, the terminology used by contemporary philosophers depends in many respects on past developments. The meaning of the terms through which we express our thought is greatly clarified when we know and understand the thought of the past philosophers who coined or modified the use of such terms. Contemporary philosophers are well aware of this historical background of our terminology. Some of them consider it an evil that can be avoided by creating an entirely new, symbolical language. Others consider it a necessary evil, and are ready to acknowledge the importance of historical studies at least in this respect.

Moreover, not only the terms but also the problems of contemporary thought depend in many points on past developments and can be more accurately understood through a study of the history of philosophy. I do not want to say, of course, that all problems of contemporary thought can be derived from philosophies of the past. Some of them can, and others cannot, and I believe that even the characteristic problems of modern thought that have no antecedents in the past can be handled much better if we are able to discriminate between old and novel problems. To become aware of the historical position and background of our own thought is a kind of philosophical self-criticism which may, to be sure, have a paralyzing effect on our own thought, but which may instead greatly improve and refine it. It may also enrich it. For our philosophical thought does not start from nothing, as some would like to believe; it rather develops through a process of discussion. We develop our own views by examining and criticizing those of others, whether they be the friends and colleagues with whom we talk or those contemporary thinkers whose works we read and study. I am inclined to think that the range of contemporary thought is limited, and that our basis of discussion might be fruitfully broadened if we included in our examination the thought of past philosophers. They discussed many problems that are still important or that may again become important, and we can learn a good deal even from their errors, just as we do from the errors of our friends or of contemporary philosophers. The history of philosophy represents a rich treasure house of ideas, true and false, from which we may derive much inspiration. Those who despise this source of inspiration because they want to be "original" and "creative" in every respect would seem to be guided by vanity rather than by a concern for truth, and I doubt that they accomplish their aim. For one does not become original by wanting to be original, nor is the ignorance of history a prerequisite of creative thought.

This leads me to another, more external consideration. I believe that the study of a subject in the history of philosophy has a disciplining effect, especially upon the mind of a young student of philosophy. Knowledge as distinct from mere opinion is not merely an expression of intellectual or emotional preferences, but an insight related to a definite subject matter in regard to which it can be called true or false. In scientific or historical knowledge, this subject matter is offered in the form of definite empirical data which our thought can coordinate and interpret with the help of its methods and categories, but which as specific data offer a kind of resistance to any arbitrary procedure. In mathematical knowledge the situation is somewhat different, but there also we have a subject matter which limits the processes of thought, which themselves follow quite definite rules of procedure. Philosophical knowledge also is determined and limited by its subject matter; yet this is of a very general and elusive character, and hence philosophical knowledge has often been mistaken for, and actually degenerated into, a mere aggregate of more or less arbitrary opinions. The history of philosophy, among other philosophical disciplines, has the advantage of a tangible and external subject matter, the texts of the philosophers we are studying, and the ideas contained in those texts. These texts offer a resistance to our interpretation; we cannot impose upon them any meaning we like, they may even contradict opinions we cherish. I believe that the habit of submitting our thought to the data of a philosophical text is a good discipline for the philosopher who wants to submit his thought to the data of reality in general, data that are much more difficult to grasp or to verify.

Finally, I should like to argue that the history of philosophy is a part, and a necessary part, of philosophy, and not merely an auxiliary discipline. There is a significant difference between the historian of philosophy and the historian of art, of literature, or of political events. The historian of art, of poetry, or of events expresses himself in the medium of the language of scholarship, narration, or criticism. This medium is different from the medium of the arts (colors and lines, stones and metals, sounds and voices), of poetry (rhythms and imagery), or of events (actions). The historian in these fields, so to speak, translates the original language of his subject matter into a different language. The historian of philosophy, however, expresses himself in the very language or medium that belongs to his subject matter, philosophy, that is, in the language of abstract or speculative thought. Hence his enterprise should be considered as a part of philosophy itself.[1]

In considering the history of philosophy as a necessary part of philosophy, I do not want to endorse the doctrine of certain contemporary philosophers who would like to identify philosophy and history. Philosophy is not identical with history, nor with the history of philosophy, as has been rightly shown by others. There is, to be sure, a mutual relation between philosophy and the history of philosophy. Every philosopher is influenced by the previous development of philosophy, and by his knowledge of it, and every historian of philosophy is influenced by his own philosophy. Yet the latter fact is a necessary condition rather than a conscious aim. The study of the history of philosophy is identical with philosophy only so long as we combine the interpretation of past philosophies with a critique of their validity. To be sure, such a critique of past philosophies is needed and will always con-

---

[1] It might be argued that the history of science is a part of science, and the history of religion a part of religion, just as the history of philosophy is a part of philosophy. To be sure, the history of science requires scientific competence, and the history of religion, religious understanding, and in both cases the medium of expression may be unchanged. However, many of the religious beliefs of the past, and most of its scientific theories, have been superseded and hence possess a merely "historical" interest. On the other hand, the philosophies of the past have not been superseded in this sense, but contain many elements at least that are pertinent to contemporary philosophical discussion.

tinue to be a part of philosophical discussion. Yet the study of the history of philosophy, as it has emerged since the last century, applies the methods of general history and philology to its particular subject matter, and tends to separate the interpretation of past philosophies from the critique of their views. To achieve this separation may be a difficult task, but it has become the aim and standard in the history of philosophy as well as in other historical disciplines. This separation emphasizes once more that the study of the history of philosophy is different from other philosophical disciplines. On the other hand, it does not refute the claim that the study of the history of philosophy is a part of philosophy. For the historian of philosophy not only uses the same medium of expression as does the philosopher, but he also deals with different approaches to the same reality with which the philosopher is concerned.

I should like to add a few remarks about the history of thought, that is, the history of philosophy in the widest possible sense. The history of thought is much broader than the history of philosophy proper: it covers wide areas in the history of literature, of religion, of science, and of the arts. Consequently, the history of thought occupies a larger place within the field of historical studies, and participates more directly and more extensively in the general significance of history. There is, moreover, a close mutual relation between the history of philosophy proper and the more general history of thought. Philosophy proper emerged from the much broader area of general thought through the development of a conscious and elaborate method and tradition. As the technical terms of philosophy are based on the words of the general language, so the problems and solutions of philosophical thought are often transformations and elaborations that correspond to the trends and currents of general thought. This is true not only for the beginnings of Western philosophy in ancient Greece, but also for practically all subsequent periods. The history of Western philosophy cannot be understood without the continual inspiration it has received from non-professional thinkers and from the successive currents of religion, of science, and of literature. Conversely, philosophy proper has at all times influenced those neighboring fields of thought. The history of philosophy may hence be properly supplemented by a study of those influences, in order to understand the changing place and significance philosophy itself has had within the civilizations of which it has been a part. The history of thought is thus of interest to the philosopher, although more indirectly than is the history of philosophy proper. The history of thought also provides its student with definite empirical data that set a limit to his imaginative opinions. Moreover, the history of thought is a storehouse of problems and ideas which are less elaborate and less methodical than those of philosophy proper, but which may stimulate philosophical thought and discussion when they are subjected to some greater methodical elaboration.

However, the history of thought would seem to present a new problem when we consider its medium of expression, and the kind of students who should pursue it. For the thought contained in this wider area not only lacks method and elaboration as compared with philosophy proper, but these "philosophical ideas" are here inseparably fused with elements of an entirely different character: poetic, artistic, religious or scientific. The question is whether the philosopher should have any share in handling this material, or whether it should not be left to the historian or critic of literature, of art, of religion, or of science. This problem is especially acute in the case of poetry and literature.

The Neo-Romantic literary historian would like to banish the philosopher entirely from this area. Without being bothered by contradictions, such Romantic critics first attribute to their poets and writers a wisdom greatly superior to that of the "professional" philosophers, and then refuse to interpret this wisdom in a rational or philosophical manner, thus fostering intellectual, and moral, irresponsibility. They are joined by those philosophers who define philosophy proper in an excessively narrow way and would like to relegate those thinkers with whom they disagree to the realm of poetry. I do not think that this is the right solution of our problem.

Of course, we must recognize the presence of those other, non-philosophical elements in the writings of poets, and leave their study quite properly to the historian of literature, admitting even that in many cases they may be more important than any contribution to thought to be found in such works of poetry. On the other hand, wherever there is an element of thought in addition to mere imagery and formal beauty, the student of philosophy has a right to isolate it and to interpret it according to his method, and even to make it more explicit and conscious than it may appear in its original context. In this sense, the history of thought is as much the business of the philosopher as of the literary historian, and the student of philosophy may make a distinct contribution to the field because he has a more universal outlook than the average literary historian, and because the philosopher is at home in the general medium of thought, although he is accustomed to a more elaborate method than that used by the thinking poet or writer. Finally, more general thinkers are trying to understand the same reality that constitutes the subject matter of the philosopher.

Nevertheless, the general history of thought is not the exclusive domain of the historian of philosophy, and it is not an integral part of philosophy, but merely an auxiliary discipline to the history of philosophy. The historian of thought has to dig into many materials and problems that lie outside the field of philosophy proper, and his results merely fill in the background of the historical development of philosophy proper.

To sum up my conclusion, the history of philosophy in the narrow sense of the word is an integral part of philosophy itself and is primarily the business of the student of philosophy. The history of thought in the broader sense is merely an auxiliary discipline of philosophy and constitutes a domain which the student of philosophy must share with the student of literature, of the arts, of religion, and of science.

Columbia University.

LOGICAL SIGNIFICANCE OF THE HISTORY OF THOUGHT

By Philip P. Wiener

Why should philosophers study the history of the kinds of thought which pervade the history of philosopy and religion, the themes of literature and the arts, the natural sciences, and the ideologies of economic and political programs? None but a sciolist, a polyhistor, or a dilettante can claim reliable knowledge of all these branches of intellectual history; why should the philosopher put himself in such suspicious company? Has he not enough to do in the foundations of the various edifices of thought—examining the logic and basic assumptions of a growing multiplicity of natural and social sciences, and viewing them in their relations to ethical, esthetic or religious values—to justify a querulous or even skeptical attitude to new-fangled studies in the *history* of the very ideas he is in the midst of analyzing and appraising? What relevance can the history of ideas have for the logical analysis of their significance? It would be fatuous optimism for me to assume that any gathering of philosophers would agree as to what is meant by *an idea,* by *logical analysis,* by *significance,* or by *truth.* But a history of thought that truly shows how and why thinkers disagree about such basic terms should throw some light on their meaning, and aid us to see things as others see them—which, I take it, is the core of humane understanding.

Those philosophers who impute the "genetic fallacy" and the evils of "historicism" to histories of thought claiming philosophical significance usually adopt one or another of the following doctrines:

(1) *Intuitionism:* Knowledge ultimately consists of infallible intuitions or direct timeless revelations of truth.

(2) *Eternalism:* Historical events are not as real as their presumed order, or historical knowledge as significant as the postulation of universal laws or categories of nature, thought or history.

(3) *Purism:* Philosophical truth transcends the subject-matter of scientific inquiry or cultural history and refers to a realm or realms of its own, not subject to historical modification nor investigable by the methods of empirical science.

Each of these doctrines is bound to lead to an antagonism to the thesis that historical researches concerning the development of thought have any logical value, for the following reasons:

(1) Since the past is irretrievable and all knowledge of it depends on memory or inferences from documents or remains, historical knowledge is thoroughly mediated and cannot be simply a matter of intuition. Memory is fallible, documents are ambiguous, remains are incomplete. Yet these are the only sources of historical knowledge. Thus they can scarcely be acceptable to intuitionists who seek certainty and immediate knowledge.

(2) The eternalist is logically bound to oppose any serious philosophical study of the history of changes of thought, for he regards all temporal phenomena as unreal, accidental, worthless or subordinate aspects of an eternal or more important or essentially infrangible pattern of history. On such an eternal view of existence, what is logically significant or valuable is the laws, the dialectical pattern, the immutable necessities of history. The rest is mere detail, embodiment, unfolding exemplification of the great cosmic pattern or organic structure in which we move and have our being. To emphasize or be unduly concerned with the historical detail by neglecting the purpose revealed in a glimpse or vision of the whole is considered to be essentially unphilosophical.

(3) Purists, including some intuitionists and eternalists, insist on logically divorcing the subject-matter of philosophy from the problems, methods, and contents of all other fields of study and human activity. Such an exclusive or esoteric position as to the subject-matter of philosophy would certainly imply that the history of thought outside that of pure philosophical thought is of no concern to the philosopher or his distinctive problems. The traditional subject-matter of philosophy—e.g., the categories, ways and limits of knowledge, the *summum bonum,* immortality and freedom—is alleged by the purist to transcend the narrow confines of the special sciences and their piece-meal methods. What the *pure* philosopher has to establish prior to meddling with the vagaries of intellectual history, we are told, is an adequate theory of the nature of existence and thought as such, the meaning of meaning, a philosophy of history that penetrates to its inner meaning and purposes, and a trans-empirical account of the relation of the eternal to the temporal.

Common to philosophical intuitionism, eternalism, and purism we thus find a logical bias against the piece-meal and exacting methods of the empirical sciences when extended to the traditionally "higher" problems of philosophy. This bias expresses itself in resistance to any possible influence on philosophic ideas by historical studies, on the ground that historical developments must be by definition irrelevant to the logical analysis of problems or the ultimate meaning of ideas. But since irrelevance is a symmetrical relation, these philosophies render themselves irrelevant to the problems of our changing civilization. My position is that even when we have attained a certain accepted degree of clarity our most reliable knowledge is still tentative, conditioned by historical evidence and subject to modification in time. In medicine, a case history leads to a diagnosis; in law, the argument from precedents or previous parallels is strong. Do we not wish to know the past record of persons to whom we entrust private or public matters? Would we not get along better with other nations and peoples if we knew more of their cultural traditions and ways of thinking and doing things? William James remarks in one of his telling blows at rationalism:

Religious thinking, ethical thinking, poetical thinking, teleological, emotional, sentimental thinking, what one might call the personal view of life to distinguish it from the impersonal and mechanical, and the romantic view of life to distinguish it from the rationalistic view, have been, and even still are, outside of well-drilled scientific circles, the dominant forms of thought.[1]

Rationalists in condemning the anti-intellectualist elements in human history often make the mistake of turning their backs on that in history or society which fails to fit their inflexible standards of rationality. This blocks inquiry, and in social matters has led to the capture of society by political demagogues and opportunists exploiting their more intimate experience of the foibles of mankind.

I believe that much of the force of the ultra-rationalist principle that the nature of a theory or idea is separate from its history derives from logically inadequate as well as uncritical histories of thought. The inadequacy resides in the failure to relate logic and historical experience. The crucial question is whether an adequate or true history of any of the ideas with which man has faced and explored the unknown could help but illuminate some of the relations expressed in any hypothesis which establishes a line of continuity between the known and the unknown. From the fact that *some* historical facts are irrelevant to the understanding or explanation of things or ideas it does not follow that *all* references to historical developments are irrelevant.

Some philosophers have maintained two conflicting doctrines: (a) history never repeats itself, (b) the same causes produce the same effects. The uniqueness of historical events or the *Eigentümlichkeit* of cultural epochs or of the *Volksgeist* of a nation is proclaimed in the same system of Absolute Reason, Will or Power which operates by means of a dialectical pattern and which violates the alleged discontinuous uniqueness by repeating itself at every moment of history. To avoid the recalcitrant facts of individuality and variety, the absolutist shows great disdain for merely empirical history and for the piece-meal methods and results of experimental sciences. The empirical alternative is to respect the continuity of history whenever we are

[1] W. James, *Will to Believe and Other Essays* (1897), 302. If Bertrand Russell knew more of the historical roots of American pragmatism, particularly its affinities with the experimental reasoning of the British empiricists, he would understand it better than he does in his spurious attacks on its "cash value" theory of truth. Unfortunately, the Latin-American Handbook of Philosophy shares this misconception of pragmatism by linking it with Wall Street; Soviet philosophers do likewise.

confronted with similar situations in the present—and to note the differences lurking in that continuity by regarding causal relations as contingent. This logical alternative requires, first, that we abandon all pretense of knowing intuitively or dialectically any historical epoch—let alone all history—as a single whole, since in fact we can know reliably only specifiable features of history that are recurrent in their isolable and recognizable features; secondly, that we abandon in scientific humility all pretense of exact *certainty* in our knowledge of causal laws; finally, that we sacrifice the attempt to grasp individuality or existence as such in publicly verifiable *knowledge* of events, persons, societies or epochs, being content with inductive generalizations or functional correlations that hold for properties common to classes of individuals. Individuals *as such* elude not only scientific knowledge, but also all historical and philosophical attempts to describe ineffable unities. It is enough for a scientist, historian or philosopher to fall so deeply in love with the particular subject he studies, that its internal structure acquires for him in that study an individuality which only similarly devoted minds can appreciate. But like all earthly loves, this intellectual love which generates the sense of the individuality of what is present to thought, will pass into the larger movements of things.

The specific and temporally conditioned sense in which history is logically internal to scientific knowledge may be illustrated from an examination of the growing structure of any science. In this sense, Newton's law of gravitation is both a mathematical *and* an historical result of the union and generalization of Kepler's and Galileo's laws. Of course, it is conceivable that, in the boastful vein of Descartes' unhistorical intuitionism, Newton might have discovered in one fell swoop of his unaided intellect all that the combined genius of Kepler's astronomical inductions and Galileo's experimental dynamics had painstakingly worked out. But considering the prior cumulative mathematical and physical knowledge which Kepler and Galileo had made use of, it is as improbable that Newton could have dispensed with their results as that Democritus could have discovered the atomic bomb. Internal to the logic of geometry is the history of the attempts to prove Euclid's parallel postulate that culminate in the non-Euclidean geometries. The very notion of logical rigor has had an internal history affiliated with the problems of the consistency, independence, and completeness of the axioms of deductive systems, so that what was once considered a satisfactory mode of proof, like the superposition of figures, is no longer acceptable to our rigorous geometers. The definition of a necessary truth given by Herbert Spencer in terms of the "inconceivability of the opposite" is sufficiently criticized by John Stuart Mill's reminder that the "history of science teems with inconceivabilities which have been conquered."[2]

[2] J. S. Mill, *System of Logic,* bk. II, ch. 5, sec. 6; quoted by C. S. Peirce, *Collected Papers,* 2. 29.

We need to distinguish in our histories of man's many-sided intellectual development the internal from the external facts. Consider the historical development of any discipline, e.g., mathematics. The religion, nationality, political ambitions, etc., of Leibniz tell us something about the social structure of Germany and Europe after the Thirty Years War, but nothing about Leibniz's contributions to logic and mathematics. For the history of the problems which in Leibniz's lifetime led him and Newton to the invention of the calculus is a mathematical affair and belongs to the internal history of mathematics, going back to the scientific thought of Eudoxus and Archimedes, whose religion, nationality, and politics were different from Leibniz's and fall within other histories of thought external to that of pure mathematics. All the achievements of mathematics as of every art and science are historical in both an internal sense and an external sense, depending on the state of our knowledge of the inter-relations. Economic and sociological historians too often neglect the internal development of ideas in the interest of "proving" that all thought and progress depend solely on external economic or social factors, which they regard as *the* driving force of all history,[3] when in fact man's cumulative knowledge is also involved as a primary factor of social progress.

The intuitionalist and eternalist fail to note the tacit reference to the cumulative history of ideas contained in both the language and content of their own eternal revelations. The main ideas and problems of man are bequeathed to him by previous efforts to state the relations of the mind of man to his environment. The claims of any particular intuition are at best those of any special hypothesis requiring verification.

The history of philosophy does not warrant the isolationist exclusiveness claimed by the purist for the subject-matter of philosophy. The categories of Western philosophy in their semantic history are linked with the forms of Indo-European grammar, the "generic traits of existence" are distilled from our scientific knowledge, the limits of knowledge are those of the growing sciences, ideas of the *summum bonum* vary with changing social and political conditions, the meaning of immortality and freedom is more adequately realized in enduring works of art, science and contributions to social progress than in esoteric realms of being or pure thought. The very nature of philosophy is hardly separable from the historical question: What problems have been regarded traditionally as answerable by philosophers? If, following Peirce, we define philosophy as the analysis of elementary concepts, then I should maintain that the "elementary" is a relative, formal character of a system of concepts whose logical arrangement or meaning varies with the historical state of our scientific knowledge, so that what is taken to be "elementary" or simple in one historical context turns out to be

[3] In this sort of economic monism, all other cultural or intellectual developments become "superstructural" or historically epiphenomenal.

composite or complex in another system; e.g., the elements of Greek physics and chemistry (earth, air, fire, water) are complexes in modern physical science. The relational character of all present-day scientific concepts has led modern logic to abandon the absolute timeless simples of classical logic underlying most systems of metaphysics, e.g., Plato's forms, Aristotle's categories, scholastic substantial forms and occult qualities, Leibnizian monads, Hume's impressions, Russellian sense-data, etc.

There are logical and epistemological lessons to be drawn from the history of science, as Peirce has shown in his extensive logical and his still unpublished historical investigations. The Ptolemaic system, though as consistent as the Copernican, yet gave way to the latter, indicating the methodological rôle played by *simplicity* in the scientific choice of hypotheses. The advent of non-Euclidean geometry throws light on the inadequacy of the classical rationalistic identification of mathematical and physical laws, and indicates the logical rôle of conventions in applying deductive systems to physical problems. Einstein's analysis of the meaning of simultaneity shows how the traditional methods of conceiving relations in space and time rested on uncriticized operational assumptions. Historical studies of biological ideas, e.g., Lovejoy's studies of pre-Darwinian evolutionism,[4] show that evolutionism is a modification of one of the most powerful ideas in the history of man's cosmological conceptions, viz., the Great Chain of Being, with its fixed species and assumptions of gradation, continuity and plenitude at the ultimate core of things. Kant revealed his *a priori* bias against historical considerations when he argued that a physical theory of the evolution of living organisms is in principle impossible.[5] Even more remote from his eternalistic conception of thought was the possibility of an evolution of the forms or categories of thought. No wonder then that he so sharply separated the history of philosophy from philosophy, assigning the former to polyhistors and the latter to transcendental logic. It is the historical evidence of the temporal character of both nature and knowledge that makes the ground quake under those time-honored edifices of metaphysics, theology and politics which are based on eternal, indubitable and self-evident axioms.

These historical lessons do not preclude philosophical speculation on the logic of science. For this there is ample room in the notion of the evolution of the laws of nature as Peirce and Whitehead have entertained it, in the evolutionary approach to morality, social institutions and religion as Dewey and Bergson have more than suggested, in the evolution and revolution of economic and political forms as Hegel and Marx proposed. Are all these potent ideas so very much alive in our own times to be dismissed with a single wave of the hand as instances of the genetic fallacy?

The much discussed problem of the use of scientific method in social prob-

[4] *Popular Science Monthly* (1904–14).

[5] *Kritik der Urtheilskraft*, IV, 161; V, 391.

lems should receive some clarification from the history of the methods and relations of the physical and social sciences. Can we learn nothing concerning what was fruitful and sterile in the social and religious controversies that raged over Newton's and Darwin's works, and today arise again over the horrible smoke of the atomic bomb? To my mind, at least one neglected relation of natural science to social philosophy emerges from these controversies, viz., the strict logical *neutrality* of scientific method, as Chauncey Wright clearly and constantly, but not always successfully, pointed out to James and Peirce. Unless we keep clearly in mind the ethical goals of civilization and cherish them loyally, science is just as likely to be used to destroy us as to solve our problems. Mechanistic or dialectical materialism and pessimistic or optimistic evolutionism are polemics for different theories of human values, and do not have the scientific import of Newton's and Darwin's contributions because the methods and concepts which scientists use to answer their delimited problems are more neutral than the interests which the metaphysical generalizations claim to support. However, the clarification of the cultural implications of the effects of great scientific discoveries has been and still is one of the chief historical functions of philosophy. The nineteenth-century logic of science in Hegel's and Marx's time was intimately fused with the rationalistic assumption that some sort of *necessity* holds for both the physical world and cultural phenomena. But what was meant by historical or empirical necessity? This is a historical *and* logical (hence philosophical) question of utmost significance, for the answers of both Hegel and Marx and their followers today are assumed by them to be a sufficient ground for drawing what they hold to be inevitable political conclusions concerning the necessity for concentration of political power in the hands of an organized minority.

The critical study of many alleged cases of "historicism"—e.g., Hegel, Marx, Savigny, Schmoller, Spengler—would show that it was not always the evidence of history that logically supported their claims, but that they often reconstructed history in order to support their social convictions or political purposes. The significance of such philosophies of history is what they reveal of the ethical or political purposes of their perpetrators. If you wish to know, for example, the political attitudes of a nation, read its approved history books or the official pronouncements of its leading statesmen and philosophers concerning the historic world mission of their nation and its culture.

The historical and logical value of the genetic fallacy is to warn us not to *identify* our own ways of thinking or looking at things with those of the past, and not to expect future generations to see things as we think they must be seen. But historical continuity does not imply such identification, and should encourage the proper kind of respect for the previous knowledge of our predecessors as well as trust in the new experiments of our successors.

We can learn what thought or mind or human nature is from its historical manifestations without limiting its future growth by narrowly restricted modes of intuition, spurious claims on eternity, or puristic notions of philosophy as a higher science.

Had we not better implement and test our epistemological theories by the rich materials provided by the historical development of the sciences, our ethical and religious theories by the historical diversity of morals and ways of living of other peoples, our aesthetic theories by the historical kaleidoscope of art styles, schools and tastes, and our political theories by the history of the successes and failures of different types of government? Would we not, in our present international dealings with the rival world powers, the United States, England and Russia, proceed more intelligently if everybody, including the American, the British, and the Russian people, were enlightened on the *historical* question: To what extent have the *governments* of the United States, Great Britain, and Russia been really working for economic and social democracy in their own and occupied countries? Ideologically, it is dangerous to forget either the common historical roots or the enemies of liberal democratic aspirations.

College of the City of New York.

Chapter VI

SOME INTERPRETATIONS OF THE HISTORY OF IDEAS

By Joseph Anthony Mazzeo

Natural species remain relatively constant. Whatever hybrids nature makes die out or are born sterile. Historical life, on the other hand, swarms with hybrids. They appear to be an essential element for fertility in the generation of great intellectual movements. The essence of history is change.—Jacob Burckhardt.

What we call the history of ideas itself has a history. Historical writing of one kind or another, whether as record—the mere recital of deeds—or as representation of event—the attempt to portray and evaluate the total configuration of actions—is as old as literature. Classical antiquity offers us many palmary examples of history as the register of the deeds of great leaders, of history as revealing the moral structure of life, of history as knowledge of the virtues, vices, and worth of men. It affords no examples and very few adumbrations of what we can call intellectual history, cultural history, or, in some broad and imprecise sense. the history of ideas. Herodotus in the fifth century B.C. gives us an absorbing account of the beliefs and customs of the Egyptians and, while his account is great literature, it is only a starting point for cultural history. The first book of Aristotle's *Metaphysics* is a review of the opinions of his predecessors, but they are introduced primarily to assist him in the definition of his own position on various philosophical issues. Diogenes Laertius wrote a book in the third century B.C., called *The Lives of the Philosophers*, but this is unreliable, gossipy, and hagiographical by turns, a work whose chief merit lies in having preserved, through quotations, extracts from the writings of philosophers whose works we have lost. Thus that most gifted of peoples, the generators of more ideas than any other nation in the history of civilization, were singularly uninterested in the history of thought, and a concept like the "history of ideas" would have struck an ancient Greek as unintelligible.

He might have asked questions like these at such a confrontation: Do ideas exist apart from the people who think them? If they do, are they not, as Plato taught, independent of the people who think them, timeless realities existing beyond the world of change and outside all processes of development and decay? If history is the representation in words of actions, how can there possibly be a history of ideas? Ideas, he might have continued, are certainly guides to action, inciters of action, but are we not much more interested in the exemplary character of the lives of the great thinkers? Surely Socrates, Epicurus the Sage, Zeno the Stoic, were really much more than the sum of their thoughts, and simple understanding of those thoughts can hardly be of much use in the conquest of true human excellence. Ideas after all, are directions for achieving a style of life, emblems of an attitude toward existence.

The Roman historians contributed little if anything that was new to the writing of history, although we find that the emergence of a universal Roman Empire led an historian like Polybius or a poet like Vergil to think of Roman history as disclosing an intelligible pattern, a grand purposeful design, of which the Romans themselves were, for a long time, unaware. In this view, the Roman historical task was to pacify the world and bring it all under the rule of law. History as a process of major change, of transformation, was presumed to have stopped with this prodigious political accomplishment.

Christian thinkers, too, found a pattern in history. They, of course, repudiated the doctrine of cyclical recurrences which dominated so much of pagan (especially Stoic) thought on the nature of historical change, and could hardly maintain that a powerful pagan Empire was the end result of God's working in the world. They read history as, in the last analysis, the story of man's creation, fall, and redemption. Christian history, in theory at least, was truly universal. It was the story of God's dealings with the whole of mankind, even if only a small fraction of mankind was going to be redeemed, and it disclosed God's providential governance of the world. God somehow, in unexpected and sometimes baffling ways, managed to work on events to bring some good out of all the evil which marks the history of mankind.

The historians of the Renaissance initiated a return to the classical models of historical writing and revived classical models remained the type of historical writing well into the eighteenth century. Thus neither the Romans nor the historians of the Middle Ages and of early modern times were interested in the history of ideas or cultural history. Indeed, they would have made no more sense of such a notion than our hypothetical ancient Greek.

So prodigious were the achievements of nineteenth-century cultural historians and philosophers of history that it became fashionable among those influenced by Romantic views to denigrate the eighteenth century as the "unhistorical century." In more recent times, we have arrived at a better appreciation of the contribution of the Enlightenment to the progress of historical thought. Indeed, Ernst Cassirer, in his classic work, *The Philosophy of the Enlightenment*, felt free to call his chapter on the historians of the period "The Conquest of the Historical World." According to Cassirer, the "conquest" begins in the closing decade of the seventeenth century with the publication of

Pierre Bayle's *Historical and Critical Dictionary* (1696). Although this encyclopedia is not an historical work in the formal sense, Bayle brought to his treatment of historical problems the analytical and critical ideals of Cartesianism. His freedom from the influence of political and religious mythology and his grasp of the "logic of historical fact" establish him as one of the founders of modern critical-historical methods.

Well into the eighteenth century, Montesquieu's *The Spirit of the Laws* combined the historical study of political institutions with a pioneering attempt to delineate a philosophy of history in terms of their development. Voltaire's *Essay on Manners* was of the greatest importance in shifting the focus of historical writing from political events and the "chronicles of kings" to the history of the human mind and its creations: religions, philosophies, morals, and customs, while Diderot's contributions on philosophers and philosophical systems to the great *Encyclopedia* initiated a new and original concern for the historical circumstances in which philosophical systems arise. All of the foregoing extended the range of historical inquiry to include cultural and intellectual matters.

Indeed, not only was the domain of history broadened during the course of the eighteenth century but historians came to seek in the thought and culture of the past for clues to those over-arching patterns which might govern the flux of history itself. Vico's grand scheme of periodic cyclical recurrences moving through characteristic cultural stages, his *New Science*, was one of the first of modern attempts at formulating a philosophy of history on an all-encompassing scale. His work exerted little direct influence on his contemporaries, and it was through Herder that his ideas reached the German Romantic philosophers. With the work of Vico, Herder, and later, Schelling and Hegel, history claimed to be a "science" in its own right, an autonomous mode of understanding. Evolutionary and developmental ideas in the nineteenth century assume an unprecedented importance for historical inquiry, and all of the historical and cultural creations of the past come to acquire a unique value in the unfolding story of the human spirit. The muse of history now requires of the historian not simply acts of erudition or of moral judgment, but acts of imaginative identification and re-creation.

This bare-boned and sketchy string of allusions to the progress of history and historiography during the eighteenth century is meant merely to suggest the great extension of the domain of history which occurred during this time. Cultural and intellectual history came, in many ways, to dominate historical thought, historians introduced regulative philosophical ideas and developmental patterns into the writing of history, and they became acutely conscious of history as an autonomous intellectual enterprise quite different from the enterprise of natural science in the methods it employs and the truth it discerns.

But before intellectual and cultural history, as we know these activities, could come into existence our conception of history and, indeed *of thought itself* had to change, and this change can be traced to the intellectual revolution accomplished by the German philosophers of the Romantic period and, in particular, to Hegel. Hegel is a notoriously difficult philosopher and what I say below about his thought will probably strike the expert as a gross simplification of the ideas of a subtle and complex mind. However, even at the risk of distortion, I think I can convey the essentials of his view of history and of thought.

Hegel's God, the Absolute Spirit, is both transcendent, contained in himself, and immanent, at work in the world. Not only does nature reflect the intelligible structure of the Absolute but so does history. Hegel's God, who is Universal Reason, is thus manifested not only in all that exists but also in all that has happened. Although he is indeed Reason, he is not such as we vaguely and ordinarily apprehend that term. The Absolute is, rather, all of the categories of thought—and they are the categories of reality as well—all of the concepts which the mind can have, all of the intelligible structures of existence, no matter how contradictory to one another they might be when viewed abstractly, and it is all of those categories in a unity. Thus the laws of common-sense logic, such as that of non-contradiction, do not really apply to the Absolute for it is the coincidence of all opposites. How then does this Absolute Spirit manifest itself in history? History, for Hegel, is nothing less than a progressive temporal revelation of the Absolute Spirit. Time or history is thus, to adapt a phrase of Plato's to our purposes, a moving image of eternity, and to understand history is to understand the unfolding of the thought of God. Much of this sounds like, and indeed is, a secularized and cerebralized version of the traditional notion of divine providence. But Hegel's Absolute is not really a judging or loving person. It is, as I pointed out, a unity of the categories of thought and being, and those categories, which exist in a transcendental unity in the Absolute *qua* Absolute, display themselves serially in time according to a law of progression by which one category generates its opposite and then unites with it in a higher synthesis which in turn generates a new opposing category, then a new synthesis, and so on.

This is the familiar law of the dialectic, so dear to Marxists, the very heart-beat of history, a rhythm which moves from thesis to antithesis to synthesis, and does so until the end of time, the achievement of Utopia, or whatever stopping-place various interpreters of Hegel chose to give it. Now for Hegel, this successive revelation of divine thoughts finds its clearest expression in the works of the great individual philosophers or schools of philosophy, and it is through the minds of the great thinkers that the divine mind manifests and realizes itself. God thinks, therefore, in and through the minds of men. The temporal process, history itself, is a kind of intellectual journey which God makes, a journey which is both a self-realization and a self-manifestation. From the human point of view, that journey began with the awakening of man's philosophical consciousness, when man first began to reflect on his experience and confronted himself with a thinking self.

Now Hegel did not reduce all of history to the history of philosophy alone. The Absolute is, after all, not only the sum of the categories of understanding and reason, but these in turn are the categories of Becoming. In fact, before the World-Spirit finds conceptual expression of a part of its life in the work of a philosopher, it has already manifested itself in a form of life, a concrete cultural fact or historical event. Thus, Hegel might have said, the Absolute generates real, live Stoics who then generate thinkers among them to give conceptual expression to that style of life and cluster of values which Stoicism really is. Indeed, the history of thought is the expression, in terms of ideas, of cultural fact, of great forms or styles of life, of a finite number of paradigmatic modes of existence which incarnate the universal categories of thought and becoming. Indeed, philosophy only comes on the scene when vitality has ebbed from a particular mode of life. Paradoxically, the theoretical foundations of Stoicism, for example, are laid precisely when living the Stoic life becomes problematic, when it is no longer powerfully, completely, and simply operative in the lives of men. As Hegel puts it, in his *Philosophy of Right*, "when philosophy paints its grey on grey, a shape of life has grown old. The owl of Minerva flies at twilight."

Now certain principles of momentous importance for the writing of history flowed from this grand poetic and philosophical vision of Hegel's. First he established intimate connections within the concrete cultural life of any epoch—its morals, values, attitudes, and their expression in art, religion, politics, on the one hand, and its philosophical and scientific thought, on the other. In fact, the latter was the conceptual expression of the former. What the latter is as thought the former is as life. Moreover, since history is, in the final analysis, the progressive revelation—the bringing to consciousness—of the categories of reason, each epoch in history, each definable phase of our civilization, or each distinguishable cultural era, is dominated by a common category or a common principle. Hence Hegelians wrote *Geistesgeschichte*, "spiritual" or cultural history, and could quite legitimately speak of a Spirit of the Age, a *Zeitgeist*.

Prescinding from the obscurities of Hegelian metaphysics and theology, we might still validly define the term *Zeitgeist* as the common sensibility of a time, a common set of assumptions, a common implicit definition of life and thought, a common style of life which underlies all or most of the apparent diversity of any cultural epoch. Hegel, with great acumen and insight, indeed found unity where many saw only diversity. The classic theist and the classic atheist, for example, are apparently at opposite ends of the spectrum. Yet the one affirms what the other denies, so that they share an identical conception of reason and of the possibilities of reason for settling certain questions. Stripped of its metaphysical and quasi-theological context, the concept of a *Zeitgeist*, of a common "Spirit of the Age," still makes good sense if we take it to mean that no particular datum of the past is fully intelligible in isolation. A poem, a philosophical or religious treatise, a scientific work, a painting or a work of architecture, has, to be sure, a kind of independent existence, but it also has, just as surely, an historical and cultural existence. We don't need to accept the Hegelian mythology to understand that the masterpieces we study as students of literature require not simply acts of judgment on our part but also acts of the historical imagination. However much they do in fact transcend their time, however powerfully they may address themselves to our condition, they were not written immediately for us, but by men with local habitations and names for their contemporaries. This is precisely why they require study and why, the Hegelians would say, the ideal context for understanding any particular work is the whole culture from which it emerged.

Unfortunately, Hegelians were so obsessed by the unity and coherence of the *Zeitgeist* that they were ordinarily inclined to oversimplify the complex conflicts and many cross-currents internal to periods of crisis or of revolutionary change. At its best, however, the treatment of literature by those writers of *Geistesgeschichte* who drew their inspiration from Hegel was not only faithful to the historical context of a work, to its "pastness," so to speak, but to its contemporaneity as well. The best practitioners of this kind of literary study, a Karl Vossler for example, could illuminate a literary work by bringing to bear on its interpretation a knowledge of the religion, philosophy, art, customs, and life of the time and place of the author. This erudition was not simply in the service of glossing an allusion, a reference or a figure of speech, but in the service of defining the sentiments and values of the author, of interpreting the ordering and particularization of general experience as that is embodied in the very style and structure of a work.

Let us recall that the Hegelian was convinced that meaning—and therefore thought—permeated all of the cultural facts of an age. The state of the language of any time, for example, its general style, carried latently those meanings explicitly realized in the works of its artists and thinkers. The great creative minds bring to actuality whatever possibilities a language may have for specifying experience, and thus expand the range of consciousness and awareness of those who come in touch with them. They are given language as a collective creation of ordinary men, saturated with what Bacon called the "Idols of the Market Place," the crudities and imperfections of an ordinary medium of exchange, and they turn it into an instrument whereby we can apprehend more of the world in its true complexity and particularity. From this point of view, no poetic achievement is fully intelligible unless we grasp how and to what degree a poet was able to use his linguistic legacy.

Out of this perspective a Vossler could ask and answer questions like the following: What possibilities for ordered intelligible experience did the state of the language and culture of a particular era afford its poets? How does their own particular style create new meanings or sharpen meanings latent in the common tongue? How did the art, philosophy, or religion of the poet's time afford his structural principles, paradigms of experience, or a body of discourse which would enable him to organize his own experience? What features in the artistic styles and sensibility of a period help to illuminate the style of a writer? How does the great poet use the knowledge of his life and time to represent experience so that it can be intelligible and relevant to later generations?

These are fairly familiar questions to the contemporary student, at least to one who has read Emil Auerbach or Leo Spitzer, but we must remind ourselves that they were unthinkable before the great intellectual revolution inaugurated by Kant and the post-Kantian German thinkers. This tradition not only produced some of the greatest workers of nineteenth-century historical scholarship, and some brilliant works of cultural-historical literary criticism, it also produced some of the most pretentious and verbose works ever written. It takes a great deal of solid erudition, sobriety of judgment, and refinement of taste to do this kind of thing well, and many lesser devotees of *Geistes-*

geschichte lost themselves in grandiose generalizations about the Baroque, the Medieval Mind, the Renaissance Spirit, and other shapeless formulae of this sort.

Burckhardt and other cultural historians of his generation rebelled against the Hegelian tradition both in its vital and its decayed forms. Nevertheless, even if Burckhardt discarded the philosophical jargon of the Hegelians and their weighty metaphysical freight, we can still detect the notion of a *Zeitgeist* in his thought, a notion rather thinly disguised as the concept of a common style or common sensibility which unified all the aspects of a cultural epoch. In his great work, *The Civilization of the Renaissance in Italy* (1860), art and artists are the key to a unified view of the age. Not only were the greatest energies and enthusiasms of the age poured into art, but Burckhardt detected a widespread impulse in the men of the time to turn life itself into an art and to assimilate other human activities to the category of art. Machiavelli thus viewed the state as something made and molded, as a work of art, and Castiglione defined the achieved self as something shaped, like a painting, into a harmony of parts. This impulse to treat both self and environment as plastic, as amenable to artistic organization, was, for Burckhardt, not simply a widespread impulse in the man of the time. It was a category of self-understanding as well. Art and artist were "models," so to speak, by which men viewed not only the world but themselves and their relation to it.

Burckhardt also repudiated the evolutionary scheme of historiography whether Hegelian, with its zig-zag and clashing patterns, or the uniform linear ascent of the proponents of indefinite progress. All of the evolutionist historiographers regarded the past as a contrast to their own time, as a preliminary stage of what is fulfilled in the present. Burckhardt, on the other hand, saw the past as filled with recurrences. Human life is fundamentally constant. Men suffer, rejoice, create, and destroy in much the same way at any time, and in the study of the past we must look for that which "echoes in us and is intelligible to us." Thus while Burckhardt accepted the notion of the unity of a culture, he did not identify that unity with some metaphysical category or try to fit any great epoch of the past into some ascending series in a transcendental scheme of things. To be sure, the art, life, and thought of a past age should all be studied together, but not simply to assist in making acts of the historical imagination. We must rise to actual acts of recognition. We must study the total civilization of an era in order to overcome its alienness and experience its life as our own. Then we realize that the various cultures of the past were but the different forms in which recurrent human experience has expressed itself. We can see why Burckhardt made art and literature rather than philosophy the center of his historical thinking. They more than any other kind of activity enshrine the recurrent and the typical, the recognizable common life of mankind.

Wilhelm Dilthey (1833–1911), a contemporary of Burckhardt, also greatly influenced the writing of cultural and, especially, of intellectual history. Like Burckhardt, he repudiated the metaphysical apparatus of Hegelianism and sought in the study of the past opportunities for acts of recognition. His work was more important for the history of ideas than Burckhardt's both because his major interests were more strictly in the sphere of intellectual history and because he gave much thought to the problems of historical method and historiography. In spite of his philosophical ambitions and interests he found literary and biographical studies more congenial, and made important contributions to our understanding of the act of criticism and its relation to acts of the historical imagination.

For Dilthey, each time we enter upon the understanding of a work of literature, we somehow reenact the life and thought of the past. What we actually do when we understand a literary work is to remove the temporal and cultural distance between us and it. This distance may be great or small, depending on the time, place, and language of the work, but when we understand a work we do so by learning that the "letter," which seems distant, really expresses a spirit which is near to our concerns and interests. This act of understanding is no more and no less than an act of interpretation, of exegesis, or literary criticism in the broadest sense of the word. For Dilthey, however, this act does not take place in an intellectual vacuum but demands the maximum possible knowledge of the cultural matrix in which the writer thought and lived.

Dilthey would have said that the whole culture is relevant to our understanding of any part of it. Only by complete immersion in the art, religions, philosophy, science, manners, and social conventions of an age do we come to know fully its style and idiom, only so do we come to understand its inner language, what it means by what it says. Our understanding of the past thus begins with a confrontation with systems of signs and symbols, and ends with the discovery of the meanings they carry. The world of culture is simply the world of meanings and, in its temporal aspect, the world of culture is history, the history of meanings. In this sense, all cultural history is, implicitly or explicitly, the history of ideas or meanings.

Now Dilthey did not conceive of meanings as simple psychological responses to stimuli. All perception of significance in human life has a temporal structure. A mind existing in a timeless moment, unaware of past or future, might well experience eternity but it could make no sense of the world around it, or, indeed, of itself. Every meaningful instant of consciousness really extends temporally both backwards and forwards. Every present event perceived as intelligible is understood as flowing from a remembered past and pointing to an unknown future. Memory is not simply a storehouse of data but an indispensable activity in our perception of present meanings. As memory is to the individual so history is to the life of mankind.

For Dilthey, literature was the record of experience, evaluated and rendered intelligible, and literary criticism was but a special form of historical inquiry, for the act of interpretation is the discovery of meaning. The quest for meanings in the records of the past unites both the historian and the critic, however different the texts with which they deal or the kinds of meanings they seek. In either case, the mind of the author and the mind of the reader meet in what Dilthey calls the reader's understanding, in his act of annihilating temporal distance.

Alfred North Whitehead is not normally reckoned among the important contributors to the progress of the discipline we call the history of ideas. Indeed, he was not primarily an historian of thought and culture. Nevertheless, he possessed a keen appreciation of the philosophic richness and value of poetry, and a remarkable sensitivity to the unarticulated motifs which affect philosophical thought. For the literary historian interested in the relations between science and literature, his *Science and the Modern World* was a seminal work. Whitehead's approach to the history of thought was guided by a realization that the systems of apparently disparate thinkers were frequently closely related by certain unconscious presuppositions of thought or by certain principles which none of the contenders in a particular intellectual struggle dreamt of questioning and which, in fact, frequently enough really united them. Such ideas, Whitehead pointed out, are usually maintained as axioms and are so deeply rooted in the minds of men that they are assumed not merely by technical philosophers but by their educated lay contemporaries. Perhaps the best example of such an idea is the principle of sufficient reason, the belief that a thing has some reason for its existence, whether teleological or not, the belief that it is at least logically grounded in something else which is logically ultimate. Thinkers as diverse in time and place as Abelard, Bruno, and Leibniz believed this principle to be utterly obvious, and it does unite them, in spite of their differences, in ways which they might not have been willing to acknowledge.

Whitehead, in studying the history of thought from the point of view of such large general ideas, found more comprehensive unifying principles and relations within it than others had discerned. More-over, he had a keen sense of the fact that ideas are not generated by philosophers only. They are born in religion, in the arts, out of the life and experience of men. Thus Whitehead gave careful attention to the thought of poets and moralists as well as to the thought of lesser minds in the pantheon of the great heroes of thought.

To A. O. Lovejoy we owe the wide currency in this century of the phrase "the history of ideas" and, although it has come to be used in a loose sense to refer to various kinds of cultural and intellectual his-tory as, indeed, I have so used it in this essay, Lovejoy meant some-thing quite precise by it. As he tells us in his classic study, *The Great Chain of Being:* "By the history of ideas I mean something at once more specific and less restricted than the history of philosophy." Lovejoy was more specific than the conventional historian of philos-ophy because he analyzed philosophical systems into what he called their unit ideas. Such systems, Lovejoy perceived, were more like religious movements than scientific hypotheses. That is, they were really heterogeneous clusters, not by any means very self-consistent, of unit ideas. On the other hand, Lovejoy was less restricted than the conventional historian of thought because he realized that an impor-tant part of the life of an idea is lived in the works of minor thinkers and of imaginative writers. The way a poet, for example, might em-ploy an idea in his work could reveal implications of it not to be found in the very system from which it was derived. Thus, Lovejoy drew heavily on literature in his interpretation of the philosophical thought of the past.

It is by no means just to Lovejoy to think that literature was for him solely a means of documenting intellectual and cultural history in terms of its more subtle movements. Rather, he felt with Whitehead that "it is in literature that the concrete outlook of humanity receives its expression. Accordingly, it is to literature that we must look, partic-ularly in its more concrete forms, if we hope to discover the inward thoughts of a generation."[1] There is, after all, a distinction to be drawn between the study of literature, whether by the layman or pro-fessional scholar, and an acquaintance with classics of literary art, however enjoyable. To penetrate fully into a work of literature is finally to make a serious effort to develop the historical imagination, to view the world, in a sense, through another culture, another time, another nationality. When we conceive of the study of literature in such historical terms, we are soon constrained to disregard the *division*

[1] *Science and the Modern World* (Cambridge, 1929), 106.

of literature by languages and nationalities, paradoxically enough, for the great beliefs and guiding ideas of our civilization have transcended such distinctions. From one point of view, then, the historian of ideas approaches literary study quite like the comparatist. Just as the myths and stories of literary tradition migrated and were diffused through different lands and different strata of society, so great philosophical systems and ideas are held by a far larger number of thoughtful people than the small circle of originators and disciples. And each movement of story or idea involves a transmutation.

Perhaps even more interesting to our psychologically minded age is the importance Lovejoy gave to motives, intellectual and emotional, which orient the thought of a philosopher. No one did more than Lovejoy to illustrate the paradoxical fact that closely related motives and reasons may help to generate completely different results at different times in the history of thought and in the minds of different thinkers, just as the same conclusions might be reached by different philosophers starting from completely divergent positions. In addition, Lovejoy revealed the dynamics of what he called dialectical motives, those tricks of logic, turns of thought, and methodological assumptions which so often dominate a thinker or, indeed, the thought of an age. Among such motives he isolated two important ones: the nominalistic motive, which is the attempt to reduce general ideas to one or another of the concrete and sensible particulars which they comprehend, and the organismic motive, the assumption that in any organized body of thought no part is intelligible except in relation to the whole.

Not only are philosophers often dominated by such intellectual motives, but they are just as often led into certain conclusions by various kinds of emotional preferences, of what Lovejoy called "metaphysical pathos." Thus some thinkers are overwhelmed by what they feel to be the sheer loveliness of the mysterious, the esoteric, or the incomprehensible. Others demonstrate the eternalistic pathos, a profound and undemonstrable conviction that anything eternal is better than anything temporal. Indeed, precisely the same cosmological vision, for example, can generate diametrically opposed attitudes so that the very vision of infinite space which terrorized Pascal aroused feelings of religious exultation in Trahearne.

Lovejoy also included under the rubric "the history of ideas" what he called philosophical semantics, the study of the varying meanings of crucial and comprehensive words such as "nature" or "art" in the history of thought. With his usual eye for paradox he showed how important but imprecise words of this kind were used, often unconsciously, to refer to entirely different concepts. Thus nature has, in the past, been lauded as an exuberantly fecund entity creating an incomprehensible variety and wealth of being, or, at other times, has been revered as a rational, restrained, ordered realm, two quite incompatible views referred to by the same word. The student of literature will probably value most Lovejoy's remarkable study of the varieties of Romanticism and his brilliant analysis of the varied and often incompatible notions that have been packed into that obscure but indispensable word.

Leo Spitzer, the next important figure in the development of the history of ideas, was in some respects a severe critic of Lovejoy but there is no doubt that his contributions to what he called "historical semantics" were influenced by Lovejoy's work in philosophical semantics. Historical semantics is Spitzer's term for a special combination of lexicography and the history of ideas proper. Spitzer would start with a word or phrase such as "mother tongue," for example, and trace its varying meanings in different cultures and eras. Or he would begin with an idea like "milieu," or "ambience," or "world harmony" as defined in a particular era and then show the variety of words and meanings which come to cluster around the concept in the course of time. He brought a vast historical knowledge to this undertaking and used material from the history of theology, philosophy, literature, music, the fine arts, science, and even the history of magic and superstition. These procedures are not to be confused with lexicographical or etymological studies in the strict sense of the word. His work, at its best, is a brilliant conflation of the history of thought with the history of words, and the organizing principle of his work lies in his notion of the "conceptual field" of ideas, a broad area of meaning in which particular groups of words, more or less synonyms, are unified.

Spitzer argued against the excessive intellectualism and the fragmenting tendencies in the work of Lovejoy. He doubted very much that "unit-ideas" could be isolated since all ideas, for Spitzer, existed to some degree in a field of related but plural meanings. He also doubted what he felt to be Lovejoy's assumption that some ideas at least come into being uncharged with emotions. Spitzer argued, it seems to me quite effectively, that all ideas are, initially at least, passionate responses to important questions and their charge of passion finds expression in the very style and shape of the utterance. Indeed, the form of expression, the particular words used to convey the thought, are part of its meaning no matter how much a philosopher might wish to be emotionally antiseptic. Spitzer also felt that Lovejoy not only abstracted ideas from their psychological context but also from the cultural context in which they arose, treating ideas as if they could be viewed as entirely separable from the life, personal and collective, in which they were generated. Spitzer emphasized against Lovejoy the totality, unity, emotional atmosphere, and cultural climate of a work rather than carefully analyzed "unit-ideas," although he was cognizant of the cluster of meanings which large philosophical concepts carry. Where Lovejoy carefully tried to separate ideas from their metaphysical pathos, the emotional charges and attitudes given to them in their origins, Spitzer treated such overtones as part of the very life of the idea itself. In effect, he denied that Lovejoy was writing the true history of an idea when he sundered it so radically from its arational context.

Spitzer also grasped, since he came from the disciplines of language and literature rather than philosophy, that Lovejoy's use of literary material, while legitimate from the point of view of some of his intentions, was essentially unliterary. This is to say that ideas as they occur in literary works are not really there essentially as intellectual propositions. Thus Brutus, in *Julius Caesar,* has Stoic ideas, but we are not asked, as readers of the drama, to decide for or against the truth of Stoicism. What those ideas do is reveal Brutus to us, just as his action and gestures and expressions would. Whether in or out of literary works, ideas, in both Lovejoy's and Spitzer's view, were the possession of individuals primarily and only secondarily and figuratively the possession of cultures. They are important when individuals feel them to be important, when they are, in fact, modes of action.

Thus Dante loved and respected ideas—scientific, philosophical, and theological—and he handled them with the kind of discipline we would expect of a philosopher. The great structure of his thought and learning acquires its literary value because it is diffracted through the action and life of the pilgrim who makes the journey through the three great realms of the beyond. To be sure, to understand the *Divine Comedy* we must have some knowledge of history, ancient and medieval, of theology and philosophy, but we do not need to believe what Dante believed or even find his ideas particularly useful outside of the context of the work. His ideas live, no matter how obsolete, because they create an intellectual vision of universal order which serves to organize and express the experience of a poet on whom no experience was wasted. The student of literature will find in the history of ideas not only the clarification of particular allusions, but will grasp how ideas come to function as organizing and structural principles in works of art, as frames which contain and define human experience.

Whatever their differences, the men whose work we have considered had the merit of recognizing that ideas have a use which goes far beyond the purely logical or strictly referential uses accorded them in technical philosophy. They are spurs to action, they harness the passions of men, they are not only propositions but also experiences, and, as such, a single idea will find multitudinously varied expression and many diverse contexts. For even if all men should abstractly understand an idea alike, no two men will experience it in exactly the same way. It is metaphor and imagery which clothe experience and when ideas really penetrate into the very life of the thinker they will emerge from his mind in some singular mode of expression.

Perhaps a better phrase for what the history of ideas is at its best, is the study of the *life of ideas*. This would enable us to include in this category such brilliant studies as Erwin Panofsky's *Gothic Art and Scholasticism* or Otto Von Simson's *The Gothic Cathedral*, works in which we discover how the great architectonic intellectual systems of patristic and scholastic philosophers furnished much of the structural themes and motifs of the great Abbey churches and cathedrals. Tracing the life of ideas would enable us to see how Whitehead came to arrive at some of the most important conceptions in his thought—"the fallacy of misplaced concreteness," the nature of an "event"—from his reading of poetry. It would enable us to understand how ideas and systems of ideas may enshrine much that is of permanent value in the record of human experience even when they are themselves untrue or obsolete. Above all, the best work of the historians of ideas has helped us to correct the simplistic but widespread notion that philosophers and scientists do all the thinking while poets and artists simply feel or perceive. They have helped us to grasp the subtle relations which obtain between mythic, religious, and poetic activities of the mind, on the one hand, and conceptual thinking of a philosophical and scientific kind, on the other. The richest result of their work, perhaps, is the possibility it creates for us of glimpsing the inner unity of a culture and tracing out the fascinating interrelationships between different works of the mind, however disparate they might seem to the untutored eye.

Bibliographical Note

The reader will find a thorough and thoughtful appreciation of Spitzer's work in Harry Levin, "Two *Romanisten* in America: Spitzer and Auerbach," *Perspectives in American Hostory,* (1968), II, 463–84. For an assessment of the method and achievements of the history of ideas see A. O. Lovejoy, *Essays in the History of Ideas* (Baltimore, 1948), his preface and his first essay, "The Historiography of Ideas," 1–13; also *Studies in Intellectual History* (Baltimore, 1953), the first essay by George Boas, "Some Problems in Intellectual History," 3–21. The classic work in the field is, of course, Lovejoy's *The Great Chain of Being* (Cambridge, Mass., 1936). For a brief perceptive treatment of the study of comparative literature and the relation of literature to ideas, see Harry Levin, "Comparing the Literature," *Yearbook of Comparative and General Literature* (1969), 5-16. A good introduction to Spitzer's methods and characteristic achievements is his *Linguistics and Literary History: Essays in Stylistics* (Princeton, 1948); also his "History of Ideas Versus Reading of Poetry," *Southern Review*, **6**, 3 (Winter 1941), 584-609. Burckhardt's statement of method is best found in his *Weltgeschichtliche Betrachtungen*, translated into English as *Force and Freedom: An Interpretation of History*, ed. J. H. Nichols (New York, 1943). A good deal of Dilthey's work remains untranslated but some of his important methodological essays are available in translation as *Pattern and Meaning in History: Thoughts on History and Society*, ed. with an introduction by H. P. Rickman (London, 1961). See also K. Müller-Vollmer, *Towards a Phenomenological Theory of Literature: A Study of Dilthey's "Poetik,"* Stanford Studies in Germanics and Slavics, **1** (1963). Hegel is a notoriously difficult thinker but perhaps the best introduction to his thought in English is still the work of W. T. Stace, *The Philosophy of Hegel* (New York, 1923; reprint, 1955).

Columbia University.

Chapter VII

THE AUTONOMY OF INTELLECTUAL HISTORY

By Leonard Krieger[*]

Intellectual historians have become cuckoos in the historical nest. To the consternation of their colleagues they like to think and to talk about method—and thereby hangs our tale. For the problem of intellectual history is not that, like political and institutional history, it has a method too long unexamined or that, like social history, it has a method modeled on more methodical disciplines and requiring adaptation. The problem of intellectual history, epitomized in the current disputes about the social relations of ideas, is that it has too many methods, that this plurality reflects the diversity of its objects, and that this diversity has raised serious doubts about its integrity as a distinct and autonomous field of history.

Indeed, the very propensity of intellectual historians for discussions of method is a symptom rather than a treatment of their problem. For the discussions are not about more or less valid ways of processing a commonly acknowledged material; they are about the appropriate way of processing more or less valid materials. The respective claims of works, propositions, ideas, styles, attitudes, and mentalities to be the authentic objects of intellectual history furnish the primary issue of controversy, and the dubiety of one or another class of this material has evoked the presentation of one or another plausible method to validate it. The hope, then, is that the means will justify the end. In any case, if the plurality of its current species defines the leading problem of intellectual history to be its generic identity, then method would certainly seem to be a derivative dimension of the problem. It is not in the infinite variety of its specific methods that a genus of intellectual history—if there is such a thing—can be found.

Nor can we deduce the integrity of intellectual history from some principle, whether from the principle of special history, abstracted from the seamless web of the past by analogy with other established special fields of history, or from the general principle of intellectual history itself considered in its universal sense of the history of man thinking as distinct from man doing. Neither principle quite holds because, as it is actually practiced, intellectual history is more general than the special histories and more specific than any categorical definition of it.

*This paper was originally delivered in a shortened version at the session on Methodology in the History of Ideas during the December 1971 meeting of the American Historical Association.

Unlike the specific fields of literary history, history of philosophy, economic history, or even history of science, intellectual history has had no special complementary discipline outside the general field of history to supply the internal analysis of its objects and thereby to define the special historical field essentially in terms of external and temporal relations. As for the generic principle of intellectual history, men have deduced from it positions as contradictory as the proposition that all history is intellectual history, that is, the history of thought, and that no history is intellectual history, since the very definition of history as *res gestae,* as past acts and events, requires that what men have thought should always be subsumed under one or another special forms of what men have done. However influential these principles may have been on the actual varieties of intellectual history they do not explain these varieties, which have in fact tended to define the realm of ideas for historical purposes to consist of something less than everything man has thought, something more than the separate compartments into which the products of thought have been traditionally divided, and something different from—albeit conditioned by and contributory to—the realm of deeds. Since the understanding of such intermediate enterprises is usually more susceptible to the historical than the principled approach, let us look beyond the principles to the history of intellectual history, with the expectation that even if we do not find there a valid ground for the autonomy of intellectual history upon which we can agree, we ought at least to discover why intellectual historians act as if they had one. This history goes back a long way and demonstrates that the current distinction of intellectual history as an historiographical field has grown out of the distinct role which has been attributed to ideas in the historical process.

The terminological discrimination between intellectual history and the history of ideas is recent,[1] but the differentiation to which it refers is ages old and has roots in the separate origin of each genre. The history of ideas refers to a category of literature in which articulate concepts have themselves been the primary historical agents, with their personal bearers and external relations adduced as conditions of them. Until recently the history of ideas in this sense has not been a discrete field; it has been closely associated with the special departments of thought and has its early model in Aristotle's metaphysical history of first principles. Intellectual history refers to an overlapping category of literature that has been more comprehensive than history of ideas in two dimensions: it has included inarticulate beliefs, amorphous opinions, and unspoken assumptions as well as formal ideas; and its

[1] Esp. Maurice Mandelbaum, "The History of Ideas, Intellectual History, and the History of Philosophy," *History and Theory,* 5 (1965), 33–66; and Franklin L. Baumer, "Intellectual History and Its Problems," *Journal of Modern History,* 21 (1949), 191–203.

primary unit of historical concern has not been the set of these notions as such but rather their external relations with the larger life of the people who have borne them. By its very orientation intellectual history has tended to go beyond the formal contours of the special disciplines and to identify the distinctive role of ideas and attitudes vis-à-vis the other historical activities of men. As such an identifiable and distinctive arena, intellectual history had its earliest model in the accounting for the role of revealed religion in our culture during the early-Christian era. The model of the two cities was articulated into the categorically separate processes of sacred and worldly history, the first subsuming men's actions and institutions under the sequential stages in the incarnation of the true doctrine, the second subsuming earthly ideas as well as earthly desires under the category of the flesh and its aimless cycles of mundane events. This scheme initiated the pattern, which would be so long-lived, of vesting the unifying threads of history in the mind, the spirit, the ideas of men. Whether such a distinctive level of intellectual history would be thought to require a distinctive method was to vary from period to period, but certainly in its early phase it did require one. The method appropriate to Christian sacred history was exegesis, usually biblical and patristic, and it was a method distinctive enough for Bodin and Vico to exclude sacred history explicitly from consideration when they were experimenting with their new methods of organizing worldly laws and cultures into some kind of loose political order.

The exclusion was symptomatic, for whatever their contributions to general history the secular historians of the early-modern period contributed little to the specific enterprise of intellectual history—a judgment, surprisingly enough, as applicable to the historian-intellectuals of the Enlightenment as to their predecessors. What contribution was made continued to be made by historians of religion, whether clerical or anti-clerical, Christian or unChristian. For through both their positive and their negative approaches confessional Christians, unorthodox Christians, and anti-Christians all alike perpetuated the traditional version of a segregated sacred intellectual history into the nineteenth century, even honing upon it the advanced techniques of authentication and criticism that were diffused through all kinds of historical research by the end of the eighteenth century, and constituted a benefaction of intellectual history for the discipline at large. But in the secular historiography of the early-modern centuries worldly attitudes, motives, and ideas were acknowledged for their historical relevance rather than for their historical autonomy. The political focus of the secular historians was too intense, or their impetus toward extended historical coherence too weak, or their feeling for the legal, cultural, and anthropological interpenetration of ideas and acts within an integral hu-

manity too strong, or their faith in the timeless source of universal historical patterns too classical for the developments in their historiography to have any discriminatory effect upon the historical status of
ideas as such. In this early-modern period we can see ideas as inseparable ingredients of ecclesiastical, constitutional, legal, and
political history; ideas as one of several sets of events comprising the
history of culture, of languages, and of the arts; and ideas as supra-his-
torical abstractions epitomizing the anthropological history of the
species. But what we do not see is a distinctly intellectual history, for if
early-modern historiography accustomed men to think of secular ideas
as part of their history it was only insofar as those ideas were tied to
and defined by the rest of men's earthly existence. At the end of the
Enlightenment as at its beginning, the only ideas with an independent
historical role were the ideas inhabiting a separate spiritual space.

The crucial modulation in the history of intellectual history was
from the spatial model prototyped in the spiritual city of the Middle
Ages into the functional model authoritative in modern times, and its
mechanics are most accessible in the historicized systems of the
nineteenth century. Comte and Mill, Marx and Engels, integrated the
realms of universal and particular history by expelling transcendent
absolute principles from universal history and positing a single social
world with a single history constituted by general laws of development.
These laws, in turn, followed continuously as scientific generalizations
from the particular facts of history. The pattern is, of course, familiar
to us all, but what may not be so familiar is the role of ideas in it. Historically relevant ideas were now considered to be functions of society
rather than a distinct level of history leading from God, the recesses of
the individual soul, or the eternal principles of human nature, but their
function for society was distinctive, autonomous, and even, by dint of
the fashionable tie of society with nature and the linguistic fashion of
patterning social on natural science, still spatialized. Comte's and
Mill's investment of intellectual history in "social dynamics," Marx's
and Engels' in "superstructure" betray the continuing tendency to
think of autonomous function in terms of spatial distinctions. For all
these thinkers the distinctive function of ideas, the function in which
they were autonomous, was their primacy in providing structural unity
to history.

But if all agreed in the formal, unifying function of ideas there was a
fundamental divergence in the kind of unity that ideas were deemed to
provide, and this divergence is important not only for the understanding
of nineteenth-century attitudes toward intellectual history but for its
origination of the division within intellectual history which would last
down to the present. In the view pioneered by Comte and given a
mantle of respectability in Mill's *System of Logic,* "the order of

progression in all respects will mainly depend on the order of progression in the intellectual convictions of mankind, that is, on the law of the successive transformations of human opinions." For ideas, operating through the intellectual elite in which they predominate, constitute "the prime agent of the social movement," the "central chain" to "each successive link of which the corresponding links of all other progressions" are "appended" and which confer "a kind of spontaneous order" upon "the succession of facts."[2] In this view, then, ideas are the determining agents in the universal laws of *progress* and they function especially as the laws of the movement *between* static epochs. Spencer characterized Comte's whole purpose as the description of "the necessary, and the actual, filiation of *ideas*" in contrast to his own purpose of describing "the necessary, and the actual, filiation of *things*." It may count as a negative proof of intellectual history's integrative function, moreover, that this same Spencer, who professed to think in terms of things rather than ideas, was contemptuous not only of most historians but of history as such, because it could not by its very nature be anything other than "heaps of stones and bricks," "material for a Comparative Sociology."[3] Here was a striking, albeit admittedly negative, testimonial to the association of intellectual autonomy with lawful history in the nineteenth-century school of progressive sociology.

In Marx and Engels the one indisputable function of autonomous ideas in history was the provision of a unity of a different kind and along another temporal axis: it was a *regressive* unity for the historical facts of the same period. The role of ideas in the progressive movement of history from stage to stage was ambiguous enough in Marx and Engels to provoke the discussions we have had in twentieth-century Marxism on the role of consciousness in revolution and on the differences between Marx and Engels in this respect. Without entering into this intricate discussion of Marxian consciousness in the *general* process of history, we must stress the undeniable attribution of autonomy to the superstructure, at first operational and then explicit, in consequence of its comparative rigidity and growing unresponsiveness to economic change *within each period* before its revolutionary progression to the next. Marx's growing concern with "fetishism" and other modes of "capitalistic false consciousness" definitely implied such autonomy. Engels' actual engagement with intellectual history—in his works on Feuerbach and Dühring—his later notice of the reciprocal "influence" exerted by the superstructure "on the whole development of society,

---

[2] John Stuart Mill, *A System of Logic Ratiocinative and Inductive* (8th ed., New York, 1881; reprinted New York, 1952), 604–06.

[3] *The Evolution of Society: Selections from Herbert Spencer's Principles of Sociology*, ed. R. L. Carneiro (Chicago, 1967), xxii,xxv. Italics in the original.

even its economic development," and his frank admission of Marx's
and his early neglect of the way in which "ideological notions" were
formed—these were express formulations of the same point, of the
braking action of the superstructure, for they were made at the very
time—around 1890—that Engels was also stressing the connection
between the dynamic movement of nature and the ineluctable
development of society's economic base.[4] The distinctive role of
ideology within the regressive superstructure, moreover, was its unifying function: it spread a conservative consensus over the fruitful
conflicts of the society. As Ernest Labrousse, a later link between
Marxism and social history, has phrased it: "movement is *par excellence* . . . economic. . . . The social retards the economic when the
social has the initiative itself. . . . But above the social the mental
retards in its turn, and the restraints of the mental are the strongest of
all. . . . The resistance of static mentality is one of the great factors of
regressive history." It is the factor, moreover, which transcends historical fragmentation: ". . . Our goal remains the restitution of global
mentality."[5]

Nor was the modified perpetuation of the distinctive unifying role of
ideas in western history embodied only in the abstract historical
systems of the nineteenth century. In the unquestionably historical
works of William Lecky, Leslie Stephens, William Draper, Andrew
White, and even of Leopold Ranke himself in his *History of the Popes*
(1834–36), ideas of religion and of scientific or utilitarian reason summarized the historical forces of regression and progression whose
conflict made western history a comprehensible whole.

Thus when, around the beginning of our century, the awareness of
historical ideas in general, the self-conscious attribution of the term
"intellectual history" and its foreign cognates to their sphere, and the
application of the recently sanctified historical methods to them,
initiated the discipline of intellectual history in the forms familiar to us,[6]
this foundation was itself a sequel to a long tradition certifying the independent role of ideas in our culture. The five easily identifiable schools
of modern intellectual history which dominated the first half of our
century and remain the bases of current developments in the field are,
indeed, reducible for purposes of analysis to two main directions, and
the relevance of the tradition to them will become readily apparent.
The five schools are: first, the German-Italian historicist school

[4]Karl Marx, *Selected Works* (London, 1942), I, 380–94, 452–62; and Engels, *Correspondence, 1846–1895* (New York, 1933), 510–11.
[5]*L'Histoire Sociale: Sources et Methodes* (Paris, 1967), 5.
[6]Felix Gilbert, "Intellectual History: Its Aims and Methods," *Daedalus* (Winter
1971), 80–82.

featuring a mix of historical philosophers and philosophical historians running from Dilthey and Croce to Cassirer, Meinecke, and Carlo Antoni; second, the group of socio-intellectual historians centering on Marc Bloch, Lucien Febvre, and the periodical *Annales;* third and fourth, the two schools which can be regarded as American counterparts of these two European tendencies, the *History of Ideas* group of Arthur O. Lovejoy and George Boas, and the New History of Robinson, Becker, and Beard; and fifth, the historians of assorted philosophical, literary, artistic, and politico-scientific theories and theorists—Bury, Barker, Randall, Sabine, Auerbach, Mornet, Hauser, Laski, and their ilk—who accommodated their special subjects to the new standard of historical research. This last group too is divisible for our purpose between the historicists and the socio-intellectuals, since its works were written within its respective special disciplines, and its historical dimension was more purely represented by one of the two main-line historical groups—the philosophers and aestheticians by the historicists, social scientists and social literateurs, like Laski and Mornet, by the historians of the *Annales.*

If we ask, then, just what it was that our immediate ancestors originated and what they carried over from *their* past, we shall look for our answers to the two main directions just indicated. Let us first limit the field of the answer and indicate what the new awareness of intellectual history was not yet, for otherwise we shall not understand what we ourselves are doing in the field. The new intellectual history was not yet a separate field of history, with its own method. Certainly there was a novel concern with method and certainly ideas were identified as distinctive objects in history, but the new methods came from outside of history—from neo-idealism and phenomenology in philosophy and especially from sociology among the newly specialized social sciences—and they were designed for integration in the method of all of history, to import principles of coherence into that method, and the awareness of the intellectual dimension of history was a function of these imported general principles. Thus while the *Annales* group and the New Historians wrote deliberate intellectual history they did not regard themselves as primarily or distinctively intellectual historians: they stressed the historical relevance of the methods and concepts of the social sciences, and they arrived at an appreciation of ideas in history by virtue of their function in retarding or advancing—but in either way in linking—the centrifugal facts on an increasingly specialized society subject to incessant change. Marc Bloch's subjects were primarily social, those of his friend and associate, Lucien Febvre, were primarily intellectual, but the essential interest of both was in the mental attitudes most closely engaged in social relations as their preservatives. Robinson, Beard, and Becker were similarly socio-intellectual historians in varying proportions, with an interest in ideas as the comprehensible measure of the relations between atavism and reform in society.

The other early schools of modern intellectual history—notably historicism and the History of Ideas—drew their methods from philosophy and used them in intellectual history to circumvent the uniqueness of every individual cultural product and every particular event which had been established for the methods both of the humanities and of general history as a humanistic discipline. Both schools revealed their philosophical origins by segregating, albeit in varying degrees, the realm of ideas from the realm of social action which had been the traditional focus of history, and if they ultimately drifted into social schematizing it was, as Antoni has shown, in betrayal of their historicist principles.[7] Further, each of these schools defined the history of ideas by a different principle of selection, according to the dimension wherein the continuity was sought. The historicist school, highlighted by Cassirer and Meinecke, looked to the configuration of ideas and found relevant, therefore, ideas that were configurable, whether they were in the form of Cassirer's attempt at what he called the "phenomenology" of the spirit of an age—that is, the essential pattern distillable from the internal relations among its ideas—or Meinecke's attempt to show the complete reflection of political conflicts in the conceptual relations of a dramatized world of interactive ideas. In Lovejoy's *History of Ideas,* on the contrary, the "unit-ideas" which were the objects of his concern were components analyzed out of the systems and combinations in which they were originally invested and followed for their continuity and development through time and discipline. Although Lovejoy seemed to provide a porosity and extensibility for his unit-ideas by admitting "implicit or incompletely explicit assumptions, or more or less unconscious mental habits" among them, his associate George Boas' recent categorical pronouncement that "ideas, after all, exist on the conscious level and their history has to stay on that level" would seem far more faithful to the logic and to the actual performance of the school.[8] To fulfill their function both within and between periods the ideas in the history of ideas must be articulate and recognizable.

It should be clear by now what was common to the men who earlier in this century identified a kind of history which they labeled variously

[7]Carlo Antoni, *Dallo storicismo alla sociologia* (Florence, 1940); Eng. trans. by Hayden V. White, *From History to Sociology: The Transition in German Historical Thinking* (Detroit, 1959), *passim.*

[8]Maurice Mandelbaum, "The History of Ideas, Intellectual History, and the History of Philosophy," *loc. cit.,* 35; George Boas, *The History of Ideas: An Introduction* (New York, 1969), 19.

as intellectual history or history of ideas, which applied to different levels of ideas, and which was worked by methods applying to more or less than the category of all ideas in history—by methods, that is, applying to all of the social past or to only certain kinds of ideas. What was common to them and new for historiography was the loss of faith in the underlying lawfulness either of the principles of human nature or the pattern of social development. What was common to them and old for historiography was their persistent faith in the immanent continuity of history itself, and it was to this continuity that they geared their methods. The connections which could be formerly assumed *for* history had now to be demonstrated *in* history.

What is distinctive about our own generation's approaches to intellectual history? A caveat is required before attempting an answer. Earlier schools and tendencies continue to be influentially represented, by those like Labrousse and Braudel who look directly to the original social and anthropological inspirations of the *Annales* school,[9] by those like Jean Hyppolite, Raymond Polin, and Ernst Nolte who still prosecute genetic and phenomenological studies of individual systems and collective ideologies in depth; and by those like Isaiah Berlin, Passarin d'Entrèves, and Heinz Gollwitzer who actively pursue the history of unit-ideas across the disciplines. Obviously, current protagonists of vintage approaches need be neither epigones nor anachronisms, and the long-lived historiographical fertility of Marxist "consciousness" together with the recent large-scale enterprise of the *Dictionary of the History of Ideas*[9a] offer impersonal confirmation of the truth that in intellectual history anteriority is not equivalent to inferiority.

What is most distinctive albeit not necessarily most distinguished, then, about the contemporary approaches to intellectual history can best be understood as counter-balancing developments from these earlier forms of it. On the one hand, we have separated intellectual history out as a discrete historical field, not only in the mechanical terms of so classifying the historians who profess it and the courses which they teach, but in the constructive terms of detaching ideas and attitudes in history both from their origins in other kinds of disciplines and from their involvement with other kinds of history and collecting them in

---

[9] Thus for Labrousse "the history of ideas" still is a history of "collective mentality"—that is, "of judgments, sentiments, and attitudes"—and "a concrete study of collective mentality can only be a study of social mentality"—that is, of the mental in its specific reference to the concrete experience of particular social groups or classes. *L'Histoire sociale*, 5.

[9a] Published by Scribner's, 4 vols. (New York, 1973), edited by G. Boas, S. Bochner, F. Gilbert, E. Nagel, R. Wellek; H. Cherniss, W. K. Ferguson, E. H. Gombrich, P. O. Kristeller, P. Medawar, M. Schapiro, H. A. Wolfson, and P. P. Wiener.

their own field, defined by their substantive function in the historical process or by the peculiar methods required to know them or by both. On the other hand, the new autonomy thus granted to intellectual history has brought the various forms and levels of man's mental life within the same universe of discourse, has evoked critical discussions over the definition of the field in terms of the relationships among its various intellectual objects, and has eventuated either in an academic struggle for domination or in a permissiveness perilous to the integrity of the field itself. Behind these current developments, helping to explain them and posing new challenges to the longevity of the older schools of intellectual history, have been two contextual developments in our own intellectual and cultural life which have set off the third quarter from the first half of the century and carry a step further the disenchantment with the orderliness of things—a disenchantment which, as we have seen, has ever been the spur in shifting our perspective on the role of ideas in history. The first of these altered cultural conditions, with a constructive effect upon the new intellectual history, has been the dramatic shrinkage in the historical branches of the substantive disciplines traditionally bordering on and overlapping intellectual history—notably of philosophy, of literature, and of the arts—with the consequence that their specific historical effluence has passed into the general pool of intellectual history.[10] The second of the altered cultural circumstances, with caustic effect on intellectual history, has been the eruption of the belief in discontinuity as a necessary condition of all human affairs. Since the earlier schools of modern intellectual history had strenuously substituted a belief in a man-made continuity *within* human affairs for the older belief in the natural continuity *behind* them, our latest cultural innovation would seem to mark an even sharper break with traditional assumptions about the role of ideas in history.

Because the various current tendencies in intellectual history have responded to both of these contemporary cultural conditions these tendencies evince common features which cut across their original variety. First, they all legitimate the field of intellectual history both by distinguishing the role of ideas from the other functions of society, unlike the older socio-intellectual history, and by building a social relevance into the ideas themselves, unlike the older philosophical history. Secondly, they all adapt the traditional function of intellectual his-

---

[10] An obvious illustration is the very topic of a recent symposium of literary scholars—"Is Literary History Obsolete?"—published, ironically, under the auspices of *The New Literary History*. Characteristically, the concluding attempt at synthesizing the fragmented answers was made by the historian, Hayden V. White, essentially through the translation of literary into intellectual history. *New Literary History*, 2 (1970), esp. 173–85.

tory to the present requirements of our culture by describing "continuities in the mode of discontinuity," to generalize François Furet's telling characterization of contemporary "serial history."[11] Because of these common features we can arrange the current approaches to intellectual history in a single spectrum composed by the various combinations of social relevance with distinct ideas, and we can hope to find in the alignment of these combinations, however different the kinds of ideas and of methods in them, a relationship among them which may help us to define their common field, or, at the least, their complementary functions.

We may distinguish three main groupings of current approaches—if we permit ourselves to distinguish for analysis what overlaps in practice—as we move from the more explicitly social to the more explicitly cultural and philosophical ends of the spectrum. The first grouping is composed of new directions in socio-intellectual history. It continues to focus on the popular levels of ideation in society and to deny special methods for ideas as such, but now it identifies ideas and attitudes as the products of a distinct function of society and takes their special requirements into account by drawing new distinctions between the method of social history, which necessarily includes intellectual history, and the method of the other social sciences. What is autonomous about intellectual history here, then, is acknowledgement of an autonomous facet in the historical role of ideas and, because of the quality that ideas contribute to history, it now insists on the autonomy of the specifically historical vis-à-vis the generic social scientific methods. The most prominent of these tendencies is represented in the current merger of the *Annales'* type of approach to socio-intellectual history with Daniel Mornet's type of the sociology of literature that appears in the work of the sixth section of the École Pratique des Hautes Études and that has been labeled by Robert Darnton, its most articulate reviewer in this country, "socio-cultural history."[12] The aspect of its work most germane to the category we are now discussing is its inquiry into the notions and attitudes of the non-intellectual classes, and the novel feature in its inquiry is its interest in the reception of articulate ideas as an autonomous component of these notions and attitudes. Obviously the most responsive tendency within intellectual history to the general democratic movement for the inclusion of the anonymous and inarticulate masses in the historical suffrage, socio-cultural history has especially developed methods of quantification and correlation of gross attitudes which are most appropriate to the measurement of mass men-

[11] Furet, "Quantitative History," *Daedalus* (Winter 1971), 161.

[12] Darnton, "Reading, Writing, and Publishing in Eighteenth-Century France: A Case Study in the Sociology of Literature," *ibid.*, 226.

tality, but this obvious feature should not obscure its recognition of the qualitative and autonomous factor in ideas that is entailed in both the diffusion of published ideas and in the variation of ideological level with the social stratification of their recipients. Furet, who works in this field of intellectual diffusion and in other dimensions of social history as well, has reformulated the *Annales'* methodology to meet the new equivalence of his interests. He categorically distinguishes the quantifying methods appropriate to the other social sciences and to homologously quantifiable kinds of history, e.g., econometric history, from the quantifying methods appropriate to "serial history," which takes definite time series as the basic realities of the past, constituted by the measurable relations of comparable homogeneous units in that series. Fed too by the extension of Namierian collective biography to include ideas and principles as independent variables and by the sophisticated Marxist stress of an E. P. Thompson on attitudes and beliefs in constituting the "logic" of the social relations which define a class,[13] the new sociocultural history both registers the distinctive role of ideas in the social past and responds to the current demand for historical discontinuity. Furet's emphasis on the series rather than the fact and Thompson's on class as a relation rather than a thing show that it is still a connection that ideas are involved in, and their stress on persistence and cohesion within a single period serves to define both the outer limits and the inner homogeneity of each of their plural series and relations.

Clustered around the middle of the spectrum which runs from mass attitudes to theoretical systems are those tendencies in intellectual history which have become most characteristic of the field—the tendencies which posit ideas and behavioral circumstances as two autonomous levels of history and apply characteristically hybrid methods to relating them. In the form of mere juxtaposition or of the provision of a social context which *ipso facto* makes ideas historical or which somehow socializes them by an invisible osmosis, the approach is scarcely new. What is new is the acknowledgment of formulated ideas and circumstantial conditions as different kinds of historical realities whose mutual relations must be conceived as an historical problem rather than an historiographical assumption, and the innovations in the methods which have been devised to discover actual relations between them. One such method—the use of psychology—is hardly new in itself, recent as Erikson's popularization of the term "psychohistory" may be. We may not go back with Frank Manuel as far as Vico for a precedent psychological history, but we must certainly agree that both Dilthey and Febvre have been our predecessors in focusing upon psychic configurations and structures as the kind of intellectual history which

[13] E. P. Thompson, *The Making of the English Working Class* (New York, 1964), 10.

119

was the matrix of men's past behavior.[14] We can go beyond these particular forbears, moreover, to note that in general the centuries-old association between psychology and philosophy in the common enterprise of investigating the origins and validity of ideas—an association persistent to the present through phenomenological psychology—continues to support the long-standing affinity between psychology and intellectual history. What is new in the current vogue of psychohistory is the prominent role of psychoanalysis, which brings two distinctive qualities to the intellectual history it features. First, because psychoanalysis organizes mental life into a process with clearly delineated temporal dimensions, it has underlined the historicity of men's ideas, the multiform vitality of the mental realm, and hence the centrality of intellectual history. Secondly, the obvious stress on the unconscious which psychoanalysis brings to the understanding of mental life has had the effect, in applications like Marcuse's, Erikson's, and Norman Brown's to intellectual history, of grounding the traditional individuality of consciously articulated ideas in the common subterranean impulses of the group or the species.

In addition to the implicit social function of the new historical psychology, there are two other methods which explicitly relate the realms of ideas and social behavior. These methods focus on the specifically intellectual classes—that is, on groups whose precise function, as groups, has been to produce or disseminate ideas. One device, at the social end of this cluster, close to the other work of the sixth section but distinct in principle, has been the expansion of inquiry from the intellectual elite to all intellectual producers, whether personally identifiable or not, with the purpose not of explaining the origin of individual ideas, but of establishing typical correlations among the ideas of intellectuals numerous enough to be considered a social group or active enough to be socially linked by an intellectual institution, such as a journal or an academy. A second socio-ideological device of this kind is the selection, for study, of those intellectual groups which have also been collectively active in those societies which have organized intellectual activities into corporate functions. In these groups there are manifested, as matters of historical fact, connections between ideas and social status, between principles and social action, between the autonomy of ideas and the imperiousness of social circumstances. Patently encouraged by Mannheim's sociological notion of the free-floating intellectual but using it rather as an historical pointer than as a general truth, this device has been especially appropriate to the histories of the German and Russian intelligentsia, a term which connotes

[14] Frank E. Manuel, "The Use and Abuse of Psychology in History," *Daedalus* (Winter 1971), 188–96.

precisely the separate social existence and distinct social function of an idea-bearing class and transfers the problem of relating idea and social action from the assumptions of the historian to the process of history.

Because this middle cluster of approaches to intellectual history is geared to register the diachronic development of the individual or group as well as the synchronic relations between ideas and their context within the individual or group, it functions not only as a structural link for the life of a society at any one time but also as a thread through changes in limited time—that is, a thread which lasts as long as the lives of the individual or the group whose personality is the mold for the change.

The final set of contemporary approaches to intellectual history is composed of those which seek within the intellectual sphere itself the larger context—preferably some linkage to society—through which alone ideas become historically knowable and historically respectable. The ideas which have evoked these approaches are still the highly individuated and articulated concepts associated with one or a few definitely identifiable historical personages that have been the stock-in-trade of the older philosophical schools of intellectual history. But new methods have been devised in response to the new emphasis upon historical discontinuity and to the growing historical indifference of the substantive humanistic disciplines, with the consequent devolvement upon intellectual historians of the responsibility to vest their philosophical, aesthetic, and doctrinal ideas with the internal dimension that was formerly supplied by the special histories of the respective disciplines. The consequence of the shift has been to dislocate the older tacit arrangement which assigned to the special historian of philosophy or the arts the internal relations of ideas and to the intellectual historian their external relations. At the same time as the intellectual historian must thus bring a new specialization and a new internality to his perception of his intellectual historical object, thereby attenuating the older connections between externally classified ideas and the respectable historical activities of men, his isolation is intensified by the contemporary cultural movement which underlines the discontinuity, both within history and between history and the historian, above all of those formal ideas, doctrines, and world-views whose historical function had traditionally been deemed to inhere precisely in their built-in continuity. The sins of continuity, whether in the form of the belief in universal truths or the belief in trans-epochal influence, loom large, for example, in the depressing syllabus of errors compiled against the historiography of such "classic texts" by the contemporary analyst, Quentin Skinner.[15]

[15]Quentin Skinner, "Meaning and Understanding in the History of Ideas," *History and Theory* (1969), 3–53, *passim.*

The intra-mural methods recently put forth for this level of intellectual history, however responsive they may be to these limiting conditions, merely take them as their point of departure, and within their limits construct new continuities and especially new bridges to the social experience of man which remains the central reference point of history as a discipline. The new movement toward the specialized, internal understanding of the art or -ology laying claim to the idea in historical question has not replaced the old awareness of temporal relations as the essence of the historical discipline. What the new movement has done is simply to displace the old awareness in the direction of stressing simultaneous rather than successive relations and of attenuating the distinction between the internal and the external relations of ideas. Again, historians now do stress the disconnectedness of their intellectual objects both from any long-range developments of ideas and from any community of constant values through or above time; and yet the traditional proclivity of intellectual historians to establish continuity persists, for they treat each disassociated idea or thinker as a microcosm that internalizes the macro-currents of past and present through its own medium, and the junctures which the historian no longer permits *between* ideas are permissibly relocated in the combinations entering into the structure *of* any particular historical idea. The methodical innovations in the service of adjusting the old role to the new conditions seem infinite in their variety, so powerful is the urge to retain the temporal axis of historical relations and to reconstitute connections. Four such innovations, representing both the diversity of practice and the community of purpose which marks this kind of intellectual history, may be mentioned here.

First, the application of linguistics, with its quantitative, analytical, and structural varieties and its range from language games to sociolinguistics, itself recapitulates the whole spectrum of intellectual history in the large. This variegated linguistic approach serves to reconstruct the socialized modes of communication which link the individual idea or syndrome of ideas, meaningless and unknowable in itself, with the contemporaries who gave it meaning and with the historian who can know it only with such mediation.[16]

Second, and most akin to the traditional methods of the historian, is the selection of social theory and theorists as the objects of intellectual history. Highlighted by H. Stuart Hughes' attention to the consciousness of society, by Frank Manuel's social prophets, and Jacob Talmon's social messiahs, this method of internal intellectual history is automatically socially relevant by virtue of its content and authentically historical when it treats its theorists as historical sources, contempo-

---

[16] John Pocock, *Politics, Language, and Time* (New York, 1971), 3–41.

rary witnesses of their society, subject to the same critical processing as any other historical source or witness.

A third method seeks to resolve the problem of the historian's new responsibility for the specialized internal relations of ideas by locating these internal relations in the historical process itself and thus converting their challenge for the historian from a problem of historiography to a question of history. The inquiry here is into the impact of a thinker's social experience upon the formation of his ideas, and the method comes into play when direct evidence fails and the pattern of his ideas affords the only extant traces of the impact.[17] The discontinuities in thought furnish the opportunities of ingress for the thinker's contemporary social experience, which becomes visible in his thought and optimally functions as a kind of bypass connecting the logically discontinuous elements of his thought—that is, precisely as a "continuity in the mode of discontinuity."

A fourth method of this internal intellectual history, finally, expands the field of ideas to include the arts in a new way. It goes beyond the older method of treating artistic works as expositions whose discursive ideas are to be abstracted from the whole composition, and it also goes beyond the older treatment of finished artistic products as intellectual events, to be aligned with other such events in the contours of an age's general style or spirit. Predicated on the insight into the implicit connection between the narrower and broader senses of culture, the new method is designed to perceive aesthetic modes of expression as autonomous kinds of thinking—as acts of thought immediate to experience, irreducible to discursive ideas or to the orthodox criticisms of their final products, and more open than either formal ideas or finished works of art are to the social matrix which cradles them all. The arts are here regarded as comprising a distinct medium of social communication, connected with other channels of ideas through the social community that sponsors them all as so many articulations of its joint existence.[18]

This set of internalized approaches thus testifies as much as the variable socialization of intellectual history to the current substantive plurality and methodic specialization in the field—but it testifies even more to the unbroken drive of intellectual historians, from the dawn of our culture until the present, to hypostatize ideas as the bridges of our history.

What answers does our survey of past and present approaches to in-

[17] Leonard Krieger, "Culture, Cataclysm, and Contingency," *Journal of Modern History,* **40** (Dec. 1968), 447–73.

[18] Carl E. Schorske's presentation in a symposium on "New Trends in History," *Daedalus* (Fall 1969), 930–33.

tellectual history yield to our initial questions about the relationship of its varieties and its integrity as an autonomous field of history?

First, if intellectual history is conceived as a field in spatial terms, requiring products more akin to one another than to products outside the field and requiring common methods of appropriate cultivation in some measure independent of methods outside the field, then it must be owned that intellectual history is not now an integral or autonomous field of history. At its social end, it studies mass attitudes with extensive methods common to other social history; at its philosophical and aesthetic end, it studies formalized terms and ideas with intensive methods common to other disciplines that are not historical.

But, secondly, intellectual historians, whatever their variety, share the attribution of a common function to ideas in history, whatever the form and level of the ideas—namely, to serve as connections, both among historical agents and between the historical agents and the historian.

Thirdly, the varieties of intellectual history may be aligned as complementary functions of their common service to continuity. The more social varieties have demonstrated their virtuosity in establishing the literal continuity of persistent attitudes; the more philosophical and aesthetic varieties have been addressed to establishing the gossamer continuity through change.

But finally—and here we pass from summary to conclusion—our survey has itself raised a further question which threatens to undercut these general answers. Socio-intellectual history and socio-linguistic history have shown themselves to be especially appropriate to the current conditions affecting the discipline of history at large: they are in tune with the democratization of the scope of history, and they have responded with special sensitivity to the requirement of discontinuity that each temporal series be known and understood in its own terms. Despite the usual fragmentation of their results yielded by the masses of their relevant agents for dimensions of ideas other than persistent attitudes and meanings, in principle the socially oriented varieties of intellectual history are surely on the side of the angels. But how can the more insulated varieties of intellectual history still be justified when to the old charge of social indifference there are now added the charges of elitism and anachronism, since the historical validity of the universal ideas on which they have traditionally depended for the long-range continuity both within history and between history and the historian is now so widely denied?

An answer to this question too can be given if we adduce a second set of functions which overlap the functions of understanding persistence and change in ideas and serve them similarly as complements to the varieties of intellectual history. It is a truism that historical knowledge is a compound of sympathy and criticism, and if we translate sympathy into truth seen from the point of view of the historical agent and criticism into truth seen from the point of view of the historian, it is clear that in principle our standard operating procedure is a combination of opposites, and that in practice there has always been a valid range of varying proportions in which historians have employed them. The diversity of these principles roughly overlaps the diversity between the more social and the more philosophical species of intellectual history—but in an unexpected way. Earlier in the century, under the aegis of continuity, historical sympathy was deemed particularly appropriate to individual change and historical criticism to social stasis. But now, under the aegis of discontinuity, the qualities are reversed: socially oriented intellectual history stresses sympathy with the past in its own terms, and philosophically oriented intellectual history assumes a critical connection between the historian and the past. For those who believe that history is the past restored, society is undoubtedly the only possible framework for its restoration. But for those who believe that history is the answer which the past gives to the questions of its successive futures, the common ground afforded by the rational forms of articulated ideas provides a communication through time that offsets their isolation from their contemporary society. And for those who believe that both reconstruction and restoration are required by the historical enterprise, conversation with the great dead joins the resurrection of the souls of the mute in a common perspective upon the autonomous role of ideas in our history.

University of Chicago.

Chapter VIII.a

ARTHUR O. LOVEJOY AND THE MORAL OF
THE GREAT CHAIN OF BEING

By Daniel J. Wilson*

Since 1933 when Arthur O. Lovejoy delivered the William James Lectures at Harvard, his study of the idea of the great chain of being has remained a consummate example of scholarship in the history of ideas. Lovejoy brought together over thirty years of study when he traced the ideas of plenitude, continuity, and gradation from their Platonic and Aristotelian genesis through the Romantic Revolution at the beginning of the nineteenth century. To view *The Great Chain of Being* as only the best exemplar of the discipline is, however, to miss much of the significance of the book. *The Great Chain of Being* is not merely the history of an idea, it is also the history of Lovejoy's ideas. The ideas embodied in the history of the chain of being had long been part of the framework of western thought and had informed the thinking of his early mentors. The implications of this history, its failure, and its moral suggested to Lovejoy as early as 1902 the outlines of a new and more intelligible world order.

As a result of his many studies in the history of ideas Lovejoy uncovered and examined the intellectual antecedents of the philosophical problem he faced throughout his career—the problem of making a pluralistic and temporal universe intelligible. In addition, the absolute idealism (e.g., of F. H. Bradley and of W. T. Harris) so prevalent at the end of the nineteenth century seemed to him incapable of explaining the rapidly changing world. Aided by the pluralistic philosophies of George Holmes Howison and William James, the young philosopher gradually developed a philosophy based on pluralism, temporalism, the existence of ideas, and faith in reason.[1] These new directions in his philosophical thought raised questions in Lovejoy's mind about man's long acceptance of a static, absolute conception of the universe and the modern values placed on change and diversity. He believed that the reasons behind this revolution in thought—a revolution vitally important to his own philosophy—could be discovered only by tracing "a part of

---

* An earlier draft of this paper was presented to the History of Ideas Club, The Johns Hopkins University, November 8, 1977. I would like to thank Professor Maurice Mandelbaum, Professor George Boas, André-Philippe Katz, and Peter A. Poggioli for their help and suggestions.

[1] For an account of Lovejoy's early years and his study under James and Howison, see Daniel J. Wilson, "Arthur O. Lovejoy: An Intellectual Biography" (Ph.D. thesis, The Johns Hopkins University, 1976), chapters 2 and 4.

the history of Western man's long effort to make the world he lives in appear to his intellect a rational one."[2]

Lovejoy's study of the history of ideas was an essential part of his philosophical effort to create a rational and intelligible account of the world. In philosophy, he argued for epistemological and psychophysical dualism, temporalism, and the principles of reason. From his earliest essays in the history of ideas, written just after the turn of the century, Lovejoy hoped to uncover the logical steps by which philosophy could move from belief in an Absolute monistic and static universe to a pluralistic and evolutionary one. If he could discover the logical grounds for this change in western thought, Lovejoy could be more certain that his pluralistic and evolutionary philosophy was not only possible, but also necessary.

In addition to unearthing the history of man's search for intelligibility, the history of ideas lent support to two of Lovejoy's most fundamental philosophical assumptions: ideas do exist and have influence, and man, as a rational animal, can use these entities called ideas to order his world.[3] Regardless of what contemporary philosophers argued, Lovejoy believed it was impossible to deny that even well before Plato people had ideas which had made a difference to their lives. Ideas were and, as history revealed, always had been a vital element in man's continuing attempt to adjust to and make sense of the universe.

Lovejoy's belief in historical inquiry was longstanding. He had decided to undertake graduate study in philosophy because it would commit him to nothing more than a "desire for reasonableness and an interest in the history of thought." In the summer of 1895 he was sure of only one thing: "I should want to make my study run largely along historical lines."[4] Thus, when faced with the problem of a pluralistic universe a few years later, he believed it was just as necessary to examine the historical antecedents of the problem as it was to investigate the contemporary philosophical systems.

Lovejoy thus began his investigations into the history of ideas contemporaneously with his initial efforts in philosophy. Several of his initial historical essays treated religious subjects, a legacy of the religious disputes with his father and his early interest in comparative religion. Even so, he very clearly addressed the question of how philosophy had accepted an absolute conception of the universe for so long and then rapidly transformed it into something very different. Before 1905

---

[2] Arthur O. Lovejoy, *The Great Chain of Being: A Study of the History of an Idea* (Cambridge, 1936), 47.

[3] See, for example, Arthur O. Lovejoy, "On the Existence of Ideas," *Three Studies in Current Philosophical Questions* (Baltimore, 1914), 42-99, and Arthur O. Lovejoy, "The Anomaly of Knowledge," *The Thirteen Pragmatisms and Other Essays* (Baltimore, 1963), 236-86.

[4] Arthur O. Lovejoy to his father Wallace W. Lovejoy, June 2, [1895], The Arthur O. Lovejoy Collection, The Johns Hopkins University.

Lovejoy had delineated the Platonic conception of the universe in a historical and critical manner which suggested the moral of the tale, and clearly anticipated his arguments in *The Great Chain of Being*.

In one of his earliest essays, "Religion and the Time-Process," published in 1902, Lovejoy began to outline the historical problem that dominated his work in the history of ideas and that he would elaborate more thoroughly in *The Great Chain of Being*. Concerned with the relationship of the temporal and the eternal, Lovejoy examined the philosophical and religious roots of the idea of "otherworldliness" so prevalent in traditional western thought. He described otherworldliness as "a disposition to define both ultimate Being and genuine Worth in terms of their 'otherness' to the characteristics of the common experience of the life in time and place." He then traced this traditional conception to Plato: "it was in Platonism that those formal preconceptions which were to determine for many centuries all the more philosophical views about divine nature and the nature of the good, got their earliest and most influential manifestation."[5]

Lovejoy had not yet discriminated the component ideas of the framework of western thought with the clarity he later achieved in *The Great Chain of Being*. He was, however, dealing with the same complex of ideas. The Good must, according to Plato, be perfectly self-sufficient: as Lovejoy described it, "the perfect must be one, simple, ontologically independent of external relations to other entities, and above all, free from all mutability, from all activity or outreaching of volition." In such a belief, "mere diversity, richness of content as such, especially in the form of change and temporal process, absolutely is not . . . valuable or interesting in itself, but only as rationalized into a formal unity."[6] Here was one side of the Platonic conception of the universe that Lovejoy was to trace in his William James Lectures.

When he turned to the fate of Platonic otherworldliness in the course of human thought, Lovejoy discovered that the idea of the Absolute underwent certain changes with the passage of centuries; new ideas about change and development appeared in western thought. In 1902 he thought that the ideas of history and of becoming had been introduced into western thought through the Judeo-Christian tradition. He had not yet asseverated the principles of plenitude, continuity, and gradation within Platonic thought which, as he demonstrated in *The Great Chain of Being,* were capable of overthrowing the tradition of which they were a part. Although in "Religion and the Time-Process" Lovejoy traced the notions of time and diversity to Judeo-Christian origins, he

[5]Arthur O. Lovejoy, "Religion and the Time-Process," *American Journal of Theology,* 6 (1902), 440, 443-44. In *The Great Chain of Being* Lovejoy described Plato as "the main historic source of the indigenous strain of otherworldliness in Occidental philosophy and religion" (35).

[6] Lovejoy, "Religion and the Time-Process," 444-47; compare with *Chain of Being*, 43-45.

also showed how the process of temporalizing the self-sufficient good paralleled the temporalizing of the Chain of Being. He believed that the deists began the weakening of otherworldliness by attempting to establish a "religion of this world." However, because their conception of the good was itself "a condition of perfected and stationary equilibrium," the deists had been unable to assign any "rational meaning or ultimate value to the time-process." The rise of evolutionary thought in the eighteenth century further contributed to the breakdown of the Platonic universe. Beginning with Gotthold Lessing, Lovejoy argued, the notion swept through western consciousness that the world, human nature, and ideas were not static entities but were constantly changing and developing.

Through the principles of evolution men believed a world of becoming could be made intelligible. The final step, Lovejoy believed, was the nineteenth-century development of a new theory of "worth" that the good consists "not in perfection, not in the arrest of forthreaching process, but has its very essence in movement and process itself." As he later argued in *The Great Chain of Being,* Lovejoy claimed that "with this radical transformation of the conception of value, the entire Platonic and Aristotelian scheme of the universe—which, as we have seen, has in its broad outlines formed the logical framework of European moral and religious thought, even where men have been least aware of it—gets now completely inverted."[7] This historical revolution in thought lay behind Lovejoy's own developing philosophy. Just as the nineteenth century had rejected a static conception of the world, so too, he rejected the absolute idealism of his philosophical mentors in favor of a philosophy based on diversity and change.

Two years later, in "The Dialectic of Bruno and Spinoza," Lovejoy returned to the Platonic influence on western thought. Philosophical scholars had long foundered on the problem of explaining how Spinoza could find in absolute substance the logical ground for "the existence of an infinity of attributes." Rather than give another analysis of Spinoza's language, Lovejoy proposed to exhibit Spinoza's "dialectical procedure through an examination of its historical sources and affinities." Lovejoy argued that "the more general and fundamental principles of Spinoza's metaphysics are in no respect original": Spinoza was a "consistent Neo-Platonist of the Renaissance type" whose approach to these problems had been "foreshadowed by Plotinus, fully worked out by mediaeval theologians and much used by Bruno." Spinoza's philosophy, Lovejoy felt, could be "understood only in the light of its relation to these earlier applications of a similar dialectic to a similar problem."[8]

Lovejoy believed that "without going back to Alexandrian Neo-Platonism little in subsequent European metaphysics can be understood

[7] Lovejoy, "Religion and the Time-Process," 448, 455-62. On the inversion of the Platonic scheme, compare with *Chain of Being,* 325-26.

[8] Arthur O. Lovejoy, "The Dialectic of Bruno and Spinoza," *University of California Publications in Philosophy,* 1 (1904), 144-45.

in its proper historical setting" and that this background was indispensable to a study of Bruno and Spinoza. Now, Lovejoy saw clearly the Platonic, Aristotelian, and Neo-Platonic origins of western thought. From Plato, of course, came the conception of the one true Being that was "perfect, simple, immutable, having no relations to anything outside itself." If true Being was perfection, what then were its relations with the imperfect world in which man lived? Although both Plato and Aristotle suggested connections, Lovejoy argued that it was the Neo-Platonists who "would find in the abstract Platonic Deity the necessary source of all being, and also the substance of all" and would thus structure much of western thought. He still thought Judeo-Christian beliefs had influenced the alteration of Platonic thought, but now he conceded that contradictions in "Platonic and Aristotelian theology" were sufficient to explain the transformation of the tradition. The Neo-Platonists, according to Lovejoy, realized that "only a Nature that included all positive being within itself could meet the requirements of the dialectic that lay behind the theology of Plato and Aristotle." The Neo-Platonists argued that all particular and relative things were "taken up within the being of the Absolute One." This idea brought the Absolute into a relationship with the relative, but it still left philosophers with a serious paradox: how could a perfect, transcendent, immutable Being "embrace within itself all the diversity of the universe?"[9]

Lovejoy discovered in Plotinus a system derivable from Platonic principles, one that sought to make the "concept of perfection and self-sufficiency . . . the ground and the necessity" for the existence of all "particular beings and the subjects of concrete predicates."[10] Plotinus had argued that the perfect Being could not remain limited within itself, but must give rise to all things. In what Lovejoy would later call the principle of plenitude, the Absolute was now conceived as the "maximum potentiality" involving "the actual existence of all possible things with all possible qualities and modes of being." According to Lovejoy, the Neo-Platonic dialectic, as worked out by Plotinus, had four elements: first, Absolute Being was transcendent, immutable and free of all limitation and relation; second, "the same Being is conceived as necessarily inclusive of all the reality that in any sense exists, and thus holding within itself the whole universe of concrete, manifold, and temporal existences"; third, the Absolute must necessarily transcend itself and become "the dynamic ground necessitating the coming into existence of all possible realities in all possible modes and scales of being"; and finally, although holding all these principles simultaneously was contradictory, to deny any seemed to involve an even "more radical and

[9] *Ibid.*, 150-52.

[10] *Ibid.*, 154-55. In *The Great Chain of Being,* Lovejoy argued that this notion of plenitude had already been present in Plato, whereas in "The Dialectic of Bruno and Spinoza" he mentions the Platonic source only in passing. "Bruno and Spinoza," 155.

offensive self-contradiction." This same dialectic, Lovejoy asserted, was also "at work in the doctrines of the Platonizing Christian theologians of the Middle Ages."[11] The dialectic of Bruno and Spinoza, of course, was only a legacy of this well established tradition. By 1904, then, Lovejoy had more fully outlined his reconstruction of the framework of Occidental thought, but the complete history would have to wait thirty years.

"The Dialectic of Bruno and Spinoza" was primarily a historical inquiry into the intellectual antecedents of the two philosophers, but Lovejoy also hoped to uncover "some general considerations capable of pertinent application to certain contemporary tendencies in metaphysics." The problem of Bruno and Spinoza, indeed in Lovejoy's view, the problem of all philosophers since Plato, was to render intelligible the relationship of Absolute Being to the imperfect world. In 1904, Lovejoy was in the midst of his own struggle to find an intelligible account of the universe. He had already rejected the notion of an Absolute as the ground of temporal existence, but the "moral" of the history he recounted in his 1904 essay lent support to his own developing theories: "The moral . . . is the hopelessness of the effort—not yet wholly given over—to make a metaphysic by framing a conception of a really 'absolute' Absolute which is at the same time to be thought as 'inclusive' of all reality, a 'comprehensive whole of experience,' the 'possessor of an infinite wealth of organized individual elements of content.' "[12] If human experience was truly pluralistic and temporal, then this real world could not be contained in a fixed absolute without self-contradiction. His historical inquiries, by revealing the contradictions inherent in an absolute, helped Lovejoy reject the Absolute idealistic philosophies of his day. The moral of his inquiries became central to Lovejoy's intellectual enterprise, and he would expound it at the end of *The Great Chain of Being.*

The philosophical framework and central problem established by Plato and described by Lovejoy in these early essays formed the background against which he constructed his own philosophy. In these early essays, in his numerous studies in the history of ideas, and most fully in *The Great Chain of Being,* Lovejoy outlined the intellectual antecedents of the philosophical problem he confronted and the temporalistic realism of his solution. The history of ideas provided ample evidence that the concept of a self-sufficient Absolute, and its corollary, the chain of being, had failed to make the universe intelligible, that time, evolution, and diversity were realities more in accord with the world as man experienced it, and that ideas are influential and are important historically. Lovejoy's temporalistic realism and his epistemological and

---

[11] Lovejoy, "Bruno and Spinoza," 154-57; cf. *Chain of Being,* 61-66.

[12] Lovejoy, "Bruno and Spinoza," 173-74. Compare the moral of this essay with that of *The Great Chain of Being,* 329-31.

psycho-physical dualism were his answers to Plato's questions about the existence of a world of becoming and the kinds of being that made up the experienced world. His essays in the history of ideas described man's attempts to answer those questions and "to show that the scheme of things is an intelligible and rational one."[13] The Absolute and the chain of being proved a failure, but out of that failure grew the ideas of evolution and the value of diversity that enabled Lovejoy to make his world comprehensible.

One needs only to look at Lovejoy's essays in the history of ideas to realize the extent to which his studies illuminated episodes in man's attempt to work out the implications of the Platonic universe. The bulk of his historical essays focused on eighteenth-century thought, evolutionism, or Romanticism (in Germany, 1790-1830). His essays on the Enlightenment pointed up the contradictions in the thought of the period, although Lovejoy admired Enlightenment thinkers for their devotion to reason and their rejection of historical and mystical religion. His studies on evolutionism traced the modern discovery of time and change, while his investigations into Romanticism eventually uncovered the transformation of the Chain of Being into a Becoming. All these studies, of course, demonstrated, if only indirectly, the importance and value of ideas to rational man.

The thinkers of the Enlightenment took the legacy of Plato to its highest development in their reliance on reason and the chain of being. At the same time, however, the contradictions inherent in their beliefs were becoming increasingly obvious. Lovejoy began his studies of the eighteenth century because the deists had been among the first modern thinkers to argue against historical Christianity and for a rational, universal religion. In their arguments, Lovejoy had found support in his dissent from the evangelical religion of his father.[14] But, the Enlightenment thinkers were more than allies in the attack on historical religion. Of all modern philosophers they had valued reason most highly and it was, of course, upon rational foundations that Lovejoy worked to build his own philosophy. The problem, as Lovejoy quickly discovered, was that the Enlightenment was too rational. As he had suggested in "The Dialectic of Bruno and Spinoza" and demonstrated at length in *The Great Chain of Being,* the contradictions inherent in the full elaboration of the ideas of plenitude, continuity, and gradation soon undermined the "hypothesis of the absolute rationality of the cosmos."[15] Reason was a key to intelligibility, but other elements of man's experience, especially time, were equally important.

[13] Lovejoy, *Chain of Being,* viii.
[14] Arthur O. Lovejoy to Wallace W. Lovejoy, April 3, 1896, and [Summer 1896], Lovejoy Collection; Arthur O. Lovejoy, "The Entangling Alliance of Religion and History," *Hibbert Journal,* 5 (1907), 265-69.
[15] Lovejoy, *Chain of Being,* 329.

At the same time that he began to write on the Platonic legacy, Lovejoy discovered the anticipation of modern, scientific evolutionism in the eighteenth century. Evolutionism was important in the history of thought because Lovejoy believed that through these ideas thinkers gained a theory whereby they "could assign rationality and spiritual significance to the temporal order of phenomena."[16] Just as Lovejoy's own reflections on the temporal process led him to reject the absolute doctrines of his teachers, so the nascent evolutionary thought of the eighteenth century did much to undermine the absolute imbedded in the chain of being.[17] Beginning with "Some Eighteenth Century Evolutionists" in 1904, Lovejoy described several episodes in the development of evolutionary thought before Darwin.[18] Although Lovejoy's essays on evolution were characteristically precise and discriminating, he was well aware of both the religious and philosophical implications of evolutionary theory. The theory had helped make possible a "religion of evolution" and ultimately temporalized the chain of being. Not solely responsible for the major shift in western thought, "the evolutionist tendency" had, nevertheless, worked "to increase the pressure towards the transformation" of the principles of plenitude, continuity, and gradation into their "temporalized form."[19] And when that had happened, especially after Leibniz, it was only a small step to the universe of Becoming celebrated by the Romantics.

The study of romanticisms and the thinkers of the early nineteenth century formed a major part of Lovejoy's work in the history of ideas. As with the Enlightenment and pre-Darwinian evolutionary thought, the ideas associated with romanticism were important in the transformation of the absolute and static world to one of diversity and becoming. Although Lovejoy did not begin his studies of the period until the mid-teens, he recognized as early as 1902 that ideas characteristic of romanticism, in at least some of its guises, were antithetical to what had come before. The new value placed on the belief in the good as

[16] Lovejoy, "Religion and the Time-Process," 457-58.

[17] Arthur O. Lovejoy, "A Temporalistic Realism," in George P. Adams and Wm. P. Montague, eds., *Contemporary American Philosophy: Personal Statements*, II (New York, 1930), 88-89.

[18] Arthur O. Lovejoy, "Some Eighteenth Century Evolutionists," *Popular Science Monthly*, 65 (1904), 238-51, 323-40; Arthur O. Lovejoy, "The Place of Linnaeus in the History of Science," *Popular Science Monthly*, 71 (1907), 498-508; Arthur O. Lovejoy, "Kant and Evolution," *Popular Science Monthly*, 77 (1910), 538-53, 78 (1911), 36-51. Several of Lovejoy's articles on evolution were brought together in Bentley Glass, Owsei Temkin, and William L. Strauss, Jr., eds., *Forerunners of Darwin: 1745-1859* (Baltimore, 1959).

[19] On the effect of religion; see "Religion and the Time-Process," 457-59; on the temporalizing of the chain of being, see *Chain of Being*, Chapter VIII, "The Chain of Being and Some Aspects of Eighteenth-Century Biology," and Chapter IX, "The Temporalizing of the Chain of Being," esp. 268-69.

"movement and process" meant that the "entire Platonic and Aristotelian scheme of the Universe" was "completely inverted."[20]

The essays on romanticism, products of Lovejoy's search for intelligibility, were valuable historical studies of the period. In his articles on "Schiller and the Genesis of German Romanticism" and "On the Discrimination of Romanticisms," Lovejoy did much to clarify the murky intellectual history of the period.[21] Only in *The Great Chain of Being* did Lovejoy explicitly connect the romantic thinkers to the overthrow of the chain of being and the absolute, uniformitarian concept of the universe of which that chain was a constituent part. Lovejoy discovered in the writings of Friedrich Schelling that the "complete and immutable Chain of Being" had "been converted into a Becoming." The ideas of plenitude, continuity, and gradation were still imbedded in western thought, but the fullness of the universe was no longer "the permanent character but the flying goal of the whole of things."[22] The way was now open for a pluralistic, temporalistic universe ordered by the principles of reason.

The existence and influence of ideas, indeed their necessity, was an integral part of Lovejoy's philosophy and the history of ideas, if only indirectly, lent support to Lovejoy's philosophical arguments. Ideas were, of course, central to any rational philosophy and indispensable in Lovejoy's representative theory of knowledge. As he put it at the conclusion of "The Anomaly of Knowledge": "I am still much inclined to believe that I have ideas, and that without them I and other men would know less than we do—would, to be precise, know nothing at all."[23] Lovejoy's working assumption in the history of ideas drew upon this philosophical position: "Whatever other definitions of man be true or false, it is generally admitted that he is distinguished among the creatures by the habit of entertaining general ideas." Not only did man have general ideas, "his thoughts have at all times had a good deal to do with his behavior, his institutions, his material achievements in technology and the arts, and his fortunes." Given the rational nature of man, the history of ideas "has its own reason for being":

To know, so far as may be known, the thoughts that have been widely held among men on matters of common human concernment, to determine how these thoughts have arisen, combined, interacted with, or counteracted, one another, and how they have severally been related to the imagination and

[20] Lovejoy, "Religion and the Time-Process," 462-63.

[21] Arthur O. Lovejoy, "Schiller and the Genesis of German Romanticism," *Modern Language Notes*, 35 (1920), 1-10, 134-36; Arthur O. Lovejoy, "On the Discrimination of Romanticisms," *PMLA*, 39 (1924), 229-53.

[22] Lovejoy, *Chain of Being*, 325-26.

[23] Lovejoy, "The Anomaly of Knowledge," 286. See also, Andrew J. Reck, "The Philosophy of Arthur O. Lovejoy (1873-1962)," *The Review of Metaphysics*, 17 (1963), 280.

emotions, and behavior of those who have held them—this, though not, indeed, the whole of that branch of knowledge which we call history, is a distinct and essential part of it, and its central and most vital part.[24]

Although the existence of general ideas justified the history of ideas, the historian must not falsely assume that man is, or was, totally rational. Lovejoy cautioned against the belief that the terms "idea" and "intellectual" implied "any assumption of the solely or chiefly logical determination of opinions and behavior and of the historical movement of thought." If man was not wholly rational, neither was he the prisoner of his subconscious, irrational desires, passions, and interests, and the historian of ideas had the responsibility to discriminate between the rational and non-rational elements in the history of thought. Despite his recognition of man's non-rational side, Lovejoy believed strongly that the historian of ideas should concentrate on the rational side: "It must still be admitted that philosophers (and even plain men) *do* reason, that the temporal sequence of their reasonings, as one thinker follows another, is usually in some considerable degree a logically motivated and logically instructive sequence."[25] And, in the sequential record of western thought, Lovejoy tried to trace man's attempt "to make the world he lives in appear to his intellect a rational one."[26]

Most of his essays in the history of ideas examined some facet of this unfolding world order, but only in *The Great Chain of Being* did Lovejoy bring together all the "general conceptions" in a masterful study of an influential complex of ideas in western thought. More importantly for the development of his own ideas, he described, more fully than before, the intellectual antecedents of the philosophical problems he had confronted throughout his career. He concluded that the history of the chain of being was the history of its failure, but a failure with a moral: no static, absolute, and completely rational conception of the universe could render the actual world intelligible. Out of the ruins of the Age of Reason, however, arose a newly dominant view of the cosmos, a scheme of things that made the temporal and pluralistic character of the experienced world intelligible. From the time he began to write philosophy at Harvard under the guidance of Josiah Royce, Lovejoy faced "a world demanding to be made intelligible."[27] Not alone in his desire to make sense of the universe, he discovered that the ideas implicit in the Chain of Being had long provided a basis for showing that the order of the world is "an intelligible and rational one."[28] When he came to

[24] Arthur O. Lovejoy, "Reflections on the History of Ideas," *Journal of the History of Ideas,* 1 (1940), 3, 8.

[25] *Ibid.,* 16-21.

[26] Lovejoy, *Chain of Being,* 47.

[27] Arthur O. Lovejoy, "Some Concluding Criticisms on the 'Total Experience' Account of Reality, with special reference to the 'Moment of Arrest,' " MS essay, June 8, 1896, Lovejoy Collection, 6-8.

[28] Lovejoy, *Chain of Being,* viii.

write *The Great Chain of Being,* Lovejoy discerned two questions at the heart of much of western thought: Why was there a "World of Becoming" in addition to the "eternal World of Ideas," and, what principle determined the character of the experienced world. These questions remained as important for Lovejoy as they had been for Plato, Plotinus, Spinoza, or the other philosophers of Occidental civilization: "For to acknowledge that such questions are necessarily insoluble or meaningless is to imply that, so far as we can judge, the world is in final analysis nonrational." If no "intelligible reason" could be given for the character of the world as experienced, then "the constitution of the world is but a whim or an accident." And that was a conclusion Lovejoy could not accept.[29]

Plato and most subsequent philosophers had assumed that these questions about the nature of the universe could and should be asked. Lovejoy shared that assumption, although he recognized that there was no assurance of success in the quest for complete intelligibility. Using an image he took from William James, he wrote: "No doubt man's quest of intelligibility in nature and in himself, and of the kinds of emotional satisfaction which are conditioned by a sense of intelligibility, often, like the caged rat's quest of food, has found no end, in wandering mazes lost."[30] If not all philosophers were successful, their failures were instructive nonetheless, and the history of the Chain of Being was part of the history of man's attempt to make his universe comprehensible.

As he had in the essays at the turn of the century, Lovejoy began *The Great Chain of Being* by turning to Plato to find the beginnings of western thought. He discerned in Plato the sharp cleavage between otherworldliness and this-worldliness that influenced the course of most subsequent philosophical and religious thought. Otherworldliness, of course, held that the "genuinely 'real' and the truly good" were radically antithetic to "man's natural life." This worldliness embodied "the chief value of existence" in struggle and development in time and "antipathy to satisfaction and finality." Lovejoy argued that Plato's otherworldliness was clearly evident in the Greek philosopher's Idea of the Good, which was the direct opposite of all change, distinct from all particular existence, and "the most indubitable of all realities."[31]

---

[29] *Ibid.,* 46-47. These sentiments are reminiscent of Lovejoy's comment to George Holmes Howison in 1901 that without an "adequate unifying principle," the "world thereupon presents itself as essentially non-rational, and unintelligible except as a brute fact." Arthur O. Lovejoy to George Holmes Howison, July 27, 1901, The George Holmes Howison Collection, University Archives, Bancroft Library, The University of California-Berkeley.

[30] Lovejoy. *Chain of Being,* 32. William James in speaking of the mind's quest of tranquility in rationality employed the same image of finding no end "in wandering mazes lost." William James, "The Sentiment of Rationality," *Mind,* 4 (1879), 341.

[31] Lovejoy, *Chain of Being,* 24-25, 35-41.

Having conceived of "an Idea of Ideas which is a pure perfection alien to all the categories of ordinary thought and in need of nothing external to itself," Plato, according to Lovejoy, grounded the "necessity and worth of all conceivable kinds of finite, temporal, imperfect, and corporeal beings" in the "self-Sufficing Being." These considerations gave rise to the two questions already mentioned: *"Why* is there any World of Becoming, in addition to the eternal World of Ideas" and what principle determines how many kinds of being make up "the sensible and temporal world"? Lovejoy believed that Plato assumed that finite and imperfect entities were "inherently desirable" and thus transformed the "Self-Sufficing Perfection" into a "Self-Transcending Fecundity." As for the number of possible beings, Plato answered: *"all* possible kinds." These two answers Lovejoy saw coming together in the "principle of plenitude"—in the notion that all conceptual possibilities must be realized in actuality.[32] Plenitude, continuity, and gradation were the three closely associated "unit-ideas" that were components of the chain of being in Lovejoy's analysis.

The second principle, that of continuity, Lovejoy found emerging in the philosophy of Aristotle, though it could also be "directly deduced" from the Platonic notion of plenitude. The idea of continuity required that if there was a theoretically intermediate type between two natural species, that type must be realized, otherwise there would be gaps in the universe implying a lack of fullness and an inadmissible inadequacy in the Good or Absolute.[33]

The principle of gradation, the third element in the complex of ideas Lovejoy studied, was also rooted in Aristotelian thought. Aristotle had suggested arranging all animals in a single *scala naturae* according to their "degree of perfection," an idea later extended to all things. This hierarchical approach gave rise to the "principal of unilinear gradation" which became attached to the principles of plenitude and continuity.[34]

The union of these three principles produced "the conception of the plan and structure of the world which, through the Middle Ages and down to the late eighteenth century, many philosophers, most men of science, and, indeed, most educated men, were to accept without question—the conception of the universe as a 'Great Chain of Being.' " This complex of ideas, according to Lovejoy, was first "fully organized into a coherent general scheme of things" in Neoplatonism. Plotinus, more clearly than Plato, deduced "the necessity of the existence of this world, with all its manifoldness and imperfection" from the self-sufficient Absolute.[35]

Although Neo-Platonism established an otherworldly conception of the universe, Lovejoy noted that elements of a this-worldly conception remained alive, even during the Middle Ages. Some philosophers as-

[32] *Ibid.*, 45-52.   [33] *Ibid.*, 55-58.   [34] *Ibid.*, 58-59.
[35] *Ibid.*, 59-66.

sumed that there was "a true and intrinsic multiplicity in the divine nature," that the good consisted of "the maximum actualization of variety" and that "the temporal and sensible experience" was therefore good.[36] These ideas, when freed from the dominance of otherworldly philosophy, would provide the basis for a new conception of the universe that celebrated the temporal, diverse world of becoming, the very conception Lovejoy attempted to make intelligible through his philosophy.

When Lovejoy wrote "The Dialectic of Bruno and Spinoza" in 1904, those two philosophers represented for him the culmination of the Neoplatonic dialectic. In *The Great Chain of Being,* he argued that Leibniz and Spinoza most clearly expressed the Chain of Being as the ruling conception of thought. The philosophy of Leibniz revealed the Chain of Being in its "most conspicuous, most determinative and most persuasive" form. However, at the very time that this world view received its grandest exposition, it revealed the paradox inherent in it. Spinoza, according to Lovejoy, had argued that the " 'fullness' " of the temporal world was necessarily grounded in "the timeless immutability" of an absolute Substance. Drawing on his own arguments against the Absolutes of the late nineteenth century, Lovejoy attacked Spinoza. "Being and change simply do not fit into an eternal rational order"— the imperfect world could not be logically deduced from an eternal Absolute.[37] In this criticism of Spinoza, Lovejoy recapitulated his earlier attacks on the eternal and foreshadowed the moral of his history of *The Great Chain of Being.*

Following his discussion of Spinoza, Lovejoy devoted three chapters of his book to the influence of the idea of the Chain of Being in eighteenth-century thought, for it was then that the conception and the three principles of plenitude, continuity, and gradation "attained their widest diffusion and acceptance." Citing examples from philosophy, theology, journalism, poetry (especially Pope's *Essay on Man*), literature, and science he traced the impact of these ideas on man's view of his place in the world, on the belief in optimism, and on the development of eighteenth-century science. The idea of the Great Chain of Being had the effect of making man aware of "his littleness in the scheme of things"—of putting him in his place; however, if that idea promoted a salutary modesty, it also discouraged attempts at reform. Reform might encourage the human species or an individual to rise above the assigned station in the chain. Eighteenth-century optimism, according to Lovejoy, was not simply blind cheerfulness in the face of obvious evil: the principle of plenitude required that goodness lie not in the paucity of evils, but in their multiplicity. A completely good universe, by this reasoning, would not be completely and fully realized. Finally, the idea of the

---

[36] *Ibid.,* 96-98.

[37] *Ibid.,* 144, 154; Arthur O. Lovejoy, "The Obsolescence of the Eternal," *The Philosophical Review,* **18** (1909), 489, 497.

Chain of Being influenced eighteenth-century biology by stimulating a search for missing links, e.g., Monboddo's ape between the lower primates and humans. Ironically, the frustrations and problems encountered in this search would soon help to overthrow the idea of the Chain.[38]

As a philosopher and historian Lovejoy clearly liked the intellectual climate of the eighteenth century and he devoted much time to studying the age.[39] His admiration for the Age of Reason was tempered by his critique of the eighteenth-century reliance on "an absolutely rigid and static scheme of things," the opposite of Lovejoy's own temporalistic and pluralistic universe. Eighteenth-century faith in reason elicited Lovejoy's admiration, but so did "the temporalizing of the Chain of Being" which, to him, was, following Leibniz, "one of the principal happenings in eighteenth-century thought." Toward the end of the century the necessary existence of all beings implied by the Chain of Being came to be seen "not as the inventory but as the program of nature, which is being carried out gradually and exceedingly slowly in the cosmic history." Difficulties and contradictions in the conceptions of plenitude, continuity, and gradation caused the "static and permanently complete Chain of Being" to break down "largely of its own weight."[40]

Lovejoy believed that one "fatal defect" of the principle of plenitude and of optimism was that "it left no room for hope, at least for the world in general or for mankind as a whole." The argument so often employed in the eighteenth century—though satirized by writers like Voltaire (in *Candide*)—held that all the evil in the world was a consequence of the universal good. To increasing numbers of thinkers in the eighteenth century and to Lovejoy "this optimistic paradox was a grotesque mockery." They felt, as did Lovejoy concerning his own efforts at social and political reform, that "it was better to admit the world to be not at present entirely rational, and retain some hope of its amendment, than to conceive of it as perfectly rational—and utterly hopeless." The growing revolt against this absolute rationality did not result in the total disavowal of the Chain of Being. Instead, the Chain was "reinterpreted so as to admit of progress in general, and of a progress of the individual not counterbalanced by deterioration elsewhere." This reinterpretation, in turn, stimulated the revival of the belief that man's destiny was a gradual ascent through all the stages toward, but never reaching, the Perfect Being. Lovejoy believed that this idea of "unending progress" had emerged "as a consequence of reflection upon the principles of plenitude and continuity." The ideas of plenitude and continuity thus contained within themselves "hidden implications" that would destroy the rational world they had supported for so long.[41]

---

[38] Lovejoy, *Chain of Being,* Chapters VI-VIII, esp. 183, 200, 204, 208, 211, 215, 232.

[39] See, for example, [Arthur O. Lovejoy], "Prolegomena," c. 1958, Lovejoy Collection, quoted in Wilson, "Arthur O. Lovejoy," 326.

[40] Lovejoy, *Chain of Being,* 242-45.   [41] *Ibid.,* 245-46, 288.

The tendency of these "hidden implications" of a principle to destroy the *"Zeitgeist* to which [the principle] was meant to minister" was, to Lovejoy, "one of the instructive ironies of the history of ideas." The ideas embodied in the Chain of Being had been used "to justify the belief in the rationality, the perfection, the static completeness, the orderliness and coherency of reality."[42] Such a static conception did provide one means of making the universe intelligible, but the denial of the reality of time proved as unacceptable to many thinkers at the end of the eighteenth century as it would to Lovejoy at the beginning of the twentieth century.[43] The temporalizing of the Chain of Being, which began in the late eighteenth century, pointed toward a new conception of the world that would recognize the reality of time.

Lovejoy went on to show that the early nineteenth-century Romantics had added a belief in the value of diversity to their recognition of temporal reality: the "substitution of what may be called diversitarianism for uniformitarianism more than any other *one* thing has distinguished, both for better and worse, the prevailing assumptions of the mind" of the nineteenth and twentieth centuries.[44] Here, then, lay the foundations of his own philosophical pluralism.

Lovejoy valued the revolt against uniformitarianism, but it was not an unalloyed good. He feared that "the revolt against the standardization of life" could easily become "a revolt against the whole conception of standards." Man, however, possessed "a reason which demands selection, preference, and negation, in conduct and in art." The task of man was not simply to succumb to Romantic diversity but to balance between rational standards and the real diversity of the world:

The delicate and difficult art of life is to find, in each new turn of experience, the *via media* between two extremes: to be catholic without being characterless; to have and apply standards, and yet to be on guard against their desensitizing and stupefying influence, their tendency to blind us to the diversities of concrete situations and to previously unrecognized values; to know when to tolerate, when to embrace, and when to fight.

Though diversity undermined the legitimate value of standards, it remained, nonetheless, "one of the great discoveries of the human mind." And, in so far as the discovery of the value of diversity was the result of the principle of plenitude, Lovejoy thought it "among the most important and potentially the most benign of the manifold consequences" of the Chain of Being.[45]

Lovejoy found in the writings of Friedrich Schelling the culmination of the revolt against the Chain of Being: "the Platonistic scheme of the

---

[42] *Ibid.,* 288-89.

[43] Arthur O. Lovejoy to George Holmes Howison, October 9, 1898, Howison Collection; cf. Philip P. Wiener, "The Central Role of Time in Lovejoy's Philosophy," *Philosophical and Phenomenological Research,* 23 (1963), 480-92.

[44] Lovejoy, *Chain of Being,* 293-94.   [45] *Ibid.,* 312-13.

universe" was "turned upside down" by Schelling who had converted the "originally complete and immutable Chain of Being . . . into a Becoming." Now, even God was identified with the Becoming. In Lovejoy's view, however, this "inversion of the Platonistic scheme of things" did "not alter its essential character." Schelling and much of the subsequent thought of the nineteenth century retained the Platonistic attributes of "insatiable generativeness, the tendency to produce diversity, [and] the necessity of the realization of the greatest possible 'fullness' of being." But things had, nevertheless, changed radically: "the generativeness is now that of an insufficiency striving unconsciously for richer and more various being; and the fullness is not the permanent character but the flying goal of the whole of things."[46]

With his discussion of Schelling and the discovery of this new and more intelligible account of the universe, Lovejoy brought his history of the Chain of Being to a close. There remained to be told only the moral of this history of man's quest for intelligibility; the last chapter, after all, was entitled "The Outcome of the History and Its Moral."

Why should Arthur O. Lovejoy, renowned for his rational and discriminating scholarship, conclude his major work in the history of ideas with a moral? That he did so suggests that the moral held great significance for him, that his history of the Chain of Being was more than an exercise in scholarship. The chief moral of the Great Chain of Being was the same as what he had outlined at the conclusion of "The Dialectic of Bruno and Spinoza" some thirty years earlier, viz., that as long as one assumed "the existence of this world of temporal and imperfect creatures" to be a "genuine good" then "the otherworldly Idea of a Good," the ideas embodied in the Chain of Being, must be "the idea of a spurious good." Furthermore, "an Absolute which is self-sufficient and forever perfect and complete cannot be identified with a God related to and manifested in a world of temporal becoming and alteration." As Lovejoy had argued in "The Obsolescence of the Eternal" (1909), the eternal was no longer necessary. The history of the Chain of Being, then, "in so far as that idea presupposed such a complete rational intelligibility of the world" was "the history of a failure," but one with "an instructive negative outcome." It revealed "the hypothesis of the absolute rationality of the cosmos to be unbelievable" because it conflicted with "one immense fact," "the fact that existence as we experience it is temporal." Finally, this history revealed "that rationality, when conceived as complete, as excluding all arbitrariness, becomes itself a kind of irrationality." The thinkers of the Enlightenment were too rational, for the "complete realization of all the possibles" excluded "any limiting and selective principle."[47]

[46] *Ibid.,* 325-26.
[47] *Ibid.,* 327-29, 331; see also, Lovejoy, "The Obsolescence of The Eternal," 497, 501-02.

In his *Great Chain of Being* Lovejoy not only traced the historical antecedents of that previous idea, but also discovered a historical justification for his own religious and philosophical beliefs. Underlying his philosophical enterprise was his assumption that "an actual world given as diverse is a world full of differences requiring to be united and harmonized; it is a world demanding to be made intelligible."[48] After 1900, Lovejoy found a large measure of the intelligibility he sought by applying his conceptions of a pluralistic and temporalistic universe, epistemological and psychophysical dualism, and the principles of reason. The actual world was "a contingent world" but that basic truth allowed men to choose rationally "among the infinity of possibles."[49] Without the legacy of the idea of the Great Chain of Being Lovejoy would not have confronted the seeming chaos of a diverse, non-rational world, but neither would he have found his way toward rendering it completely intelligible.

Muhlenberg College.

[48] Lovejoy, "Concluding Criticisms," 6-8.   [49] Lovejoy, *Chain of Being,* 332.

Chapter VIII.b

ARTHUR O. LOVEJOY AND THE EMERGENCE OF NOVELTY

By Kathleen E. Duffin

In the methodological prologue to *The Great Chain of Being*, A. O. Lovejoy urges historians of ideas to include in their scope of interest a search for the implicit and explicit assumptions, or *"unconscious mental habits,"* of an individual, a generation, or an era.[1] Lovejoy turns to the elusive concept of "metaphysical pathos" in order to illuminate the animating impulses of individual, generational, and epochal thought-habits: there are minds that simplify and minds that diversify; those that migrate perpetually toward the esoteric and those that crave the utterly comprehensible. The relative abundance of different casts of mind determines to a great extent the philosophical climate of an age. Lovejoy claims that such innate propensities for particular kinds of thinking are a basic subject matter for intellectual history. They guide an individual philosopher's logic and determine the popularity of different approaches in different eras.

Philip P. Wiener has pointed out that Lovejoy's reliance on the "congenital diversity of types of human nature" to explain the historically divergent views of philosophical schools is rather anomalous for in his own philosophy he insists on the central position of temporal processes. A more consistent "temporalist" position would have to "challenge the fixity of types of human nature and even, as C. S. Peirce did, deny the absolute invariability of the laws of nature."[2] Lovejoy's particular concept of historical change may have something to do with the anomaly. As an ardent supporter of the doctrine of emergent evolution, Lovejoy stresses the appearance of entirely new qualities not logically derivable from what has preceded them. Thus significant evolutionary change is effected by leaps or chance mutations; Lovejoy generally avoids the term "mutation" and prefers "novelty" instead. For Lovejoy, then, the most distinctive feature of significant change is not continuity. His concept of evolution is reflected in his notion of "fixed" beliefs: human nature *is* subject to change, but significant change is accomplished by virtually inexplicable shifts in metaphysical pathos, and not by gradual modification. While the notion of innate proclivities does not necessarily indicate the intrusion of the irrational into the bedrock of all intellectual endeavor, it does imply that the "nonsystematic" aspects of philosophy deserve careful attention. Lovejoy's advocacy of a genetic method of historical analysis and his particular brand of temporalism are both based upon his concept of an emergent evolutionary process.

His work serves to remind us that it is not only as self-contained and formal structures that philosophical doctrines are factors in intellectual history; certain basic assumptions and inclinations in Lovejoy's own philosophy

---

[1] Arthur O. Lovejoy, *The Great Chain of Being* (Cambridge, 1936), 7.
[2] Philip P. Wiener, "The Central Role of Time in Lovejoy's Philosophy," *Philosophy and Phenomenological Research* **23** (1963), 491.

may be considered as forming a metaphysical pathos of his own, especially in his conception of emergent evolution. In line with Lovejoy's legitimation of the philosophical search for such underlying assumptions, I wish to turn back upon Lovejoy his concept of a predisposing "metaphysical pathos," and thus highlight a basic animus of his thought. Isolating this important thread can perhaps contribute to a greater understanding of Lovejoy's own distinctive approach to the history of ideas.

The nature of Lovejoy's analytical method in historiography—the tracing back of "unit ideas" to their historical points of origin—might lead one to suspect that Lovejoy's work partakes of the metaphysical pathos of excessive concern for uniformity and continuity. Nothing could be further from the truth. The excessive urge to simplify and to unify is often the target of his trenchant criticism. While he maintains, for example, that the aim of science is to look for continuity and identity in the natural world, it is not, he asserts, the duty of philosophy to "assume *a priori* that nature must to an indefinite degree lend itself to the gratification of this ambition."[3] Lovejoy analyzes seemingly uniform concepts and theories into their diverse components. Diversity, the true state of affairs, is obscured by a deceptive univocality; continuity is often imposed upon the situation from without. Lovejoy's staunch dualism in his theory of knowledge, his fundamental anti-reductionism in the life sciences, and his historical study of pre-Darwinian evolutionary ideas all reflect his acceptance of discontinuity as an ever-present feature of the world. In *The Great Chain of Being* he traces a process of ideational change: the movement from static conceptions of being to temporal conceptions of becoming. His historical work can be viewed as a descriptive account of prescriptive philosophical tenets ascribed to by Lovejoy himself, for he clearly believes in the superiority of philosophies that celebrate the temporal and thus firmly deny the existence of eternal and absolute realities of any kind. Temporal diversity results from the emergence of novelty in the evolutionary process. Despite a formal methodology that stresses the pervasive domination of unit ideas and the mere juxtaposition of pre-existing elements, intellectual history in the Lovejovian sense has as part of its task the eventual determination of the nature of intellectual change:

> . . . it is a part of the eventual task of the history of ideas to apply its own distinctive analytic method in the attempt to understand how *new* beliefs and intellectual fashions are introduced and diffused, to help to elucidate the psychological character of the processes by which changes in the vogue and influence of ideas have come about; to make clear, if possible, how conceptions dominant, or extensively prevalent, in one generation lose their hold upon men's minds and give place to others.[4]

Philip P. Wiener provides another insight into Lovejoy's philosophy by stressing the close relationship between the latter's theory of knowledge as formulated in *The Revolt Against Dualism,* and his concern with evolutionary ideas.[5] In Lovejoy's conception of "temporalistic pluralism," he

---

[3] Arthur O. Lovejoy, "The Meanings of 'Emergence' and its Modes," *Proceedings of the 6th International Congress of Philosophy* (New York, 1927), 27.

[4] A. O. Lovejoy, *Great Chain*, 20.

[5] Philip P. Wiener, "Lovejoy's Role in American Philosophy," in *Studies in Intellectual History,* ed. George Boas (Baltimore, 1953), 165.

seeks to expound a philosophy that comes to terms with change. A controversial aspect of his method in intellectual history is his removal of venerated figures from their pedestals, and the revelation of an entire corps of secondary thinkers who appear to be retrospectively reflecting or anticipating major discoveries and achievements. By concentrating on a program that seems to minimize the importance of the seemingly novel, Lovejoy does not neglect the importance of true novelty in intellectual history. He merely concedes its rarity. His distaste for scholastic Aristotelianism centers upon its intrinsically static character.[6] A static conception of the universe is not only an inaccurate one, according to Lovejoy, but a pessimistic one. Progress is not considered by Lovejoy to be a natural concomitant of evolution but the possibility of change in the natural world and of perfectibility are cited by him as reasons for hope.

Lovejoy's concern with the temporal and his attendant emphasis upon the emergence of the utterly new in a discontinuous world appear on four related levels. (1) On the epistemological level he opposes all forms of postulated eternal realities; he is concerned about the very possibility of knowledge, and believes that ideas exist apart from the material world although emergent from it; and he has a critical realistic belief in the existence of a world outside the mind. (2) On the ontological level he argues for the discontinuity of nature, or more precisely, he defends a form of vitalism that stresses the unique aspects of the emergence of life, humans, and ultimately, ideas in the natural world. (3) On the causal level Lovejoy asserts that there is an essential discontinuity between the subject matters of disciplines; he maintains that laws are not necessarily related logically, and that causality itself has been misconstrued in a priori fashion to imply the inclusion of all qualites of the effect in the cause. (4) On the historical level, Lovejoy chooses discontinuity and change as the subject matter of his own investigations, by concentrating upon evolutionary theory. By examining Lovejoy's thought on each of these levels, it may be possible to elucidate another level, the methodological, and to see how Lovejoy's particular interest in the emergence of novelty affected his approach in several areas.

That Lovejoy's concern with the temporal afforded support for his epistemological dualism is a fact already discussed by Wiener and others. Knowing, as a phenomenon with which we have intimate acquaintance, is possessed of intentionality, and "self-transcendent reference"; in other words, knowing implies the presence, within our own experience, of entities which must be simultaneously conceived as existing *outside* of experience. The possibility of "intertemporal cognition" is evidence in favor of Lovejoy's particular form of dualism.[7] "To all theories about the nature of reality or of knowledge I early began to apply one touchstone before any other— that of congruence with the most indubitable fact of our experience, namely, that experience itself is temporal."[8] It was this predisposition that set Love-

---

[6] John Herman Randall, Jr., "Arthur O. Lovejoy and the History of Ideas," *Philosophy and Phenomenological Research,* **23** (1963), 477.

[7] A. O. Lovejoy, *The Revolt Against Dualism* (LaSalle, 1930), 303-21.

[8] A. O. Lovejoy, "A Temporalistic Realism," in *Contemporary American Philosophy: Personal Statements,* eds. George P. Adams and William P. Montague 2 vols. (New York, 1930, 1962), II, 87.

joy apart from many of his philosophic contemporaries. The dominant meta-physical position in American universities at the turn of the century could be termed "idealistic," which Lovejoy defines as maintaining that "to be real, or even barely to exist, is to fall within sentience; sentient experience, in short, is reality, and what is not this is not real."[9] Gradual disillusionment with that position, according to Lovejoy, resulted in a move toward the polar viewpoint that all experience carries with it the "extra-mentality" of its object. Lovejoy finds neither extreme philosophically compelling, and asserts that " 'reality' may be of a mixed character, and that the 'objects' apprehended in sensory or other experience may be in some cases purely 'mental' and in others 'extra-mental'."[10] The contemporary philosophical de-bate exhibited, for him, "the entirely gratuitous dilemma of an absolute idealism or an absolute realism."[11]

The primary feature of Lovejoy's philosophy is that no assertion of any "supra-temporal" realm of being can be reconciled with the fact that "we mortals *live*—that is, have a transitive, perpetually lapsing and yet continuing mode of being under the form of time, and with what is implied even by the theory of eternal realities itself—namely, that the knowing of such realities by us occurs in time."[12] Lovejoy rejects all systems that seek to reconcile the eternal and temporal realms, as, for example, in the conciliation offered by George Holmes Howison. The latter's professed ethic of personal idealism seeks to maintain both the temporal and eternal realms, postulating no "traffic" between them, but asserting that somehow the temporal tends to move toward the static perfection of the eternal.[13] Such a reconciliation tries to preserve some semblance of the absolute, separate from temporal things. Lovejoy finds fault with the resultant fatalism of such doctrines, for they postulate an end toward which everything is moving and assert that there is a greater perfection beyond this world. Lovejoy, in 1916, praised Josiah Royce for not succumbing to the moral indifference of the Absolute in most "idealist" systems. Royce, he claims in a eulogizing paragraph, felt, despite his idealism: "Intolerable wrongs done in the order of time seemed. . . , in truth, no whit less intolerable when looked upon as necessary elements in an order transcending time."[14] For Lovejoy, idealism was merely a way-station in philosophy's process of maturation: "The eternal is, then, I think, the characteristic but not necessarily incorrigible distemper of ado-lescent metaphysics."[15]

In his 1909 article, "The Obsolescence of the Eternal," Lovejoy draws a clear sketch of the concept of evolution that stands behind his repudiation of the eternal in all of its philosophical guises. His early statement appeared, significantly, during the semi-centennial of the publication of *The Origin of Species,* and reflected an attempt to separate two grand concepts of nine-teenth-century thought: Kantian idealism and the scientific formulation of evolutionary theory. In Lovejoy's opinion, these two philosophical strands

---

[9] *Ibid.,* 85, quoting Bradley.   [10] *Ibid.,* 86.   [11] *Ibid.*   [12] *Ibid.,* 88.

[13] A. O. Lovejoy, *Bergson and Romantic Evolutionism* (Berkeley, 1914), 47-50.

[14] A. O. Lovejoy, "On Some Conditions of Progress in Philosophical Inquiry," *Philosophical Review*, 26 (1917), 125.

[15] A. O. Lovejoy, "The Obsolescence of the Eternal," *Philosophical Review*, 18 (1909). 501.

exhibit but a superficial harmony and are bound to come into opposition. An evolutionary world-view would eventually triumph in philosophy, as it had in science, but before that would come to pass, the confusions inherent in the evolutionary process itself would have to be resolved. The Kantian position implies that the temporal aspect of the world stressed in evolution is but a secondary one. Lovejoy argues that evolutionary thought cannot be superimposed upon a species of eternalism without inconsistency.

Lovejoy's own definition of evolution is a very general one, revealing the fact that he opposes more specific, "mechanistic" descriptions of the process because he equates them with an unacceptable determinism. He defines evolution as "a process of real temporal Becoming; and by real Becoming I desire to imply not only change, but also the emergence into existence, at diverse moments, of new items of reality which did not previously exist and which, therefore, by their appearance bring an actual augmentation of the total content of the universe."[16] Thus temporality and the evolutionary process are integrally bound up with the appearance of new entities: the emergence of novelty. No concept of the qualitative or quantitative constancy of the universe, implied in various eternalist doctrines, can be consistent with such an evolutionary process. Lovejoy's temporally-based challenge to the idealist edifice is indirect: "The direct argument for the existence of this idealistic eternal we shall not challenge; we shall only inquire whether that eternal can conceivably be correlated in any logically consistent or practically pertinent way with the empirically undeniable existence of the temporal and the evolving."[17]

Lovejoy qualifies his view by limiting it to a nonmechanistic version: "That 'evolution' follows as a natural implication from the mechanistic conception of the physical world seems to be assumed by many as an obvious commonplace. But it is not difficult to show that in reality the notion of evolution and the notion of a closed mechanical system are inherently incompatible."[18] Lovejoy seeks to discredit the concept of the perfect Laplacean calculator; perfect foreknowledge of all the particles in the universe would not permit the prediction of new complexes, for "there will therewith pop into existence something, *other than that arrangement merely defined as such,* which was not in the universe at all at the preceding moment."[19] The sum total of entities in the Lovejovian universe cannot remain the same, and such an entity as consciousness itself must have appeared "quite literally out of nothing."[20] The Kantian realm of the eternal is incompatible with the "unexpected universe" that Lovejoy sees as coincident with open-ended evolution. We must trust our intuitive perception of the reality of temporal transition; any difficulties in conceiving the absence of an eternal realm prove only the "inability of the principles governing our processes of conceptual thinking quite to cover or exhaust the whole nature of reality."[21]

This stress upon the actual human experience of temporal transition is the basic structure upon which Lovejoy builds his conception of the possi-

---

[16] *Ibid.,* 482.   [17] *Ibid.,* 484.
[18] *Ibid.,* 485.   [19] *Ibid.,* 487.   [20] *Ibid.,* 488.
[21] A. O. Lovejoy, "The Place of the Time Problem in Contemporary Philosophy," *Journal of Philosophy,* 7 (1910), 693.

bility of knowledge, especially of past and future events. It is in accounting for the possibility of such knowledge transcending immediate experience that Lovejoy develops his own form of epistemological dualism. The entire enterprise of knowledge is indirect: a system where a present idea about a past event is distinct from the past event itself. Because Lovejoy does not define knowledge as congruent with experience itself, a fundamental discontinuity between the past and the present does not negate the possibility of knowledge. Thus the problem of knowledge of the past is not confined to history: all disciplines are enmeshed in the same anomaly of knowledge, for they "rest upon the postulate of the reality of past events and of the possibility of now knowing something of what they were—be they only the operations performed at an earlier moment of an experiment which a physicist is now conducting, or the results of the experiments of his predecessors."[22]

Lovejoy's theory of knowledge asserts that knowledge itself contains an unbridgeable chasm. It is an event of a highly anomalous sort when considered from the viewpoint of physical and biological science alike; a cognitive animal can be affected by events that have already occurred, and by events that have not yet taken place. Thus an organism exists that is itself physical, yet capable of having an entity in its experience that cannot be described as part of the physical world; this is the "lesser anomaly of knowledge."[23] An even greater anomaly is that knowing seems to entail having to do with entities that do not coexist with the perceiving organism. How can a physical being have something to do with something that does not exist at all as a reality contemporaneous with the act of knowing? If we do grant that something that is in some way a *simulacrum* of the absent event is present, we cannot escape the former or lesser anomaly of knowledge, namely, that mediating ideas are indeed psychical entities, and that an animal has appeared during the course of evolution that can produce such "intangible" and "imponderable" secretions.[24]

Instead of denying the chasm between physical and psychical entities, Lovejoy acknowledges it to be a product of the evolutionary process. That process is "creative" and characterized by "saltatory innovations" of which conciousness itself is one.[25] We can escape the greater anomaly of knowledge by accepting the lesser: the occurrence of specifically mental entities in nature.[26] Constrained by the limits of temporal existence, we know the past vicariously by means of existent representative ideas, themselves a product of evolution. To attempt an escape from the resultant implication of psychophysical dualism "is to invest one's doctrine with the sort of metaphysical pathos which always attaches to assertions of the inseparability of things."[27]

Thus far we have delineated three major features of Lovejoy's thought that have grown out of his belief in the primacy of temporal experience and the emergence of novelty as a product of evolution: the

[22] A. O. Lovejoy, "Present Standpoints and Past History," *Journal of Philosophy*, **36** (1939), 487.

[23] A. O. Lovejoy, "The Anomaly of Knowledge," *University of California Publications in Philosophy*, 4 (1923), 3-43.

[24] *Ibid.*, 15-22.   [25] *Ibid.*, 32.   [26] *Ibid.*, 43.

[27] A. O. Lovejoy, "Pastness and Transcendence," *Journal of Philosophy*, **21** (1924), 608.

revolt against eternals; a concern with viewing the past as distinct from the present and the attendant epistemological considerations of this view; and the theory of representative ideas, themselves an emergent in the evolutionary process. In *The Revolt Against Dualism,* the realist implications of Lovejoy's temporalism are set out. Lovejoy's dualistic realism asserts a belief in "the existence of a real and at least in some measure knowable physical world."[28] For "the history of man's reflective experience gives some ground for the surmise that there are congenital diversities among human minds" as regards the relative persuasiveness of the critical realist position.[29] What reasons, other than the purely instinctual, does Lovejoy offer as support for a belief in a world of existing particulars that are *not* human ideas? Here, the first "essential" of an object's physicality has to do with the time of its existence; the belief in "real" objects helps us regard the universe as more coherent than sense-experience would tend to indicate, and consists in their filling "the temporal gaps between actual perceptions. The 'independence' of a thing means, concretely, its continued existence, or the continuance of a connected series of events of which it is a member, at times when it is not being attended to. . . ."[30] For Lovejoy, then, the starting point of the argument for physical realism "is the plain man's normal and reasonable belief that the processes of nature do not stop when he stops noticing them."[31] Because the realist belief is at base "a natural and almost universal prejudice of mankind," the burden of proof rests with those who demand that it be abandoned.[32]

Lovejoy brings his *Revolt Against Dualism* to a close by a retelling of the *Timaeus* creation myth as Plato might have recast it "if he had been enough of an evolutionist to conceive of the production of living creatures as proceeding from lower to higher, and if he had been more definitely mindful of the problem of the character and genesis of natural knowledge."[33] The ability to transcend the present is an ability that makes its "radically discontinuous" appearance along with man, in the natural order. "What is needful is that the nature which belongs to one region of being shall be not only reproduced in another, nor merely, when so reproduced, be beheld by a creature having its existence in that other region, but . . . shall be reproduced and beheld as if present in the region in which it first existed, and as belonging to a thing which had or has its being there; only so can any creature see another as being another, and the mutual blindness of the parts be in a certain measure overcome."[34] Lovejoy's allegory is a fitting reflection upon the centrality of emergence; discontinuity is an inevitable by-product of change, and Lovejoy's ideas about the very structure of knowing come to terms with it.

Lovejoy's thoughts about the evolutionary process from which we ourselves have emerged give greater insight into his thoughts about emergent evolution in general. His recognition of the problem of discontinuity determines the way in which he approaches the problem of life. The Darwinian formulation of evolution provided a mechanism for change comprised of two essential features whose roles were differently stressed in different philos-

---

[28] Lovejoy, *Revolt Against Dualism,* 259.
[30] *Ibid.,* 267. [31] *Ibid.,* 268.
[33] *Ibid.,* 319-320.

[29] *Ibid.,* 258.
[32] *Ibid.,* 297.
[34] *Ibid.,* 321.

ophies: the production of variation, and the action of natural selection upon that variation. The inherently random nature of available variation was emphasized by James and Peirce, who sought to maintain a large element of "indeterminism" in their respective philosophies.[55] The growing supremacy of evolutionary thought left philosophers with three fundamental choices: they could continue with an older legacy of evolutionary thought, namely, the idea that progress was evolution's inevitable concomitant; they could banish ideals of all sorts from science, including the ideal of progress; or they could admit the probabilistic status of all scientific laws and seek elsewhere for support of the human hope for "progressive" change.[35] Lovejoy chose a different position: in his conception of the emergence of novelty, one can find something of a replacement for the Absolute of conventionally idealist evolutionary schemes such as that of Schelling, although progress is not inevitable in Lovejoy's conception of emergent evolution. Still, the fact remains that in much of his discussion of "novelty" Lovejoy concentrates on the *possibility* of progress rather than of "regression." The human hope for progressive change is still accommodated within a scientific perspective.

In Lovejoy's lectures on Bergson we find more extensive discussion of ideas central to the theme of emergent evolution. Bergson's system, expounded in *L'Evolution Créatrice* (1907) provides for an indeterminate yet progressive evolutionary process. Bergson examines and finds wanting contemporary interpretations of the evolutionary process with their respective emphases upon change via small increments or via mutations. The intricacy of the results of the evolutionary process seems to defy the randomness of the available variation. While Lovejoy casts a critical eye on parts of Bergson's scheme of creative evolution, he finds that much of what Bergson expresses echoes his own ideas about the inadequacy of idealist thought, and the supremacy of the temporal. Lovejoy recognizes in Bergson's thought an apotheosis of the temporalist quarrel with idealist tenets. He sees Bergsonianism as a "condition" of the times as well as a self-contained philosophy; thus Bergson's speculations have, for that reason, "an importance which is not necessarily dependent upon, nor proportional to, their logical value."[36] Bergson's definition of creative evolution is in certain respects similar to Lovejoy's, i.e., "a process in which genuinely new reality is ever coming to birth, in which the universe is not merely altered and rearranged, but positively augmented and enriched with fresh and unprecedented and unpredictable types of being and novel potencies of action, undeducible from any so-called 'laws of nature' manifested in antecedent stages of cosmic history."[37] Lovejoy, however, seeks to prove that Bergson's emphasis upon the "indivisibility" of time would not be compatible with the very creativity of the evolutionary process that he postulates. A truly emergent evolution can only take place in a time scheme in which later moments are truly external to earlier ones. Bergson's elaboration upon the concept of *la durée* is thus simply an ingenious substitution of indivisibility for the formerly expunged concept of the eternal.[38]

[35] Philip P. Wiener, *Evolution and the Founders of Pragmatism* (Cambridge, 1949), 124.

[36] Lovejoy, *Bergson*, 7.   [37] *Ibid.*, 7.   [38] *Ibid.*, 11.

Bergson's radicalism, for Lovejoy, lies precisely in Bergson's affirmation not only of the reality of temporal experience, but of its dynamic efficacy. Bergson accomplishes the substitution of *se faisant* for *tout fait.* "the idea of a reality which is actually and literally making itself moment by moment as it goes along, in place of the idea of a reality which—even if it is supposed to be temporally and successively experienced—is yet regarded as already *made.*"[39] Bergson advocates a radical indeterminism that forever lays to rest explicitly end-directed conceptions of evolutionary change, and his notion of creative emergence confirms the capacity of each moment to produce novel entities not contained in antecedent states that "could not have been forseen even by one who had analyzed those states beforehand down to the last bit of *then* present content which belonged to them."[40] The past may have a role in shaping what is to come, and in any complex may account for the bulk of seeming novelty, but the fact of genuine novelty, small though it may be, creates a true disjunction between past and present. This is similar to Lovejoy's own vision: a realm where indeterminacy can dwell contentedly without necessitating a radical excision of all notions of causality.

The Bergsonian element that ensures the continuation of the creative process is the *élan vital,* a veritable counterpart of the Schopenhauerian will-to-live. Because it is not assured that in Bergson's system the *élan* will indeed triumph over material elements antithetical to change, Lovejoy finds his system "pessimistic." To make Bergson consistent, Lovejoy argues, one would have to assume that matter itself manifests a similar impulse to "forge ahead." Such a more consistent form of Bergsonian thought revives aspects of evolutionary thought that antedate the alliance of mechanism and evolution in the nineteenth century.[41] The Darwinian or mechanistic conception of evolution, or what was popularized as such, implies, in Lovejoy's words, waste, disharmony, and cruelty on a "monstrous" scale: a perpetual cycle in which all is trapped. The less mechanistic strain of what could be termed "Schellingism" in Bergson, is one that appeals in many ways to Lovejoy. The assumption that given events in time are fully explicable as effects of prior events implies that "it is really the same old atoms shuffling about in accordance with the same old laws," that history is merely the unfolding of a pre-determined plan, and that human volition in any form is ultimately insignificant.[42] Bergson's key point is that "there remains at every moment a *marginal* freedom; each present adds *something* which the past knew not of; and therefore the future cannot be assumed to be completely predictable."[43]

Lovejoy's own beliefs about creative emergence in evolution are given expression in writings that deal specifically with emergent evolution. In two articles published in *Science,* in 1911, Lovejoy seeks to analyze the concept of vitalism in biology. While he maintains that he is merely presenting such an analysis and not promulgating a particular viewpoint, it is evident that his own affinities lie with those who assert, in some manner, the autonomy of laws governing living things. Vitalism, as Lovejoy defines it, is the belief that the apparent discontinuity between the inorganic and the organic worlds is not due to our temporary ignorance of connections but is a fundamental

[39] *Ibid.,* 15.   [40] *Ibid.,* 16.   [41] *Ibid.,* 28.

[42] A. O. Lovejoy, *The Reason, The Understanding, and Time* (Baltimore, 1961), 150.   [43] *Ibid.,* 162.

reality. Lovejoy relates this basic form of vitalism to beliefs in the autonomy of the life sciences, and "pluralism" in general. The vitalist thus asserts the doctrine of "logical discontinuity" while maintaining that "this discontinuity does not necessarily imply any breach of the principles of causal uniformity."[44]

Lovejoy's own position is more clearly stated in his article of 1924, "The Discontinuities of Evolution": ". . . the evolutional process, the sequence of temporal changes constituting, for example, the total history of our solar system from nebula to man, is not, properly speaking, continuous," for "it does indeed, in certain respects, show breaks or 'chasms'," and "it exhibits the 'emergence' from time to time of absolute novelties, discontinuous variations in no way deducible from, or explicable by, any characters of the prior members of the series."[45] Lovejoy buttresses his position with evidence of new perspectives within the biological sciences themselves, mentioning E. B. Wilson's *The Cell in Development and Heredity* (1909) and J. B. S. Haldane's *Mechanism, Life and Personality* (1923) as examples of contemporary dissatisfaction with mechanistic views of life within the biological community itself. The relative importance of discontinuity in evolution and the concomitant emergence of novelty was a much-debated issue in scientific circles in the first two decades of the twentieth century. C. Lloyd Morgan's *Emergent Evolution* (1923) was a focal point in this debate: emergent evolution stressed the incoming of the "new." "Emergent" was initially employed by G. H. Lewes in *Problems of Life and Mind* (1875), where he contrasts it with "resultant," the former indicating an "unpredictable" relationship of effects to causes, and the latter, a predictable one. It is ultimately to J. S. Mill's discussion of "heteropathic laws" in the *System of Logic* (1843), that Lloyd Morgan traces the concept of emergent entities in nature.[46] The mechanistic assumption of "total predictability" was being weakened by current developments in genetics.[47] Such events within biology led Lovejoy to maintain: "Certainly when any competent physiologist can write in this fashion, a philosopher may legitimately believe that there is at least some presumption, in the present state of our knowledge, against the assertion of the continuity of the laws of the organic and the inorganic—that the bridging of this chasm is not only unachieved but improbable."[48] Lovejoy goes on to state the fundamental position of the emergent evolutionist: "The union of the conception of evolution with the conception of reality as a complex of which all the parts are theoretically deducible from a very small number of relatively simple laws of the redistribution of a quantitatively invariable sum of matter and of energy—this union the 'emergent evolutionist,' if I may call him so for

[44] A. O. Lovejoy, "The Meaning of Vitalism," *Science,* 33 (1911), 612; see also, Lovejoy, "The Import of Vitalism," *Science,* 34 (1911), 75-80.

[45] A. O. Lovejoy, "The Discontinuities of Evolution," *University of California Publications in Philosophy,* 5 (1924), 175.

[46] C. Lloyd Morgan, *Emergent Evolution* (London, 1923), 1-3.

[47] H. Wildon Carr, "Life and Matter," *Proceedings of the 6th International Congress of Philosophy* (New York, 1927), 19.

[48] A. O. Lovejoy, "Discontinuities," 205-06. Lovejoy here refers to Haldane's rejection of a "mechanistic" theory of heredity, and not specifically to Carr, although the later holds a similar position.

short, now declares to be a *mésalliance,* of which the progeny are hybrid monsters incapable of survival."[49] Emergent evolution thus considers "as curious aberrations of great scientific minds the ingenious hypotheses which have been devised solely in order to avoid admitting the spontaneous generation of life at some remote past juncture in stellar evolution."[50] The urge to unify and to simplify militates against non-reductionist interpretations of biological experiments: Lovejoy also asserts that some of the evidence put forth in biology for "non-vitalist" positions, such as Loeb's achievement of the artificial fertilization of the sea urchin, is inadequate because the results can equally be construed as demonstrating that the critical juncture of discontinuity has merely been successfully reproduced by human intervention.[51] Lovejoy's own question remains: "Is there any real emergence of novelty, any creative evolution, in the dynamic or executive part of nature, in the modes of behaviour of those entities which physical science regards as having been longest upon the cosmic scene and of which our bodies consist?"[52] The answer is relevant, according to Lovejoy, not only to our interpretation of biological phenomena, but to philosophy itself: "The doctrine of emergent evolution is a revolt of temporalistic, and usually realistic, philosophers against . . . features of the older evolutionism."[53]

Lovejoy defines "novelty" in three ways: the appearance of qualities not previously found in a system, at certain points in its history; the appearance of types of objects, or events not previously found; the appearance of new laws or modes of action not previously exemplified.[54] It is Lovejoy's argument that all of these criteria can be fulfilled in our observations of many aspects of the natural world. He amplifies his opinions in perhaps his most complete statement on emergent evolution, "The Meanings of 'Emergence' and its Modes," a paper delivered to the International Congress of Philosophy in 1926, in a symposium on "The Hypothesis of Emergent Evolution, its Meaning and the Present State of the Argument Concerning It." Rather than defend the acausal nature of the emergent viewpoint, Lovejoy attacks the currently accepted definition of "causal" as a prejudice that contradicts experience. He opposes the position that the causal relation must be conceived as "rationally explanatory."[55] It is necessary that we modify our logic on the basis of the gaps we observe in nature. General antipathy toward the notion of "an absolute epigenesis" (the term Lovejoy finds more agreeable in some senses than "emergence") can be traced to the hampering belief that "a cause . . . does not 'account for' its effect, unless the effect is a thing which the eye of reason could somehow discern *in* the cause, upon a sufficiently thorough analysis."[56]

Lovejoy characteristically provides an historical perspective on the rise of this particular viewpoint and points to the seventeenth century as the age ushering in a view of natural events as mere combinations or rearrangements of pre-existing entities of invariant quantity. Such is the philosophical heritage of biological concepts of preformation, and the genesis of the "mechanist" conception of causality that Lovejoy seeks to repudiate. The problem whether

---

[49] *Ibid.,* 177. [50] *Ibid.,* 207. [51] *Ibid.,* 206.
[52] *Ibid.,* 182. [53] *Ibid.,* 177. [54] *Ibid.,* 178.
[55] A. O. Lovejoy, "Meanings of 'Emergence,'" 20. [56] *Ibid.*

our own experience seems to contradict the "causal" assumption is disposed of, says Lovejoy, by too neatly relegating all of the data of experience to the "subjective" realm, i.e., the physical world is purged of anything that does not seem to fit an *apriori* causal framework.[57]

Emergence, as Lovejoy defines it, signifies "any process in which there appear effects that, in some one or more of several ways yet to be specified, fail to conform to the maxim that "there cannot be in the consequent anything more than, or different in nature from, that which was in the antecedent."[58] Lovejoy's "ways yet to be specified" are five in number: instances of some general type of change which are not describable or predictable by laws sufficient to cover such cases in the antecedent; the appearance of new qualities in entities that were already present in the antecedent; the appearance of entities not having all the essential characteristics of their counterparts in the antecedent; the appearance of an event, a type of event "irreducibly different in kind" from any in the antecedent, and having distinctive characteristics of their own; the existence of a greater number of instances of one or more types of "prime entity" common to both the antecedent and the subsequent states, but not explicable by the transfer of those additional entities from outside the system.[59] The first criterion is what Lovejoy terms a "functional" one, and it presents the most difficulties for those seeking to establish the possibility of a complete unification of science.[60]

This application of the concept of emergence to scientific laws themselves has it antithesis in Henri Poincaré's assertion that "we can know nothing of the past, except under the condition that it is admitted that laws have not changed. If we admit this, the question of an evolution of laws cannot arise. If we do not admit it, that question, like all the others relating to the past, becomes insoluble."[61] Lovejoy with his firm belief in the manifestation of temporal diversity, states that we must not confuse "heuristic" devices with statements of fact; that science has a stake in viewing everything as capable of simple causal formation with intrinsic consistency does not mean that such an assumption should be adopted by the philosopher as well.[62]

Lovejoy's other four criteria for the emergence of novelty are termed "existential"; while the causal prejudice grates most sharply against admitting the emergence of "laws," the emergence of entities is still opposed by the very same argument. The entire concept of emergence can be divided in another way: a concept of "general" emergence and one of "specific" emergence. Lovejoy argues that the former is more often opposed than the latter, primarily because specific instances of "gaps" and novelties are more amenable to empirical observation. The former assumption is something of a leap of faith.[63] Such an overall scheme of emergence "asserts a genuine progressiveness in the cosmical processes—in the sense, at least, of an increase of versatility in nature's fundamental activities—as the presupposition of the otherwise incomprehensible diversification of her products and the ascending scale of *their* powers."[64]

[57] *Ibid.*, 21.
[58] *Ibid.*, 22.
[59] *Ibid.*, 27.
[60] *Ibid.*
[61] *Idem*, "Discontinuities," 193.
[62] A. O. Lovejoy, "Meanings of 'Emergence,' " 27.
[63] *Ibid.*, 25.
[64] Lovejoy, "Discontinuities," 195.

Lovejoy claims that preformational concepts that have been opposed to emergence are not only contradictory of experience, but bereft of hope, entailing a form of the staticism Lovejoy finds pessimistic in Aristotelian concepts. For Lovejoy, preformational notions are not only prejudices, but unfortunate ones: "Metaphysical preformationism" in any of its guises has "less edifying and cheering implications than are sometimes attributed to it."[65] Any such doctrine would imply, according to Lovejoy, that "the whole movement and travail of the creation is but a barren shuffling-about of the same pieces; an increase or ascent in one region must be simultaneously compensated by an equivalent decrease or decline elsewhere."[66] The possibility of the emergence of novelty replaces what is clearly a "barren" scheme to Lovejoy by one in which we can continue to expect the unexpected.

Attempts to refute the claim that a particular entity is indeed emergent can take either of two methodological routes according to Lovejoy: (1) the "reductive," which tries to reduce the entity to what is sufficiently described as its antecedents, and (2) the "retrotensive,"[66a] which seeks to find the "novel" features of the entity in the antecedents. The emergent phenomena crucial for Lovejoy's epistemology are "trans-physical entities," psychical events and objects produced "as effects of the formation of certain complex and late-evolved integrations of living matter, when acted upon by certain forms of radiant energy."[67] This is as succinct a statement as any of Lovejoy's desire to integrate the entire category of ideas into an ontological order that is itself the product of the evolutionary process. Both the reductive efforts of behaviorism and the "retrotensive" efforts of "pan-psychism" have, according to Lovejoy, utterly failed to refute this specific case of emergence so crucial to his philosophy. Pan-psychism has found itself in the awkward position of equating mind and awareness to such an extent that it must "strain at an emergent gnat and swallow an emergent camel."[68]

Perhaps the clearest statement of Lovejoy's "optimistic" interpretation of emergent evolution comes at the close of his 1926 paper:[69]

"Yet, even though no knowledge which we possess concerning evolution justifies that generalized or cosmic meliorism which now so widely does duty for a religion, there nevertheless lies before our terrestrial race in its own little corner of the world a future which, if dim with uncertainties and beset with perils, is not necessarily devoid of possibilities immeasurably transcending all that the past has brought forth. There perhaps yet remain to mankind, we are told, some thousand million years; if it be so, before this long day ends it is possible that, besides all man's laboring reason may achieve, there may yet emerge out of the latent generative potencies of matter as there quite certainly have emerged before our strange planetary history, new and richer forms of being, such as no prescience of ours could foresee and no contrivance of ours create." If Lovejoy has precious little faith in the plasticity of human thought, he does have faith in the workings of an evolutionary process that seems to promise "new and richer forms of being."

[65] *Idem,* "Meanings of 'Emergence,' " 24.   [66] *Ibid.*

[66a] *Ibid.,* 29. "Retrotensive" appears to be Lovejoy's own term, describing the process of admitting that an "emergent" does indeed have the characters attributed to it, and seeking to find those characters in the emergent's antecedents.

[67] *Ibid.,* 30.   [68] *Ibid.,* 31.   [69] *Ibid.,* 32-33. See n. 55 above.

The stress upon the importance of novelty seems to be at odds with the usual picture of the Lovejovian critical and analytical method, employing, not denigrating, the very causal notions he relegates to "prejudice" in his discussions of emergent evolution; he stresses the recombinative nature of most supposedly "new" systems. Lewis S. Feuer remarks that Lovejoy's early articles on theological history may hint at some religious longing that Lovejoy preferred not to reveal. Feuer also mentions that Lovejoy was drawn to the doctrine of emergence, and wrote "some of his most brilliant articles in defense of that theory" although he found fault with thinkers who had tried to attach some "theistic" basis to the evolutionary process.[70] It would perhaps be simplistic to maintain that the doctrine of emergent evolution appealed to Lovejoy as a possible surrogate for religion, especially when one recalls that Lovejoy himself remarked: "One may have strong emotions about certain things, but that has nothing to do with the cogency of the argument."[71]

Lovejoy, in his historical writings, seeks to demonstrate almost disparagingly, how much man has been a "backward-looking animal."[72] A belief in chronological primitivism[73] and a belief in progress are juxtaposed: "If such a natural law of the augmentation of value in time is assumed, on the one hand all the past phases of the historic process will appear to afford encouragement and instruction—and they can be regarded as showing the general direction of a curve of progress which can be hypothetically projected into the future; while, on the other hand, that assumption will chiefly make for a forward-looking habit of mind."[74] Lovejoy states that ". . . evolutionism is in essence of course, the logical opposite of primitivism. . . ."[75] His quotation from Monboddo could well be the motto of Lovejoy's own emergent evolutionism; "nothing *is* at first what it afterward *becomes*."[76]

The conclusion of *The Great Chain of Being* separates the "utility" of various philosophical conceptions from their "validity." The concept of continuity, Lovejoy concludes, was perhaps useful throughout its long history, but is ultimately invalid. Lovejoy traces the odyssey that has revealed ". . . the hypothesis of the absolute rationality of the cosmos to be unbelievable. It conflicts, in the first place, with one immense fact, besides many particular facts, in the natural order—the fact that existence as we experience it is temporal."[77] Faith in a rational, connected order is perhaps "invalid," but as the history of philosophy has shown, it is an eminently useful concept and one that we abandon at our peril. The split that Lovejoy sees between the philosophically useful and the philosophically valid helps to elucidate the relationship between his philosophical tenets and historical methodology. The

---

[70] Lewis S. Feuer, "Arthur O. Lovejoy," *The American Scholar* (Summer 1977), 366.   [71] *Ibid.*

[72] George Boas and Arthur O. Lovejoy, *Primitivism and Related Ideas in Antiquity* (Baltimore, 1935), 7.   [73] *Ibid.*   [74] *Ibid.*

[75] A. O. Lovejoy, "Monboddo and Rousseau," in his *Essays in the History of Ideas* (Baltimore, 1948), 40.

[76] Boas and Lovejoy, *Primitivism,* 190.

[77] A. O. Lovejoy, *Great Chain of Being,* 329.

rationalist assumption, the "prejudicial" cause and effect apparatus, and the simplifying animus that make science functional are all given a place in Lovejoy's pluralism. These assumptions form for Lovejoy the core of historical and philosophical methods. That in their exercise they do not exhaust the realm of possibilities in the natural world is a sign not of human incapacity, but of the unfathomable nature of the universe in which every appearance of genuine novelty is inscrutable and unpredictable. The goal of Lovejoy's logical analysis of words and concepts, the methodological hypothesis of unit-ideas, is the application of a test to determine whether a candidate, psychical or physical, for the status of "novelty" is indeed "emergent" and not merely a juxtaposition of antecedents, for "absolute novelty" is "a good deal rarer than is sometimes supposed."[78] To explain change in general the human mind requires the causal assumption. If this were not the case, the useful roles of prediction and logical analysis could never be understood, but to determine what is truly novel in human history as well as in evolution itself all of our philosophical arsenal needs to be employed. The methodology of the history of ideas is thus indebted to Lovejoy's reflection on the import of the theory of evolution; his belief in the occurrence of irreducible novelty in a world that is not always predictable does not conflict with his use of an eminently rational historical method. The classification of that method as "genetic" finds favor with Lovejoy; indeed he refers to it as the essence of his approach. But it must also be remembered that Lovejoy means something quite specific by "genetic": ". . . it is of the nature of really genetic theories *not* to explain. If the thing to be accounted for is truly something new, an 'emergent' or pure 'mutation,' then, though the theory may correctly describe the circumstances preceding or attending its emergence, it cannot deduce the necessity of its emerging from those circumstances."[79]

Harvard University.

[78] *Ibid.,* 4.
[79] A. O. Lovejoy, *Reflections on Human Nature* (Baltimore, 1961), 85-86.

Chapter IX.a

LOVEJOY'S *THE GREAT CHAIN OF BEING* AFTER FIFTY YEARS

BY DANIEL J. WILSON

Fifty years ago Harvard University Press published *The Great Chain of Being* by Arthur O. Lovejoy. Hailed by reviewers at its publication, the book has remained a volume to reckon with over the past half century. Still in print, *The Great Chain of Being* is regularly cited and still frequently analyzed and criticized.[1]

It is appropriate on this anniversary to study briefly the history of this influential book. Although many scholars have relied on Lovejoy's scholarship whatever their reservations, critics have attacked his interpretations of particular thinkers and his methodology. It should not be surprising that more recent and specialized scholarship questions some of Lovejoy's readings of particular texts; it would be more surprising if there were no such criticisms. Are there common themes linking these interpretative criticisms? Are the errors charged to Lovejoy matters on which reasonable scholars might disagree, or were there fundamental flaws in his approach which produced the alleged mistakes? Potentially more damaging to *The Great Chain of Being* and to Lovejoy's reputation are the methodological critiques which critics have leveled primarily in the last twenty years. The concept of a "unit-idea" and the methodology of tracing such ideas as exemplified in the book have been most heavily criticized. These methodological criticisms are potentially more serious; if Lovejoy's method is flawed, the critics undermine not only the analysis and conclusions of *The Great Chain of Being*, but the history of ideas as an approach to intellectual history.

The methodological critics have focused on Lovejoy's concept of the "unit-idea." These critics, for a variety of reasons, attempt to modify or to abandon the concept. The "unit-idea," they believe, is neither a useful analytical tool nor an applicable heuristic device. Even Lovejoy's defenders modify the concept through the idea of family resemblance. The critics, however, have failed to distinguish clearly between the ordinary connotation of a unit-idea as an atomistic entity—a view encouraged by some of Lovejoy's language—and the more flexible way the concept is employed in *The Great Chain of Being*. The criticisms can be resolved

I would like to thank Darrell Jodock, Ludwig Schlecht, and Larry Shiner for their useful criticism.

[1] The most complete bibliography of Lovejoy's writings and criticism is Daniel J. Wilson, *Arthur O. Lovejoy: An Annotated Bibliography* (New York, 1982). A recent computer search of the literature uncovered 138 citations to *The Great Chain of Being* from 1980 to July 1985.

in part by turning away from the name of the concept to Lovejoy's actual use of it in the book.

The Great Chain of Being was originally given as the second series of William James Lectures at Harvard in the spring of 1933. Lovejoy hoped his historical lectures would appeal to philosophers, historians, and literary critics. The philosophers at Harvard, however, found little of interest in the lectures and the audience grew noticeably smaller for the later lectures. Literary scholars, though, found more value in Lovejoy's remarks.[2]

Lovejoy's correspondence reveals an apparent reluctance on the part of Harvard University Press to publish the manuscript. Lovejoy recognized that the book would "find its largest sale among readers chiefly interested in modern literary history" rather than among philosophers. In the fall of 1935 Lovejoy was still trying to build support for publication by suggesting Marjorie Nicolson and George Sarton as readers who would address "the expectations of the appearance of the book, in non-philosophical circles." Marjorie Nicolson did, in fact, write William Ernest Hocking, who was shepherding the manuscript through the Press, to support publication. Her letter suggests that financial considerations had delayed a decision, in part because Lovejoy was insisting on an expansion of his original lectures. The volume, she asserted, was "eagerly awaited by students in so many different fields." Noting its certain appeal to historians and literary critics, Nicolson concluded that publication "will justify the expense put into it."[3]

When the book finally appeared in 1936 it was warmly received by the initial reviewers. Clifford Barrett in the *New York Times Book Review* described Lovejoy's arguments as "not only highly enlightening but, frequently something near to exciting." The reviewer for the *Journal of Philosophy* declared that this was a book which no "serious student of philosophy" could neglect. John Laird, writing in *Mind*, concluded that the book was "what a book should be—very good to read," but also raised some questions about Lovejoy's interpretation of Thomas Aquinas. The most critical review was perhaps that of Ernest Nagel who thought Lovejoy had slighted psychological and social factors; Nagel also questioned the concept of the unit-idea.[4]

The reviews of Laird and Nagel thus hint at the major lines of criticism

[2] Daniel J. Wilson, *Arthur O. Lovejoy and the Quest for Intelligibility* (Chapel Hill, 1980), 191.

[3] Arthur O. Lovejoy to Ralph Barton Perry, June 18, 1935; Arthur O. Lovejoy to William Ernest Hocking, October 5, 1935; Marjorie Nicolson to William Ernest Hocking, October 5, 1935; all in the Philosophy Department Files, Harvard University Archives.

[4] Clifford Barrett, "The Great Chain of Being Through the Ages," *New York Times Book Review*, May 9, 1937, 11; H[arry] T[odd] C[ostello], *The Journal of Philosophy*, 33 (1936), 580-81; John Laird, *Mind*, n.s., 46 (1937), 400-405; Ernest Nagel, *Science and Society*, 1 (1937), 252-56.

as they have developed: critiques of Lovejoy's interpretations of particular thinkers and of his methodology, particularly of his reliance on the unit-idea. I shall not take up all the criticisms leveled at *The Great Chain of Being* or at Lovejoy's method in the history of ideas. Instead, this essay will focus on selected themes in the criticism that seem most important. Since the methodological issue is the more important, I shall begin by discussing the critiques of Lovejoy as interpreter. The errors charged to Lovejoy in this regard are not random, but reflect his approach to subjects and his philosophical and temperamental orientation.

The earliest critique of Lovejoy's reading of a particular thinker and the most extended dialogue between disputants centered on his treatment of St. Thomas Aquinas in the third chapter of *The Great Chain of Being*. Lovejoy focused on two "dialectical motives" which produced internal strains in the thought of even the greatest of medieval theologians. According to Lovejoy, Aquinas accepted the principle of plenitude which required of God's goodness the necessary creation of all genuine possibilities, with the implication that God had no choice in the kind of world He created. But Aquinas, as an orthodox theologian, must also accept the absolute freedom of God's will to choose and to select. Lovejoy argued that Aquinas never resolved this contradiction in his thought: "we witness the painful spectacle of a great intellect endeavoring by spurious or irrelevant distinctions to evade the consequences of its own principles, only to achieve in the end an express self-contradiction."[5]

Anton C. Pegis and Henry Veatch attacked Lovejoy on the question of contradictions in Aquinas's thought. The debate opened in 1939 with Pegis's short book, *Saint Thomas and the Greeks* and continued with a three-way exchange in *Philosophy and Phenomenological Research* in 1947-48. Both Pegis and Veatch were committed Thomists and defended Aquinas vigorously. The debate centered on the meaning of particular texts and on the viewpoint and expectations of the interpreter.

Pegis originally charged that Lovejoy misinterpreted Aquinas by bringing to his analysis preconceptions inappropriate to a study of the medieval theologian. Lovejoy expected classical authors, such as Plotinus, and medieval authors, such as Aquinas, to be dealing with the same idea of plenitude and, consequently, to face the same dilemmas. But, Pegis argued, Plotinus and Aquinas did not inhabit the same philosophical world and could not be expected to share the same ideas, problems, or contradictions. The Thomistic account of creation is quite different from the classical account and Lovejoy erred in holding to an "extremely syncretistic notion of creation." Aquinas, Pegis believed, recognized that his doctrine of creation differed from the Greeks whereas Lovejoy did not. Aquinas would not be seen as contradicting himself if we allow "to

[5] Arthur O. Lovejoy, *The Great Chain of Being: A Study of the History of an Idea* (Cambridge, Mass., 1936), 78, esp. 73-82.

the Greeks and to Christian thinkers their own unique visions of the world." If we do that, then "there is no inherent contradiction between goodness and liberty or between liberty and self-sufficiency in their worlds."[6] Thus, for Pegis, it was Lovejoy's expectation of a uniformity of meaning on the question of creation as embedded in the idea of plenitude that produced the apparent contradiction. Remove the expectation, and the contradiction disappears from Thomistic thought.

Lovejoy did not immediately respond to Pegis's essay. Pegis, however, had, by implication at least, raised a question of methodology as well as of interpretation. Lovejoy assumed a stability of meaning in the unit-ideas he traced. The type of unit-idea he traced in *The Great Chain of Being* consisted of "a single specific proposition or 'principle' expressly enunciated by the most influential of early European philosophers, together with some further propositions which are, or have been supposed to be, its corollaries." Lovejoy was convinced that "there *is* a great deal more that is common to more than one of these provinces than is usually recognized, that the same idea often appears, sometimes considerably disguised, in the most diverse regions of the intellectual world."[7] Lacking the fundamental unity of meaning, there would have been no unit-ideas to trace. For Lovejoy, then, Aquinas had confronted, as had Plotinus, a real contradiction on the question of creation.

The issue returned in 1947 with the publication of Henry Veatch's essay. He charged Lovejoy with "rather serious errors of interpretation" regarding Aquinas and in particular with confusing a creationist theory, such as that of Aquinas, with an emanationist theory, such as that of Plotinus. Veatch wanted to avoid having "to choose between a God who creates the world by necessity and a God who creates it by sheer chance." God, he argued, is not bound by the logical constraints of earthly philosophers. Drawing on Aquinas, he concluded that God "has a reason for creating the world, but not a necessarily determining reason."[8] Theologians, presumably, could escape logical constraints, at least in their official capacities.

Lovejoy defended himself against Veatch's new charges and Pegis's earlier ones in "The Duality of Thomistic Theology." Thomas, he argued, contained both an indeterminate thesis, which Veatch conceded, and a determinate one, which Veatch contested. What was at issue according to Lovejoy was whether there were the two sides to Thomistic thought, and like his adversaries he cited texts to assert that there were. In responding to Pegis as well as to Veatch, Lovejoy provided examples of

---

[6] Anton C. Pegis, *Saint Thomas and the Greeks* (Milwaukee, 1939), 48-49, 80-81.

[7] Lovejoy, *The Great Chain of Being*, 14-15.

[8] Henry Veatch, "A Note on the Metaphysical Grounds for Freedom, with Special Reference to Professor Lovejoy's Thesis in 'The Great Chain of Being,' " *Philosophy and Phenomenological Research*, 7 (1947), 402, 407-8, 411-12.

what he considered to be both creationist and emanationist thought in Aquinas. He concluded that part of the dispute lay in the unwillingness of Pegis and Veatch to recognize that even so great a thinker as Aquinas might have fallen into contradictory thought. For his part, Lovejoy refused to dismiss the possibility of contradiction, especially when to him it seemed evident in the texts:

> But it is not a permissible practice in the historiography of ideas to force an author into the appearance of harmony with himself by treating one set of passages as if they meant the opposite of what they plainly say. For it cannot be assumed *a priori* to be impossible for a writer—even a philosophical writer— to be attracted by mutually incompatible ideas, to be responsive to conflicting strains in his intellectual heritage, and therefore to give expression sometimes to one, sometimes to another.[9]

Following further exchanges between Veatch and Lovejoy that do little to advance the argument, Anton Pegis entered the lists to support his Thomistic colleague. The basic question was the existence, as Lovejoy asserted, or nonexistence, as Pegis and Veatch believed, of a "necessitarian strain" in Aquinas's theology. Pegis argued that Lovejoy had failed to prove that the God of Plato, Plotinus, and Aquinas were the same God and thus that Aquinas's God suffered from the same disabilities as the God of the Greeks. The key fact for Pegis was that "Plato, Aristotle, and Plotinus do not hold creation: St. Thomas does." Since there is no unity of idea, there can be for Pegis no contradiction, or more precisely the contradiction was Lovejoy's not Aquinas's: "In the end, the problem posed by Mr. Lovejoy is not at all the meaning of the Thomistic texts; it is the meaning which, in his interpretation, certain Thomistic doctrines are forced to have." In a reply to Lovejoy's rejoinder, Pegis is even more explicit: "For Mr. Lovejoy, necessity and liberty are opposed divine attributes: *The Great Chain of Being* is built on that opposition; but for St. Thomas, they are not opposed. . . . [T]he Thomistic God is necessary *without* being determined and free *without* being undetermined."[10]

Perhaps only another Thomistic scholar could referee the authority of textual interpretation in this dispute, but he might simply add another voice to the fray. A more recent scholar, Florestano Centore, has suggested that the debate as it was framed by the principals was ultimately unresolvable. Aquinas, Pegis, and Veatch on one side and Lovejoy on the other were doomed to disagree because they brought to the texts in question very different assumptions: "each thinker is presupposing a different assumption about the relationship between the Creator and

[9] Arthur O. Lovejoy, "The Duality of Thomistic Theology: A Reply to Mr. Veatch," *Philosophy and Phenomenological Research*, 7 (1947), 421-22.

[10] Anton C. Pegis, "*Principale Volitum*: Some Notes on a Suggested Thomistic Contradiction," *Philosophy and Phenomenological Research*, 9 (1948), 52, 54, 69; Anton C. Pegis, "Autonomy and Necessity: A Rejoinder to Professor Lovejoy," *ibid.*, 90.

creation. . . . Presupposed by Lovejoy's imagery is the notion that there is somehow a homogeneity between the Creator and the creation. Presupposed by Aquinas's view, on the other hand, is the notion that there must be an absolute break between the Creator and the creation." Because he was a theologian, Aquinas had available to him certain resources unavailable to Lovejoy. Centore notes that we must remember that "Aquinas is primarily a theologian who *begins* with an assent to the basic truths of Scripture." Aquinas can and does accept the consequences of revelation, but "Lovejoy, of course, is not willing to begin in such a fashion."[11]

Centore is certainly correct on the opposing assumptions of Lovejoy and Aquinas. His suggestions are also applicable to Lovejoy's dispute with Pegis and Veatch. The two Thomists not only accepted Aquinas's assumptions and theological modes of resolving apparent contradictions, they also in some measure accepted St. Thomas himself as an authority, as a source of theological truth. Lovejoy granted Aquinas's greatness but held him to the standards Lovejoy expected of any philosopher. The disputants debated whether Aquinas and the Greeks inhabited separate worlds, but that debate arose in part because Lovejoy and his Thomistic adversaries themselves inhabited different intellectual worlds.

The Great Chain of Being has continued to inspire medievalists despite their reservations about Lovejoy's particular interpretations. These scholars largely accept the method of the history of ideas and bring it to bear on thinkers or ideas Lovejoy ignored, or use it to qualify Lovejoy's own findings. The result is not so much a rejection of the conclusions of *The Great Chain of Being* as a qualification, a modification, or perhaps an addition to Lovejoy's book.

Bernard McGinn, in *The Golden Chain*, finds that Lovejoy's treatment of the idea of the chain in medieval thought was based on a too "narrow viewpoint" on philosophy. Lovejoy, he charges, did not "take into account all the dimensions of the systems of thought under investigation." In addition McGinn argues that "Lovejoy's continued stress on the plenitude and continuity of the Chain of Being as its most dominant characteristics may be legitimate for eighteenth-century usage, but is less valuable for explaining most of the Neoplatonic and medieval uses." McGinn proposes to redress this deficiency by examining "certain essential areas" of "the full range of implications of the symbol of the Chain of Being in the medieval period." He demonstrates that the Golden Chain of Homer in medieval thought represents other significant manifestations of the Chain of Being and that these manifestations need to be seen in a "symbolic mode" rather than "measured by a narrow

---

[11] Florestano Centore, "Lovejoy and Aquinas on God's 'Need' to Create," *Angelicum*, 59 (1982), 34, 31.

conceptual yardstick."[12] The problem with *The Great Chain of Being* was not so much what Lovejoy had done, but what he had not done.

Other medieval historians have taken a similar approach to Lovejoy's study. Ewert Cousins, for example, in his essay "Fecundity and the Trinity," acknowledges that "Lovejoy's book is a remarkable achievement" but then goes on to note a "major omission." Lovejoy, he argues, "failed to take into account data from Christian Trinitarian theology." This failure is particularly significant according to Cousins because Trinitarian theology was important to many of the thinkers considered by Lovejoy and because Trinitarian "speculation adds an entirely new dimension to the problematic" of *The Great Chain of Being.* Cousins concludes that Trinitarian theology made it possible for "the divine fecundity . . . to express itself in a variety of cosmological schemes and not merely in the rigid chain of being that resulted from situating the principle of plenitude within the world."[13] He explores this theme in the writings of the Pseudo-Dionysius, Anselm, and Bonaventure. Edward Mahoney proposes to examine a "conceptual framework" involving ideas of the "hierarchy of being" which "at some point or other invoke God in some way as the measure of the scale and explain that a thing has its place or grade in the scale according as it approaches to God and recedes from non-being and matter, or, . . . as it falls away from God and approaches matter or non-being." Lovejoy, Mahoney argues, does not study this theme in The Great Chain of Being, though Lovejoy did repeatedly allude "to the gradations of all things upward from matter to God."[14] Finally, Francis Oakley, in his recent *Omnipotence, Covenant, and Order,* sets out explicitly to qualify "Lovejoy's vision of European intellectual history while at the same time . . . vindicating the validity, efficacy, and fruitfulness of his improperly maligned approach to intellectual history." Oakley's theme, neglected by Lovejoy, is "the distinction between the absolute and ordained or ordinary powers of God." He proposes to trace "the vision of an order . . . grounded not in the very nature of things but rather in will, promise, and covenant."[15] The thrust, then, of the recent medieval scholarship relating to *The Great Chain of Being* has been to explore areas of thought untouched by Lovejoy, to trace related

[12] Bernard McGinn, *The Golden Chain: A Study in the Theological Anthropology of Isaac of Stella* (Washington, D.C., 1972), 76, 79, 81, 101.

[13] Ewert H. Cousins, "Fecundity and the Trinity: An Appendix to Chapter Three of *The Great Chain of Being,*" in *Studies in Medieval Culture,* XI, ed. John R. Sommerfeldt and Thomas H. Seiler (Kalamazoo, 1977), 103, 105.

[14] Edward P. Mahoney, "Metaphysical Foundations of the Hierarchy of Being According to Some Late-Medieval and Renaissance Philosophers," in *Philosophies of Existence: Ancient and Medieval,* ed. Parviz Morewedge (New York, 1982), 165, 212, n. 1.

[15] Francis Oakley, *Omnipotence, Covenant, and Order: An Excursion in the History of Ideas from Abelard to Leibniz* (Ithaca, 1984), 10-11.

ideas and themes in medieval thought, and to see this work largely as a qualification of and supplement to Lovejoy's study.

Another area of dispute concerning the principle of plenitude involves the Greeks themselves, especially Aristotle and Plato. Jaakko Hintikka and Erkka Maula have questioned whether Lovejoy read the ancient texts correctly. Hintikka notes that Lovejoy in *The Great Chain of Being* asserted that the principle of plenitude is not found in Aristotle and is in fact rejected by the Greek. Hintikka, however, believes that Aristotle "accepted and used some form of the principle of plenitude." His readings rest on two passages in the *Metaphysics* which Hintikka admits are "ambiguous."[16] Lovejoy's misreading of Aristotle, Hintikka argued, rests in Lovejoy's consideration of "the principle of plenitude almost exclusively in one context only." Lovejoy, in his book, focused only on "the relation of the creator to his creatures and more generally to the idea of creation." A broader contextual view, according to Hintikka, would have enabled Lovejoy to read Aristotle as subscribing to the principle of plenitude rather than rejecting it.[17]

If Hintikka sought to include Aristotle among those thinkers who held to plenitude, then Erkka Maula sought to qualify Lovejoy's attribution to Plato of a belief in the principle. Lovejoy's problem lay in his conception of the Demiurge as a creative being. Lovejoy, according to Maula, fused "the Creator in the *Timaeus* with the Form of the Good in the *Republic*," but this "identification is a notoriously suspect way of reading Plato ... and has frequently been rejected altogether." The principle of plenitude, however, can still be found in a modified and, to Maula, more reasonable reading of Plato.[18]

None of these criticisms raise significant methodological problems, though they do raise questions about the quality of Lovejoy's classical and medieval scholarship in the light of more recent views. His scholarship on later thinkers has attracted fewer critics. Hintikka, however, has suggested problems in Lovejoy's approach to Leibniz. Here, again, the cause is the alleged narrow focus of Lovejoy's work on the role of plenitude "in philosophical and theological ideas of creation and of the perfection of the world." Hintikka and Heikka Kannisto revive the charge in an article on Kant where they note that "the idea of creation is important for Lovejoy's outlook on the Principle of Plenitude." They do concede that the views of the early Kant, at least, "are well in line with

[16] Jaakko Hintikka, "A. O. Lovejoy on Plenitude in Aristotle," *Ajatus*, 29, (1967), 5; Jaakko Hintikka, "Aristotle on the Realization of Possibilities in Time," in *Reforging the Great Chain of Being: Studies of the History of Modal Theories*, ed. Simo Knuuttila (Dordrecht, 1981), 60.

[17] Hintikka, "A. O. Lovejoy," 9-10.

[18] Erkka Maula, "On Plato and Plenitude," *Ajatus*, 29, (1967), 18.

Lovejoy's main emphasis."[19] The problem here, as with the Greeks and Aquinas, is the interpretative framework which Lovejoy brought to the texts.

Lewis S. Ford mixes praise with his criticism of Lovejoy's interpretation of Friedrich Schelling. Lovejoy's views as expressed in the book remain "the most exciting interpretation of Schelling available in English." The Romantic philosopher and his American counterpart share the problem of resolving the conflict between divine self-sufficiency and the necessity for God to create the world. Lovejoy, following Schelling, resolved the conflict in favor of a world and a God of Becoming. When Ford turns to Lovejoy's account of the dispute between Schelling and Jacobi, however, he finds the "reconstruction" to be "based on several significant factual errors." These problems do not seriously undermine Ford's confidence in the basic correctness of Lovejoy's reading of Schelling: "His intuitive grasp of the central thrust and significance of Schelling's thought is still valid despite its faulty historical foundation."[20]

Hans Eichner, like Ford, finds much to praise and criticize in *The Great Chain of Being*. He cites Lovejoy's study and Michel Foucault's *Les Mots et les choses* as two influential works that support "the general recognition that something fundamental did happen" to European intellectual life during the Romantic Era. Lovejoy and Foucault, from their very different perspectives and methods, both argue "that the decades around 1800 mark a turning point in Western thought, the beginning of an era that has continued into the present."[21] Where Eichner faults his predecessors is on their failure to measure the impact on the modern world both of science and of men who "took no notice of Romantic theory and carried on in the spirit of Copernicus, Harvey, Newton, and even La Mettrie." This failure to account adequately for science must qualify Lovejoy's and Foucault's thesis that the Romantics "ushered in a way of looking at the world that still dominates our own times."[22]

By pointing to the emphasis on creation and the crucial importance

---

[18] Jaako Hintikka, "Leibniz on Plenitude, Relations, and the 'Reign of Law,' " in *Leibniz: A Collection of Critical Essays*, ed. Harry G. Frankfurt (Garden City, N.Y., 1972), 156-57; Jaakko Hintikka and Heikka Kannisto, "Kant on 'The Great Chain of Being' or the Eventual Realization of all Possibilities: A Comparative Study," in *Reforging the Great Chain of Being*, 289.

[20] Lewis S. Ford, "The Controversy Between Schelling and Jacobi," *Journal of the History of Philosophy*, 3 (1965), 76-78; see also, Lovejoy, *The Great Chain of Being*, 325-26.

[21] Hans Eichner, "The Rise of Modern Science and the Genesis of Romanticism," *PMLA*, 97 (1982), 8, 19; Michel Foucault criticized the history of ideas for creating irrelevant anachronisms and for disregarding the way general rules of discourse overshadow individual thinkers. If Foucault is right, it would invalidate most intellectual history as traditionally practiced. See Michel Foucault, *The Archaeology of Knowledge*, trans. A. M. Sheridan Smith (New York, 1972), especially 135-40.

[22] Eichner, 24-25.

of the Romantic period to Lovejoy's own thought, these critics have uncovered the source of the blinders Lovejoy wore when he approached certain texts. When Lovejoy wrote *The Great Chain of Being*, he had been wrestling with the historical and philosophical problems for thirty years. As a graduate student and young professor Lovejoy sought to develop a justification for abandoning a wholly rational world in favor of a contingent one in which evolution was a distinguishing characteristic. Lovejoy found in Schelling the solution to the dilemma of the two Gods which had bedeviled western civilization since Plato. Unable to believe in the two Gods, desirous of demonstrating the contradictions he saw in western thought and anxious to find support for his faith in "Becoming" and in a God "placed in, or identified with, this Becoming," Lovejoy wrote more than a history; he wrote a historical justification for his own philosophical position. Lovejoy recognized that his historical study had traced a "long series of 'footnotes to Plato,' " but we must realize that it was also a preface to Schelling and to Lovejoy and to their faith in an evolutionary, temporal world in which God was part of the process.[23] When Lovejoy read Plato, Aristotle, Aquinas or any of the other thinkers whom he discussed, he was prepared to find in their work the unresolved, because unresolvable, contradiction between the two conceptions of God as creator. We should not be surprised that so careful a scholar as Lovejoy found what he was looking for. As even his critics concede, some of the passages are ambiguous and susceptible to such a reading. Lovejoy, like the men he studied, was susceptible to "dialectical motives"—the "endemic assumptions" and "intellectual habits"—which shaped his thought and his history. Temperamentally unable to resolve logical contradictions by non-logical means, Lovejoy saw the two-God problem as unresolvable, whereas others found ways to deal with or to evade the problem. If, then, we are aware of the "dialectical" motives operative in Lovejoy's own thought, we can understand why critics have found fault with some of his interpretations.[24]

Potentially more challenging to Lovejoy's enterprise are the methodological critiques of the past twenty-five years. They have focused on Lovejoy's conception of the "unit-idea" calling into question the very existence of such entities and the ways in which Lovejoy used the concept. This criticism has not been totally negative, for even those scholars who dismiss the "unit-idea" have found value in Lovejoy's emphasis on "dialectical motives" and "metaphysical pathos," the nonrational factors affecting thought, and in the interdisciplinary thrust of his study. The critiques of the unit-idea bear close examination because the unit-idea distinguishes Lovejoy's approach from others in intellectual history. If

---

[23] Lovejoy, *The Great Chain of Being*, 325-26.
[24] *Ibid.*, 10; for the influence of biographical factors on *The Great Chain of Being*, see Wilson, *Arthur O. Lovejoy and the Quest for Intelligibility*, especially 139-56.

it is untenable, then the history of ideas as practiced by Lovejoy is undermined.

The first significant challenge to the unit-idea came from Lovejoy's colleague at Johns Hopkins, Leo Spitzer. Responding to Lovejoy's essay, "The Meaning of Romanticism for the Historian of Ideas," Spitzer characterized the unit-idea as "an idea detachable from the soul of the man who begot or received the idea, from the spiritual climate which nourished it; an abstract idea that survives in history from generation to generation; a separate idea, always identifiable to the eye of the historian, in whatever period." He asserted that "the assumption that an idea in history is a completely separate element is inconceivable to me." Lovejoy, bound by his adoption of "the analytic method of the chemist," emphasized "continuity" in ideas. But for Spitzer, this "procedure of tracing the career of individual, abstract ideas as isolated units . . . seems to me erroneous, and bound to lead to erroneous conclusions." Spitzer proposed, instead, "a *Geistesgeschichte*, in which *Geist* represents nothing ominously mystical or mythological, but simply the totality of the features of a given period or movement which the historian tries to *see as a unity*—and the impact of which . . . does in fact amount to more than that of the aggregate of the parts." The virtue and value of *The Great Chain of Being*, according to Spitzer, lay in those chapters where Lovejoy supposedly ignored his analytical method in favor of "a world history of spiritual climates" focused on the ideas embedded in the chain.[25]

Lovejoy was quick to reply to his colleague and to defend his method in the history of ideas. Lovejoy reiterated his conception of his method as "two very simple and . . . innocent working hypotheses": he described unit-ideas as "certain discriminable factors or 'units,' both ideational and affective, logical and alogical, which may be, and often are, recurrent or persistent," and he remained convinced that thought, whether of an individual, a school, or a period "may, and usually does, contain a number of such distinct conceptual and affective components." His method "primarily consists simply in carefully scrutinizing the textual evidence to see whether or not an identical component recurs in two or more contexts."[26]

Spitzer's arguments foreshadow the line of criticism developed by hermeneutical and deconstructionist critics. The hermeneutical critics emphasize understanding the text in relation to the reader. There is no objective knowledge to be obtained, only understanding. For the hermeneutical critic there are no atemporal ideas or truths; ideas or truths, if they exist at all, are embedded in a particular text subject to interpre-

[25] Leo Spitzer, "*Geistesgeschichte* vs. History of Ideas as Applied to Hitlerism," *Journal of the History of Ideas*, 5 (1944), 194, 198-200, 202-3.

[26] Arthur O. Lovejoy, "Reply to Professor Spitzer," *Journal of the History of Ideas*, 5 (1944) 204-5.

tation and reinterpretation. Furthermore, for a critic like Jacques Derrida "no single interpretation can claim to be the final one, and the practice of deconstruction leads to the proliferation of interpretations."[27]

Lovejoy's method, on the other hand, is rooted in his epistemological dualism. Ideas do exist as separate, atemporal entities which can be known to us. An idea, such as plenitude, is seldom if ever known to us in its pure elemental form; our knowledge of it is mediated by a variety of factors, rational and non-rational, social and ideational. When an idea appears in a particular context it mirrors more or less well the abstract concept of the idea. The task of the historian of ideas is to analyze how well or how poorly a particular instance of the idea mirrors the abstract form and to discover what forces and factors have produced the distortion.[28] There is thus a fundamental philosophical difference between Lovejoy and critics like Spitzer and the hermeneuticists. For Lovejoy knowledge of the idea and its history is possible because ideas have an existence separate from the texts in which they appear. For the hermeneuticists, there are no atemporal ideas; ideas have no existence beyond a particular text and their interpretation of it. The two approaches to history, then, are incompatible not only in terms of their methodology but even more fundamentally in terms of their underlying philosophical assumptions.

Maurice Mandelbaum, writing some twenty years after Spitzer, also raised questions about the unit-idea. This concept, he argued, was at once "the more original and the more problematic" aspect of Lovejoy's approach to history. Mandelbaum felt that Lovejoy's stress on "*the continuities of the elements*" could blind him to the larger patterns of a philosopher's thought into which those elements fit. Focusing on the elements of a system made it difficult to "yield an interpretation of the basic aim and motivating power of that system." Since originality often lay in the pattern of thought, emphasis on the unit-ideas could easily lead the historian to miss what was most original about a thinker or to underestimate or misconstrue the question of influence on subsequent philosophers. Mandelbaum proposed a modification in the concept of the unit-idea to alleviate these difficulties. Some unit-ideas may be "*continuing ideas*," such as the chain of being, and these could profitably be traced backward in time. Others, however, might be "*recurrent ideas*," which were those which "human beings are apt to entertain on many different occasions, quite independently of whether or not others had previously entertained them." Part of the task of the historian of ideas, then, would be to distinguish between these two types of unit-ideas in

[27] David Hoy, "Jacques Derrida," in *The Return of Grand Theory in the Human Sciences*, ed. Quentin Skinner (Cambridge, 1985), 54.

[28] Richard Rorty develops the mirror imagery in *Philosophy and the Mirror of Nature* (Princeton, 1979), especially 12-13, 357.

the thinker under scrutiny. Mandelbaum also noted the value of Lovejoy's method in "indicating historical *parallels*" and in demonstrating "the ambiguities and confusions" inherent in key concepts. But, he cautioned that too heavy a reliance on Lovejoy's methods could lead the historian to underestimate the central motivating factors in an author's work and "to minimize the independence of an author's thought." These weaknesses he traced to Lovejoy's "passion for drawing distinctions in order to gain analytic clarity."[29]

If Mandelbaum proposed to modify the unit-idea in the interests of greater precision and accuracy, Louis Mink argued that unit-ideas as conceived of by Lovejoy could not properly be said to have any history at all. Mink charged that the history of ideas tended to treat "ideas as if they were things," timeless and unchanging, and that Lovejoy's methodology contained both "a doctrine of elements and a doctrine of forces," which are incompatible. The doctrine of elements conceives of unit-ideas as if they were physical things, whereas the doctrine of forces considers ideas intelligible in terms of "our experience and understanding of human thought and feeling." Mink argues that "Lovejoy's doctrine of forces explains why there is a *history* of ideas; but his doctrine of elements characterizes ideas in such a way that (like physical constants or the number 2) they cannot have a history at all, that is, undergo development and change." Lovejoy's method, which he viewed as "analogous to that of analytical chemistry," results in an atomism which precludes unit-ideas from having a history "in the sense of a connected development." The unit-ideas, by definition, remained essentially unchanged as they take their place in various thought complexes.[30]

Mink finds Lovejoy's doctrine of forces to be "essentially correct." These forces can be reduced to two: "the logical 'pressure' of ideas," and "individual propensities of feeling, taste and temperament." This doctrine is "throughout dialectical, although it is a dialectic without laws, which is to say a dialectic in which outcomes are historically intelligible although not theoretically deducible." But nothing in a history based on this doctrine of forces requires "the postulation of unit-ideas identical over time and over differences of thought and culture." Although Lovejoy, according to Mink, linked the two conceptual systems (of elements and forces), there is no necessary linkage, and Mink proposes to eliminate the doctrine of elements and to favor the doctrine of forces. Ideas cannot be understood in a vacuum or as some sort of elemental unit; they are comprehensible only when "they are apprehended and made internal to consciousness in some way." Causation, properly speaking, ends when

[29] Maurice Mandelbaum, "The History of Ideas, Intellectual History, and the History of Philosophy," *History and Theory, Beiheft* 5 (1965), 35, 37-38, 41.

[30] Louis O. Mink, "Change and Causality in the History of Ideas," *Eighteenth-Century Studies*, 2 (1968), 7-9, 11; Lovejoy, *The Great Chain of Being*, 3.

an idea is perceived. What the historian seeks to trace is not causation but "influence." Properly done, then, "the history of ideas is not a chronology of things, but the story of the development of consciousness."[31]

Mink's analysis points to one of the puzzles of *The Great Chain of Being*, the absence of a clear, unambiguous definition of a unit-idea. Referring to philosophical systems, Lovejoy notes that the historian of ideas "breaks them up into their component elements, into what may be called their unit-ideas." He also seems to conflate unit-ideas and dialectical motives and to place greater emphasis on the second. Lovejoy suggests that the historian of ideas is most interested in "the persistent dynamic factors, the ideas that produce effects in the history of thought." Finally, he declines to "attempt a formal definition" of "the elements, the primary and persistent or recurrent dynamic units, of the history of thought." In lieu of a definition, he lists the principal types, most of which refer to factors rather than to elemental units: "implicit or incompletely explicit *assumptions*, or more or less unconscious mental habits, operating in the thought of an individual or a generation"; "dialectical motives," which include such things as the "nominalistic" and "organismic" motives; "metaphysical pathos"; "philosophical semantics"; and, finally, "a single specific proposition or 'principle' expressly enunciated by the most influential of early European philosophers, together with some further propositions which are, or have been supposed to be, its corollaries."[32] The emphasis, it seems, is to be on the dynamic factors that influence thought. Even in offering a definition of the unit-idea Lovejoy hardly achieves the elemental solidity so often attributed to it. Note that the unit-idea in its original formulation is enunciated as a principle or proposition complete with certain corollaries. Either Plato was not the source of unit-ideas, or unit-ideas, even as conceived by Lovejoy, were not atomistic units, but rather congeries of ideas. Lovejoy's own attempted definition of a unit-idea and the emphasis he gave to the dynamic factors in his history would suggest that Louis Mink was right to emphasize the dynamic forces in Lovejoy's methodology.

Philip Wiener, however, defended Lovejoy against Mink's charges that he treated ideas as things. The things and events of the past are "irremediably gone" though the ideas of them are not according to Wiener. Lovejoy pursued "an inquiry not into the history of things but into the abstract but inferential ideas that composed the variety of its philosophical and literary appearances in different minds at different times." Unit-ideas, Wiener argued, are "*analytical* components of com-

---

[31] Mink, "Change and Causality," 14-15, 25; see also, R. S. Crane, "Philosophy, Literature, and the History of Ideas," in *The Idea of the Humanities and Other Essays Critical and Historical*, I (Chicago, 1967), 173-87.

[32] Lovejoy, *The Great Chain of Being*, 3, 5, 7-14.

plex ideas which have undergone historical development and change."
These were not units which could be treated numerically; rather they
were akin to Bertrand Russell's "atomic propositions" which could be
analyzed as components of more inclusive "molecular propositions." An
understanding and analysis of these ideas, Wiener asserted, was not
"destructive of their historical development or of their aesthetic qualities
or potentialities."[33]

Replying to Wiener, Mink noted that no one could accuse Lovejoy
of believing that ideas could be identified with things. His point, rather,
was that Lovejoy's proposed analysis of "idea-complexes" into their
"component 'unit-ideas' is a realization, with respect to ideas, of the
same a priori conceptual system which is realized differently with respect
to physical objects; the form, so to speak, is the same, although the
content is different." Mink reiterated his view that in relying on the
dynamic forces Lovejoy wrote persuasive history, but that historians
seldom required the concept of unit-ideas or the notion of causation. In
this regard, he saluted Lovejoy as a "brilliant pioneer" in developing
"what are virtually paradigms of the non-causal understanding of the
development of ideas."[34]

Quentin Skinner, writing in *History and Theory*, developed an argument that in some ways parallels Mink's and in other ways Spitzer's.
Like Mink, he was alert to the danger that treating ideas as Lovejoy did
meant that "the doctrine to be investigated so readily becomes hypostatized into an entity." Seeking this entity leads the historian "to speak
as if the fully developed form of the doctrine was always in some sense
immanent in history." The "reification of doctrines" produces "two
kinds of historical absurdity": the search for "earlier 'anticipations' of
later doctrines" and the "endless debate" about whether a particular
doctrine really exists in a particular thinker or at a particular time. The
historian, in consequence, is unable to discuss the relationship between
what an author said and what he might have meant. Skinner concludes
that "the notion that any fixed 'idea' has persisted is spurious." Histories
which focus on supposedly persisting ideas can "never go right."[35]

Skinner proposes a more complex study of the uses of words and
doctrines: "we must study all the various situations, which may change
in complex ways, in which the given form of the words can logically be
used—all the functions the words can serve, all the various things that
can be done with them. . . . we should study not the meaning of words,
but their use." The historian should focus not on the "*occurrence*" of

[33] Philip P. Wiener, "Some Remarks on Professor Mink's Views of Methodology in the History of Ideas," *Eighteenth-Century Studies*, 2 (1968), 312, 315, 317.

[34] Louis O. Mink, "Reply to Philip Wiener," *Eighteenth-Century Studies*, 2 (1968), 319-20.

[35] Quentin Skinner, "Meaning and Understanding in the History of Ideas," *History and Theory*, 8 (1969), 10-12, 35.

certain words but on "the *use* of the relevant sentence by a particular agent on a particular occasion with a particular intention (*his* intention) to make a particular *statement*." What we are left with, then, is not the history of an idea, but "only a history necessarily focused on the various agents who used the idea, and on their varying situations and intentions in using it."[36] Skinner's approach, as Francis Oakley rightly points out, is not that different from some of Lovejoy's own statements of method. Lovejoy recognized that an adequate interpretation of a text was "dependent upon a knowledge—or an assumption—about what he [the author] was trying to do." As Oakley notes, Lovejoy was himself a champion of "a historical, contextual approach to literature."[37]

Nonetheless, Skinner's and Mink's criticisms help illuminate the controversy surrounding Lovejoy's interpretations of Plato, Aristotle, Aquinas and the others. Lovejoy was looking for the expression of a particular idea and no doubt had in mind an idealized form of the doctrine. What he found, of course, was that the various thinkers seldom, if ever, employed the idea in its ideal form because of dialectical motives, metaphysical pathos, or semantical confusion. Thus, it was easy to find Aquinas in contradiction with himself. What Lovejoy's critics such as Pegis and Veatch have done is to examine the use of the idea by a particular thinker in a particular context with little regard for the supposed persistence of the idea over time. For these critics the context was more important than the persistent idea. Thus, what made sense in the medieval and theological context in which Aquinas wrote appeared hopelessly contradictory to Lovejoy.

Some years later, Jaakko Hintikka's presidential address to the American Philosophical Association launched an assault on Lovejoy's conception of the unit-idea. Acknowledging that *The Great Chain of Being* has been "the most influential single work in the history of ideas in the United States during the last half century," Hintikka nonetheless questioned both certain details of the history and the methodology which lay behind it. He asserted that although the principle of plenitude "is perhaps as close to a unit-idea as we can hope to get in history, in the last analysis *it is not a unit-idea*." If true, this "casts serious doubts on Lovejoy's whole methodology." He argued that "the Principle of Plenitude is not *one* idea, but a conglomeration of several interrelated ideas." It fails on a second account as well, for "its implications are not independent of its conceptual and theoretical environment." Lovejoy's narrow focus on certain aspects of plenitude led him to overlook other manifestations of the concept with the consequence that he often misinterpreted particular thinkers, such as Aristotle. The "moral" which Hintikka reaches is that

---

[36] *Ibid.,* 37-38.
[37] Arthur O. Lovejoy, "Reflections on the History of Ideas," *Journal of the History of Ideas,* 1 (1940), 13-14; Oakley, *Omnipotence, Covenant, and Order,* 33.

"there just are no such unit-ideas." But if there are no unit-ideas, the historian of ideas does have a role to play in the "teasing out of hidden ambiguities and in the discovery and clarification of the frequently surprising interrelations of different ideas." Hintikka concludes, somewhat in the manner of Skinner but with less precision, that we ought to focus on "ideas that can accurately reflect different thinkers' outlook."[38]

With Mink, Skinner, and Hintikka lined up against it, the unit-idea was in deep trouble. But Moltke Gram and Richard Martin defended Lovejoy's methods against Hintikka's attack. In an essay published in the *Journal of the History of Ideas*, they noted that Hintikka's claim that unit-ideas did not exist was "at once strikingly ambitious, comprehensive—and quite wrong." They assert that Hintikka's evidence gives them "a strong reason" to believe in the existence of unit-ideas. After rehearsing Hintikka's argument they conclude that his claims regarding the nonexistence of unit-ideas is based on "a pervasive methodological error." Hintikka has "confused the *sense* with the *significance* of an idea in the study of its historical contexts." Plenitude would have to exist as a unit-idea, otherwise Hintikka, or Lovejoy for that matter, could not "locate the environments in which *P*[lenitude] is supposed to have been either asserted, assumed, or repudiated." Gram and Martin argue that Hintikka was wrong to conceive of the unit-idea as an "atom-like unit," and they assert that Lovejoy saw plenitude as part of a set of complex ideas "interrelated in just such and such a way." They conclude their defense of Lovejoy by arguing that unit-ideas may have different formulations depending on the "conceptual or linguistic context. *But ... there are always family resemblances sufficient to justify bringing them all under a common rubric.*"[39]

The notion of family resemblance as the proper way to conceive different formulations of a unit-idea was also developed simultaneously by Nils Bjorn Kvastad. Kvastad argued that the proper task of the historian of ideas was not that of "a spiritual chemist breaking up compounds into irreducible units." Rather, such a historian was to analyze "ambiguous" terms through a sensitivity to similarities and differences in definition. The resemblances, then, "can often be elucidated by means of Wittgenstein's so-called theory of 'Family Resemblance.'" Though Kvastad modified Lovejoy's view of unit-ideas, he found his emphasis on the dynamic forces, "dialectical motives," and "metaphysical pathos" particularly valuable. In this he was joined by Thomas Bredsdorff who praised Lovejoy's "demonstration of the tremendous importance of am-

[38] Jaakko Hintikka, "Gaps in the Great Chain of Being: An Exercise in the Methodology of the History of Ideas," *Proceedings and Addresses of the American Philosophical Association*, 49 (Nov. 1976), 24, 27-30, 34-37.

[39] Moltke S. Gram and Richard Martin, "The Perils of Plenitude: Hintikka Contra Lovejoy," *Journal of the History of Ideas*, 41 (1980), 497, 508-10.

biguities, imprecisions, and contradictions in the actual use of language."
In his use of these motive forces and in his interdisciplinary emphasis
Lovejoy "produced an invaluable body of work."[40]

Thus, although the notion of the unit-idea as an atomistic element
capable of analysis analogous to that performed in chemistry has been
almost uniformly rejected or substantially modified by critics, a suggestive
modification in the concept of the unit-ideas has been made by Gram,
Martin, and Kvastad in their notion of family resemblance. Here the
recurring expressions of the supposedly identical idea are really slightly
different expressions appropriate to altered contexts, yet closely enough
related that they can be brought together under a similar rubric. If
accepted, this view would alleviate some of the interpretive problems
discussed earlier; the principle of plenitude in Plotinus and that in Aquinas
could be different, though related. Is such a view, however, consistent
with Lovejoy's conception of the unit-idea in *The Great Chain of Being*?

The problem, I would suggest, lies more in the name which Lovejoy
gave to the phenomenon than in his conception of it. By calling it a
"unit-idea" and by making the analogy to analytic chemistry, Lovejoy
put the emphasis on a kind of elemental solidity that his own use of unit-
ideas does not support. There seems to have been some uncertainty in
Lovejoy's mind as to the precise nature of these units. He asked, "Of
what sort, then, are the elements, the primary and persistent or recurrent
dynamic units, of the history of thought?" Since they are "rather heterogeneous," Lovejoy did "not attempt a formal definition" but described
five "principal types." Even when he came to the fifth type, the classic
"unit-idea," the description lacks the fundamental unity one might expect: "It consists in a single specific proposition or 'principle' expressly
enunciated by the most influential of early European philosophers, together with some further propositions which are, or have been supposed
to be, its corollaries." This is certainly a strange definition of a supposedly
fundamental and atomistic unit. It is, to be sure, a single "proposition"
or "principle," but those descriptive terms suggest more complexity than
does "unit-idea." Further, this proposition or principle comes trailing
attached corollaries. The "unit-idea," as Lovejoy defined it, is less unitary
than many have assumed.[41]

Clearly there was something which Lovejoy found in Plato and which,
in some measure, could be traced through the history of thought. The
various expressions of plenitude shared something in common, a word,

---

[40] Nils Bjorn Kvastad, "On Method in the History of Ideas," *International Logic
Review*, 9 (1979), 100-101, 104; Thomas Bredsdorff, "Lovejovianism—or the Ideological
Mechanism: An Enquiry into the Principles of the History of Ideas According to Arthur
O. Lovejoy," *Orbis Litterarum*, 30 (1975), 7, 24.

[41] Lovejoy, *The Great Chain of Being*, 7, 14. Francis Oakley also recognized that
Lovejoy's analogy with analytical chemistry created problems for the history of ideas;
Omnipotence, Covenant, and Order, 39.

a philosophical issue or problem, a perceived similarity or usefulness. But as the critics have pointed out these different expressions appeared in different contexts were given different meaning or emphasis and may in fact have been different, though related, ideas. Given the lack of elemental solidity and the aggregate nature of Lovejoy's own definition of a unit-idea, the concept of family resemblance among key ideas in western thought gains support. If we treat ideas such as plenitude, continuity, and gradation not as solid, unchanging particles but as aggregates which may be slightly different, though still closely related, at each recurrence, then the historian of ideas can more precisely analyze what is persistent and what is new or original in a thinker's work. To conceive of the idea of plenitude, for example, as part of a congerie of closely related ideas each of which finds expression in particular thinkers, for particular purposes, in particular contexts, makes the idea more clearly one of the "persistent dynamic factors" which Lovejoy saw as the special interest of the historian of ideas.[42] To reconceive the unit-idea in this fashion reduces the opposition between the history of ideas on the one hand and *Geistesgeschichte* and hermeneutics on the other. It downplays Lovejoy's emphasis on continuity, without eliminating it entirely, in favor of a greater emphasis on understanding the idea as situated in a particular text in a particular context.

The notion of the unit-idea as a collection of family resemblances is certainly at odds with the name "unit-idea" but not, I would suggest, with the way Lovejoy *used* the term in *The Great Chain of Being*. It is the term "unit-idea" which needs to be abandoned, not the methodology of identifying families of closely related key ideas in western thought and analyzing the continuation or recurrence of those ideas with a heightened sensitivity to the multifarious influences on the expression of the idea in a particular context by a particular thinker. By giving up the word "unit-idea" we will be less distracted by the name and can devote more attention to the substance of Lovejoy's achievement. That, I think, would be more in line with his own emphasis in *The Great Chain of Being*.

After fifty years *The Great Chain of Being* remains a provocative, important, and substantial piece of scholarship. It is still frequently cited for the light it sheds on particular periods and thinkers, especially in the eighteenth and early nineteenth centuries. It has also provoked a substantial body of critical literature which has modified some of Lovejoy's interpretative judgments and called into question aspects of his methodology. But even here the critics have pointed to a resolution of the problem of the "unit-idea" if we but pay closer attention to Lovejoy's definition and use of the concept than to the name he gave it. Whatever its alleged problems and deficiencies, the book cannot be and has not been ignored and that, perhaps, is Lovejoy's greatest achievement in *The*

---

[42] *Ibid.,* 5.

Great Chain of Being, producing a text that after half a century still rewards close study and provokes scholarly debate.

Muhlenberg College.

Chapter IX.b

LOVEJOY AND THE HIERARCHY OF BEING

By Edward P. Mahoney

Throughout his justly celebrated and highly influential work Arthur Lovejoy constantly refers to a conceptual scheme according to which all beings find a place in an ascending order, namely, the "Great Chain of Being."[1] They are ranked in a series that rises from nothingness through the inanimate world into the realm of plants, then into that of the animals, then humans, and above that through angels or other immaterial and intellectual beings, reaching its goal or terminus in God.[2] Lovejoy appears to believe that this conceptual scheme finds its roots in the writings of Plato with perhaps some additions from Aristotle.[3] Of particular importance are Lovejoy's remarks in Chapter II, entitled "The Genesis of the Idea in Greek Philosophy: The Three Principles" (24-66). Lovejoy insists against Burnet that Plato did indeed accept the "Theory of Ideas" or Forms which culminates in a "frank mysticism." He sees this doctrine as set forth by Plato both in the *Republic*, Books VI and VII, and in the *Phaedrus* (34). For Lovejoy, Plato's crucial move is to have postulated an Idea of Ideas, from which the other Ideas "seem to be conceived as in some obscure manner derivative" (39). In fact, Lovejoy himself sees more than just the other Ideas (or Forms) as derivative from the Idea or Form of the Good. He goes on to say that for Plato in the *Republic* the Good is, first of all, "the most indubitable of all realities" and that, secondly, "it *is* an Idea or essence in distinction from the particular and changing existences which in varying degrees participate in its nature" (40). Lovejoy thus appears to take *Republic* 507b to propound a hierarchy of good things in this changing world which are put into varying levels according as they participate in greater or less degree in Goodness itself.

This observation seems to be verified by Lovejoy's own remarks on the following pages. He suggests that the Good can be identified as Plato's

---

[1] See Arthur O. Lovejoy, *The Great Chain of Being, A Study of the History of an Idea* (Cambridge, Mass., 1936). Other general and more recent surveys in English of the topic of metaphysical hierarchy are Lia Formigari, "Chain of Being," in *Dictionary of the History of Ideas*, I (New York, 1973), 325-35; C. A. Patrides, "Hierarchy and Order," in *ibid.*, II, 434-49. Neither they nor Lovejoy pay attention to the conceptual scheme that I analyze in this article and that dominated medieval and Renaissance discussions regarding metaphysical hierarchy.

[2] Lovejoy, *The Great Chain*, 58-59.

[3] For scholarly literature on the supposed intimations of the notion of the chain of being in Plato and Aristotle, see my article, "Metaphysical Foundations of the Hierarchy of Being according to Some Late Medieval and Renaissance Philosophers," in *Philosophies of Existence, Ancient and Medieval*, ed. Parviz Morewedge (New York, 1982), 216-18, n. 1.

God—a rather questionable proposal—if by "God" is meant "what the Schoolmen called the *ens perfectissimum*, the summit of the hierarchy of being, the ultimate and only completely satisfying object of contemplation and adoration. . . ." (41-42). The only qualification that must then be made, to follow Lovejoy, is to characterize goodness in the highest degree as what is an "absolute self-sufficiency" (43). "The essence of 'good,' even in ordinary human experience, lay in self-containment, freedom from all dependence upon that which is external to the individual. And when 'the Good' is hypostatized and made the essence of the supreme reality, the term has the same connotation, except that it is not taken in an absolute and unqualified sense" (42).

In his analysis of Plato, Lovejoy sees this "otherworldly" aspect of Plato's "Absolute," namely, the Idea of the Good (42) balanced by "the contrary tendency" of "a peculiarly exuberant kind of this-worldliness" (45). According to Lovejoy's account, Plato finds in the "Idea of Ideas," which needs nothing outside itself, "the necessitating logical ground of the existence of this world." Plato was looking for the "ground or explanation of the existence of mundane things, and of the number and diversity of their several modes and degrees of imperfection" (45). The only place where he could have found "any reason for the being of the sensible world" was "in the very nature of the sole Self-Sufficing Being." As Lovejoy understands Plato, "The self-same God who was the Goal of all desire must also be the Source of the creatures that desire it" (45). Lovejoy apparently takes Plato in the *Republic* 509b to say that the Good is the cause of the existence not only of the other Ideas or Forms (which is what one would think is the true meaning of the passage) but also the cause of the existence of all the things in this sensible and material world about us (46).

Lovejoy confirms this reading of the passage on the Good in the *Republic* by drawing upon the *Timaeus*. He attempts a reconciliation of the two passages that closely resembles a Neo-Platonic reading, though he would distinguish his from theirs. Since he assumes without question that the doctrine of the *Republic* and the *Timaeus* must be reconcilable, he concludes that what is said about the Demiurge in the latter dialogue cannot be taken literally. However, he refuses to interpret the Demiurge as the poetic personification of the Idea of the Good, which is "the ground and source of all being" according to the *Republic*. Nor will he follow the Neo-Platonists' lead and view the Demiurge as a subordinate emanation just below "the Absolute and Perfect One." He suggests rather that Plato originally had two series of supersensible beings, namely, Ideas and Souls. The former were the everlasting objects of thought, the latter eternal thinking beings. Lovejoy presents as "a probable conjecture" that "Plato in the end conceived of the highest members of both series as somehow identical." This would entail that the Demiurge possesses all the attributes of the Good of the *Republic* (48). However, as Lovejoy reads the *Timaeus*, the Demiurge would lack some perfection if the world did not come to be. Consequently, the "other-worldly Absolute," that is, the Idea of the Good which is identical with the Demiurge, now becomes "a Self-Transcending Fecundity" after having been conceived as a "Self-Sufficing Perfection." Lovejoy concludes in almost Neo-Platonic fashion: "A timeless and incorporeal One became the logical ground as well as the dynamic source of the existence of a temporal and material and extremely multiple and variegated universe" (49).

An even more striking conclusion derived from the *Timaeus* is that every possible kind or type of thing present in the World of Ideas must in fact be found in our spatio-temporal world: ". . . it takes all kinds to make a world," he remarks (51). He sets this conclusion and some others that follow from Plato's assumptions under the general rubric of "the Principle of Plenitude." One of the other conclusions that Lovejoy lists merits special attention: ". . . the extent and abundance of the creation must be as great as the possibility of existence and commensurate with the productive capacity of a 'perfect' and inexhaustible Source. . . ." (52). Lovejoy here again has made the questionable reading that Plato's Good is the direct causal source of the existence of everything in our sensible, material world.

There is, according to Lovejoy, a striking implication latent in Plato's enunciation of the Principle of Plenitude (52). It is that the "expansiveness and fecundity of the Good" involves a necessity. That is to say, the Idea of the Good as a necessary being "must, by virtue of its own nature, necessarily engender finite existents." The Good or Absolute would not be what it is by nature if it did not give rise to all the possible things found in the totality of "ideal Forms" (which Lovejoy seems to view as either contained within the Idea or Form of the Good or as somehow identical with the Idea or Form of the Good). Although Plato did not fully draw out this implication, he bequeathed it to later philosophy and theology. There must be a cosmic determinism as regards the various kinds of things that do exist, and so God cannot do other than what he has done (54).

When Lovejoy turns from Plato to Aristotle, he is careful to distinguish the sort of God that Aristotle held from that Absolute or Good that he appears to attribute to Plato. The God of Aristotle "generates nothing" since his self-sufficiency would be compromised by the dependence on others implied by the need to produce them. On the other hand Lovejoy believes that Aristotle's "Unmoved Perfection" is the cause of all motion and the cause of all activity of imperfect things (presumably including things here on the surface of the earth) as their final cause (55). All things other than God yearn and strive for the Good that is the bliss that God enjoys in his self-contemplation.

But the Unmoved Mover is no world-ground; his nature and existence do not explain why the other things exist, why there are just so many of them, why the modes and degrees of their declension from the divine perfection are so various. He therefore cannot provide a basis for the principle of plenitude. And that principle is, in fact, formally rejected by Aristotle in the *Metaphysics* [II, ch. 5, 1003a2 and XI, ch. 6, 1071b13]: "it is not necessary that everything that is possible should exist in actuality"; and "it is possible for that which has a potency not to realize it." (55).

Aristotle provides Lovejoy with the key to the continuity that characterizes the concept of the hierarchy of things. Lovejoy correctly observes that Aristotle did not formulate the law of continuity with the generality given to it by later thinkers, nor did he set forth with any definitiveness that the qualitative differences among things provide the foundation for a continuous series. But Lovejoy considers it worthy of note that Aristotle did set forth the notion of a continuum and that he introduced the principle of continuity into natural history (55-56). Lovejoy wisely emphasizes that Aristotle never set down any one particular "ascending sequence of forms," since he realized that there are various criteria or determinate attributes according to which organisms, and animals in particular, can be ranked or graded (56). Nonetheless, he considers Aristotle rather than Plato to be the source of the concept of a hierarchic order of things. Although there are "occasional intimations" in Plato's *Dialogues* that the Ideas and their sensible instances in this world "are not all of equal metaphysical rank or excellence," such a conception of hierarchically ordered existences (in this world) and essences (in the Intelligible World) is only a "vague tendency" in Plato and not a "definitely formulated doctrine" (58).

In spite of Aristotle's recognition of the multiplicity of possible systems of natural classification, it was he who chiefly suggested to naturalists and philosophers of later times the idea of arranging (at least) all animals in a single graded *scala naturae* according to their degree of "perfection." For the criterion of rank in this scale he sometimes took the degree of development reached by the offspring at birth; there resulted, he conceived, eleven general grades, with man at the top and the zoophytes at the bottom [*De generatione animalium*, II, ch. 1, 732a25-733b16]. In the *De anima* [II, ch. 3, 414a29-415a13] another hierarchical arrangement of all organisms is suggested, which was destined to a greater influence upon subsequent philosophy and natural history. It is based on the "powers of the soul" possessed by them, from the nutritive, to which plants are limited, to the rational, characteristic of man "and possibly another kind superior to his," each higher order possessing all the powers of those below it in the scale, and an additional differentiating one of its own. Either scheme, as carried out by Aristotle himself, provided a series composed of only a small number of large classes, the subspecies of which were not necessarily capable of a similar ranking (58-59).

Surely it is noteworthy that Lovejoy does not suggest that for Aristotle

all the *species* of living things or all the *species* of animals are arranged
in an ascending or descending order. On the contrary he is careful here
to stress that only large classes are distinguished and ranked. But this
result seems not wholly to agree with Lovejoy's observation in the first
sentence of the previous quotation that Aristotle suggested to later naturalists and philosophers that all animals could be ranked "in a single
graded *scala naturae* according to their degree of 'perfection.' " Such a
statement suggests some sort of metaphysical grading according to species. Lovejoy does in fact claim to find such a grading scheme implicit
in Aristotle's natural philosophy and metaphysics, for he goes on to
observe, following in part a discussion of W. D. Ross:

But there were in the Aristotelian metaphysics and cosmology certain far less
concrete conceptions which could be so applied as to permit an arrangement of
all things in a single order of excellence. Everything, except God, has in it some
measure of "privation." There are, in the first place, in its generic "nature" or
"essence," "potentialities" which, in a given state of its existence, are not
realized; and there are superior levels of being, which, by virtue of the specific
degree of privation characteristic of it, it is constitutionally incapable of attaining.
Thus "all individual things may be graded according to the degree to which
they are infected with [mere] potentiality." This vague notion of an ontological
scale was to be combined with the more intelligible conceptions of zoological
and psychological hierarchies which Aristotle had suggested; and in this way
what I shall call the principle of unilinear gradation was added to the assumptions
of the fullness and the qualitative continuity of the series of forms of natural
existence (59).

It is open to debate whether there is such a scheme in Aristotle,
according to which all the species of things are set out in a single
metaphysical ordering according as they differ in degree of privation from
the species just above and just below them. Just as debatable is that there
is in Aristotle the metaphysical conception of the universe as a "Great
Chain of Being" precisely as Lovejoy then goes on to describe it. Lovejoy
continues:

The result was the conception of the plan and structure of the world which,
through the Middle Ages and down to the late eighteenth century, many philosophers, most men of science, and, indeed, most educated men, were to accept
without question—the conception of the universe as a "Great Chain of Being,"
composed of an immense, or—by the strict but seldom rigorously applied logic
of the principle of continuity—of an infinite, number of links ranging in hierarchical order from the meagerest kind of existents, which barely escape nonexistence, through "every possible" grade up to the *ens perfectissimum*—or, in
a somewhat more orthodox version, to the highest possible kind of creature,
between which and the Absolute Being the disparity was assumed to be infinite—
every one of them differing from that immediately above and that immediately
below it by the "least possible" degree of difference (59).

Lovejoy has on his mind the conception of the Great Chain of Being not so much as it was articulated in the Middle Ages but rather as it was found in a blander version in the early modern period. Although he had just spoken of this conception as accepted unquestionably by many in the medieval period, he cites no medieval philosophers and theologians. On the contrary, he simply goes on to quote "by way of anticipation . . . out of many, two or three modern poetic phrasings of these conceptions." The authors cited are respectively George Herbert, Alexander Pope, and James Thomson, all of whom are basically literary figures and not philosophers or theologians. Lovejoy quotes from Pope's *Essay on Man* that God in his wisdom must form the best of all possible systems and that the ascending order must "rise in due degree," that is, there can be no jumps or gaps in the "vast chain of being," lest one step be broken and "the great scale's destroyed." But what is crucial for our discussion here is that the Chain of Being is conceived by Pope as starting from God, who is the Infinite, descending down through angels, men, brute animals, birds, fish, insects to nothing (60).[4] This same picture of a "mighty chain of being" reappears in Thomson's *The Seasons*. The brief text presented by Lovejoy (61) makes more precise that the chain involves a decrease of perfection as one descends down from God, "Infinite perfection," until one reaches nothing. Thomson speaks of "The mighty chain of being lessening down/From Infinite Perfection to the brink/Of dreary nothing, desolate abyss!"[5]

By starting with these authors and ignoring at this point a medieval thinker of the stature of a Thomas Aquinas, Lovejoy has, in my judgment, skewed the discussion regarding development of the conception of the Great Chain. The point is not simply that Lovejoy could not include everyone but that he has omitted central aspects of the conception of the Great Chain of Being as it was heatedly debated throughout the late medieval and Renaissance periods. He also seems innocent of the fact that some of the problems thrown up against the conception of the Chain in the modern period had already been raised by medieval and Renaissance thinkers.

In Lovejoy's presentation of the origins of the concept of the Chain of Being, Plato and Aristotle are seen to have provided the "ingredients," but "it is in Neo-Platonism that [this complex of ideas] first appear as fully organized into a coherent general scheme of things" (61). At the beginning of a later chapter in his book, he characterizes the conception of the Chain of Being as "a group of ideas which owed its genesis to

[4] See Alexander Pope, *Essay on Man*, ed. Maynard Mack (London, 1950), 19 (Epistle I, lines 43-46) and 44-45 (lines 237-46) for the quotes given by Lovejoy. Also relevant are 31-34 and 92-95 (Epistle I, lines 31-34, and III, lines 7-26).

[5] See James Thomson, *The Seasons*, ed. Henry D. Roberts (London, n.d.), 48 (lines 333-37), "Summer," for the quotation given by Lovejoy. Also relevant is 88 (lines 1743-48).

Plato and Aristotle and its systemization to the Neo-Platonists" (183). And finally, in the concluding chapter he refers back to his earlier analysis of the "formation of those conceptions of metaphysical theology which ... first clearly manifested themselves in the *Republic* and the *Timaeus* of Plato and were developed and systematized by the Neo-Platonists" (315). One was the idea of a God "whose essential nature required the existence of other beings, and not of one kind of these only, but of all kinds which could find a place in the descending scale of the possibilities of reality ..." (315). Once again the *Timaeus* is read in such fashion as to provide the notion that "that which is more perfect necessarily engenders, or overflows into, that which is less perfect, and cannot 're-main within itself' " (315). Lovejoy explicates the significance of this notion by stating its agreement with an assumption that "seems natural to the human mind—that the 'lower' must be derivative from the 'higher' " (316). But what Lovejoy does not make clear about the causal implications of the Great Chain of Being is whether the lower beings all come directly from the one highest Being, that is, God, or from beings intermediate on the scale. The latter would of course be the basic thrust of the Neo-Platonic presentation of the Chain of Being, and it would provide one of the thorniest problems to those medieval theologians who adapted the concept of the Chain to their creationistic world-view. It is remarkable that Lovejoy slights discussion of this thorny and central problem. [6]

In Chapter II, entitled "The Genesis of the Idea in Greek Philoso-phy," Lovejoy does in fact devote several pages to summarizing key notions from Plotinus. He appears to take "the theory of emanation" as central to Neo-Platonism and as "essentially an elaboration and extension of the passages in the *Timaeus* which have been cited" (61). Through the key concepts worked out in his own analysis, Lovejoy describes the evolution of the scheme of the Great Chain of Being as "an attempt at a deduction of the necessary validity of the principle of plenitude, with which the principles of continuity and gradation are definitely fused" (62). Plotinus makes it clearer than Plato, as Lovejoy sees things, that the necessary existence of this world and its manifoldness and imperfec-tion are deduced "from the properties of a rigorously otherworldly, and a completely self-sufficient, Absolute ..." (62). The One, which is the First Good, "overflows" and produces an Other, since it cannot remain in itself, as if jealous or impotent. Lovejoy takes the emanation from the hypostasis of the One to the hypostasis of Intelligence to the hypostasis of Soul to involve the necessary production of every kind or type of thing in a descending serial order, but he leaves unclear whether this means every possible *species* and not just large areas or spheres of reality. Re-ferring to *Enneads* IV, 8, 6, he remarks, "And this generation of the

---

[6] See (note 3 above), my "Metaphysical Foundations," 166 and 218-19, n. 5.

Many from the One cannot come to an end so long as any possible variety of being in the descending series is left unrealized" (62). Other passages from Plotinus that he cites (*Enneads* II, 9, 13 and II, 2, 11) also suggest that there is a series of grades of being in a descending order (64-65). Lovejoy goes on to write of the "specification of differences among creatures through distinctive limitations" and refers to "the specific class of logically possible animals whose 'nature' it is to be eaten" (65). Consequently, when he remarks that for Plotinus the world is "so 'full' that no possible kind of being is wanting in it" (66), he may in fact consider Plotinus's descending hierarchy to involve a descending series of *species* in the sensible world. The problem is that in Chapter II Lovejoy is himself rather vague and ambiguous on this issue.[7]

If any chapter in *The Great Chain of Being* is meant to set forth a sampling and analysis of medieval discussions of the hierarchy of being, it would presumably be Chapter III, which is entitled "The Chain of Being and Some Internal Conflicts in Medieval thought" (67-98). Lovejoy sees two major sources for the medieval Christian adaptation of "the principle of plenitude," his basic organizational concept, and "the group of ideas presupposed by it or derivative from it" (67). They are Augustine and Pseudo-Dionysius. He thus omits all reference to the *Liber de causis* and Proclus's *Elements of Theology*, both of which were known in Latin versions and had great impact on the history of metaphysics from the late thirteenth century onwards.[8] Lovejoy's sampling of medieval and Renaissance philosophers from the thirteenth century through the end of the sixteenth century is disappointing to anyone who has studied even a few of the many distinguished thinkers of the period. Albert the Great is cited only once and then solely from his commentary on the *De animalibus*, a reference taken from a monograph on Leibniz (79 and 340, n. 19). One might assume from Lovejoy's presentation that Albert's interest in hierarchy and his application of the principle of continuity were limited to the realm of nature and species of animals, when in fact he discusses the hierarchical arrangement of all things, including that of the Intelligences. Lovejoy does mention John Duns Scotus on one occasion (81) and alludes to him indirectly (70), when he refers to Scotists, but nowhere presents Scotus's discussions on metaphysical hierarchy or his important doctrine of the "essential order" (*ordo essentialis*). Nor does he treat Marsilio Ficino and Giovanni Pico della Mirandola.[9] In

---

[7] For literature on Plotinus and Proclus, see *ibid.*, 215-16, n. 2. For an indication of passages in Plotinus's *Enneads* where he refers to the One as the measure that things imitate in a nearer and more distant manner, see my article, "Neoplatonism, the Greek Commentators, and Renaissance Aristotelianism," in *Neoplatonism and Christian Thought*, ed. Dominic J. O'Meara (Albany, 1982), 169-77 and 264-82, at 275, n. 43.

[8] For scholarly literature on the two works, see "Metaphysical Foundations," 214, n. 2, and 219-20, n. 9.

[9] Patrides, "Hierarchy and Order," 442, does discuss both Ficino and Pico.

various respects Lovejoy's discussion of hierarchy must be supplemented as well as corrected.

Although there are references in this chapter to various of the writings of Thomas Aquinas, Lovejoy never presents in a straightforward fashion Thomas's own account of how the grades or levels in the hierarchy of being are distinguished. Lovejoy's overriding aim seems to be to pursue his own thesis regarding the "principle of plenitude" and the way in which it supposedly causes a thinker to hold to a completely "full" universe, one in which all possible kinds of things have been actualized.[10] It is striking that Lovejoy quotes Thomas from his *Summa contra Gentiles*, I, ch. 45 (76), where Thomas clearly takes the various *grades* (*gradus*) of being to be *species* (75), but never notes that this is a different reading of the hierarchy than that of Plotinus, for whom the levels were spheres of being and not species.[11]

Lovejoy's uncertainty as to whether the Great Chain involves a descending series of great spheres of being or a descending series of species appears to emerge in his presentation of Dante's views on angels as found in *The Divine Comedy*. Lovejoy refers to Dante's "explanation of the angelic hierarchies," but he then calls it "one order of beings" and says that there is an infinite number of them created, or at least (quoting *Paradiso*, XXIX, 130-35 and 142-45) a number greater than any number that a finite intellect could conceive. Lovejoy thus leaves in doubt whether there are rankings among the angels or whether they are all on the same level of being. But in lines 136-38, which Lovejoy omits, Dante himself states that the First Light of God radiating on all the angels is received by them in as many ways as there are "splendors." Angels differ one from another in species according as they differ in their modes of cognition and therefore as they differ in illumination from God. But what then follows is somewhat disturbing. Lovejoy remarks that for Dante divine production extends not only to the "creation of an infinity of spiritual beings" but also to mortal things; ". . . the emanation of existence from its fount descends by degrees through all the levels of potentiality" (69). He then quotes from Longfellow's translation of the *Paradiso*, XIII, 52-55 and 58-63, but emends the Italian text at line 59 to read *nuove* instead of *nove* (339, n. 5). The result is that the light of the "Idea" or Word in the Trinity is reflected in "new subsistences" (presumably what Lovejoy would understand to be temporal, physical things) and not in "nine subsistences," that is, the nine orders of angels who turn the various heavenly spheres. Since Longfellow's commentary is very precise on this

---

[10] On the dispute between Lovejoy on the one side, and Anton C. Pegis and Henry Veatch, on the other, whether Thomas's conception of God involves a necessitated God, see "Metaphysical Foundations," 213, n. 1.

[11] On rare occasion Thomas uses *gradus* of divisions of reality that do not match genera or species; see *ibid.*, 225, n. 39.

score, it is puzzling why Lovejoy made such an emendation. It may perhaps be wondered whether he wholly understood the place of the angels in Dante's hierarchy or the doctrine of the orders of angels.[12]

The conceptual scheme that did in fact dominate discussions of metaphysical hierarchy from the thirteenth through the sixteenth century originated in Proclus, an author mentioned only once by Lovejoy (64).[13] Medieval authors knew of this scheme through William of Moerbeke's translation of Proclus's *Elements of Theology*, Pseudo-Dionysius's *De divinis nominibus*, and the *Liber de causis*.

Proclus takes the Good or the One, which is beyond Being, to be the principle and cause of all things, their measure ($\mu\acute{\epsilon}\tau\rho\upsilon\nu$).[14] The more something participates in what is above it, the higher is its place in the hierarchy. The "nearer" something is to the One or the Good, the more it will be like it, that is, it will be in a greater measure good and universal. It will also be a more powerful cause in the series of causes or principles. A procession ($\pi\rho\acute{o}o\delta\varsigma$) involves a descent such that there is a ranking in an order through a remission away from the principles just above each member of a series and also away from the first in a series. Such a procession involves a going from what is a unity to a plurality and a dispersion. Consequently, that which is nearer to the One is itself more one, whereas that which is more remote from the One is more multiple or composed. And even the last or lowest kinds of existents depend on something above them, for if they did not they would withdraw into non-being ($\epsilon\grave{i}\varsigma\ \tau\grave{o}\ \mu\grave{\eta}\ \grave{o}\nu$) and vanish. For Proclus there is a kind of mathematical aspect to the series of things as they are measured by their approach to or their receding away from the One. Moreover, Proclus would seem to accept a principle of continuity whereby there are no gaps in series but intermediate principles which unite the extreme terms.[14] Granted that there are hints of some of these ideas in Plotinus, it is only in Proclus that these hints harden into axioms and that the descending series from the One involves what appeared to be species or comparable to species and not large realms or levels of being.

---

[12] On Dante's doctrine of the nine orders of angels, see Kenelm Foster, *The Two Dantes and Other Studies* (Berkeley, 1977), 120-22; Patrick Boyde, *Dante Philomythes and Philosopher, Man in the Cosmos* (Cambridge, 1983), 181-88; and for a helpful general discussion regarding the orders of angels in the Middle Ages and the Renaissance, C. A. Patrides, *Premises and Motifs in Renaissance Thought and Literature* (Princeton, 1982), 3-30.

[13] Lovejoy was not unacquainted with Proclus's *Elements of Theology*. He cites it in his study, "The Dialectic of Bruno and Spinoza," in *University of California Publications: Philosophy*, I (Berkeley, 1904), 153, n. 1. But in this study and also in *The Great Chain of Being*, it is Plotinus who represents Neo-Platonism for Lovejoy and to whom he gives his scholarly attention. Proclus's name does not appear in the index of Lovejoy's book. Formigari ("Chain of Being") does not appear to refer to Proclus at all. She seems to rely heavily on Lovejoy and to accept his account of Plato's *Republic* and *Timaeus*.

[14] See my "Metaphysical Foundations," 215, n. 2 for the relevant texts.

Although there is a close similarity between Proclus and the Pseudo-Dionysius, the latter eliminates the causal role that the intermediary beings play in Proclus.[15] Moreover, Dionysius identifies being with God himself and holds that all other beings have their being by directly participating in God himself, who is their creator. God serves as the principle (ἀρχή), the measure (μέτρον), and number (ἀριθμός) of all other things. Just as every natural number is generated in some fashion from the "one" or unit (μονάς) and is more multiplied the further away it proceeds from the unit, so all circles exist in the center and are more joined one to the other the closer they are to that center. In like fashion all things are more composed the "further" away they are from God, who gives all creatures their being. Dionysius's adoption of spatial language to explicate metaphysical hierarchy is particularly noteworthy, since it will be reflected in various medieval and Renaissance thinkers. In like fashion, his acceptance of a principle of continuity, according to which the lowest in a higher rank of things touches the highest in a lower rank, would be reflected in medieval discussion.[16]

The *Liber de causis* was translated from Arabic into Latin before 1200. Although it is derivative from Proclus's *Elements of Theology*, it maintains, against Proclus, both that God is Being as well as the One and the Good and also that God is a creator. Once again God is taken to be the "measure" (*mensura*) of all things. Everything other than God participates in unity and has more intense power and higher operations as it is more united with God and approaches more closely to him, that is, to pure Unity. The degree of a thing's "closeness" (*propinquitas*) to God determines the mode of that thing's being (*modus esse sui*). Intelligences and sensible things receive according to their "quantity" (*quantitas*).[17]

Albert the Great reflects some of these ideas from Dionysius and the *Liber de causis* in his commentary on Dionysius's *De divinis nominibus* and in his *Liber de causis et processu universitatis*.[18] God serves as principle, cause and measure (*mensura*) of all things. The more an Intelligence approaches (*accedit*) God, the simpler and more one it is. Participation and approaching God are interrelated in such a way that everything participates more or less in being according as it approaches (*accedit*) to the likeness of God. Albert repeats these ideas in his commentary on the *Sentences*, where he also cites both Dionysius's *De divinis nominibus* and the *Liber de causis*. God is an exemplar and excelling measure. The greater the distancing (*elongatio*) of creatures from the First Being, so much the less do they participate in him. There is an intension and

---

[15] *Ibid.*, 166 and 218, n. 5.
[16] *Ibid.*, 166-67 and 219, n. 6-8.
[17] *Ibid.*, 167, and 219-20, n. 9 and 13.
[18] *Ibid.*, 167-68.

remission (*intensio et remissio*) in God and creatures, a more and a less (*magis et minus*) of being and goodness insofar as there is an approach and a receding (*accessus vel recessus*) of creatures, which are good and exist by participation, with respect to God, who is good of his very substance and who exists through himself.

But it is Thomas Aquinas, Albert's student, who makes more consistent and systematic use of Dionysius, the *Liber de causis*, and even Proclus himself.[19] The conceptual scheme that he works out is more nuanced than that of Albert and is presented repeatedly in his various works, from the early *De ente et essentia* and commentary on the *Sentences* through and various *Quaestiones disputatae*, namely, *De veritate, De potentia dei*, to the later *Summa theologiae*.[20] Thomas carefully explains that the notion of "measure" (*mensura*) has been "transferred" from the genus of quantity to other genera, so that what is first and simplest in each genus can be called the measure of everything else in that genus.[21] Consequently, just as the unit measures all natural numbers, so God measures all things in all genera. As something approaches (*accedit*) the measure in a genus it has more of the nature of that measure, just as it has less of that nature as it recedes (*recedit*) from that measure. In the case of God and creatures, the more a creature approaches (*accedit*) to God, the measure, the more it has of being, while the more it recedes (*recedit*) from him, the more it has of non-being (*tantum habet de non esse*). Such an "approaching" is simply the finite thing participating in God, and Thomas underscores that there always remains an infinite distance (*distat in infinitum*) between the finite thing and God. The various grades of perfection (*gradus perfectionis*) in finite things are determined by their retreat (*recessus*) from potentiality and their approach (*accessus*) to God, who is pure actuality and something wholly one. The further a thing is from God and the closer it is to matter, the more that thing has of potentiality.

Adapting a passage from Aristotle (*Metaphysics*, VIII, ch. 3, 1043b36-1044a2), Thomas states that the different species of things (*species rerum*) are like natural numbers, which differ through the addition and subtraction of unity. Beings are constituted in differing species, insofar as they are determined to some special grade (*specialis gradus*) or determinate grade (*determinatus gradus*) among the things that exist. There is even a more or less (*magis et minus*) among the angels that establishes them in different grades and therefore in different species. In like fashion, Thomas sees among minerals a gradation through various species up to gold, a gradation among plants up to the species of the perfect trees

[19] *Ibid.*, 219, n. 7.
[20] *Ibid.*, 169-73 and 222-29, n. 26-52.
[21] *Ibid.*, 169 and 223, n. 27 and 29.

(which he does not identify), and a gradation among the animals up to the human species.[22]

Thomas's elaboration, from hints in Proclus, Dionysius, and the *Liber de causis*, of the nuanced conceptual scheme sketched here had a noticeable impact on medieval and Renaissance discussions regarding metaphysical hierarchy. The notion that God is the basic measure and that things take their places in the hierarchy of being as they "approach" toward him or "recede" away from him is of major significance. One of the basic weaknesses of Lovejoy's presentation is precisely that he does not present and discuss this constantly debated doctrine.

Siger of Brabant sets forth Thomas's scheme in his own questions on the *Metaphysics* and on the *Liber de causis*.[23] He appears to accept the notion of a measurement as things "approach" God, and he speaks of a measurement as things approach closer to matter. The scheme is also set forth and discussed in the works of Giles of Rome and Henry of Ghent, who disagreed so sharply on the problem of the distinction of essence and existence. Giles argues that there can never be a rest in creatures' approaching God, since he is infinitely distant from all of them, and that therefore there is the possibility of an infinite number of created things between God and prime matter or nothingness. But while God can always create another more perfect species of angels, there will in fact never be an actual infinite number of creatures.[24] Godfrey of Fontaines (d. 1306/1309) discusses the conceptual scheme but stresses that he does so tentatively and without committing himself to it. He compares the hierarchy of beings to the essential order (*ordo essentialis*) of numbers but concludes against Giles that one cannot go to infinity in creatures who are closer and closer to God since there must be a halt in some particular creature than which there can be no other more perfect.[25] John Duns Scotus accepts the doctrine of participation and considers the whole range of beings, both infinite and finite, to comprise an "essential order" (*ordo essentialis*) in which ascent necessarily comes to a halt in a single and completely highest being, namely God. Finite things will be more or less perfect as they approach more or less (*magis et minus appropinquantes*) to the First Being. But what Scotus appears to reject is that

[22] *Ibid.*, 170-71 and 229, n. 47.

[23] *Ibid.*, 172-74 and 229-30, n. 53-65.

[24] *Ibid.*, 174-77 and 230-32, n. 66-81. For a major addition to the bibliography on Giles and the concept of hierarchy, see now the fine study of Barbara Faes de Mottoni, "*Mensura* im werk *De mensura angelorum* des Aegidius Romanus," in *Miscellanea Mediaevalia*, ed. Albert Zimmermann, Band 16/1 (Berlin, 1983), 86-102.

[25] *Ibid.*, 177-79 and 233, n. 83-86. To the scholarly literature cited there should be added John F. Wippel, "Possible Sources for Godfrey of Fontaines' Views on the Act-Potency 'Composition' of Simple Creatures," *Mediaeval Studies*, 46 (1984), 222-44. Godfrey's frequent use of Proclus's *Elements of Theology* when discussing the conceptual scheme is especially noteworthy.

matter or non-being plays any role as a measure of things in the hier-archy.[26]

The conceptual scheme of God and matter or non-being as the two termini or measures of the metaphysical hierarchy received much atten-tion during the Italian Renaissance and led to some acrimonious inter-changes. George of Trebizond denies that one creature could be any closer to God than another, since all of them are infinitely distant from him. Bessarion, his distinguished adversary, replies by suggesting that God can be considered not only as infinite but also as that being which is more perfect than all other beings and the highest being, though not infinite. God as creator must be taken in the latter sense and is therefore not infinitely distant from creatures.[27]

Marsilio Ficino accepts this solution and makes constant and enthu-siastic use of the scheme of God as the measure of all things in the metaphysical hierarchy of being as they approach toward him or recede from him.[28] Matter too serves as a pole measuring the various grades of perfection (*gradus perfectionis*) of things, since it is closest to non-being and further from God. And while Ficino does map out large spheres in the hierarchy of being, following here the thought of Plotinus, he does in fact make species to be the building blocks of the hierarchy of being and compares them to the series of natural numbers. Contemporary scholars have noted the presence within Ficino of these two rather dif-ferent conceptions of metaphysical hierarchy.[29] But while Ficino does accept both God and matter as the two poles measuring, he clearly views God as the dominant measure in the scheme. For that reason he is contemptuous of those "barbarians" (*barbari*) who reject God as a measure and who argue that since God is infinitely distant from all creatures none will be any closer to him than another. These unnamed opponents hold that things differ according to their "receding" (*recessus*) from privation or non-being.[30]

One of Ficino's targets is almost certainly Paul of Venice (d. 1429), whose ideas on metaphysical hierarchy were heavily influenced by four-teenth-century discussions, notably those of Richard Swineshead (fl. ca. 1340-1355) and John of Ripa (fl. ca. 1355), regarding the measurement of the intension and remission of forms. For Paul the scale of being (*latitudo entis*) begins with the zero grade of being (*non gradus entis*) and runs through species insofar as each species is at a different distance

---

[26] *Ibid.*, 179-82 and 233-36, n. 87-105.

[27] *Ibid.*, 187-88 and 240-41, n. 122-25.

[28] *Ibid.*, 188-92 and 241-42, n. 126-39.

[29] See Paul Oskar Kristeller, *The Philosophy of Marsilio Ficino*, trans. Virginia Conant (New York, 1943), 75-76; idem, *Il pensiero filosofico di Marsilio Ficino* (Florence, 1953), 67-68 and 72-75; Michael J. B. Allen, "The Absent Angel in Ficino's Philosophy," *JHI*, 36 (1975), 219-40.

[30] See my "Metaphysical Foundations," 191.

from the zero grade. This serial ordering is likened to that of natural numbers. Since God is at an infinite distance from creatures, a horse and a human will be equally distant from him. Nonetheless, they and all other finite things can be put in a ranking according to their distance from the zero grade (*distantia a non gradu*).[31] But this position and its reputed source, namely, Swineshead's treatise *De intensione et remissione qualitatis*, which is found in his *Calculationes*, are attacked and rejected by Cardinal Domenico Grimani (1461-1523) in his commentary on the treatise.[32] Grimani defends the view that the perfection or intension of things is measured by their nearness (*propinquitas*) to the most perfect being and their imperfection or remission is measured by their distance (*distantia*) from that being. God is then the sole measure of all things and no other measure, whether matter or the zero grade (*non gradus*), is required to account for the grades in the hierarchy of being. Swineshead's view, at least as it is applied to the question of metaphysical hierarchy, is also rejected by Pietro Pomponazzi,[33] who maintains that God is the measure of all things according as they approach to or recede from him, since he is the highest grade in the latitude of beings.

Three early sixteenth-century Thomists, Thomas de Vio (1469-1534), Giovanni Crisostomo Javelli (ca. 1470-ca. 1538), and Jacobus Brutus, continued to maintain the conceptual scheme of two termini that determine the grades of all things as they approach to or recede from these two measures, namely God and matter.[34] The scheme is elaborated at great length in Agostino Nifo's commentary on Averroës's *Destructio destructionum* and doubtless reflects his close study of Albert and Thomas. It is significant that he cites the *Liber de causis*. He repeats the scheme in other early writings. What is startling is that Nifo attributes this conceptual scheme to Averroës, due no doubt to passages in the *Destructio* which appear to involve the acceptance of a metaphysics of participation.[35] Marcantonio Zimara (1460-1532) follows Nifo closely on this topic, accepting the conceptual scheme and attributing it to Averroës. He attempts to evade the problem of how creatures could be at different distances from an infinite being by maintaining that when God is taken as imitable or participable by creatures he is not taken as infinite. Zimara attacks the *Calculatores* for having based the hierarchy of being solely

---

[31] *Ibid.*, 192-94 and 242-43, n. 140-44. Another philosopher who may have influenced Paul is Albert of Saxony. See n. 142.

[32] *Ibid.*, 195-97.

[33] *Ibid.*, 197-98 and 244-45, n. 154.

[34] *Ibid.*, 197; 245, n. 156-57; and 247-48, n. 182.

[35] *Ibid.*, 198-99 and 246-47, n. 161-70. For discussion of Nifo's conception of the order of the universe, see my study, "Philosophy and Science in Nicoletto Vernia and Agostino Nifo," in *Scienza e filosofia all'Università di Padova nel quattrocento*, ed. Antonino Poppi (Padua, 1983), 135-202, at 194-95 and 198-200.

on reference to the zero grade.[36] Another contemporary, Alessandro Achillini, also accepts tentatively the conceptual scheme of the two measures, but he apparently does so only on the assumption that God is finite. Revealing his heavy debt to Swineshead and the *Calculatores* tradition, he expresses his own preference for measuring things according to the zero grade (*non gradus*). Since no two species are equally distant from the zero grade, they are like the series of natural numbers, no two of which are equally distant from the unit.[37] Pomponazzi's student, Gaspare Contarini, also rejects the zero grade as a measure and takes God, considered as "finite," to be the measure of the latitude of being.[38]

Although the celebrated Aristotelian philosopher of the mid-sixteenth century, Jacopo Zabarella, appears to avoid all discussion of metaphysical hierarchy in his works, the scheme of the two measures and the problem of how creatures could approach nearer and nearer to an infinite God continued to be debated.[39] Cesare Cremonini, who succeeded Zabarella as the major philosopher at Padua, discusses in detail the various approaches to measures of metaphysical hierarchy. He explicitly refers to the positions of Nifo and Zimara. But he too appears to eliminate all metaphysical grounds for the hierarchy of things and definitely rejects God as a measure of the Intelligences.[40] On the other hand Francesco Buonamici, Galileo's teacher at Pisa, discusses metaphysical hierarchy at great length in his mammoth *De motu libri decem*.[41] He himself takes God alone to suffice as the measure of all things. He too escapes the objection that an infinite God is equally distant from all creatures by saying that in this context God is to be considered as finite. Buonamici attacks both Swineshead and Achillini by name for teaching that the zero grade alone suffices to measure the hierarchy of being. Another acquaintance of Galileo, Iacopo Mazzoni, also takes God to be the sole measure of other things. To the objection that an infinite God cannot serve as a measure, he replies that "closeness" and "distance" here mean simply more or less participation in infinite perfection.[42] In his *Juvenilia*, Galileo Galilei himself argues against the notion of God serving as a measure of things according to their distance or receding from him. He

[36] *Ibid.*, 199-202.

[37] *Ibid.*, 202-3 and 247, n. 178-81.

[38] *Ibid.*, 247-48, n. 182.

[39] On Zabarella, see the fundamental study of Antonino Poppi, *La dottrina della scienza in Giacomo Zabarella* (Padua, 1972).

[40] See my article, "Il concetto di gerarchia nella tradizione padovana e nel primo pensiero moderno," in *Aristotelismo veneto e scienza moderna, Atti del 25° anno accademico del Centro per la Storia della Tradizione Aristotelica nel Veneto*, ed. Luigi Olivieri, II (Padua, 1983), 735-37.

[41] *Ibid.*, 737.

[42] See "Neoplatonism, the Greek Commentators, and Renaissance Aristotelianism," 176. On Galileo's relations with Mazzoni, see Frederick Purnell, Jr., "Jacopo Mazzoni and Galileo," *Physis*, 14 (1972), 273-94.

thereby rejects the position of Buonamici, his own teacher, and that of his friend and colleague at Pisa, Mazzoni. On the other hand, he frequently refers to the perfect order (*ordine*) of the universe in his major work, the *Dialogo sopra i due massimi sistemi del mondo*, and states that it is the product of the omnipotent maker (*Artifice onnipotente*), who is the creator and guide (*Facitore e Rettore*) of the universe. Although he does refer to the different species in the universe, namely, minerals, plants, animals, and humans, he nowhere proposes anything like the conceptual scheme in which God alone or God and matter serve as measures of an ascending or descending order of species. There seems to be no "metaphysical" explanation for the order of things other than what lies hidden in the Divine Mind.[43]

By reason of his mechanism, René Descartes rejects the notion of a hierarchical ranking of physical beings and he reveals himself uninterested in the question of an order among the angels.[44] Although Spinoza sets forth a metaphysical system that is markedly anti-hierarchical, he does speak on one occasion of all things extending from the highest to the lowest grade of perfection.[45] In contrast, a clear and decided commitment to the hierarchy of being is to be found in Leibniz, who openly adopts the language of the conceptual scheme, that is, "chain," series, grades of perfection, "quantity" of an essence and the descent from the infinite being down to the lowest grade, non-being. But Leibniz completely ignores the notion of God and non-being playing the roles of measures of the grades and the hierarchy of being.[46] In general, seventeenth-century figures lost or deliberately rejected the notion of God and non-being as measures, though some do in fact continue to speak of things "approaching" to or "receding" from God or nothingness. Indeed there are quotations giving such views scattered through Lovejoy's *The Great Chain of Being.*[47]

The most striking acceptance of the hierarchy of being according to grades among early modern philosophers is that by John Locke. In this instance, his source was not Richard Hooker, since the latter observes

[43] See "Neoplatonism, the Greek Commentators, and Renaissance Aristotelianism," 176 and 280, n. 83; "Il concetto di gerarchia," 738. On the manner in which Galileo substituted his own conception of the order of the universe for that of Aristotle, see Maurice Clavelin, *The Natural Philosophy of Galileo*, trans. A. J. Pomerans (Cambridge, Mass., 1974). For a general examination of the term "order" in Galileo's various writings, see Paolo Galluzzi, "Il tema dell' 'ordine' in Galileo," in *Ordo, Atti del II Colloquio Internazionale*, ed. M. Fattori and M. Bianchi, *Lessico Intellettuale Europeo*, XX (Rome, 1979), 235-76.

[44] See "Metaphysical Foundations," 249, n. 187 for the scholarly literature.

[45] Spinoza, *Ethica ordine geometrico demonstrata*, I, Appendix, in *Opera*, ed. Carl Gebhardt (Heidelberg, 1925), 83. See "Metaphysical Foundations," 250, n. 188.

[46] "Metaphysical Foundations," 250, n. 189; "Il concetto di gerarchia," 739, n. 23 for references in Leibniz and to the scholarly literature.

[47] For a list of passages and authors, see "Metaphysical Foundations," 249, n. 186.

that species in the physical world will have different dignities, and therefore rankings, according to the criterion adopted for evaluating them.[48]
At most, Hooker accepts an ordering of the angels disposed according
to higher and higher grades.[49] On the other hand, the conceptual scheme
is quite evident in Christoph Scheibler (1589-1653), one of Locke's scholastic sources. He maintains that God is the measure of creatures, that
creatures approach God according to a more and less (*magis et minus*),
that species proceed from God like numbers, and that God could always
produce another species more perfect than the most perfect species now
existing.[50] But while Ralph Cudworth speaks of a gradation or scale of
beings which rises from the lowest to the highest and uses the terms
"order," "steps," and "grades," the conception of hierarchy that he
proposes is rather vague.[51]

Locke himself allows in *An Essay concerning Human Understanding*
that God has in "an unlimited degree," that is, infinitely, as angels have
in "a higher or lower degree," those operations that we find on reflection
in ourselves, for example, existence and knowledge. The First Being is
"infinitely more remote . . . from the highest and perfectest of all created
beings" than the "purest seraph" is distant "from the most contemptible
part of matter." Locke takes it as "probable" that there are more species
of angels above us than there are species below us. The descent by "easy
steps" in a "continued series" and without "gaps" in the physical world
should be matched, given God's providence, by an ascent upward from
us "by gentle degrees." Locke thus adopts the spatial language of the
conceptual scheme, namely, infinite distance, ascent, and descent; and
he refers to the lowest state of being as that "which approaches nearest
to nothing." He also accepts the principle of continuity, even referring
to mermaids and sea-men. What is altogether missing, however, is that
either God or non-being serves as measure of the "degrees of perfection"
or "ranks of being."[52] That notion of measurement is also missing in

---

[48] Such an observation had already been made by John of Jandun ("Metaphysical
Foundations," 237, n. 117).

[49] *Ibid.*, 250, n. 190.

[50] Christoph Scheibler, *Metaphysica*, I (Oxford, 1637), 441-51 (Bk. I, ch. 25); *idem,
Liber sententiarum* (Marburg, 1631), 135, 139, 226-28.

[51] Ralph Cudworth, *The True Intellectual System of the Universe* (2nd ed.; London,
1743), I, 421 (ch. 4); 728, 858, 862 (ch. 5).

[52] John Locke, *An Essay concerning Human Understanding*, ed. Peter N. Nidditch
(Oxford, 1975), 444-47 (III, ch. 6, #9-12); 656-66 (IV, ch. 16, #12). See "Il concetto
di gerarchia," 740-41 and n. 27. Lovejoy has noted the first of these two passages (*The
Great Chain of Being*, 184, 190, 228-29). Since Locke holds that we do not know the
real essences of things, but only nominal essences, it has been argued that "Locke's scale
is not really a metaphysical scale of 'entities' or 'being'. . . ." See Michael R. Ayers,
"Mechanism, Superaddition, and the Proof of God's Existence in Locke's Essay," *The
Philosophical Review*, 90 (1981), 237-38. See also his "Locke versus Aristotle on Natural

George Berkeley's allusion in *Siris* to the chain or scale of beings which rise upwards by "gentle uninterrupted gradations."[53] It is also lacking in his *Alciphron*, where he refers to the Pseudo-Dionysius, speaks of "innumerable orders of intelligent beings" that are "more perfect than humans" and refers to God as "infinitely above" man.[54]

If we now turn back to Lovejoy himself and *The Great Chain of Being*, there seem to be some conclusions that we may draw. First of all, Lovejoy appears to have defined the central meaning of the chain in terms of the way in which it was presented by seventeenth- and eighteenth-century writers. This means that he imposed on the medieval and Renaissance periods a description that failed to capture the major thrust of the conceptual scheme of the two poles that measure the grades or ranks in the hierarchy of being, namely, God and matter or non-being. The incomplete survey presented here of philosophers and theologians who accepted or debated such a conception of metaphysical hierarchy surely demonstrates that this conceptual scheme dominated discussions on hierarchy from the late thirteenth through the late sixteenth century. By neglecting or ignoring this rich tradition, Lovejoy failed to give an adequate and accurate account of the development of the concept of the Great Chain during that period. Moreover, he appears not to have realized that the medieval and Renaissance philosophers and theologians had themselves heatedly debated the whole question of how creatures could approach closer and closer to God if he always remained at an infinite distance from even the most perfect of them. Although I cannot develop the topic here, Lovejoy also overlooked the interesting discussions on the metaphorical nature of the language adopted in speaking about things "approaching" or "receding" from God.[55]

Another major criticism to be made of Lovejoy follows from our examination of the origins of the concept of the Chain of Being. There seems little justification for turning Plato's Form of the Good into a God from whom all things flow, unless one wants to reaffirm Neo-Platonism or a variant of it. Lovejoy's reading of Plato's *Republic* and the *Timaeus* is simply mistaken. In like fashion Lovejoy seems to impose on Aristotle a particular concept of hierarchy suggesting a metaphysics foreign to his

Kinds," *The Journal of Philosophy* 78 (1981), 257, where Locke's nominal essence and the concept of a hierarchy of distinct species are discussed. Ayers cites Lovejoy.

[53] George Berkeley, *Siris*, ed. T. E. Jessop, Sects. 274 and 284, in *The Works of George Berkeley, Bishop of Cloyne*, V (London, 1953), 129 and 133. But see also 137 (Sect. 296); 140 (Sect. 303); and 155-57 (Sects. 341-47).

[54] Berkeley, *Alciphron*, ed. T. E. Jessop, in *The Works*, III, 166-68, 170 and 172. See "Metaphysical Foundations," 250, n. 193-95 for the relevant secondary literature on Berkeley.

[55] There are interesting discussions in Aquinas, Maimonides and Pomponazzi, among others. See my "Metaphysical Foundations," 171, 227-28, n. 44 and 244-45, n. 154.

thought.[56] Granted that Aristotle does propose an ordering among the animals, it is based on physical considerations, and the most plausible explanation for the hierarchical ranking of the Intelligences is the ranking of the respective sphere that the individual Intelligence causes to move as a final cause.

Lovejoy did discern some of the elements in the conceptual scheme that we presented, but he went astray in trying to find them in Plato and Aristotle. More to his credit is his concentration on Plotinus. But here he should have seen in Proclus some important notions regarding metaphysical hierarchy that are only vaguely hinted at by Plotinus or that are simply not there. What is unfortunate is that scholars still draw confidently on Lovejoy's presentation of the concept of the hierarchy of being as it is supposedly found in Plato and Aristotle and remain innocent of the importance and influence of Proclus. Others take his presentation of medieval authors as accurate and fairly comprehensive when it is neither. Needless to say, Lovejoy himself should not be faulted for those who uncritically accept his book as the gospel on hierarchy. *The Great Chain of Being* remains a provocative account of some absorbing ideas regarding metaphysical hierarchy. Although I did not myself read it until I was well advanced in research on the topic, I must confess that I find that it almost always raises new questions on each rereading. Perhaps that is the highest compliment that can be paid to any contribution to the enterprise of "the history of ideas," a scholarly enterprise to which Lovejoy contributed so impressively.[57]

Duke University

---

[56] Aristotle does not hold to a creator God, a metaphysics of participation in the being of that God, or grades of being established by "distance" from God. Whether he held that all things down to the lowest can be related directly to God as final cause is another matter. For helpful literature on hierarchy and Aristotle, see *ibid.*, 217, n. 1, especially the contributions of Friedrich Solmsen and G. E. R. Lloyd.

[57] Part of the research on which this article is based was done during the tenure of a fellowship from the John Simon Guggenheim Foundation for 1979-1980.

Chapter IX.c

LOVEJOY'S UNEXPLORED OPTION

By FRANCIS OAKLEY

The past year has seen the appearance in print of two volumes of essays focusing on the role played in European intellectual history by the notion of divine omnipotence.[1] The growth of interest in the subject is manifest also in its recurrence as a persistent theme in articles published of recent years in the pages of this journal.[2] But if the current degree of preoccupation with that particular divine attribute is certainly something of a novelty, the preoccupation itself is not. While Arthur O. Lovejoy was preparing his William James Lectures for publication in 1936 as *The Great Chain of Being*, an Oxford philosopher, Michael Foster, published in *Mind* three magisterial articles exploring the relationship between the concept of the divine omnipotence and the rise to prominence in the early modern era of the philosophy of nature undergirding the Newtonian natural science.[3] But the thesis they propound is foreign to Lovejoy's preoccupations in *The Great Chain of Being*, and nowhere does he refer

---

[1] Tamar Rudavsky (ed.), *Divine Omniscience and Omnipotence in Medieval Philosophy* (Dordrecht, 1985); Mariateresa Beionio-Brocchieri Fumagalli *et al.*, *Sopra la volta del mondo: Onnipotenza e potenza assoluta di Dio tra medioevo e età moderna* (Bergamo, 1986), with "Bibliografia essenziale"; cf. Amos Funkenstein, *Theology and the Scientific Imagination from the Middle Ages to the Seventeenth Century* (Princeton, 1986), esp. 117-201.

[2] See the following articles in the *JHI*: P. M. Heimann, "Voluntarism and Immanence: Conceptions of Nature in Eighteenth-Century Thought," 39 (1978), 271-83; Kathleen M. Ashley, "Divine Power in Chester Cycle and Late Medieval Thought," 39 (1978), 387-404, and "Chester Cycle and Nominalist Thought," 40 (1979), 477; James R. Royce, "Nominalism and Divine Power in the Chester Cycle," 40 (1979), 475-76; Margaret J. Osler, "Descartes and Charleton on Nature and God," 40 (1979), 445-56; Michael Heyd, "From a Rationalist Theology to Cartesian Voluntarism: David Derodon and Jean-Robert Chouet," 40 (1979), 527-42; Richard C. Dales, "The De-Animation of the Heavens in the Middle Ages," 41 (1980), 531-50; John Barnow, "The Separation of Reason and Faith in Bacon and Hobbes, and Leibniz's Theology," 42 (1981), 607-28; William J. Courtenay, "Late-Medieval Nominalism Revisited," 44 (1983), 159-64; Henry Guerlac, "Theological Voluntarism and Biological Motivation in Newton's Physical Thought," 44 (1983), 219-27; Margaret J. Osler, "Providence, Divine Will, and the Theological Background to Gassendi's Views on Scientific Knowledge," 44 (1983), 549-60, and "Eternal Truths and the Laws of Nature: The Theological Foundations of Descartes' Philosophy of Nature," 46 (1985), 349-65; Heiko A. Oberman, "*Via Antiqua* and *Via Moderna*: Late Medieval Prolegomena to Early Reformation Thought," 47 (1986), 23-40.

[3] M. B. Foster, "The Christian Doctrine of Creation and the Rise of Modern Science," *Mind*, 43 (1934), 446-68, "Christian Theology and Modern Science of Nature (I)," *ibid.*, 44 (1935), 439-66, and "Christian Theology and Modern Science of Nature (II)," *ibid.*, 45 (1936), 1-27.

to it. If in that classic work he was certainly concerned with the divine attributes, they were the attributes proper to a Platonic rather than any specifically Christian understanding of the divine, and the role of the biblical notion of God in the development of European thought was treated as a source rather of confusion than of creativity.[4]

Lovejoy's point of departure, it will be recalled, was the Platonic notion of the necessary realization of all conceptual possibilities, itself the outcome of the conflation of the idea of the Good (outlined in the *Republic*) with the figure of the divine *demiurgos* (introduced in the *Timaeus*). The self-sufficing perfection being by that strange alchemy transformed into a self-transcending fecundity, it could begrudge existence to nothing that could possess it. It was from the linking together of this Platonic notion (which he called "the principle of plenitude") with two other fundamental principles or "unit ideas" drawn from Aristotle—the principles of continuity and of "unilinear gradation"[5]—that was formed the idea complex which constituted, Lovejoy said, "the conception of the plan and structure of the world which, through the Middle Ages and down to the late-eighteenth century, many philosophers, most men of science, and indeed, most educated men, were to accept without question." Nothing other, in fact, than "the conception of the universe as a 'Great Chain of Being,' composed of an immense, or ... [even] ... infinite, number of links ranging in hierarchical order from the meagerest kind of existents, ... through 'every possible' grade up to the *ens perfectissimum.*"[6]

To that great conception the Jewish notion of "a temporal Creator and busy interposing Power working for righteousness through the hurly-burly of history" was clearly antithetical.[7] Similarly the views of those later-medieval thinkers, such as "the Scotists, William of Ockham, and others," who, placing their stress on the biblical notion of God, "held the arbitrary and inscrutable will of the deity to be the sole ground" not only of the existence of the world but also "of all distinctions of value" in that world.[8] Such men were "extreme anti-rationalists," and Lovejoy leaves one with the distinct impression that they were in poor position to reach for any vision of order in the universe, let alone that overarching conception of the great chain of being which, by the eighteenth century, its period of greatest diffusion, had come to sustain the intellectual and imaginative world of "writers of all kinds—men of science and philosophers, poets and popular essayists, deists and orthodox divines."[9]

---

[4] Arthur O. Lovejoy, *The Great Chain of Being: A Study of the History of Ideas* (Cambridge, Mass., 1936), ch. 2, 67-98 ("The Chain of Being and Some Internal Conflicts in Medieval Thought").

[5] *Ibid.*, 58-59.

[6] *Ibid.*, 59.

[7] *Ibid.*, 157.

[8] *Ibid.*, 69-70.

[9] *Ibid.*, 183.

In this, however, Lovejoy was wrong. Preoccupied as he was with the Platonic and Neoplatonic contribution to the shaping of the later European conception of the world as a rational and ordered one, he was naturally disposed to see the biblical notion of God as mighty will and irresistible power above all as serving to introduce an element of "arbitrariness," "contingency" and "unpredictability" into the world, as promoting the idea of a cosmos "lacking in orderliness, . . . characterized by a kind of incoherency and whimsicality."[10] But in order to be omnipotent an omnipotent being must possess the power freely to bind itself. And as I have argued at length elsewhere,[11] from the recognition of that possibility there emerged in the Middle Ages and flourished until the eighteenth century a durable theme on which pivoted a coherent scheme of things contrasting sharply with the picture evoked by the notion of the great chain of being but rivalling it by its own imaginative force. The theme in question is a distinction drawn by so many late-medieval theologians, scientists, and lawyers concerning the power of God (*potentia dei absoluta; potentia dei ordinata*)—and by frequently invoked analogy, of popes, emperors, and kings. The scheme: the vision of an order—natural, moral, salvational, political—grounded not, like the great chain of being, in the very nature of things but rather in will, promise, and covenant. Only if historians recognize that in so many of the texts confronting them this vision of order jostles side by side with that embodied in the antithetical vision of the great chain of being will the perplexities generated by some segments of early modern theological, legal, and scientific thinking be successfully dissipated. But ironically, it was only by the pursuit of Lovejoy's own approach to the history of ideas that I was led to that conclusion. Hence the further conclusion that that approach can lay a much greater claim to our respect than most historians seem currently willing to concede.

In what follows, then, I propose to attempt three things. First, to sketch in the outlines of the covenantal understanding of order. Second, to illustrate the degree to which the recognition of its presence can illuminate some segments of early-modern thought. Third, to defend the validity, efficacy, and fruitfulness of Lovejoy's improperly maligned approach to intellectual history.[12]

I. In a sermon published in Boston in 1726 the Reverend Samuel Willard wrote that

---

[10] *Ibid.*, 328-29.

[11] Francis Oakley, *Omnipotence, Covenant, and Order: An Excursion in the History of Ideas from Abelard to Leibniz* (Ithaca, 1984).

[12] For a more fully and precisely developed version of this intricate argument see my *Omnipotence, Covenant, and Order.*

Divines do from Scripture observe a twofold Power ascribed to God, viz. 1. An unlimited and absolute Power, by vertue of which he can do all possible things, even such things as he never actually doth. . . . 2. An ordinate Power, which is not a Power different from the former, but the former considered, as God hath pleased to set limits or bounds to it by the Decree. . . .[13]

In this passage Willard was invoking a remarkably durable scholastic distinction the origins of which can be found in the efforts of such eleventh- and twelfth-century thinkers as Peter Damiani, Peter Abelard, St. Anselm, Hugh of St. Victor and Peter Lombard to solve the puzzle of how God's power was to be related to his other attributes of will, reason, and goodness. Only in the early-thirteenth century, however, does the distinction itself appear finally to have crystallized. Coming to the fore in the writings of such prominent theologians as Albertus Magnus, Thomas Aquinas, Duns Scotus, and William of Ockham, it enjoyed a continuing vogue among philosophers and theologians in the fourteenth and fifteenth centuries, survived the ideological turbulence of the Reformation era, and was still being invoked in the seventeenth century by such Catholic thinkers as Francisco Suarez and by such Protestant divines in Old and New England as William Ames and John Norton.[14]

From its inception the distinction between the absolute and ordained power evolved from the attempts of the early scholastic theologians fully to honor the goodness and wisdom of God without being led thereby (in the unhappy footsteps of Abelard) to impose limits on his freedom and omnipotence by asserting what Lovejoy dubbed as "a necessitarian optimism."[15] The arena of debate (and the arena, therefore, within which the distinction came into play) was that of the order of creation. That is to say, the questions that were generating the difficulty probed the matter of the divine omnipotence by raising such issues as God's capacity to create a different or better world than he had in fact created. At the start the absolute power was understood to refer to "the total possibilities *initially* open to God, some of which were realized by creating the established order" with "the unrealized possibilities ... [being] ... now only hypothetically possible."[16] The stress, therefore, lay on the realm of the ordained power, which evokes the stable, concrete arrangements

[13] Samuel Willard, *A Compleat Body of Divinity* (Boston, 1726), qu. 4, serm. XXII, 70, col. 2.

[14] Francisco Suarez, *Metaphysicarum Disputationum*, (Mainz, 1605), II, 140-41, 289 (disp. XXX, sec. 17, disp. XXXIV, sec. 7). William Ames, *The Marrow of Sacred Divinity*, bk. 1, chap. 6, secs. 16-20, in *The Marrow of Divinity*, ed. John D. Eusden (Boston, 1968), 93. John Norton, *The Orthodox Evangelist or a Treatise wherein many Great Evangelical Truths are briefly Discussed, cleared and confirmed* (London, 1654), 19-20.

[15] Lovejoy, *Great Chain of Being*, 70-71.

[16] Thus William J. Courtenay, "Nominalism and Late Medieval Religion," in *The Pursuit of Holiness in Late Medieval and Renaissance Religion*, ed. Charles Trinkaus and Heiko A. Oberman (Leiden, 1974), 19.

that the good God, who never acts in a disorderly or arbitrary fashion, has preordained in his creation, has actually chosen to effect, and that we humans, then, can safely rely upon. At the same time the absolute power remained as it were on dialectical standby, a matter of abstract possibility periodically evoked to underline the contingency of creation, the world's dependence, that is, on the untrammeled decision of the divine will, the fact that it does not have either to be what it is or even to be at all. Thus, for example, Albertus Magnus and Thomas Aquinas.

In the wake, however, of the thirteenth-century reception of the writings of Aristotle and of his Arab commentators, Avicenna, Al-Farabi and Averroës, the arena of debate came to be widened and the reach of the distinction concerning the divine power lengthened. Those writings forced upon the attention of scholastic philosophers and theologians an understanding of the divine and its relationship with the natural world even harder to reconcile with the biblical God than the Platonic and Neoplatonic vision had been. As a result and in an attempt to protect the biblical doctrine of God against the philosophical necessitarianism or determinism that appeared at least to many to be part and parcel of Aristotle's thought, philosophers and theologians were led to place a heightened emphasis on God's freedom and omnipotence in relation not only to his creation of the world but also to his governance of created things. Thus, when the distinction between the absolute and ordained powers was invoked (as it was with increasing frequency), the line tended now to be drawn between the ordained, ordinary, or common law, in accordance with which God normally condescends to work within the framework he has freely willed and established by his promise or covenant, and the absolute power whereby he can do anything that does not involve a contradiction—whereby, therefore, he can transcend (and, on occasion, actually *has* transcended) that established order, whether it be salvational, moral, or natural.

The beginnings of this shift were evident at the turn of the thirteenth and fourteenth centuries in the formulations of thinkers of as different philosophical tendency as Aegidius Romanus, a man of quasi-Thomist sympathies, and Duns Scotus, founder of the philosophical tradition that, during the remainder of the Middle Ages, rivalled Thomism in its strength and appeal.

For Aegidius, while God (like the pope) possesses a "regulated" power whereby he governs things in accordance with "the common laws" he himself has put into nature, such as permitting fire to burn, water to moisten, and so on, he possesses also an absolute power or plenitude of power whereby he can set aside the operation of such secondary causes and act "apart from [*praeter*] the common course of nature."[17] Similarly,

---

[17] Aegidius Romanus, *De ecclesiastica potestate*, ed. Richard Scholz (Weimar, 1929), 149-50, 152, 156-59, 181-82, 190-94 (lib. III, caps. 2, 3, 7, 9).

though perhaps not quite so bluntly, Scotus distinguished (by analogy not only with kings but with man as a free agent within whose power the law falls) between the ordained power whereby God acts *de jure*, in accordance with the rightful law he has himself established, and the absolute power whereby *de facto* he can act apart from or against that law.[18]

As the royal, papal and legal analogies suggest, the surfacing of such formulations is associated with the emergence among the canon and civil lawyers of a parallel tradition which distinguishes between the absolute and the ordained, ordinary, civil, or regulated power (the latter terms tend to be used interchangeably) of popes, emperors and kings.[19] Such, moreover, was the later currency of those formulations that they seemed to Pierre d'Ailly at the end of the fourteenth century to convey a "more proper" understanding of the ordained power than did the older usage that limited God *de potentia ordinata* to being able to do "only those things which he himself ordained that he would do." Hence, in his own very frequent use of the distinction d'Ailly does not hesitate to illustrate the operation of God's absolute power by invoking the analogy of the king's absolute power, and he was prone to speak of God as acting "naturally" when he acts in accordance with his ordained power and as acting "supernaturally or miraculously" when he acts by his absolute power, breaching thereby "the common law" or "common course of nature."[20]

[18] John Duns Scotus, *Oxoniense scriptum in librum primum Sententiarum Magistri Petri Lombardi* (Coimbra, 1609), 677-78 (I, dist. 44, qu. unica).

[19] That tradition stretched from the canonists Hostiensis and Johannes Andreae in the late-thirteenth century, via Baldus de Ubaldis in the fourteenth, Innocent Gentillet, Barthélemy de Chasseneux, Jean Bodin, Sir John Doddridge, and others in the sixteenth, to William Barclay, Albericus Gentilis, John Cowell, Edward Forset, Sir John Davies, and James I of England in the seventeenth. This important tradition of prerogative thinking calls into question Charles Howard McIlwain's classic interpretation of Bracton in particular and medieval constitutionalism in general (see Francis Oakley, "Jacobean Political Theology: The Absolute and Ordinary Powers of the King," [1968], 323-46) and undercuts the attempts of W. H. Greenleaf and James Daly to demonstrate that James I's divine-right ideas can be "properly understood" when one sees them as "derived from a range of metaphysical notions which collectively may be called 'the idea of order' " (or "cosmic harmony") "best described," even classically so, in Lovejoy's *Great Chain of Being*. See Greenleaf, "The Thomasian Tradition and the Theory of Absolute Monarchy," *English Historical Review*, 79 (1964), 747-84, 748, and *Order, Empiricism, and Politics: Two Traditions of English Political Thought, 1500-1700* (London, 1964), 60-67, 14-15; James Daly, *Cosmic Harmony and Political Thinking in Early Stuart England*, (*Transactions of the American Philosophical Society*, n.s. 79, pt. 7, Philadelphia, 1979); cf. Oakley, *Omnipotence, Covenant, and Order*, 73-118.

[20] Pierre d'Ailly, *Quaestiones super I, III et IV Sententiarum* (Lyons, 1500), I, fol. 56 (qu. 1, art. 3 JJ), fol. 120 (qu. 9, art. 2 M) (fol. 159 r-v) (qu. 13, art. 1 C-D) fol. 188 (IV, qu. 1, art. 2N); also his *De Trinitate* and *De libertate creaturae rationalis*, in *Joannis Gersonii: Opera omnia*, ed. Louis Ellies Dupin (5 vols.; Antwerp, 1706), I, 619, 632.

By the sixteenth century, according to Suarez,[21] the usage which d'Ailly had thought to be more appropriate had come to be the more common one, a development reflected in the fact that the ordained power was now sometimes referred to as the *ordinary* power. Thus Martin Luther, who had once dismissed the distinction as a piece of scholastic sophistry, later used it in much the same way as had d'Ailly, employing interchangeably the terms "absolute" and "extraordinary" on the one hand, and "ordained" or "ordinary" on the other, treating the former as God's miraculous power of intervening in the prevailing order established by his will.[22] And out of this usage, in turn, appears to have developed in the writings of some of the great Puritan divines of the seventeenth century the distinction between "the ordinary and usual" or "extraordinary and unusual" providence of God. The former consisted in "God's observance of that order in things which was appointed from the beginning" and which "in natural things is the law of nature common to all things"; the latter consisted in "God's provision for things beyond the usual and appointed order" i.e. miracles.[23]

II. Such, in brief outline, is the history of the distinction between the absolute and ordained power of God around which crystallized, or which itself gave expression to, an understanding of the order of things, not as something indwelling in the very nature of reality and reflecting an hierarchical chain of being but as an imposed order grounded in will, promise, and covenant. Grounded, that is to say, in an omnipotent God's unconstrained decision to bind himself to follow a stable pattern in dealing with his creation in general and with human beings in particular. The importance of recognizing just how widespread this rival vision of order was in the late-medieval and early-modern era can best be illustrated, I believe, by focusing on the notions of order in the natural world prevalent among the early-modern natural scientists.

For Lovejoy, of course, "the features which differentiated the new from the old world-picture most widely . . . owed their introduction and, for the most part, their eventual general acceptance" to "the influence of those originally Platonic metaphysical preconceptions" which had given birth to the vision of order embodied in the notion of the great chain of being."[24] When it came to the early modern scientific thinkers, then, his interest lay with men who sympathized with that notion or with one or other of its component ideas—men like Giordano Bruno, Kepler, William Derham, the great naturalist John Ray, or Leibniz.

[21] Suarez, *Metaphysicarum Disputationum*, II, 140-41, 289 (disp. XXX, sec. 17, and disp. XXXIV, sec. 7).

[22] Martin Luther, "*Vorlesungen über I Mose*," cap. 19, 14-20, and cap. 20, 2, in. Luther, *Werke, Weimar Ausgabe*, 43. 70-71, 106.

[23] Thus William Ames, *Marrow*, I, chap. 9.

[24] Lovejoy, *Great Chain of Being*, 99.

Above all Leibniz, in whose writings the notion found its clearest expression, and who, despite elaborate disclaimers, was committed to "the proposition that the existence of everything that does exist, and also its attributes, behavior, and relations, are determined by a necessary truth, or a system of such truths."[25]

So far as the order of nature is concerned, such a philosophical stance clearly precluded any determinative role for the divine *will*, and some commentators have taken the critique of the Newtonians that Leibniz mounted in the celebrated Clarke-Leibniz correspondence of the years 1715 and 1716 as correctly pointing up the degree to which "the concept of a mechanical, geometric universe threatened the primacy of God in the creation."[26] They have been disposed, that is, to question the judgment of such a "Christian *virtuoso*" as the great chemist, Robert Boyle, when he spoke so glowingly of the harmony between Christian theology and the new science of the day. Seeing the central bone of contention between the natural philosophers and the Christian traditionalists to be the question of God's relationship to the universe and the nature of his authority within it, they find Boyle's extensive analyses of that topic, of the operation of divine providence, and of the status of miracles to be neither fully persuasive nor fully coherent. "Boyle's opinion about miracles," we are told, "stood in absolute contradiction to the rest of his thought. It was an arbitrary and artificial reconciliation of two positions that could not be reconciled satisfactorily"[27]—namely, his scientific view of the world as a great machine possessed of an unchanging order and his Christian commitment to belief in the providential activity of a personal God. For that commitment involved belief not merely in the general divine concourse whereby God sustains in being the whole order of the universe but also in those particular providences whereby God miraculously interferes with that order and touches the lives of individuals.

Other points of tension there doubtless were. But this, we are told, was the central issue, and Boyle's failure was symptomatic. Throughout the seventeenth century the *virtuosi* were condemned to fight an increasingly desperate and ultimately doomed rearguard action. Maneuver frantically though they might, they proved unable finally to reconcile their biblical notion of an all-powerful, loving, and personal God, from whose providential intervention not even the might of a Nebuchadnezzar was

[25] Thus Lovejoy, *Great Chain of Being*, 174. Lovejoy also argues (176) that "one, and perhaps the principal, tendency of Leibniz's insistence upon his principal of sufficient reason . . . was to promote the doctrine of universal necessity and to diminish the horror of the hobgoblin which had so terrified even Leibniz himself, the metaphysics of Spinoza."

[26] Richard S. Westfall, *Science and Religion in Seventeenth-century England* (New Haven, 1958), 23-24.

[27] Westfall, *Science and Religion*, 89; cf Franklin L. Baumer, *Religion and the Rise of Scepticism* (New York, 1960), 78-90; E. A. Burtt, *The Metaphysical Foundations of Modern Physical Science* (London, 1925), 187-96.

proof, with their own scientific understanding of the universe as a great and wondrous machine, grinding on its inexorable course in accordance with those immutable and necessary uniformities to which they gave the name of laws of nature and which they took it to be their task as scientists to identify. In the Clarke-Leibniz correspondence, Dr. Samuel Clarke, Newton's apologist, might splutter angrily at Leibniz's sneering intimations that the Newtonians were being inconsistent with their own mechanistic principles in teaching the possibility, indeed the necessity, of God's intervention in the world of nature after the creation in order to reform the notions of the planets, perhaps also to conserve the total amount of notion in the world. But Leibniz (we are told) was correct; he had identified the central dilemma. The story of the relationship between science and religion in the seventeenth century was, in its most fundamental aspect, the story of the progressive exile of the sovereign God of Abraham, Isaac, and Jacob to the remote and inaccessible post of the First Cause, to whom eighteenth-century deists were to accord a thin and sanitized respect.

Told in this way, as a story of progressive secularization and with the eighteenth-century culmination and Leibniz's viewpoint positioned well to the foreground, this stretch of history takes on an impressive coherence. As Franklin Baumer has said, "it is a fascinating thing to watch this *reductio* [whereby "divine activity in nature was significantly reduced if not eliminated"] proceed, almost ineluctably it would seem, from Galileo to Newton and Leibnitz."[28] The question remains, however, if the story should be told in that way. And, in fact, an acquaintance with the long history of the distinction between the absolute and ordained power and the covenantal understanding of order which it sustained would strongly suggest the wisdom of setting the story in the context not of what came after but of what went before, of the struggle of medieval theologians, not, indeed, with any mechanistic philosophy of the seventeenth-century type, but with deterministic or quasi-deterministic notions of Neo-Platonic and Aristotelian provenance. The more so in that the thinking of late-medieval scientific thinkers had reverberated to that theological struggle. The more so, too, in that so much of the emphasis on divine omnipotence in the writings of the early modern scientific thinkers is rather self-consciously linked with the need to reject any trace of necessity either in God or the world he has created. Thus Descartes, Walter Charleton, the Newtonian, Roger Cotes,[29] and above all Boyle himself, who, pondering the old scholastic question concerning God's

---

[28] Baumer, *Religion and the Rise of Scepticism*, 85.

[29] Descartes, *Meditationes de prima philosophia*, in *Oeuvres de Descartes*, ed. Charles Adam and Paul Tannery (Paris, 1897-1910), VII, 434-36; Walter Charleton, *The Darknes of Atheism Dispelled by the Light of Nature: A Physico-theologicall Treatise* (London, 1652), 217; Newton, *Philosophiae Naturalis Principia Mathematica*, in *Opera quae exstant omnia*, ed. Samuel Horsley (London, 1779-85), II, xx, xxiii.

ability to make a better world than he has in fact created, and evoking God's "immense power and unexhausted wisdom," answered in contrast both to Abelard before him and Leibniz after him that "the divine architect" could indeed "make [such] a greater master-piece"—or who again, citing the Aristotelian denial to God of either the creation or the providential government of the world (which had so exercised his medieval predecessors), confessed that he took "divers of *Aristotle's* opinions relating to religion to be more unfriendly, not to say pernicious, to it, than those of several other heathen philosophers."[30]

It is hardly surprising, then, that if one glances at the sort of arguments Boyle typically makes in fighting his alleged rearguard action, one finds oneself on familiar ground. Responding as he is, not to fears about the implications of the mechanical view of nature but to a long-established worry about the threat posed by Aristotle's (and other cognate) ideas to Christian orthodoxy, it is understandable that he makes his case within the terms of a tradition of theological, philosophical, and scientific discourse dating back already in his day three centuries and more. That is to say (and in common with Descartes, Charleton, and Gassendi), he invokes the old scholastic distinction between the absolute and ordained power, or extraordinary and ordinary providence of God, which continued to reverberate through the writings of seventeenth-century theologians, generating echoes and harmonies in the thinking of Francis Bacon, John Locke, and the great Newton himself.[31] The implication is that a miracle like that which delivered Daniel's three companions from Nebuchadnezzar's fiery furnace results from an interposition of God's "absolute and supernatural power," by which he withholds "his ordinary and general concourse," suspending "the ordinary or usual course of things." For "the laws of motion, without which the present state and course of things could not be maintained, did not necessarily spring from the nature of matter, but depended on the will of the divine author of things," who, being omnipotent, can "do whatever involves no contradiction."[32]

To Leibniz, admittedly, Boyle's apparatus of mechanical forces and divinely imposed laws of nature was inadequate to explain the nature

[30] Robert Boyle, *A Free Inquiry into the Vulgarly Received Notion of Nature*, in *The Works of the Honourable Robert Boyle*, ed. Thomas Birch, (London, 1972), V, 195-96, 163-64.

[31] Boyle, *Free Inquiry*, in *Works*, V, 216, 223; *Some Considerations about the Reconcileableness of Reason and Religion*, in *Works*, IV, 161-62. For Gassendi, see Osler, "Providence, Divine Will, and the Theological Background to Gassendi's Views on Scientific Knowledge," 549-60; for the pertinent views of Descartes, Charleton, Bacon, and Newton, see Oakley, *Omnipotence, Covenant, and Order*, 84-87, and for those of Locke, Francis Oakley and Elliott W. Urdang, "Locke, Natural Law, and God," *Natural Law Forum*, 11 (1966), 92-109.

[32] Boyle, *Some Considerations*, in *Works*, IV, 159-62; *Christian Virtuoso, ibid.*, V, 521; *Free Inquiry, ibid.*, V, 170, 216, 223.

and behavior of things. To him that approach, with its externalism, and its fixation on "the divine volition and command," smacked of Malebranchian occasionalism. It simply would not suffice.[33] What was needed was the recognition within the world of natural things of a creative but "indwelling force," an "indwelling law" from which "actions and passions proceed," a willingness to ascribe to natural phenomena a certain independence of God, a certain "self-sustaining efficacy."[34] But it would be anachronistic to try to explain the disagreement as one between a scientific thinker who was clear about the logical implications of the "mechanical philosophy" and another who, because of religious inhibitions, was not. I would suggest, rather, that what one is seeing here (as in the clash with Clarke) is an encounter between two men each possessed of one of the radically different understandings of the nature of things so often to be found jostling side by side in early-modern scientific thinking.[35] One was that of Leibniz, redolent of Lovejoy's great chain of being and teetering on the edge of Spinozist determinism, the other, that of Boyle or Clarke, responding, rather, to what I have called the covenantal vision. And if, for good theological reasons, and in accordance with that vision, the natural world was no longer conceived as a luminous world fraught with purpose by virtue of its own indwelling rationality, it was conceived, nonetheless, as possessing a contingent but stable order that God, by virtue of his ordained power had freely imposed upon it and to which the empirical investigations of the scientists, though certainly not proof against the incursions of omnipotence, could be taken to be a safe guide.

III. "Methodology," Max Weber once remarked, "can only be self-reflection on the means which have proven to be valuable in actual research." To the degree to which that is true, the argument outlined in the preceding pages witnesses to the fruitfulness of Lovejoy's approach to the history of ideas. For while that argument aims to engineer a significant qualification of the overall picture of European intellectual history outlined in his *Great Chain of Being*, it is only by the continued

[33] Leibniz, *De ipsa natura*, §§ 3 and 5; in *Die philosophischen Schriften von Gottfried Wilhelm Leibniz*, ed. C. J. Gerhardt (Berlin, 1875-90), IV, 505-7.

[34] *Ibid.*, IV, 505, 507-9 §§ 2, 5, 7 and 9. See also J. E. McGuire, "Boyle's Conception of Nature," *JHI*, 33 (1972), 539. For a similar appraisal see Carolyn Merchant, *The Death of Nature: Women, Ecology, and the Scientific Revolution* (New York, 1980), 275-89; for a different one see Amos Funkenstein, *Theology and the Scientific Imagination from the Middle Ages to the Seventeenth Century* (Princeton, 1986), 123 n.22.

[35] As in the thinking of Newton himself, which, voluntarist though it was, bore also the clear imprint of Henry More's view of nature. See Alexandre Koyré, *From the Closed World to the Infinite Universe* (Baltimore, 1957), 190; J. E. McGuire, "Neoplatonism and Active Principles: Newton and Corpus Hermeticum," in *Hermeticism and the Scientific Revolution*, ed. Robert W. Westman and J. E. McGuire (Los Angles, 1977), 93-142.

exploitation of the methodological approach he himself pioneered that it succeeds (to whatever extent it does) in realizing that aim.

That approach, it will be recalled, was distinguished by three motifs. The first was its interdisciplinary quality. "Ideas," Lovejoy said, "are the most migratory things in the world." "The presence and influence of the same presuppositions or other operative 'ideas' " should be detectable "in very diverse provinces of thought and in different periods." As a result, the working of a given idea needs, "*if* its nature and its historic role are to be fully understood, to be traced connectedly through all the phases of a man's reflective life in which those workings manifest themselves, or through as many of them as the historian's resources permit."[36] Hence the second motif, the need for cooperation or collaboration among specialists in all the pertinent fields, for no one "can be a competent original investigator in many provinces even of history."[37] The more so if, in accordance with the third of his motifs, one pursues one's study of the history of ideas not by focusing on periods, schools, systems, or -isms, all of which involve "ideas-complexes" or compounds, frequently unstable, but by breaking those complexes down into their component elements or "unit-ideas" (such as specific propositions or principles along with their corollaries) and tracing them across time as he himself did in his classic work.[38]

All three motifs recur in my own attempt to chart from the twelfth to the eighteenth centuries and across the boundaries dividing nations and differing fields of thought, the history of the distinction between the absolute and ordained power and the vision of the nature of things that pivoted on it. That being so, perhaps I may be permitted simply to dismiss as a trifle premature the obituary for this "Lovejovian" genre of intellectual history recently proclaimed by Lawrence Stone.[39] But the critiques mounted by J. G. A. Pocock, John Dunn, and (especially) Quentin

---

[36] Arthur O. Lovejoy, *Essays in the History of Ideas* (Baltimore, 1948), xii; "The Historiography of Ideas," *Proceedings of the American Philosophical Society*, 78 (1938), 530-35; "Reflections on the History of Ideas," *JHI*, 1, (1940), 4; *Great Chain of Being*, 15.

[37] Lovejoy, "Historiography of Ideas," 536-40; "Reflections," 6-9.

[38] Lovejoy, *Great Chain of Being*, 3-15; "Historiography of Ideas," 537-39. Louis Mink, "Change and Causality in the History of Ideas," *Eighteenth Century Studies*, 2 (1969), 7-25, has plausibly criticized the degree to which Lovejoy, misled by the analogy he had drawn from physical chemistry, treated his unit-ideas as if they were things, unchanging atomic particles, incapable themselves of possessing a history; but Mink himself concedes that in his actual historical practice, if not in his programmatic methodological statements, Lovejoy either focused his attention on idea-complexes such as the great chain of being, which certainly do change across time, or tended to treat his unit-ideas less as elements than as dynamic forces—that is, as idea-complexes.

[39] See Lawrence Stone, *The Past and the Present* (Boston, 1981), 85-86.

Skinner are of a more substantive nature.[40] If intellectual historians can risk a twinge of wry amusement at Stone's born-again willingness to confess that "ideas, culture and individual will" can indeed function in history as "independent variables," and as "important causal agents of change,"[41] they can draw cold comfort from the heavy freight of mythology, fiction, conceptual confusion, distortion, and even absurdity generated by the ahistorical or inadequately historical goals and procedures that these fellow intellectual historians regard as characteristic of the history of ideas as traditionally pursued. And even colder comfort, if they are admirers of Lovejoy, from Skinner's blunt conclusion that the Lovejovian methodology for the history of ideas is not only prone to produce the type of "conceptual morass" that Dunn deplores[42] but is itself misguided, is wrong in principle, "rests on a fundamental philosophic mistake," producing not just histories that "can sometimes go wrong" but histories that "can never go right."[43]

But in this, or so I would argue,[44] Skinner is simply mistaken. Misled, it would seem, by too selective a reading of Lovejoy's methodological discussions, perhaps also by a tendency to assume that Lovejoy himself shared the historiographical failings ascribed to others,[45] he misses the precise thrust of Lovejoy's approach as well as the degree to which the latter's concerns coincide with his own.[46] Although the claims he makes are applied on a broader front, Skinner himself has testified to the fact that the intellectual context of his own methodological enterprise was the way in which the history specifically of *political thought* was being written, and it was, in fact, from the crimes real or alleged of the historians of political thought that he compiled his formidable syllabus of errors.[47] What he was reacting to, in effect, were "two prevailing assumptions about the study of the classic texts in the history of political thought."

[40] For these critiques, their underlying assumptions, and the responses they have stimulated, see Oakley, *Omnipotence, Covenant, and Order*, 27-30, and 127-28 n.41.

[41] Stone, *Past and Present*, 80-81, 83.

[42] John Dunn, "The Identity of the History of Ideas," *Philosophy*, 43 (1968), 97.

[43] Quentin Skinner, "Meaning and Understanding in the History of Ideas," *History and Theory*, 8 (1969), 35, 37.

[44] See *Omnipotence, Covenant, and Order*, 27-40.

[45] Skinner refers to the opening (methodological) chapter of *The Great Chain of Being* but does not illustrate from Lovejoy's writings any of the numerous errors he attributes to the practitioners of the traditional history of ideas ("Meaning and Understanding," esp. 35-39). Other critics of that genre usually refer to Lovejoy's approach only in the most general terms and sometimes in such a fashion as to suggest that they could comfortably plead innocent to the charge of having read him.

[46] See Oakley, *Omnipotence, Covenant, and Order*, 32-34.

[47] Set forth in "Meaning and Understanding," 3-53, a listing of faults compiled with a degree of polemical zeal about which he himself later conceded a twinge of mild regret. See Skinner, "Some Problems in the Analysis of Political Thought and Action," *Political Theory*, 2 (1974), 279.

The first assumption is akin to that made by the proponents of the New Criticism in literary studies, namely, that "the source of a text's intelligibility lies within itself and its understanding does not require the commentator to consider its context." The second is that "a satisfactory history can be constructed out of the 'unit-ideas' contained in such texts, or else out of linking such texts in a chain of alleged influences."[48] The second assumption, you should note, he appears to have regarded as a *consequence* of the first, and, when he attacked it, it was in an attempt to argue his claim that the first assumption constitutes "a wholly inadequate methodology for the conduct of the history of ideas," one "incapable in principle of considering or even recognizing some of the most crucial problems which arise in any attempt to understand the relations between what a given writer may have *said*, and what he may be said to have meant by saying what he said."[49]

That claim I am not disposed to dispute. But while such a methodology may conceivably have been characteristic of the way in which the history of political thought has frequently been written, I see no grounds at all for equating it with the methodology that Lovejoy himself proposed or that he and his collaborators attempted to apply. The intellectual context of his methodological enterprise was a much broader one, and the precision with which he formulated his own stance was of a much higher order. Certainly, it is misleading to represent him as concentrating simply on "studying the form of words involved" and wholly inaccurate to depict his enterprise as constituting "little more than a very misleading fetishism of words."[50] There is every reason to believe, indeed, that he would have felt a good deal of sympathy with the views of Dunn and Skinner, with their negative appraisal of much that has passed as history of ideas, their sensitivity to the ease with which the historian can impose on the texts he is reading a spurious unity or coherence, their preoccupation with the way in which people actually use words, and their antipathy, therefore, toward any treatment of ideas across time that smacks even remotely of any sort of "fetishism of words."[51] Hence his explicit *rejection* of the approach to literary studies being promoted in his own day by the advocates of the New Criticism. Good reading, he argued, was dependent on more than a scrutiny of a text's "own literal and explicit content"; it was dependent "upon a knowledge—or an assumption—about what he [the author] was trying to do," something that

---

[48] Skinner, "Some Problems," 279; cf. "Meaning and Understanding," 31.

[49] Skinner, "Meaning and Understanding," 31.

[50] Skinner, "Meaning and Understanding," 36 and 39.

[51] He does not appear, for example, to have appraised very highly either the historical or the philosophical respectability of J. B. Bury's *Idea of Progress* (a work frequently adduced in the recent literature as an example of the traditional approach to the history of ideas). See Lovejoy, "Historiography of Ideas," 541-42. *Essays*, xiv, and "The Meaning of Romanticism for the History of Ideas," *JHI*, 2 (1941), 259.

cannot "always be safely or fully inferred from the obvious content of the work."[52] As a result, he himself championed a historical, contextual approach to literature. And in literary history as also in the history of philosophy, where he detected parallel problems, he stressed the danger of too obsessive a preoccupation with masterpieces and the importance, accordingly, of studying minor writers and thinkers and of grasping the "collective thought" of a given age. Only thus, indeed, is a truly *historical* understanding of the "few great writers of that age possible."[53]

Neither the approach to the history of ideas that Lovejoy championed nor his actual attempts to pursue that approach can be faulted, then, on the grounds that Skinner adduces. For they reflect no disposition to slight the meanings intended by the authors of the texts under scrutiny or to ignore the contextual studies necessary if those meanings are to be identified with any sort of precision. Indeed, there is a sense in which Lovejoy's particular program enriches that context and eases that task of identification. The context in which a text is to be understood, after all, is no more a simple given than is the meaning we ascribe to that text.[54] It is the product, rather, of historical reconstruction, reflecting inevitably the interpretative choice of the historian. One of the great strengths of Lovejoy's approach to the history of ideas is that it adopts an interpretative strategy in the absence of which some texts—notably those embodying the more migratory of ideas—are doomed to be improperly or inadequately understood. For it is particularly sensitive to the impact of the written word, cognizant of the degree to which an author may be responding to questions posed by thinkers predating him by centuries, or may be nudged along his path by the pressure, the logical promptings, and the "particular go" (Lovejoy's phrase)[55] of an idea he has appropriated. It is a program mindful of the extent, therefore, to which the community in the context of which that author does his thinking includes not only those presently living but those who have gone before. And though intellectuals often but oddly overlook the fact, it was Lovejoy's great achievement to have reminded us of how large a part books play in their lives, of how, through books, their society is peopled with the dead, of how often they hear or make the dead to speak in new and frequently vibrant ways.

Williams College

---

[52] Lovejoy, "Reflections," 9-16; "Historiography of Ideas," 531-35.

[53] Lovejoy, *Great Chain of Being*, 19-20; cf. "Historiography of Ideas," 533-55.

[54] Endorsing here the view stated by Bhikhu Parekh and R. N. Berki, "The History of Political Ideas: A Critique of Q. Skinner," *JHI*, 34 (1973), 182-84, though not necessarily all the claims they choose to affiliate with that view.

[55] Lovejoy, "Reflections," 23.

PART THREE

QUESTIONS

Chapter X.a

NOTES AND DOCUMENTS

HISTORY CHANGING FORM[1]

By J. Huizinga

In a previous essay[2] I have defined history as an intellectual form, i.e., a form in which the mind masters a domain lying within its grasp. Similar intellectual forms would be literature, music, philosophy. But *form* is a word covering a wide range of meaning. Thus it could be said that history as a type of mental inquiry *is* a form. Yet histories also *have* form, shapes and appearances as individual as the times they interpret; the history of the Roman Empire or of the city of New York, for instance, has a special pattern of its own, distinguishable from all others and instantly recognizable by one who knows the subject even slightly.

This latter interpretation suggests, however, still a third variant of the meaning of *form*. For though any history has of necessity an individual form, some histories have a more interesting form than others. The mind passes an aesthetic judgment in these matters. It is of *form* in the sense of something aesthetically arresting that I would speak here. I want to consider history as a form of knowledge with power to fill the imagination.

In fact, the chief historical talent seems to me to be *imagination*—not fancy, but that image-making force which recreates an original thing so that others may seem to see the features and hear the voices of the billions of people who once lived. Then it is as if the words of Michelet came true: *"L'histoire c'est une résurrection."*

Curiously enough, photography with its thousands of images has often done disservice to our power to imagine the past. Our heads have become kaleidoscopes of pictures of everything on earth—pictures we have seen in

---

[1] A communication read in the Netherlands Academy of Sciences, Section of Letters, on January 15, 1941. Condensed from the author's own translation by Bert and Emily Wabeke.

[2] Professor J. Huizinga of Leiden University, the well-known medievalist and author of *The Waning of the Middle Ages,* has made notable contributions to the philosophy of history. The present essay is a specific development of the general theory of history embodied in an article "On a Definition of History" which was first printed in the *Communications of the Royal Netherlands Academy of Sciences, Section of Letters,* vol. 68 (1929), and reprinted in the same year in the author's *Cultuurhistorische Verkenningen* (Haarlem, Tjeenk Willink, 1929). A slightly modified version was published in English as a contribution to *Philosophy and History: Essays Presented to Ernst Cassirer,* ed. by Raymond Klibansky and H. J. Paton (Oxford, Clarendon Press, 1936), 1–11, and in Dutch in the latest edition of the Winkler-Prins *Encyclopedia, art.* "Geschiedenis."

movies, in books, in all the myriad displays of photographic skill. But the miscellaneous snapshot gallery is not to be confused with the power of historical imagination which is able to see through all these glimpses to the true form of the past, and reveal it anew, though never perfectly, to the minds of the readers.

This image of any part of history is, of course, little more than a potentiality. The history of the Roman Empire, taken as a whole, can hardly be more than an indefinite multitude of notions, accessible to the mind through reading or research. It is ore waiting for the labor of man to fashion it into form. Philosophy can speculate on whether or not the real form will ever be revealed. But the living desire of the historian is not to speculate, but to see this form, this shape of things gone by, and to create its image.

Perhaps, however, it would be better to drop this provocative word *image,* and to use another, obviously more closely allied to history. For the function of history can be described quite accurately as narration, a *story-telling.* Certainly in former times history took form as a *relatio.* However much the genius of historians might differ, they treated their subject-matter as a story : Thucydides as well as Herodotus, Machiavelli as well as Villani, down to Voltaire in his *Charles XII,* and even to Macaulay's *History of England* or Motley's *Rise of the Dutch Republic.* This form of historical narrative is closely connected with the ancient literary affiliations of history in times when its profession was hardly to be called scientific and when its product still mainly bore a static character, that of a direct rendering of the material offered by tradition.

But modern scientific treatment of history has often apparently invalidated this term *story.* Unless its express aim is to provide popular reading matter, a modern historical monograph is not a relation, but a disquisition. This does not mean that the contemporary work is not excellently written, but that the reader must follow the author in another mental fashion than formerly. He must keep a critical eye on the writer; he must weigh his arguments. Nevertheless, if the author is eminent and the reader's fancy lively, even the most logical scientific monograph will be enjoyable in a literary sense. In spite of all, it will be as if the author told a story rich in entanglements, suspense, and dénouement.

History, even in its severest scientific form, should always be readable. Unreadable history is no history at all, but at best a sample of historical research lacking aesthetic form. For history is not simply logical; it is epic and dramatic. Of course I am not speaking of an intentional embellishment of historical narrative with dramatic or romantic motifs, of *histoire romancée.* My assumption is that history in itself shares the aesthetic essence of the epic and the drama. No intelligent reader can read a tolerably well-written bit of history without being touched constantly in his epic or dramatic sensibilities. This response comes not just from the way in which the materials are presented, but seems to appertain to the events themselves.

As we approach our own times, however, this element of the epic and dramatic in history seems to fade, even to vanish. It is as if former stages of civilization exhibited something which is lacking today. I find this especially true of American history, which, because it has passed in less than two centuries from rustic simplicity to a highly technical complexity, exhibits my point in striking fashion. As I speak of the gradual loss of form inherent in the material of modern history, particularly in the history of the United States since the Civil War, I should like to make it clear that I find this increasing shapelessness due not to an optical illusion nor to a deficiency in the forces or fashions of historical imagination, but to a change in the components of history itself. This view implies, of course, that in the technical and ideological composition of the present world there is little place left for the fine and venerable product of the mind over which Clio stood sponsor. So gloomy a view warrants scepticism, even my own; nevertheless the thought persists.

The history of North America before the War of Independence shows all the features proper to colonial history in general; viz., a certain lack of unity, a certain disparity, a certain rusticity. Its pattern becomes visible only from close by. The general reader, who incidentally counts for much in matters of history, will not be struck by particular beauty of line or color in the story of the thirteen separate colonies. Only the specialist who has an abundance of detailed knowledge will recognize in it those traits which make history a living thing. But it is not enough for history that the specialist should understand and enjoy it. History reaches its full function of fecundating civilization only when its general idea is available to all. This condition was fulfilled for American history from the moment the thirteen colonies wrested their freedom from the mother country. Henceforth instead of being a number of disparate units, the young states of America stand formally united. It was, to be sure, a defective cohesion which the Articles of Confederation had been able, after much trouble, to give the new commonwealth. The Federal Congress had no right to lay taxes and levies upon the several states nor means of coercion to enforce its resolutions. Economic crises within and diplomatic troubles without complete the picture of confusion and distress, which would make the history of those years indistinct to the eye but for the swiftness of the transition from disorder and crisis to order and stability. It is superfluous to recall the sequence of events. But it is interesting to note that when the delegates from the states met in the 1787 convention, they had on their official agenda no plan for far-reaching reforms. Yet two years after their meeting, the most important document of modern political history, the cornerstone of the mightiest commonwealth, had become law. Almost simultaneously the French Revolution began a new era of history in Europe and George Washington's oath of office inaugurated a great period in the history of America.

In the first period after 1789 the historical lines are relatively simple. The persons acting are of a marked type, and the conditions and the conflicts are easy to grasp. In short, the history of those years shows shape and color. Even the economic problems, indissolubly mixed up with the political factors in American history, still display a simple structure. Capitalistic enterprises of trade, navigation, and industry in the northern states are contrasted with the landed estates in the aristocratic South, and with the rising agrarian interests in the regions then called the West, with their population of pioneers ever moving farther on. These western people, however, hardly as yet affect the history of their country. Lacking statehood and inexperienced in politics, they do not play a large part in the government, which is still in the hands of an *élite*—for such are the Yankees as well as the slave-holders. Now it is nearly always a fact that the history of a period has a distinct form when its public life is conducted by an *élite*. The masses still remain in the background.

A pronounced *form* is characteristic of American history during the first half of the nineteenth century. This epoch abounds in distinct, even picturesque types which easily fasten themselves in one's memory. There are not only men like Jefferson and Andrew Jackson, but also political leaders of the second rank like Daniel Webster, Henry Clay, and John Calhoun. Although the period is already dominated by such economic issues as free trade *vs.* tariff, banking and currency, and internal improvements, the resultant conflicts present themselves in political form, as constitutional disputes, nearly all involving the essential rivalry between the federal authority and states' rights. The antagonism between opposing interests and opinions still takes an almost classic shape. It seems very likely that in those days oratory and debate in Congress had a far greater effect and a much more direct influence on important decisions than in later times. The fame of men like Clay and Webster rests even now upon certain great speeches in the House or in the Senate.

Notwithstanding its simple and clear structure, American history during the period from 1820–1850 presents rather less marked features than European history of the same period. The reason is evident. Where a state is almost *continental* in extent, one mighty nation ruled by a fundamental law, one of the principal themes of history is missing; namely, that of ever repeated strife between independent powers for supremacy, prestige, or material advantage. This theme had filled all the epochs of Antiquity, the Middle Ages, and modern times in the old world. But American history no longer yielded anything fully equivalent to the fascinating and changeful play of diplomacy and violence going on among the competing units of political Europe. A continent-state of this type ceases, as a rule, to produce history of the classic pattern; the element which we call epic-dramatic hardly finds room for expression. Only a crisis which breaks the political unity itself can bring again to the fore the *story* quality of history. This is what happened when the conflict over slavery became unavoidable and bloody war between North and South filled four tragic years of American life. Then at once the epic shape of history reappears. This form is not the result of literary fancy. It lies in the facts themselves. Abraham Lincoln and Robert E. Lee bear the true features of an Agamemnon and a Hector. Neither Lincoln's heroism nor Lee's chivalry may be made light of as the mere effects of romantic worship or of artful grouping of the facts. It is history itself which in these two characters takes form. The surrender at Appomattox and the shot in Ford's theatre meant the end of a tragedy in the fullest sense of the term.

After the Civil War, the history of the United States not only loses dramatic pathos, but is also robbed of comprehensible and striking form. The general reader at least will find it more or less confused, perplexing, and without unity. Its image is obscure; its outlines hard to remember. This loss of visual pregnancy is important to our theme. We have been wont to see the happenings of the past as a series of scenes; we have been accustomed to interpret history as the acting of well-defined rôles of *dramatis personae*. One has only to recall some of the famous paintings of the historical *genre* to be convinced of this. But this concept of a special personnel of players for each chapter of history, which clung to our interpretation of former periods, no longer serves modern times. We are hindered in such a vision by our strong consciousness of collective processes as the real basis of our history. We instinctively refuse to reduce them to pictorial form. However, this *impersonalization* of history is dearly bought, for in losing its pictorial form, history has lost its capacity to be retained in memory as a lively and lasting image. American history after the Civil War is exceptionally well suited to illustrate this loss.

When reading accounts which portray the decades of 1870–1890, one can hardly escape the impression that the history of the United States is losing its former charm. The story of those years leaves a sense of weariness, of confusion. Yet it is not historical importance that is wanting. The scene is as full of passionate conflicts as ever before. Public life is as loud, the problems are as weighty. The struggle for silver, the movements of Grangers and populists, the particularly bitter and bloody strikes of the epoch, the rise of the monster trusts—all these subjects would seem to supply ample material for history in the grand style. Nevertheless the subject-matter fails to make a captivating story. Is it because corruption and vulgarity loom larger in that period than before or after? The cause, it would seem, lies deeper. There is an indistinctness in the sequence of events; there is no form to be visualized in the whole. Of course, an American well versed in the particulars of his country's past and present will doubtless perceive features here more clearly than a foreign historian could do. Still I doubt whether even the best student of American history could trace an historical portrait of persons like Conkling or J. G. Blaine as vivid and striking as he might draw of Jefferson or Andrew Jackson. A real difference in the historical factors of the two eras makes the historical perceptions different.

I feel sure that the main reason for this difference lies in the continual domination of the economic factor over the political in later American history. Consequently history has had to change its record of personal happenings to one of collective phenomena. In the economic process individuals may play a special part—as inventors, as promoters, as tycoons, as legislators, but never as *persons,* and never as *masters* of the process. In political events, however, individuals emerge as personalities, fully human in their aspects. This circumstance implies that in a history dominated by the economic factor—as American history undoubtedly is, far more so than European—the human element recedes into the background. I can but call this an objective change in the historical process itself, a change which is part of the awesome phenomenon we are now witnessing with foreboding: the mechanization of all social life.

If my conclusion is correct, a history which has become diffuse and indistinct because of such an excess of the economic factor may resume its dramatic tension and marked outline only when the political process regains a primary importance, when events come to gravitate around a striking personality as protagonist in some violent strife. This is what happened in modern American history when the conflict over Cuba arose, when war with Spain was declared and Theodore Roosevelt burst upon' the scene with his surprising actions and great success. This remarkable man electrified American history not because he was the first to fight the trusts, but because he was Teddy, a vivid and inimitable type of man for all time to come. Whereas W. J. Bryan, with all the fulminant pathos of vigorous oratory in his early years and with all his serious later work for international peace, has long been a vague shadow, whereas even Woodrow Wilson remains too much a painful recollection, Theodore Roosevelt keeps shape—and this in spite of that other who bears the same surname and whose authority and vast responsibilities now exceed those of his predecessor. Once more in our day great names are rising, and political issues overtower economic ones. And once more a vast scene of dramatic history—and tragedy—has been revealed.

Let us now summarize and conclude. Several decades of increasing shapelessness in American history can be explained by the fact that a political unit covering the main part of a whole continent loses, by its very homogeneity, the most fertile of all themes for history: the conflict between independent powers, be they peaceful rivals or hostile opponents. Furthermore, the ever-increasing preponderance in such a continent-commonwealth of economic forces is likely to obscure the human being as an actor in history. It is of course true that an American living in the midst of his country's throbbing life will feel the excitement of the presidential campaigns, for instance, and find in them the drama that the historical process should provide. And yet has such a focus given him a vision of true history, comparable to what the world still keeps of Salamis, of Luther before the Diet in Worms, or of the eighteenth of Brumaire? I doubt it.

There is one thought to be added. The modern world is becoming more and more accustomed to thinking in numbers. America has hitherto been more addicted to this, perhaps, than Europe. But now even in Europe men of science, technologists and statisticians, have driven almost all thought into the corner of purely quantitative valuation. Only the number counts, only the number expresses thought. This shift in the mode of thinking is full of grave dangers for civilization, and for that civilizing product of the mind called history. Once *numbers* reign supreme in our society, there will be no story left to tell, no images for history to evoke. Already many historical writers have moved to the periphery of Clio's domain and concern themselves with those regions which belong in a sense to history without actually being history (archaeology, anthropology, history of art and literature, etc.). Does this indicate that the tree which once bore the fruits of epic political history is bound to wither? Or will a coming generation win back the classic form of history?

University of Leiden.

DISCUSSION

A REPLY TO J. HUIZINGA ON THE FORM AND FUNCTION OF HISTORY

BY JOSEPH KATZ

In an essay entitled "History Changing Form," published in the April, 1943, issue of this *Journal*, J. Huizinga, the eminent Dutch historian, raises some fundamental questions with regard to contemporary civilization. He notes an increasing *impersonalization* of politics and speaks with alarm about the "awesome phenomenon" of the mechanization of all social life. History is said to be losing the former "charm" which any account of it, even in the severest scientific form, ought to reveal; for an aesthetic quality seems to appertain to the events of history themselves. To this objective change corresponds a similar subjective change in the treatment of history. The tendency among historians is to concern themselves "with those regions which belong in a sense to history without actually being history," such as archaeology or anthropology. In general, thought seems to be driven by "men of science, technologists and statisticians" into the corner of purely quantitative valuation. "Only the number counts, only the number expresses thought."

Such are Huizinga's assertions, and they ought not to pass unchallenged. I shall try to show that his evaluation of contemporary history involves some inconsistencies and depends upon questionable standards. His conception of the function of history seems to rest on an illegitimate concern for its aesthetic form.

The events of contemporary history, according to Huizinga, betray an increasing "shapelessness." His test case is American history between 1870 and 1890. He finds that in spite of its passionate conflicts the history of these two decades is poor in drama and its outlines hard to remember. He contrasts the leaders of that period with such personalities as chivalrous Lee, heroic Lincoln, electrifying "Teddy" Roosevelt. On the one hand are men who serve as mere exponents of an impersonal "economic" process, on the other are dramatic personalities who show themselves masters of a process where the "political" element dominates.

There are a number of objections to Huizinga's way of reasoning. In the first place, it is hardly legitimate to single out a relatively uneventful period and by contrasting it with some of the more dramatic occurrences of history to take its lack of drama as an indication of increasing "loss of form." Moreover, Huizinga seems to contradict himself when he states that in our day great names are again arising and *political issues overtower economic ones.* "And once more a vast scene of dramatic history—and tragedy—has been revealed.'' In the immediately preceding paragraph he has declared that the domination of the economic over the political factor constitutes an *objective* change in the historical process itself, which is supposed to have taken place already or to be in the process of taking place.

Huizinga asserts that in consequence of the domination of the economic over the political factor history was forced to change its record of personal happenings to one of collective phenomena. Moreover, it seems to me that when he contrasts personal with impersonal factors he implicitly also makes a distinction between objective and subjective determinations in history. Thus it is significant that when speaking of the leading figures in political events he designates them not only as *persons* but also as *masters* of the process. He says: ''In the economic process individuals may play a special part—as inventors, as promoters, as tycoons, as legislators, but never as *persons,* and never as *masters* of the process.''[1] Recent history is characterized as mainly an economic process, and certain features of it are rejected. He designates them, not very fortunately, by the phrase ''impersonalization of history,'' by which, if our interpretation is correct, he also seems to signify a weakening of the subjective element. It is difficult to accept this phrase in either of the two senses. Obviously the tendency which Huizinga criticizes has its very beneficial side when viewed as an effort to eliminate so far as possible the arbitrary and harmful elements inherent in the amassing of power in the hands of an individual or a selected group. It can, therefore, hardly be called an ''impersonalization'' of *history;* especially as an ''impersonalization'' of politics may give to the human person a more pronounced stature in other fields. Likewise this development does not seem to indicate that the subject-object relation in history (a distinction which requires much elaboration) has fundamentally changed. This latter question ultimately leads back to a discussion of free will (frequently involved in similar approaches to an analysis of civilization) and calls for separate treatment which falls outside the scope of this reply.

When Huizinga regrets the ''impersonalization'' of politics, his view seems to be above all influenced by his concern for the *story quality* of history. He asserts that the historical process *should* provide drama, and he finds that even the excitement of presidential campaigns compares poorly with the vision of ''true history'' the world still keeps of Salamis, of Luther before the Diet of Worms, or of the eighteenth of Brumaire. Throughout Huizinga shows himself immensely concerned with the aesthetic character of history. He speaks of ''the fascinating and changeful play of diplomacy

---

[1] This interpretation seems to be confirmed by an earlier work of Huizinga entitled *In the Shadow of Tomorrow* (New York, 1936). He asserts (*op. cit.,* 225 ff.), that a spiritual katharsis of culture cannot be expected from a structural change of society or social planning, but only from an internal regeneration of the individual, an individual who, it appears, masters objective conditions.

and violence,'' and with some relief he notes that ''the epic shape of history reappears'' when ''bloody war between North and South filled four tragic years of American life.''

Apparently, according to this view, the standard by which history is to be evaluated is conceived in terms of the narrative quality of the events.[2] True history is supposed to take the form of the epic and the drama. Yet it is evident that whether this assertion is true or not, these aesthetic effects are merely incidental to the events (and often less obvious to the participants than to the spectators). One might be attracted by the entertainment history provides. But one can hardly wish for the continuation of violence simply because it gives history ''visual pregnancy'' and ''pictorial form.'' Misery makes a good story. But it was an unfortunate abstraction which elevated an incidental characteristic to a normative level. Conflicts spring from antagonistic ideals and interests. To advocate conflict for conflict's sake would only betray a lack of other significant ideals. Huizinga fears that politics will no longer be ''the acting of well-defined rôles of *dramatis personae.*'' But he can hardly mean that human actions ought to conform to the standards of a well-acted tragedy, even though it provide enjoyment for future generations. Obviously this attitude, in spite of its contrary intentions, would be very unkind to man's aspirations and deprive real issues of that significance and seriousness which alone moves men to fight.[3]

Huizinga has devoted several writings to a discussion of contemporary problems. The most comprehensive statement of his views on this subject is to be found in the book already mentioned, *In the Shadow of Tomorrow* (New York, 1936; Dutch edition, 1935), with which may be compared *Der Mensch und die Kultur* (Stockholm, 1938), and the last chapter of *Homo ludens* (German edition, Amsterdam, 1939). His general position may be summarized as follows: He finds that with the exception of the various sciences contemporary thinking is characterized by a weakening of judgment in spite of, and partially because of, the spread of universal education and the facilities of communication. He believes that the ''mechanism of modern mass-entertainment'' is inimical to concentration and absorption,

[2] In other writings Huizinga shows himself primarily concerned with the spiritual and moral meaning of history. For a discussion of his views on this subject see the second part of this reply and also *note 3*.

[3] Elsewhere Huizinga himself rejects vigorously the notion of war for war's sake as an attempt to set up ''evil as a beacon and a guiding star for a misguided humanity'' (*In the Shadow of Tomorrow*, 127). It is surprising, therefore, that in this recent note he emphasizes the dramatic qualities of strife and war without a note of caution. It seems that his concern in the present context for the story character of history makes him neglect the ethical implications of his view. But it is significant that these implications would lead him in the end to conclusions which he utterly rejects.

and instead fosters passivity. Other crisis-symptoms are the widespread renunciation of rationality (in art and politics especially) and a puerile worship of life. In contrasting our time with similar periods of upheaval and seeming decline he notes one characteristic difference. Whereas the Christian system of morals, apart from certain exceptions, remained unshaken by the fall of the Roman Empire, the turmoils of the Renaissance and Reformation, and even the Revolution of 1789, our own civilization no longer seems to be orientated toward a transcendent ideal. This change is of primary importance; for the historical evaluation of different cultures "appears ultimately to be determined by its spiritual and ethical rather than its intellectual and aesthetic value-content. A culture which does not boast technical achievements or great sculptural art may still be a high culture, but not if it lacks charity" (*In the Shadow of Tomorrow*, 41–42). Thus Huizinga favors a return to "eternal truths, truths that are above the stream of evolution and change" (*op. cit.*, 238) which he finds expressed in the spirit (though not always in the institutions) of Christianity. He frequently speaks of moral principles as "unalterable and absolute," and in a letter to J. Benda entitled *L'esprit, l'éthique et la guerre* (Paris, 1934), he endorses M. Benda's view that these principles are to be regarded as the "trésor des âges passés perdu au XIXᵉ siècle." He admits that in favoring conversion and *return* he contradicts what he had said about the *irreversibility* of the historical process. But he thinks that this contradiction is due to "the antinomic determination, the inconclusiveness of all our judgment" (*In the Shadow of Tomorrow*, 237–238).

In surveying Huizinga's arguments it is characteristic to find him upholding a belief in "eternal" and "absolute" moral values. Moreover, in spite of the fact that he recognizes the irreversibility of the historical process, he demands revulsion and return if these values are to be realized again. On this twofold assumption our judgment must naturally remain "inconclusive." When we ask what Huizinga considers to be truths which are "above the stream of evolution and change," it is difficult to find an answer. Frequently it seems that he is referring to Christian standards of valuation. But as these principles themselves have had a history, they could hardly confirm his point. In reading such passages the suspicion seems to be warranted that Huizinga's "eternal truths" resemble too much certain definite features of the past which, though they are irrecoverable now, may still be regarded with that kind of longing which hopes that their day may not yet be gone. The notion of history as an *irreversible process* does not lead him to recognize at crucial points that values, whatever their "eternal" aspects, manifest themselves in temporal forms. This becomes particularly clear when he speaks of "transcendent ideals," in lacking which he thinks our time compares most unfavorably with other periods. Had his eyes been less fixed on the past, on that "treasure of bygone ages lost in the 19th century," he might have given more credit to the aspirations of contemporary society, which reveal features not dissimilar to what he calls orientation on transcendent ideals, "surrender to all that can be conceived as the highest," though present ideals have a different form and surrender may be more cautious and, in some quarters, more enlightened.   In other words, Huizinga does not explicitly recognize the historical process as cumulative and continuous.   (This recognition, by the way, affords a simple explanation why our age, like any age, differs from all preceding ones.)   But it is only after this recognition has been made and the material of history viewed accordingly that Huizinga's method of seeking guidance for the present in the past becomes really fruitful and the past affords illumination as well as direction.

Though there is a certain amount of indecision in Huizinga's approach to contemporary problems, he seems to be certain that our civilization is ailing and reveals particularly "grave evils and shortcomings."   Similar and more extreme views have been expressed.   The fear that our present civilization faces decline was a dominant theme of Continental thought in the era following upon the first world war.   It represents a late negative outgrowth of evolutionism, and must be distinguished from fin-de-siècle pessimism, since it asserts the specific corruption of our own time rather than the dubiousness of man's existence in general.   It has played a most important rôle in recent political thinking, where it frequently resembles an obsession.   But it has even invaded the field of cultural analysis to such an extent that one is not surprised to find in Huizinga recurrent phrases calling for redemption and salvation.   His view undoubtedly receives support when one considers the far-reaching and often disastrous effects of violence manifested in our time.   We must, therefore, concede to him that it was not an idle fear which prompted him to his warning, even though we must disagree with him as to the extent and nature of the disease.

Columbia University.

Chapter XI

TWO MEANINGS OF HISTORICISM IN THE WRITINGS OF DILTHEY, TROELTSCH, AND MEINECKE

By Calvin G. Rand

The meaning of the word "historicism" remains unsettled for many writers in the English-speaking world. A variety of definitions exists, and consequently, the concept is vague and ambiguous. Few attempts have been made to introduce order into these conflicting opinions.[1] There is no doubt that the concept of historicism has great plasticity, and it could be argued cogently that there can be no one meaning, only several. But just as a concept like empiricism is spoken of in different senses, yet still retains a comprehensive meaning, so for historicism, I shall contend, there are two closely related meanings which allow us to use the word intelligibly and more precisely.

In this enquiry into historicism I have followed the writings of Wilhelm Dilthey (1833–1911), Ernst Troeltsch (1865–1923), and Friedrich Meinecke (1862–1954).[2] These German authors are acknowledged authorities of the historicist tradition, and their particular explication of historicism is generally supported by other scholars (especially in Europe).[3] They are, moreover, historicists, themselves,

[1] Two of the better recent comments on historicism are D. E. Lee and R. N. Beck, "The Meaning of Historicism," *American Historical Review*, (April 1954); and H. Meyerhoff's introductory chapter to his anthology, *The Philosophy of History in Our Time* (New York, 1959).

[2] Of particular importance for the meaning of historicism are Dilthey, *Gesammelte Schriften*, Vols. III, VIII; Troeltsch, *Gesammelte Schriften*, III, *Christian Thought: Its History and Application* (New York, 1957) which comprises an English translation of *Der Historismus und seine Überwindung. Fünf Vörtrage*, and "The Ideas of Natural Law and Humanity in World Politics," in O. Gierke, *Natural Law* (Boston, 1957); Meinecke, *Die Entstehung des Historismus* (Munich, 1936), *Zur Theorie u. Philosophie der Geschichte* (Stuttgart, 1959), *Die Idee der Staatsräson in der neuren Geschichte* (Munich, 1924)—translated as *Machiavellism* (New Haven, 1957).

[3] To mention a few: E. Cassirer, *The Problem of Knowledge* (New Haven, 1950); F. Engel-Janosi, *The Growth of German Historicism* (Baltimore, 1944); W. Hofer, *Geschichtschreibung und Weltanschauung* (Munich, 1950); W. Bodenstein, *Neige des Historismus* (Berlin, 1959); E. Fulling, *Geschichte als Offenbarung* (Berlin, 1956); C. Antoni, *From History to Sociology* (Detroit, 1959); H. S. Hughes, *Consciousness and Society* (New York, 1958); H. Butterfield, *Man and His Past* (Cambridge, 1955); P. Geyl, *Use and Abuse of History* (New Haven, 1955); Ortega y Gasset, *Concord and Liberty* (New York, 1946); R. N. Stromberg, "History in the 18th Century," *J.H.I.* (April 1951); G. G. Iggers, "The Image of Ranke in American and German Historical Thought," *History and Theory*, Vol. II, No. 1.

writing from within the tradition; yet their accounts are not without criticism and comprise a balanced appraisal. The period of their productive scholarship (1880s to 1930s) represents the culmination of the historicist movement—a standpoint which allows them to survey the entire tradition and to point out and wrestle with severe difficulties raised by historicist thought. In this literature, then, there can be discerned two ways in which the term "historicism" is used. I am interested primarily in discussing these two meanings and only secondarily in setting forth actual historicist doctrine and its problems. While my intention is not to deal with the history of historicism, a few introductory comments on the word, itself, are in order.

The German "Historismus" originated in the XIXth century, although it did not enter into technical vocabulary much before the early XXth. It only became widely known in the 1920s through Troeltsch's writings.[4] Meinecke finds the term first used in Karl Werner's book on Vico (1879), in which "the philosophical historicism of Vico" (*philosophischen Historismus Vicos*) is mentioned, but with little comment on its meaning.[5] Shortly later, a more definite, yet disparaging use occurred in Carl Menger's polemic against G. Schmoller and the historical school of economics. Menger deplored their historical approach to political economy and spoke of "the false dogma of historicism in the domain of our science" (*das falsche Dogma des Historismus auf dem Gebiete unserer Wissenschafte*).[6] Subsequent interpretations, positive and negative, can be traced in the early XXth century,[7] until Troeltsch in 1922 gave a comprehensive definition of

[4] Particularly the collection entitled, *Der Historismus u. seine Probleme* (Tübingen, 1922), which comprises Vol. III of Troeltsch's *Gesammelte Schriften*.

[5] Meinecke, *Die Entstehung des Historismus*, 1. Werner's book, *G. Vico als Philosoph u. Gelehrte Forscher* (New York, n.d.), does, however, on p. 310 speak of "a one-sided historicism . . . which excludes a rational self-elevation above the temporal-historical process" (*einseitige Historismus . . . der eine denkende Selbsterhebung über zeitgeschichtliche Strömmungen . . . ausschliesst*). This passage foreshadows the historicism of Troeltsch and Meinecke and especially the problem of relativism, that is to say, man and his creations dissolved in the historical flow with no certainty on which to stand.

[6] C. Menger, "Die Irrtümer des Historismus in der deutschen National-Oekonomie," 1884, in *The Collected Works of Carl Menger* (London School of Economics #19, London, 1933), 4–5. Menger is not attacking the historical point of view, per se, but rather its introduction into the specific discipline of economics. He argues that progress in economics will come through a sharpening and deepening of its own methods and concepts, not through the outside assistance of the historian, the mathematician or the physiologist. See *ibid.*, 4. As Meinecke puts it, Menger is criticizing "the excessive valuation upon history in political economy" (*the übertriebene Bewertung der Geschichte in der National Ökonomie*). *Enstehung*, 1.

[7] See e.g. Karl Heussi, *Die Krisis der Historismus* (Tübingen, 1932), 1–15; also Walter Hofer, *Geschichtschreibung u. Weltanschauung* (Munich, 1950), 321f. and Lee and Beck, *op. cit.*

historicism as "the historicizing of our entire knowing and experiencing of the spiritual world, as it has taken place in the course of the XIXth century." [8] This very general definition grasped the point common to most earlier ones, in that it held historicism to mean: thinking in a *specific* historical way, or the assuming of a *specific* historical point of view in comprehending and experiencing the world of man's activities. The result of man's purposeful and creative actions is what is meant by "spiritual world" (*geistige Welt*). And, as Troeltsch asserts, this historical point of view had become rooted in our thinking and experiencing by the end of the XIXth century. Following Troeltsch, Meinecke in his classic *Enstehung des Historismus* (1936), traced the XVIIIth- and XIXth-century origins of this new orientation in thought. Earlier in 1901, Dilthey had made a similar analysis to which Troeltsch and Meinecke are both indebted.[9] Although Dilthey did not employ the word "Historismus," he was quite clearly writing about the same intellectual movement as his successors. Hence, this XIXth-century development, nurtured by the new German Historical School and by the many facets of the Romantic movement, a development praised by Meinecke as "one of the greatest spiritual revolutions that Western thought has experienced," [10] came to be called "historicism" in the following century. Writers like Meinecke have regarded it a liberating step forward; Croce even constructed a type of historicist philosophy, although a distinctly Hegellian version. Yet others like Karl Löwith and Karl Popper have deplored the consequences of historicism and, partly through misinterpretation, have dismissed it as pernicious. The arguments, pro and con, in the last seventy-five years have distorted whatever clear meaning the term might have developed. Still, the writings of Dilthey, Troeltsch, and Meinecke, in spite of many obscurities, are able to provide a basis upon which to construct an objective analysis.[11]

[8] (. . . *die Historisierung unseres ganzen Wissens und Empfindens der geistigen Welt, wie sie im Laufe des 19 Jahrhunderts geworden ist*), *Die Neue Rundschau* (1922), 573.

[9] W. Dilthey, "Das Achtzehnte Jahrhundert u. die Geschichtliche Welt," *G.S.* III.

[10] (*eine der grössten geistigen Revolutionem, die das abendländische Denken erlebt hat.*) *Enstehung*, 1.

[11] One confusing terminological point, plaguing even Meinecke and Troeltsch, is the occasional interchanging of "historicist" and "historical." It must be kept in mind that while these words overlap they also have separate meanings. "Historical" broadly denotes the past or an account of the past. "Historicist" is a narrower term referring to a particular way of considering the past, a way which certain writers claim will provide the fullest knowledge of the past. Historicist principles are, however, associated with the ideas of the XIXth century–German Historical School (from Niebuhr to Ranke); thus, that School of historical thought could be called "historicist." Yet, confusion arises when historicism is generally said to involve an

Now when historicism is said to mean a *specific* historical way of thinking, several items are open to analysis: the phrase "way of thinking," the content of this procedure, and the meaning of a *specific* historical way of thinking. Vagueness of terminology has played no small part in confusing readers of historicist literature.

The phrase "way of thinking" is a literal translation of the German "Denkweise," "Denkart," and "Denkform," which abound in Meinecke's writings. Other terms having analogous meanings are "Betrachtungsweise" (way of considering) and "Behandlungsweise" (way of treating).[12] Such English words as "view," "approach," "way of dealing with" convey the same sense. There are also involved affective connotations which could be summed up in the phrase "attitude toward." These broad terms suggest the manner in which an investigator (the subject) generally seeks to apprehend his subject matter (the object or content). If the subject matter be records of past events and the investigator an historian, then a way of thinking suggests a methodology of history, method conceived in a very pervasive sense. If the investigator be a thinking and perceiving man in general, and his content the world around him, there arises the question of a *Weltanschauung*. It will be argued that historicism as a way of thinking can justifiably be defined as a methodology at the least and a *Weltanschauung* at the most.[13] As a methodology, historicism will mean a body of formal concepts and principles to guide the historian in his study of past events. As a *Weltanschauung*, historicism will designate a comprehensive view of man and his world, based upon an analogous body of concepts.

First, historicism as a method of apprehending past events. It is clear that method in this context does not have to do with precise techniques of gathering empirical data, documentary analysis, and the like.[14] It means here a general procedure of investigation, and the

---

historical way of thinking. This terminology is not necessarily incorrect, but unprecise. It would be better to designate historicism as a *specific* historical way of thinking as in this study.

[12] See Meinecke, *Entstehung*, 5; and in the same volume Carl Hinrich's "Einleitung," xxvii. See further "Historismus" in J. Hoffmeister's *Wörterbuch der Philosophischen Begriffe* (Hamburg, 1955); the first definition is based upon the term "Denkweise."

[13] Note how Otto Hintze criticizes Troeltsch's lack of clarity as to whether he means historicism to be a "concept of a methodological direction of thinking in the sense of a logical conceptual structure" (*Begriff einer methodischen Denkrichtung im Sinne einer logischen Kategorial struktur*) or a general "World and life view" (*Welt- und Lebensanschauung*). "Troeltsch u. die Probleme des Historismus," *Historische Zeitschrift*, Vol. 135 (1927).

[14] On this point see Troeltsch, *G.S.* III, 3; also Meinecke, *Zur Theorie u. Philosophie der Geschichte*, 341.

concepts and principles involved should be looked upon as leading to broad, heuristic directives to the historian. They are meant to assist him in his orientation toward the past. They are to influence his aims and goals and to help determine what he must look for in his subject matter and what questions to put to that subject matter. Certain principles of investigation might not be strictly historical but, let us say, philosophical or anthropological; and the historian must be able to distinguish between them clearly. The XXth-century historian, G. P. Gooch, illustrates this difference when he writes:

the *treatment* (my emphasis) of law and institutions may be absolute or relative. The former sets up a system in conformity with an ideal formed by reason; the latter studies legal principles and methods in relation to the social needs from which they spring. The 18th century was dominated by the philosophic conception, the 19th by the historical.[15]

Historicists would similarly claim that a particular "treatment" of the past is required for a proper historical understanding, and would confirm Gooch's "relative" approach.

The methodological concepts of a *specific* historical way of thinking (i.e. historicist) can be summed up as individuality, development, and relatedness. Following in the Rankian tradition, Dilthey, Troeltsch, and Meinecke hold these concepts and the principles resulting from them the most pervasive and indispensable in any historical consideration.[16] Such concepts represent not only an analysis of the able historian's theoretical categories, but as well a prescription of the way in which he should view his subject matter. Hence, the historian, in studying and organizing the panorama of the past through records and other empirical evidence, is directed to look upon each person, event, nation, or era as a unique individual, which develops over a period of time through its own internal means and through causal interaction with other developing individuals. He must select characteristics which distinguish a particular individual from all others as well as characteristics common to all; he must note the different stages of an individual's development, what has led to these changes

---

[15] G. P. Gooch, *History and Historians in the Nineteenth Century* (Boston, 1959), 39.

[16] On Ranke, Meinecke writes: ". . . the principles which make his historical writing so vital and fruitful, namely, the feeling for the individual . . . for its particular individual development, for its common basis of life which ties all of these, one with another . . ." (. . . *die Prinzipien, die seine Geschichtschreibung so lebendig und fruchtbar machen, nämlich, der Sinn gemeinsamen, alles miteinander wieder verknupfenden Lebensgrund . . .*"), *Enstehung*, 601. The two major sections of Troeltsch's collection on historicism (*G.S.* III) deal with historical individuality (Chap. 2, pp. 111f.) and the development concept and universal history (Chap. 3, pp. 221f.). Likewise, Dilthey singles out the sense for the individual and for the genetic as the essence of the new historical point of view. *G.S.* III, 246–247.

and whether internal or external causes are in question; and he must determine, if significant, the influence of external causes, which may be other individuals or more general environmental factors. Putting it in another way, the historian notices that each individual is rooted in its own time and place in the course of history and that it grows out of the specific circumstances of the times.[17] The genetic principle is particularly obvious here and is deemed essential to the historian.[18] As Dilthey remarks, he must have "a sense for the genetic, for the true nature of development" (*Sinn für das Genetische, für die wahre Natur der Entwicklung*).[19]

In addition to these principles and concepts, the historian's feeling, emotion, and imagination are of major importance to historicists from Vico and Herder to Troeltsch and Meinecke. When Dilthey speaks of "Sinn," [20] he means more than pure cognition; the reference is in large part to the emotional attitude of the historian. "Sinn" translated as "interest in," "taste for," or "feeling" conveys this meaning. In another passage Dilthey, following Ranke, explicitly says "feeling" when correlating the two main principles of historicism, "genetic understanding" (*genetische Verständnis*) and "the feeling for the individual worth of every historical manifestation" (*das Gefühl des Eigenwertes jeder geschichtlichen Erscheinung*).[21] The historian's attitude, similar to the aesthetic, must be so innate or cultivated as to feel an appreciation and an affection for each historical phenomenon, solely for its own self, not as a means to a further end—that is to say, not as a case in point for a moral teaching in didactic history, nor as an instance of a law in types of scientific history. Likewise, Troeltsch, in addition to mentioning the importance of feeling (*Einfühlung*), cites further the historian's need for imagination and insight in order to grasp the novel and significant in the records of the past. Here lies the creative freedom, the genius, the magic of the great historian.[22]

[17] Herder, one of the forefathers of historicism, writes: "As the botanist cannot obtain a complete knowledge of a plant, unless he follows it from the seed, through its germination, blossoming and decay; such is Greek history to us. . . ." "The whole history of mankind is a pure natural history of human powers, actions, and propensities, modified by time and place." P. Gardiner, *Theories of History* (Glencoe, Ill., 1959), 38–39.

[18] Hoffmeister's first definition of historicism as a "Denkweise" is based upon the genetic principle (*op. cit.*).

[19] Dilthey, *G.S.* III, 247.

[20] See also above Meinecke's "Sinn für das Individuelle," f.n. 16.

[21] Dilthey, *G.S.* III, 246. Cf. Ranke's statement about the historian: ". . . first he must feel participation and pleasure in the particular for itself . . . a real affection for the human race in all its manifold variety. . . ." F. Stern, ed., *The Varieties of History* (New York, 1956), 59.

[22] Troeltsch, *G.S.* III, 38–39.

Historicism as a method, therefore, is decidedly humanistic and reflects the creative, subjective side of the historian's trade—that which he brings to his subject matter. And, of course, historicists contend that these categories and attitudes will result in the greatest objectivity as far as it is possible. The historical object, if defined as the content of the historian's account, remains a synthesis of the historian's activity and the records at his disposal. Likewise, history, itself, as the historian's written account, is, in Meinecke's words, "a creative mirror" (*eine schaffender Spiegel*) of the past. Historicism deals with the requirements on the historian's side of the synthesis.

The questions might now arise: have not historians always worked according to the principles and assumed the attitudes advanced by historicism? Is historicism contributing anything new and significant? Does the word, itself, have a distinct meaning? To these questions Meinecke would answer that it is true that great historians have, consciously or not, approached their material in these ways. In this case historicism concerns what the successful historian has done and is doing; and in a sense it might appear superfluous to add that this activity is historicist.[23] On the other hand, Meinecke would argue that more often than not history was incompletely and inaccurately written prior to the late XVIIIth-century revolution in historical writing and that certain definite principles of writing history, growing out of that revolution, represent in his opinion the best criteria for the enterprise. This body of principles constitutes historicism as a methodology and can be contrasted with other principles of historical writing representative of XVIIth- and XVIIIth-century rationalism.[24] Similarly, Ranke's followers advanced these same ideas, which were later called historicist, in contrast to certain positivistic methods of approaching history (e.g. Karl Lamprecht's theories at the turn of the century). Meinecke would further argue that bad historical writing can occur at any time through neglect of proper procedures and attitudes. For example, an historian might overstress the importance of a great personality and fail to see his relation to the general forces of the times.[25] Or conversely, an historian might erroneously seek to discover long-range uniformities in history, and by looking for common characteristics miss or deliberately ignore unique differences between peoples.[26] Historicism as a methodology is, therefore, a position to be de-

[23] For more on this point see Lee and Beck, *op. cit.*

[24] See Meinecke and the "pragmatic" history of XVIIIth-century rationalism. *Entstehung*, 3.

[25] See the criticism of Erich Brandenburg's overemphasis on great men in Meinecke's "Ein Wort über geschichtliche Entwicklung," *Theorie*, 102f.

[26] Pieter Geyl, reflecting historicism, challenges Toynbee on this point in *Debates with Historians* (New York, 1958), Chap. 5.

fended over against others, a position which its adherents claim embodies the most adequate way of grasping history. We can meaningfully speak of an historicist as opposed to other approaches to history. And, although the word, itself, might not be acknowledged, the tradition lives on in such modern writers as Carl Becker, Pieter Geyl, Herbert Butterfield, and C. V. Wedgewood.

In regard to contemporary problems in the methodology of history, however, historicism can provide few concrete answers, at most some general directions in thinking. For example, concerning the relationship between history and the natural sciences, historicist writers would largely affirm the late XIXth-century distinction between history as idiographic and the natural sciences as nomothetic; Ranke and Dilthey are, indeed, the immediate sources of this theory. Historicists would base this distinction on such points as: 1) The traditional goal of the historian to narrate individual events; 2) the undesirability of the historian to seek general laws (even if possible), since this would tend to ignore unique individual characteristics; 3) the special historical subject matter—man's conscious, purposeful activity —in contrast to the uniform natural object of science; 4) the ability of the historian to approach his subject matter in a particularly intimate way, because man qua man, is in a special position, sympathetically or analogically, to understand his fellow man's thought and action. Yet the distinction is often not decisive. Thus Troeltsch speaks of a spectrum of the sciences (*Wissenschaften*) and sees a great gulf between the extremes (e.g. historical biography and physics); toward the middle, however, the gap partially disappears in contrasting economic history, natural history, geology, and the like.[27] Moreover, the importance of the social sciences for history is often stated, but never is the relationship clearly formulated.[28] Likewise, in regard to the rôle of generalization in history and to the nature of historical explanation little precise knowledge can be gained. Causation, causal efficacy is clearly stressed; but the details of historical causation remain unclear.[29] Class concepts and uniformities are held essential, but nowhere is their function in an explanation discussed, except that they are means to throw light on the particular, the end.[30] It is true that Dilthey's notorious "Verstehen" places the historian in a special position, but even this notion is open to considerable interpretation, while Troeltsch and Meinecke hardly add to our knowledge of it. So, in spite of the fact that historicist thinking continues and may well

[27] Troeltsch, *G.S.* III, 29–30.

[28] *Ibid.*, 45; also, Meinecke, *Entstehung*, 2.

[29] See e.g. Meinecke's "Kausalitäten u. Werte," *Theorie* (translated and reprinted in Stern, *op. cit.*).   [30] Troeltsch, *G.S.* III, 62f.

have influenced present issues, it should not be conceived as an exact enough methodology to be consulted for solutions to such issues. In fact, most historicist literature predates their present formulation.

If the method of historical interpretation, embodying the historicist concepts, be broadened and applied to man's view of the world in general, then historicism can be conceived as a *Weltanschauung*. This has been its most widely known meaning in Europe. By *Weltanschauung* I mean a unified and comprehensive view of the world around us and man's place within it, again, a way of looking at and experiencing the world as a whole. The term "philosophy" seems too definite; a *Weltanschauung* may include philosophical concepts, but is more general than any particular philosophy. A phrase like "direction of philosophical thinking" (*Richtung des philosophischen Denkens*),[31] would be better. In some senses metaphysics could be equated to *Weltanschauung* if the former be interpreted as referring not to the super-sensible, but to the pervasive characteristics of the empirical world. Now an historicist *Weltanschauung* interprets the world through the categories already noted. The nature of our world appears to be flux and change, a process and development of newly emerging individuals, each in its unique position in time and place, rising and falling and non-recurring. The process contains nothing but large and small, developing and intertwining individuals. It moves to no goal, only individual ends and values appear momentarily within the process.[32] The adoption of such an historicist Weltanschauung, moreover, leads to the possible "historicizing" (*Historisierung*) of any body of thought, for example, politics, economics, or religion.[33] It was this approach to economics that led to Menger's diatribes.[34] And Troeltsch, himself, was forced to wrestle with the relativistic difficulties stemming from an "historicizing" of the religious tradition.[35]

Although historicist writers are often unclear in their meanings, historicism as a *Weltanschauung* best fits many of their statements. Troeltsch undoubtedly means a *Weltanschauung* when he writes of the "crisis of historicism."[36] As one commentator puts it: "It is a

[31] This is Hoffmeister's phrase which he uses in his second definition of historicism (*op. cit.*).

[32] See Troeltsch, *Christian Thought: Its History and Application*, 44; "Natural Law and Humanity," in O. Gierke, *Natural Law*, 204; also Meyerhoff, *op. cit.*, 11.

[33] The natural sciences are generally omitted in this connection by the historicists under discussion. Also, it obviously does not make sense to speak of "historicizing" history. Yet, as explained above, it is meaningful to speak of an historicist approach to the past, in contrast to other methods of interpreting the same content.

[34] See above, f.n. 6.

[35] See *Christian Thought*, part 1.

[36] This "crisis," he explains, has to do with the "general philosophical foundation

crisis of the world-view based upon history, a crisis of the whole culture." [37] Troeltsch's definition of historicism as the "historicizing of
our knowing and experiencing" points to this interpretation. For
man's total apprehension of his world is oriented toward an historical
viewpoint. He speaks further of the "historicizing of our thought" following in the late XVIIIth century the "mathematicizing" (*mathe-
matisierung*) and "naturalizing" (*naturalisierung*) of the previous
century, or the replacing of one *Weltanschauung* by another. In the
first part of the XIXth century the German historical *Weltanschauung* was a profound and progressive view of the world; but by
the end of the century it had degenerated, according to Troeltsch, into
a sceptical and ennervating outlook, largely through the relativistic
consequences of interpreting all things historically. By 1920 Western
culture had been so permeated by these harmful results that its *Weltanschauung* or historicism, itself, could be called in a state of crisis.[38]
Troeltsch's dilemma, never to be successfully resolved, hung upon his
general affirmation of historicism and his realization of the consequences to which it had led. These thoughts, nevertheless, demonstrate his broad conception of historicism—in this instance, more than
a methodology, and less than a speculative philosophy.[39]

Meinecke's writings, moreover, make explicit that the historicist
Weltanschauung is not only a "principle of knowledge" (*Wissen-
schaftsprinzip*), but also a "life principle" (*Lebensprinzip*). To be
sure, the "life principle" was the predecessor.[40] The specific historical
view of the world, which developed in the German states during the
early XIXth century, was prepared by a new and subtle orientation
in mood during the previous two centuries. A feeling and vital appreciation for all aspects of the life processes were developing in the Age
of Rationalism and provided the ground upon which an historicist
way of thinking was founded. This is why Meinecke focuses upon
Leibniz and especially Goethe as precursors of historicism. They have

---

and elements of historical thinking" (*allgemeinen philosophischen Grundlagen and
Elementen des Historischen Denkens*). *G.S.* III, 4.

[37] (*Es ist eine Krise der auf die Geschichte gegrundeten Weltanschauung, eine
Krise der gesamten Kultur.*) W. Bodenstein, *Neige des Historismus*, 145.

[38] Troeltsch, *G.S.* III, 1–11.

[39] Later in *G.S.* III, 102–110, Troeltsch, reflecting Vico, contrasts naturalism and
historicism as the two great creations of modern thought, both stemming from
Descartes. Naturalism, based upon the XVIIth-century revolution in mathematics
and physics, applies to the natural world; and historicism, arising from the analysis
of consciousness and from the genetic principle, is concerned with the world of
human life. Both are conceived as comprehensive directions of philosophical thinking, not as systematic philosophies.

[40] Meinecke, *Theorie*, 341; *Enstehung*, vii.

little to say about history proper, but they do represent the change in attitude that he is seeking in the origins of the movement.[41] A philosophy is not in question here—neither Leibniz's nor Goethe's system of ideas could be called historicist; rather an undercurrent of feeling about life is hinted at, in the dynamism of the monad and in the Sturm und Drang.

With Dilthey there is a lack of clarity on these points. On the one hand, he clearly discerns a "new historical *Weltanschauung*" developing toward the end of the XVIIIth century.[42] His studies precisely foreshadow the detailed research into this development later carried out by Troeltsch and Meinecke. On the other hand, when Dilthey discusses [43] his three principal types of philosophical or metaphysical *Weltanschauungen*—naturalism, idealism of freedom, and objective idealism—an historical *Weltanschauung* is omitted. Two answers to this problem are possible. First, there are many affinities between an historical *Weltanschauung* and that termed "objective idealism"; the latter appears to be in some senses a philosophical counterpart of the former.[44] But secondly and more important, the specific historical point of view, subsequently historicism, is not precisely philosophical and furthermore quite definitely underlies all three *Weltanschauungen* as well as any further ones that might arise. The historicity of all man's creations, physical and mental alike, lies at the heart of Dilthey's thought; and in this sense historicism becomes a more general type of metaphysical thinking concerned with the most comprehensive traits of the human world. These thoughts are concisely presented in his imaginative lecture, "The Dream." Here the "historical consciousness" suggests the relativity of all speculations; and the further thought that each point of view represents one side and perspective of the unattainable truth is a source of liberation and joy for

[41] B. Croce, more rationalist and Hegelian, discounts this factor. He considers Leibniz and Goethe basically unhistorical and at most on the bare fringe of the movement (*History as the Story of Liberty* [New York, 1955], 72–73).

[42] When referring to Möser, Winckelmann, Hamann, and Herder, Dilthey writes that a "wholly new conception of the historical world broke through in them, a truly new historical world-view originated" (*eine ganz neue Auffassung der geschichtlichen Welt bricht in ihnen durch, eine neue wahrhaft historische Weltanschauung entsteht*), *G.S.* III, 247.

[43] *G.S.* VIII, 100–118. An English translation of this section can be found in Kluback and Weinbaum, ed., *Dilthey's Philosophy of Existence* (New York, 1957), 31f.

[44] The representatives of "objective idealism"—Shaftesbury, Leibniz, Goethe, Herder—are precisely those thinkers whom Meinecke was later to designate as precursors of historicism. The pantheistic and Neo-Platonic tendencies of this metaphysics are likewise quite similar to the idealistic ingredients in the speculative thought of Troeltsch and Meinecke. See Dilthey, *G.S.* VIII, 115–118; also Troeltsch, *G.S.* III, 211f.

Dilthey.[45] Man's "consciousness" of the character of the world grows out of the immediate or "lived" experience (*Erleben*) of his surroundings. From this elemental awareness is built a comprehensive view of his total experience, that is, a *Weltanschauung*.[46] The relation between an historical *Weltanschauung* and the three types remains, however, uncertain. The former is at least more pervasive and forms their background.

In the thought of Dilthey certain issues and problems of historicism appear quite clearly. An initial contrast with the more intellectualist theories of Windelband and Rickert is evident in Dilthey's stress upon immediate experience (Meinecke's life principle).[47] The artistic element in the historian's trade is seen to balance his objective and empirical procedures. The relativistic difficulties, soon to plague Troeltsch, are set forth, but in Dilthey's case held advantageous. And for Dilthey, as for his successors, an historical *Weltanschauung* (i.e. historicism) is neither a science of man and nature, nor a religion, nor a systematic philosophy. The natural world is not their real concern; and the achievements of the sciences are generally accepted. Only the attempt to treat the discipline of history as analogous to the sciences is opposed. Religion, too, is considered separately from history. For Dilthey, religion is a particular interpretation of experience, whereby meaning is given to the observable world by reference to an unseen realm. In the beliefs of Troeltsch and Meinecke the Christian Deity exists and remains a vague but ultimate hope for the overcoming of moral relativism; but the historical world is accepted fully, with all of its consequences, and the attempts by either author to reconcile the two realms are generally unsuccessful.[48] Finally, historicism is not a systematically formulated philosophy for any of the three. At most it could be called a general historical view of man and his activities in which several broad categories of philosophical interpretation are stated. Still, "direction of philosophical thinking" seems the most adequate way of designating historicism as a *Weltanschauung*.

[45] A translation of "The Dream" is reprinted in Meyerhoff, *op. cit.*, 37f. For the "historical consciousness" underlying all *Weltanschauungen*, see Kluback and Weinbaum, ed., *op. cit.*, 44f.

[46] Dilthey, *G.S.* VIII, 78–84.

[47] Troeltsch discusses this point at length when criticizing Rickert, *G.S.* III, 119f., 151f.

[48] Troeltsch and Meinecke occasionally mention a type of Neo-Platonism or monodology whereby divine essences are embodied in historical individuals, thus establishing an absolute in each case. See Troeltsch, *G.S.* III, 211f. Carlo Antoni discusses this point in *From History to Sociology*, 118. In his final lectures, Troeltsch sees the individual's moral personality and conscience as the point of reconciliation. *Christian Thought*, Part II, Chap. 1 and 2.

To clarify further the meaning of historicism, it may be helpful to point out formally what I do not mean by the term. The following interpretations can be derived from historicist ideas; but they remain excesses or by-products, not the crux of the movement, itself. To be sure, historicism is open to interpretation, but to interpret it in ways contradictory to the accepted views of most scholars in the last fifty years adds unnecessary confusion to an already complicated concept. It is not always evident what Dilthey implies and what Troeltsch and Meinecke mean by historicism, but it is certain that they would not accept the points now to be enumerated.

First, historicism should not be conceived as a specific logic of history or a systematic philosophy. Croce, following in Hegel's footsteps, is the most obvious representative of this position. It is true that Croce expresses many enlightening thoughts about historicism; yet when he remarks that historicism represents the strict "logical principle" of the "concrete universal" and, as the new humanism, regards the natural sciences with "indifference or aversion," [49] he is then moving far beyond traditional meanings. He is turning historicism into a distinct philosophy, comprising a unique body of knowledge. Vico and Herder may have foreshadowed this development, but Hegel and Croce represent a considerable extension of their ideas. In fact, a new dialectical rationalism is created to take the place of, ironically, the XVIIIth-century rationalism which Vico and Herder vigorously attacked.[50] Contrary to Hegel and Croce, the concept of historicism advanced in this study recognizes the vital, non-rational processes of experience, the importance of the other sciences, and the generality and heuristic nature of historiographical principles. Historicism as a *Weltanschauung* is the most philosophical view of the term, but even in this case, as suggested already, a systematic historicist philosophy is not implied, nor can it be found in the literature.

Secondly, historicism does not mean a theory of inevitable historical laws or cycles.[51] Once again, suggestions of these ideas can be discerned in the writings of Vico and Herder who were interested in the development of groups and nations against the background of God's providence. But to say that historicism is an "approach to the social sciences" aiming at "historical prediction" through laws of the evolu-

[49] Croce, *History as the Story of Liberty*, 63f., 74–75, 316.

[50] Croce, for example, criticizes Meinecke's historicism in that it recognizes the "irrational" in life. For Croce true historicism is "more profoundly rational"; it formulates the "irrational" in a "rational light." *Ibid.*, 64.

[51] This is Karl Popper's interpretation in *The Open Society and Its Enemies* (Princeton, 1950), and *The Poverty of Historicism* (Boston, 1957). Furthermore, J. Passmore terms Toynbee an historicist "if ever there was one" (*Philosophical Review* [1959], 96). See Meyerhoff's harsh words on such interpretations. *Op. cit.*, 299–300.

tion of history [52] goes as far as to contradict many genuine historicist principles and remains quite contrary to the spirit of even Vico's and Herder's historical thinking. The holistic and deterministic implications in these earlier thinkers belong more to their philosophical or theological speculations than to their interpretation of history. It is rather the rational dialectic of Hegel and Marx, along with the positivistic aims of J. S. Mill and Comte, which have attempted to introduce law and prediction into history. Ranke speaks of trends and tendencies in the historical process, but not in a long-range, predictable sense.[53] And Ranke in this instance is followed by Dilthey, Troeltsch, and Meinecke.[54] Their many references to accident, chance, and the unpredictability of men's decisions, as well as their view of history as a continual mixing of individual lines of development in a system of external relations, all preclude any sense of law, prediction, or total evolution.

Third, historicism has been erroneously interpreted as a way of writing history in a purely objective, impersonal, and factual manner.[55] This view of historicism has been derived in part from a one-sided interpretation—in fact a misinterpretation—of Ranke's historiography.[56] Its partial truth lies in the fact that historicism does reflect Ranke's interest in each historical individual, solely for itself, and his strict use of empirical records. But the falsity of the view consists in its neglect of the subjective and interpretative side of the historian's trade [57] and the historicist's insistence that complete ob-

[52] Popper, *Poverty of Historicism*, 3. Ironically, Popper's "piecemeal" approach and his "situational logic" of history represent in many ways a defense of the historicism of Dilthey, Troeltsch, and Meinecke.

[53] Ranke specifically denied the possibility of general laws in history; see "Dialogue on Politics," reprinted in T. Van Laue, *Ranke* (Princeton, 1950), 163.

[54] For example, see Dilthey against Hegel's "group mind," *G.S.* VII, 284–285; Troeltsch on historical development, *G.S.* III, 54–55, and on the dialectic of Hegel and Marx, 244f.; also Meinecke, "Eine Wort über geschichtliche Entwicklung," *Theorie*. See also Frederick Engels' "The End of Classical German Philosophy" which traces how Hegelianism developed into a dogmatic, non-historical system, necessitating the rise of the then historically-minded Left-Wing Hegelians; reprinted in L. S. Feuer, ed., *Political Writings of Marx and Engels* (New York, 1959), 195–242.

[55] See Heussi, *op. cit.*, 18–20; also Charles Beard, "That Noble Dream," reprinted in Stern, *op. cit.*, 317f. Hoffmeister, *op. cit.*, also gives this interpretation as his third definition of "historicism."

[56] See Iggers, *op. cit.*

[57] Ranke, for example, stresses the historian's "point of view" in his Preface, reprinted in Stern, *op. cit.*, 55f.

jectivity is never possible. And to add that historicism implies a colourless, dry-as-dust type of historical writing is far-fetched, indeed.[58] Such writing belongs to the pedant of any age, whether a follower of Ranke or an historian of today. The many historicist remarks on feeling, imagination and inspiration are quite to the contrary. An equally justifiable response to historicist writing would be Goethe's, who on first reading Herder, exclaimed, "God knows how you make one feel the reality of the world." [59]

Fourth, historicism sometimes appears to be equated to relativism.[60] This is misleading. There is no doubt that relativism is bound up with historicism; but it would be more accurate to say that contextualism is an elemental historicist precept, while relativism is a consequence *of* historicism *for* other disciplines, like morality or religion. The case of Troeltsch is instructive. As an historian he was to observe each historical phenomenon, for example, the Christian religion, as rooted in its particular time and place in the historical process; but it is Troeltsch, the theologian, who was subsequently forced to wrestle with the problem of the relativity of Christianity.[61] Likewise, he deplored the relativistic effect of an historical *Weltanschauung* on Western morality. Hence historicism by directing the historian to consider everything in its particular context contributes to a general point of view which may, for better or worse, lead the observer to regard all elements of his culture as non-absolute and continually subject to change.

A final point must be made. I have designated historicism as a general methodology and a *Weltanschauung*, based upon the concepts of individuality, development, and relatedness. I have, moreover, attempted to distinguish *Weltanschauung* from philosophy as a systematic discipline, and from religion. While there is evidence for these distinctions, it must be emphasized that in historicist literature they are often unclear and that there is considerable overlapping of methodology and *Weltanschauung*, *Weltanschauung* and philosophy.

[58] Nietzsche, in his influential *Von Nutzen u. Nachteil der Historie für das Leben* (*Gesammelte Schriften*, Vol. VI, Munich, 1922), attacks this type of writing; yet he is not so much denouncing the objectivity of research as the pedant, himself, and the excess of "history" when it dulls the vital instincts.

[59] Quoted in Cassirer, *The Problem of Knowledge*, 219.

[60] See Lee and Beck, *op. cit.*; H. A. Hodges, *The Philosophy of Dilthey* (London, 1952), 362; R. Aron, *La Philosophie Critique de l'Histoire* (Paris, 1950), 9; A. Stern, *Philosophy of History and the Problem of Values* (The Hague, 1962), 138. Fritz Stern points out this error in *op. cit.*, 23.

[61] See Troeltsch, *Christian Thought*, Part 1.

Meinecke is particularly unprecise, Troeltsch and Dilthey to lesser extents. All three possess philosophical beliefs which needlessly interfere with their historical theorizing.[62] Yet with little violation to the thought of these authors, it is possible to advance their specifically historicist principles without resorting to speculative interpretations of these principles. Only by a cutting off of the philosophical dimension do I feel that historicism as a point of view or attitude can be clearly presented. This process, however, is difficult to accomplish for historicism as a *Weltanschauung*. Thus, it appears best to regard historicism more formally and only as a broad methodology. The relevance of historicism for the mid-XXth century is another question. But, if it is judged relevant by historians and philosophers, it will more than likely be done so on the basis of its methodological value.

State University of New York at Buffalo.

[62] For example, Meinecke's philosophical thought is derived from the idealistic assumptions of XIXth-century romanticism. His actual historical writing is quite free from these assumptions. But when he begins to philosophize about history in general or about a concept like historical individuality, then idealistic intrusions occur. He remarks, for instance, that the individual is ultimately "ineffable" and that an inner form or "entelechy" accounts for its unified structure. See, e.g. *Machiavellism*, 9.

Chapter XII

SEMANTICS IN THE METHODOLOGY OF THE HISTORY OF IDEAS

By Nils B. Kvastad

Ideas are studied in all branches of history. In political history the complexes of ideas known as political ideologies are central; economic history deals with ideas like "mercantilism," "socialism," etc.; and religious history is inseparable from the study of theological ideas. But the importance ascribed to ideas varies from Hegel who regarded ideas as the major force in history to those Marxists who look upon them as parts of a mere superstructure. Some scholars focus on various ideas by defining them and describing their origin, development, and mutual influence. This is especially true of the study called "history of ideas." It is a vast historical discipline that treats ideas in all areas, but its methods are often diffuse and need clarification.

Semantics and History of Ideas.—Methodologists of the history of ideas usually agree that semantics is relevant for it. E. Skard says that the history of ideas to some extent is the history of words.[1] G. Aspelin has stressed the necessity of a thorough analysis of the peculiarities of the language of the scientists and philosophers one studies, as understood during the time when the texts were written.[2] Arthur O. Lovejoy, the grand old man of the history of ideas and its chief inspirer in modern times, said that this field is studied under at least twelve different labels, among them "some parts of the history of language, especially semantics."[3] A semantical approach is reflected in the titles of some of his essays, e.g., " 'Pride' in Eighteenth-Century Thought"; " 'Nature' as Aesthetic Norm"; " 'Nature' as Norm in Tertullian"; and "The Meaning of 'Romantic' in Early German Romanticism."[4] Such an approach one also finds in many other works in this field, as in Leo Spitzer's *Essays in Historical Semantics* (New York, 1948), and in H. Gotthard, *Geschichte des Begriffes "Romantisch" in Deutschland* (Berlin, 1927). Many semantical studies also exist about various ideas in Latin literature, like "pietas," "dignitas," and "auctoritas."

What are ideas?—Most scholars will say that the subject matter of the history of ideas consists of "ideas." But this term is ambiguous. Sometimes the same author also seems to use it with different meanings, e.g., Plato who often uses it in a way that implies that ideas have an existence of their own, independent of everything human. Sometimes "ideas" for him seem to be equivalent to "concepts." Hegel regards ideas as a creative force. For him, ideas or concepts give rise to other ideas in a three stage dialectical develop-

---

[1] Eiliv Skard, "Innlegg ved Paulus Svendsens doktordisputas" (Discourse in connection with Paulus Svendsen's thesis for a doctor's degree), *Edda* (Oslo, 1941), 424.

[2] G. Aspelin, "Idehistorien som vetenskap" (The history of ideas as a science), *Lychnos* (1948-49), Annual of the Swedish History of Science Society (Uppsala, 1950), 138.

[3] A. O. Lovejoy, *Essays in the History of Ideas* (Baltimore, 1948), 1.

[4] *Ibid.*, Table of Contents, v.

ment, whose goal is the "Absolute Idea." For Berkeley, however, "ideas" signify that which is immediately perceived.

I think the most useful meaning for the history of ideas is to identify ideas with concepts. To use Plato's interpretation of ideas as extramental would commit the scholar to a particular ontology. Berkeley's definition is too narrow.

The study of concepts will therefore be central in the history of ideas. But it must be understood that a concept usually is an abbreviation for a proposition or a system of propositions. One may therefore regard concepts in this field as guidelines or clues to the kind of propositions being investigated. Historians of ideas must therefore study propositions expressing the meanings of concepts.

Not all concepts belong to the subject matter of the history of ideas. Concepts of things like a nose or a watchdog seldom do, whereas pervasive notions like romanticism, history, and art do. I do not think it is possible to define the class of concepts discussed in the history of ideas so precisely that one would always know whether a particular concept belongs to the history of ideas or not. The definition has to be rather open-ended, but this does not make it useless so long as it provides some rough guidance. I shall assume that the concepts discussed by the historians of ideas are those which have some broad cultural or philosophical relevance. This is meant as a descriptive definition of those ideas that actually have been discussed in this field.

In semantics one distinguishes between concepts or ideas, on the one hand, and terms, words, and expressions, on the other. A concept or idea is the meaning which a term, word, statement, or act expresses. The same concept can be expressed by different terms from different languages. Thus the words "dog," "chien," and "Hund" express the same concept 'dog.' As is common in semantics, concepts and ideas are put in single quotation marks, and terms, words, and expressions in double ones. Thus the term "idea" expresses the concept 'idea.' I will, however, omit the quotation marks when no serious misunderstanding arises from doing so.

Lovejoy uses the distinction between a word and what it expresses in the following:

But since the word ["nature"] is one and the ideas it may express are prodigiously numerous and various, it is, for the historian, often a task of difficulty and delicacy to determine what, in a given writing or passage, the idea behind the word is.[5]

Definitions—Definitions are important for ideas and concepts as well as for terms and words. It is common in logic to distinguish between normative definitions (N-definitions), descriptive definitions (Ds-definitions), and real definitions (R-definitions). An N-definition is a sentence proposing or prescribing that some expression "a" shall be used with the same meaning as another expression "b" within a specified context. An example is in Russell's *History of Western Philosophy:* "Catholic philosophy, in the sense in which I [i.e., in that book] shall use the term, is that which dominated European thought from Augustine to the Renaissance."[6] That which is defined is called the *definiendum,* while the defining expression is called the *definiens.*

[5] *Ibid.,*xv.
[6] B. Russell, *A History of Western Philosophy* (New York, 1945), 301.

A Ds-definition is a sentence stating that some expression "a" actually is used with the same meaning as another expression "b" within a certain context. Scholars commenting on the works of others, as philosophers and historians of ideas often do, frequently use Ds-definitions. When, for instance, W. Stegmüller writes the following in a chapter about the philosophy of Karl Jaspers, it must be regarded as a Ds-definition: "Transcendence is for Jaspers also here (i.e., in the context of his book *Von der Wahrheit*) again the Absolutely Other, that only can be heard by someone experiencing existence."[7]

R-definitions may be roughly explained as definitions giving a condensed characterization of all objects subsumable under a concept. Sometimes R-definitions are catchwords or slogans: "man lives not by bread alone, but chiefly by catchwords,"[8] Lovejoy once observed. When Sartre in his popular lecture "Existentialism is a Humanism" in 1946 defined "an existentialist" as "one who holds that existence precedes essence," this can probably be regarded as a R-definition.

The distinction between N- and Ds-definitions is important in the history of ideas, because authors often use quite another definition of a term in practice than the one they may say in advance that they will apply. This means that their professed N-definition of a term differs from the Ds-definition of it as it is actually used. This usage also often characterizes ordinary speech. Empirical research in semantics has shown that one seldom can rely on what people say about their own verbal behavior. Instead, one has to find out how in practice they use certain words. It is therefore a task for the historian of ideas to find out if an author actually follows his own N-definitions, i.e., if the Ds-definition of some term in a text is identical with his professed N-definition of it in that text.

Most historians of ideas focus on philosophical or literary texts. N-definitions are generally more frequent in the former group than in the latter. In some philosophical works, as in Spinoza's *Ethics*, N-definitions are very common indeed. In literature one generally looks for Ds-definitions, but such definitions are seldom explicitly given. Often one has to construct the *definiens* of a term from what is implicitly said about it in a text. Methods to do so will be mentioned later.

Synonymity.—A central concept in semantics is synonymity. One can say that two concepts are universally synonymous when they are interchangeable in all contexts in which they appear without change in the cognitive meaning of these contexts. One may also say that the term "a" is universally synonymous to the term "b" when "a" always means the same as "b," or when "a" and "b" always express the same meaning.

Historians of ideas often try to point out synonymity, e.g., that pleasure and happiness were synonymous for Bentham. Lovejoy also often discusses synonymity. In his essay "The Meaning of 'Romantic' in Early German Romanticism," he says: "According to this explanation . . . 'romantisch' was to Schlegel equivalent in meaning to 'romanartig.' "[9] Commenting on the younger

---

[7] W. Stegmüller, *Hauptströmungen der Gegenwartsphilosophie* (Stuttgart, 1960), 219 (my translation).
[8] Lovejoy, *op.cit.*, xiv, xv.   [9] *Ibid.*, 184.

Schlegel, he says: "The word ['romantisch'] here being expressly declared to be a synonym of 'modern, in contrast with the classical poetry of antiquity.' "[10]

The definitions of synonymity just given express so-called universal, indiscriminate synonymity, i.e., that a term "a" always, in all contexts, and for all persons, means the same as "b." This, however, is seldom the case, but such an assumption, explicit or implicit, of universal synonymity between two terms, is a common source of error in the history of ideas. The scholar makes general, sweeping statements about synonymity and seems to imply, at least implicitly, that this relation is accepted by everyone and is valid in all contexts. But too often this is not so. Claims of universal synonymity are often easy to refute, because one needs only one contrary instance to invalidate them.

Also the view that all occurrences of the same term are universally synonymous frequently causes mistakes in the history of ideas. That the occurrences of the same term are universally synonymous means that all of them express the same meaning.

This is often assumed when a scholar traces an idea throughout history in numerous texts. He then often assumes that a particular term always expresses the same idea, but this is frequently not so. He ought to prove in each case that this assumption is valid. Some philosophers, who praise the Greeks as scientific pioneers, write as if the term "atom" is a universal synonym that meant the same in Ancient Greece as in the present century, but this is, of course, not so. Probably these writers also know the difference; nevertheless they often write as if they did not.

When a scholar wants to prove a universal synonymity relation between occurrences of the same term or between any occurrence of the term "a" and any occurrence of the term "b," he will get the most reliable results if he can consider all occurrences of the term or terms for which the relation is assumed to be valid, which is usually impossible. When this is so, he should investigate enough occurrences to justify drawing an inductive inference. He may, e.g., have found that n occurrences of the term "a" all express the same idea, then he concludes that all occurrences of "a" are synonymous. If n is sufficiently great, the inference may be fairly reliable, but of course never certain. It is no less legitimate to use such a procedure in the history of ideas than in science, where induction is constantly used.

In fact, induction is often employed in the history of ideas. When someone, e.g., says that a term "a" always means the same as "b," he seldom has read all occurrences of "a" and "b." He often has simply drawn an inductive inference from the occurrences he has read, stating that the synonymity observed between them is always valid. Such a procedure is often discernible in the use of the expressions "my general impression," "my reading has convinced me," etc. What is too often forgotten, however, is that inductive inferences are only probable, never certain. The probability increases as the number of confirming relevant occurrences in different contexts increases. Moreover, many scholars have not meant that a universal synonymity relation exists, but only that such a relation is valid in some historical period, in certain texts, or for certain authors. In such cases he ought to mention the context in which the

[10]*Ibid.*, 201.

synonymity relation is assumed to be valid. Historians of ideas frequently forget to specify the contexts.

Many synonymity relations should therfore have the form: the term "a" in the context U and the term "b" in the context V are synonymous in U and V when they are interchangeable everywhere in U and V without change of cognitive meaning in the contexts. If $U = V$, synonymity is studied within the same context. In the history of ideas the ultimate contexts, i.e., the places where the ideas actually are studied, are generally texts, even when the contexts are periods or authors. Lovejoy thus mentions as contexts "eighteenth century thought," "early German Romanticism," and "Tertullian" in his essays mentioned above; but what he actually has studied, are the *texts* from or about these periods, and *texts* by or about Tertullian. To say that a period or an author has been studied, is generally an abbreviation for the fact that certain texts relevant to the period or the author have been studied.

Historians of ideas often choose contexts that are too wide. This may lead to much disagreement and to many rival theories, because the number of occurrences becomes unsurveyable. Although induction may be used in such cases, it is usually advisable to narrow the context. Then the chances for getting valid results are better. The most accurate results generally come from confining oneself to texts in which one can study all occurrences of the terms one will investigate. Semantical methods like subsumption and occurrence analysis can then be applied. Some may object that in these cases the context will be too small and the conclusions may therefore be uninteresting; but in building a house, one places one brick at a time. A reliable, but perhaps trivial result inferred from many small contexts, can be used to draw important conclusions valid in a wider context.

Too many historians of ideas tacitly assume that some synonymity relations hold for both the same person in all situations and for different persons; i.e., that there is both intrapersonal and interpersonal synonymity, which is not always true.

I define two types of intrapersonal synonymity relations as follows: (1) the term "a" in the text U is intrapersonal synonymous to the term "b" in the text V for the author P when all occurrences of "a" in U and all occurrences of "b" in V mean the same for P; (2) an occurrence of the term "a" at the occurrence place p_1 in the text U is intrapersonal synonymous to another occurrence of "a" at the occurrence place p_2 in the text V for the person P when both occurrences of "a" mean the same for P.

Scholars often try to prove intrapersonal synonymity relations as defined in (2). Some have, e.g., attempted to find out if various occurrences of "idea" in Plato's dialogues were intrapersonal synonymous for him. Many think that some of them were not. Lovejoy warns against "over-unifying" and harmonizing an author's views too much. He may then—at least partly—have in mind the danger of too readily assuming intrapersonal synonymity.

Some interpersonal synonymity relations important in the history of ideas can be defined as follows: (3) the term "a" in the text U for U's author P is interpersonally synonymous with the term "b" in the text V for V's author Q when all occurrences of "a" in U for P mean the same as all occurrences of "b" in V for Q; (4) the instances of the term "a" occurring at the place p_1 in the text

U and at the place p_2 in the text V are interpersonally synonymous for U's author P and V's author Q if and only if "a" at p_1 for P means the same as "a" at p_2 for Q.

If all occurrences of "a" are intrapersonally synonymous for each author within his own works, one can say that: (5) the term "a" occurring in U and V is interpersonally synonymous for U's author P and V's author Q when it means the same for both of them.

When historians of ideas compare authors writing in different languages, the historians often assume falsely interpersonal synonymity relations in the sense that some term in one language is believed to mean the same as another term in a different language. Certain controversies about Spinoza exemplify this: critics believe that his Latin terms, such as "*libertas*," meant the same to him as the corresponding term "freedom" in other European languages meant to many of his contemporaries. This interpersonal synonymity hypothesis is not valid.

Most theories in the history of ideas seem tacitly to assume that certain in-, terpersonal synonymity hypotheses are valid. When a scholar, for instance, says that some term expresses the same idea in some period, he usually means that it does so in the works of different authors, i.e., that it is interpersonally synonymous for them.

Concepts often used in connection with synonymity are 'synonymic alternative' and 'heteronymity.' To say that the term "a" is a synonymic alternative to the term "b" means that "a" and "b" express the same idea in at least one case. When one translates, as historians of ideas often do, the main task is to find synonymic alternatives in one language for words of another. Synonymic alternatives are also often used for stylistic purposes, to modify a text without change of meaning.

That a term "a" is heteronymous to a term "b" means that "a" expresses another meaning or idea than "b." Most terms are of course heteronyms. Students of religious ideas sometimes try to show that terms that are assumed to be heteronyms really are synonyms or vice versa. Philosophers with a syncretic view on religion may thus try to show that the terms "God," "Allah," and "Brahman," generally assumed to be heteronyms, really are synonyms. Christian philosophers tend to deny this.

Methods to determine Synonymity.—A problem for the scholar making synonymity hypotheses, is: How shall one in *practice* determine if some terms are synonyms?

In empirical semantics one may use questionnaires, but such methods have limited value in the history of ideas because most texts that are studied were written by noncontemporaries. When an author is living and willing to be questioned, such procedures can be used. If one in this way will investigate if some term "a" in a text of a living author is synonymous for him with another term "b," one invites him first to read the text. Then he is asked to replace "a" by "b" and read it again. If he says that the cognitive meaning of the text does not change, "a" is assumed to be intrapersonally synonymous to "b" in the text for its author (provided he is honest), but if he says that the meaning changes, this synonymity hypothesis has been falsified. If, however, one does not use questionnaires, other methods can be tried. One method has to rely on consulting competent persons. When the historian of ideas, e.g., studies an idea in some science, it will often be necessary to rely on scientists in the field. If they say that some term "a" can replace the term "b" in some texts without change in cognitive meaning, this is often sufficient to regard "a" and "b" as interpersonally synonymous in these texts.

In the less scientific fields of literature and the humanities, however, one will not be so inclined to rely on competent persons, because concepts are not so rigidly defined here, and there is often little consensus among scholars in these areas. The use of this method therefore depends on the field being investigated.

A third method to verify synonymity hypotheses is to see if there is a rule which states or implies that the expressions involved are synonymous. Such rules are often N-definitions. In fields where N-definitions are strictly followed, as in mathematics and logic, one can therefore prove a synonymity hypothesis by referring to an N-definition stipulating that the expressions involved will be used as identical. Historians of scientific ideas often use this method. They may wonder whether two expressions "a" and "b" are synonymous in the text of some scientist. Then they find that "a" and "b" are the *definiendum* and *definiens* in an N-definition he gives and consistently follows. Consequently, "a" and "b" are synonymous in the text. Perhaps this procedure can be used some day in connection with Pythagoras. An ancient writer states that he used definitions. Maybe he was the first mathematician to do so explicitly. So if one should find some of his texts containing two terms "a" and "b," which he in another context linked by an N-definition that he followed consequently, then this method may be used.

Ambiguity.—Ambiguities exist in the works of most thinkers. N. Kemp-Smith says that hardly any technical term employed by Kant in his *Critique of Pure Reason* is not used in many different senses.[11] An example of an ambiguous concept from Kant's ethical writings is his famous "categorical imperative." Its most important senses are quoted in the article "Imperativ" in Eisler's *Wörterbuch der philosophischen Begriffe* (Berlin, 1930).

Lovejoy believed that the ambiguity of words, especially of the great catchwords of an age, is important in history and said that the multivocality of a word might facilitate or promote changes in the reigning ideas. He also stressed that semantics should clear up the ambiguities of important words of a period and investigate how the confused associations of ideas arising from these ambiguities have influenced the development of doctrines.[12] In some essays he tried to point out the various meanings of central terms like "romanticism" and the confusion that often followed their ambiguity.

Especially analytical philosophers stress ambiguities and confusion in the texts of previous thinkers, which in their view often characterize metaphysical doctrines. Thus Russell in his discussion of Berkeley in *A History of Western Philosophy* points out the ambiguity of the word "pain," which in Russell's view leads Berkeley astray.

As historians often overrate the importance of plan and wisdom in history and underrate the role of sheer foolishness, so the historians of ideas often

---

[11]N. Kemp-Smith, *A Commentary to Kant's "Critique of Pure Reason"* (London, 1918), xx.

[12]See, e.g., A. O. Lovejoy, *The Great Chain of Being* (Cambridge, 1942), 14.

overestimate the amount of clear thinking in their field and underestimate the role of confusion and ambiguity. In the history of ideas this latter aspect is often more dominant than in the history of philosophy, because historians of ideas deal more with minor thinkers and writers who usually are the most obscure and ambiguous, but who frequently reflect the diffusion of ideas more than the major thinkers who originate or develop them.

Ambiguity is not always something to be avoided. In science and philosophy it generally is, but not always in literature. Here a skillful use of ambiguities may heighten the artistic effect. Many great poems are very ambiguous indeed, but this does not decrease their value as art. Historians of ideas are concerned with literature. A term "a" is ambiguous when there is at least two instances of "a" such that the first expresses a different meaning or idea from the second. One can also say that ambiguity is lack of synonymity among instances of the same term.

Ambiguity in communication between author and reader can be defined in this way: the term "a" in the text U is ambiguous in communication between U's author P and U's reader Q, when "a" has a different meaning for P from what it has for Q. We then assume that all occurrences of "a" are intrapersonally synonymous for each person. In common usage "ambiguity" is regarded as something to be avoided. "Ambiguity" is then generally associated with important differences in meaning between various occurrences of the same term. In semantics, however, one generally assumes that any pair of occurrences of the same designation is ambiguous, if sufficiently small shades in meaning are taken into account. Absolute unambiguity is a fiction. One is instead interested in eliminating important ambiguities that cause serious misunderstandings. It must be noted, however, that what is an "important" ambiguity cannot be determined exactly. It is based on a rather rough estimate.

Interpretation.—Ambiguity is closely connected with interpretation. The more interpretations of a designation or a term, the more ambiguous it is. If a term "a_0" is ambiguous and sometimes has the same meaning as "a_1," sometimes as "a_2," sometimes as "a_n," and all these meanings are different, then "a_1," "a_2,". . . "a_n" are called *interpretans* designations expressing interpretations of "a_0," or in short, interpretations of "a_0." If no pair of interpretations are synonyms for a person P listing them, they make up a so-called intrapersonally heteronymous reference list of "a_0" for P.

Interpretations are important influences in history. Various interpretations of passages in the Bible and of Marx's writings have caused much bloodshed. Other debates about interpretations have been less bloody, but nevertheless heated. An old dispute in the Middle Ages was whether Aristotle can be interpreted as teaching immortality or not for the individual soul.

Most great philosophers have been interpreted in many different ways. An example is Kant who is the basis of a multitude of schools, all with their own interpretations of him. Plato has also given rise to many different interpretations. His teaching became the basis of the four so-called minor Socratic schools, among them the Cynic, as well as for the skepticism of the Academy, advocated by Arcesilaos, for example.

Other philosophers, like Hume, have not been interpreted in so many ways. In Hume's case a reason may be that he is a clearer writer than Kant, but it is probably more important to indicate that Hume, until this century, has not been studied as much as Kant or Plato. It seems that the less interest is focused on a thinker, the less interpretations are suggested of his views.

Many of Lovejoy's views are interpretations. An example is his interpretations of "pride" in eighteenth-century thought. He stressed that the term was equivocal, for it was often used to designated two distinct, though kindred, types of feeling or desire: "self-esteem, or the craving to think well of oneself, in its many degrees and forms, especially its emulative form [1st interpretation]; and the desire for, and pleasure in, the esteem, admiration or applause of others, especially the craving for 'distinction' [2nd interpretation].[13]

Not all interpretations are of equal interest; some are more important than others. Lovejoy gave an example when he wrote: " 'Pride,' then, in an especially important sense, meant a sort of moral overstrain, the attempt to be un-naturally good and immoderately virtuous, to live by reason alone."[14] Usually those interpretations are most important that occur most frequently. And when an author is studied, one generally regards his own interpretations as more important than those of commentators.

A scholar usually regards interpretations of some designation with large internal divergencies as more important than interpretations where the differences are small, because the former will generally cause greater difficulties for his understanding of a text in which the designation appears. In this case he will often have to eliminate some of the interpretations as unlikely to enable one to comprehend the text, but if the various interpretations of the designation only vary slightly, he need not care about that. Several interpretations of "war" as used by Nietzsche exemplify interpretations with large internal divergencies. Some, like Mussolini and many Nazis, interpreted "war" in Nietzsche's works in a strict military sense. Others, like August Messer, believed that by "war" Nietzsche meant primarily moral and spiritual struggles.[15]

A historian of ideas will also, like a scientist, tend to be more interested in original and unusual interpretations than in trivial ones, because the former will generally have greater consequences. But an interpretation must not be so original that it becomes unreasonable. An example is perhaps Heidegger's interpretation of Kant as mainly concerned with ontology. In polemics unreasonable interpretations are common. Meanings are then ascribed to a person which his text in no way bears out.

Terms have no fixed set of interpretations since it is common knowledge that people interpret the same terms differently. When they do, this is due to many factors, such as their personality, their group, religion, nation, and language community, as well as the period in which they live. Their interpretations are often colored by their prejudices, their feelings towards the author of the text, etc. There are other reasons why interpretations differ and misinterpretations arise. Sometimes a reader who has not understood an author, views the text through interpretations and commentaries which naturally differ from the interpretations of those who have grasped the author's intentions. Often widely different interpretations are due to faulty translations, as when Aristotle was

[13]Lovejoy, *Essays in the History of Ideas, op. cit.*, 62.   [14]*Ibid.*, 67.

[15]A. Messer, *Erläuterungen zu Nietzsches Zarathustra* (Stuttgart, 1922), 41.

translated from Greek into Arabic and then into Latin during the Middle Ages, or to not knowing the linguistic conventions of a certain time. Sometimes new interpretations seem to arise because some wish to give increased authority to their own views by claiming that they are the true interpretations of some great thinker or text. In Indian philosophy it thus seems as if many philosophical innovations have to be disguised as the true interpretation of some old text. Something similar seems to happen frequently in the Marxist camp.

Frequently one comes to believe that some expression can be interpreted in several equally plausible ways. Or it may be that one does not understand it at all, due to one's own fault or because the text in which it appears is too obscure. Sometimes one suspects that the author is the only one who understands the text. In such cases one usually suspends judgment concerning the meaning of the expression. Such suspension of judgment is frequent when the texts one studies are so short or fragmentary that it is impossible to have any well-founded opinion about the meaning of many terms, e.g., when one studies the fragments of ancient philosophers like Heraclitus and other pre-Socratics.

In the history of ideas it is fruitful to distinguish between the author's intentions and readers' interpretations. An author may intend to express a different meaning with a term from many of his readers' interpretations of it, i.e., the problem of ambiguity in communication arises. If a term expresses the same idea for both reader and author, one can say that a successful communication occurs between them. If not, there is a communicational failure. Both communicational successes and failures are frequent in the history of ideas.

Precision in interpretation.—Historians of ideas put much effort into clarifying texts. This they often do by eliminating some possible misinterpretation of a term, i.e., they make its meaning more precise. A term "a" is more precise than a term "b" when all interpretations of "a" also are interpretations of "b," and there is at least one interpretation of "b" which is not also an interpretation of "a," assuming that there is at least one correct interpretation of "a." Such precision cannot always be obtained because a scholar may feel that a term is so obscure that it is impossible to make it more precise. This was Russell's view about Aristotle's concept 'essence.'

Most expressions can be given many precise forms, which can be used to make a kind of pedigree. As an example, one can take an expression "a_0" that is given the more precise forms "a_1" and "a_2"; "a_1" and "a_2" can also be given two more precise forms each, "a_{11}" and "a_{12}" for "a_1," and "a_{21}" and "a_{22}" for "a_2." Each of these four more precise forms of "a_1" and "a_2" can in their turn be given two new ones, so that they have eight "more precise" forms together. In this way one can continue and obtain a so-called pedigree of preciseness with various levels: "a_1" and "a_2" represent the first level, "a_{11}," "a_{12}," "a_{21}," and "a_{22}" the second one, and so on. One does not have, however, always only two such "more precise" forms of each expression. Sometimes a term is given more than two so that a certain level has more expressions than twice the number of the previous one.

"A_1" and "a_2" are called the main directions of increased precision, while the expressions after them indicate subdirections. If one pools together all the forms of greater precision from the different levels into one list, one gets a so-called branched reference class for "a_0." To make such classes is often useful in the history of ideas. Lovejoy has given one in his essay " 'Nature' as Aesthetic Norm."[16] His reference class may be made into a precision pedigree of the expression " 'Nature' as Aesthetic Norm" as "a_0," and five precise forms of it as the first level class, labelled by him A, B, C, D, E. Some of these forms of precision are given various new grades so that one also gets a second level class. Only one number of this second level class, however, is divided once more (in two more grades), so a third level is the last level of this pedigree. Such reference classes should be more frequently used in the history of ideas, because they make the various forms of preciseness more surveyable, and reveal the relations among them.

Definiteness of Intention.—A historian of ideas should not be too precise in his interpretations; otherwise he will transcend the author's alleged definiteness of intention. This concept can be clarified in the following example.

If someone asserts a proposition containing an expression "a_0," one may ask: "Do you by a_0 mean a_1 or a_2?" (Or, more correctly: "Do you by the expression 'a_0' mean the idea or meaning expressed by 'a_1' [i.e., 'a_1'] or the idea or meaning expressed by 'a_2' [i.e., 'a_2']?" But in ordinary speech such formulations are considered too clumsy or pedantic.) He may say: "a_1." "But do you by a_1 mean a_{11} or a_{12}?" Here one of two things may happen. Either he says that he meant either a_{11} or a_{12}, or he may be at a loss to know what to answer. He has never analyzed a_0 sufficiently to have become aware of the distinction between a_{11} and a_{12}. It is new to him. He did not intend a_{11} any more than a_{12}. In this case the limit of his definiteness of intention in relation to the direction of precision represented by the reference class a_0, a_1, a_2, a_{11}, a_{12} exists between the first and the second level of greater precision. The precision of the second level transcends his definiteness of intention concerning the reference class of "a_0."

In general, one can say that if a person P has a limit of definiteness of intention in relation to a particular pedigree with some term as its starting point, which exists between the n'th and the $(n+1)$th level of precision, another person Q has a limit between the $(n+m)$th and the $(n+m+1)$th level of precision, when m is equal to or greater than one, then Q has a greater definiteness of intention than P in relation to this pedigree.

Thus one can distinguish between two kinds of misinterpretations: first, to attribute to a person some particular precise form of a_0, say a_1, while he actually means a_2, not a_1 (intraintentional misinterpretation); second, to ascribe to him the precise form a_{12} as contrasted to a_{11}, when neither has been considered (transintentional misinterpretation).

Plato's dialogues illustrate definiteness of intention. In them Socrates frequently tries to find the definition of some expression, and proposes various precise forms among which he asks his interlocutors to choose. If one of them at once chooses one alternative, his definiteness of intention is not transcended. But when he does not know what to say, Socrates will help him. In most of these cases, the limit of the interlocutor's definiteness of intention has been transcended. Berkeley's *Three Dialogues between Hylas and Philonous* has also many instances illustrating this concept of definiteness of intention.

By use of questionnaires the definiteness of intention of a living person can

[16]Lovejoy, *Essays in the History of Ideas, op. cit.,* 70–73.

be fairly accurately estimated. But in the history of ideas, dealing mostly with
dead authors, this is in general impossible. A historian of ideas for this and
other reasons is seldom sure about an author's definiteness of intention. Sometimes an author gives precise alternatives of some terms and chooses among
them, which helps to determine his definiteness of intention in relation to these
terms. But most judgments of an author's definiteness of intention concerning
his terms are uncertain. Yet a scholar ought to keep this concept of definiteness
of intention in mind as a brake on offering clarifications too quickly. It is of little
use to try to clarify and make precise a vague text if it just reflects the vagueness of its author's thoughts when he wrote it, and the suggested precise interpretations would have been transintentional for him. Many authors analyzed
by historians of ideas have less definiteness of intention concerning their terms
than the philosophers mostly trained in general philosophy have concerning
theirs. One reason is that the history of ideas, as mentioned, to a greater extent
includes second- and third-rate thinkers who generally are more superficial
than the major philosophers.

Symmetry, Transitivity, Reflexivity.—The various semantical concepts we
have discussed have certain elementary logical properties. It can be proved
that the synonymity relation is symmetrical, transitive, and reflexive, that the
interpretation relation is neither symmetrical, transitive, nor reflexive, and that
the preciseness relation is transitive, asymmetrical, and irreflexive.[17]

A relation is symmetrical if and only if it holds between the concepts A and
B, it must also hold between B and A, e.g., when A and B are synonymous. A
relation is transitive if and only if it holds between A and B, and between B and
C, it must also hold between A and C, e.g., if A is more precise than B, and B
more precise than C, then A is more precise than C. A relation is reflexive if
and only if it holds between A and B, it also holds between A and A, e.g., A is
similar to A. A relation is not reflexive when it does not hold between A and A,
e.g., A is the mother of A.

These logical properties of the semantical concepts we have discussed imply
that it is often important to know if a term is a synonym, an interpretation, or a
more precise form of another term in order to avoid mistakes. If one thus
thinks that the terms A and B are universally synonymous, while B actually is
an interpretation of A, this may cause invalid conclusions in connection with
translations. If the interpretation B is translated into C, being always a
synonym for B, one may assume a transitive relation between the supposed
synonyms A, B, and C, and that A means the same as C. But because B is an interpretation of A and not a universal synonym, this conclusion is not justified.

Another example would be if a scholar misunderstood an author P's commentary on the text of another author Q and believed a term "a" used by Q to
be a synonym for the term "b" used by P, while "b" actually is a more precise
rendering of "a." The scholar would then confuse his "elucidation" by treating
"a" and "b" as symmetrical and reflexive.

Agreement and Disagreement.—The historian of ideas is witnessing and
reporting a process of communication and discussion ranging over centuries,
which is sometimes successful, but often not. I will now consider problems of
communication more in detail in connection with agreements and

[17] A. Naess, *Interpretation and Preciseness* (Oslo, 1953), 93–100.

disagreements. Agreements and disagreements are especially important in philosophy and political history, not so much in literature, although ideological and philosophical debates also exist there.

In semantics, agreements and disagreements are studied in relation to sentences that express propositions containing ideas. A sentence is often the definiens of a term expressing some idea. Therefore a discussion of (dis)agreement in relation to sentences is also relevant to the history of ideas. There are many forms of agreement and disagreement. I mention some of the most important ones for our field. If the writer A in a text U asserts a sentence s, and the writer B in his text V states that he agrees to the proposition he believes A expresses by s, and s means the same for both A and B, then there is so-called "expressed propositional agreement" between A and B concerning s in the texts U and V. But if B says he disagrees with the proposition he believes A expresses by s, and s means the same to both, then there is expressed propositional disagreement between A and B concerning s in U and V.

History abounds in examples illustrating this. When two schoolmen in the Middle Ages discussed the sentence "God exists," there was expressed propositional agreement between them. But when a schoolman discussed the sentence "Jesus is God" with a rabbi, there would be expressed propositional disagreement between them. If, however, there is verbal agreement between A and B, but s does not mean the same for A in U as for B in V, they have different propositions in mind, and the verbal agreement does not tell us whether B really agrees to the proposition A intended to express by s. In this case there are two possibilities. Either B agrees to the proposition that A expresses by s, or he does not. The first possibility may be called "pseudoexpressed propositional agreement," and the second "pseudoagreement." In the latter case B apparently agrees with A, but he would have disagreed if he had known what A really meant.

Sometimes pseudoagreement is consciously intended. When treaties are formulated between two parties by a go-between, different views can intentionally be slurred over so that both can sign, because they interpret the text differently, both reading their own views into it and both disagreeing with the interpretation of the other. Then one can claim that agreement has been reached which is in fact pseudoagreement. Kissinger's diplomacy seems to some degree to be characterized by such devices.

Then we have those cases when A in U asserts s, B in V verbally disagrees with the proposition he believes A expresses by s, and s does not mean the same for both of them. Here the mere verbal disagreement does not tell us if B really disagrees with the proposition that A intends by s. If, however, B would have disagreed with s if he had known what A in U meant by it, there is "pseudoexpressed propositional disagreement." Some parts of Kant's *Critique of Pure Reason*, which aimed at refuting Hume and Leibniz, may exemplify pseudoexpressed propositional disagreement. Russell believed that Kant had not assimilated Hume's arguments, so what Kant disagreed with was not actually Hume's views. On the other hand, if Kant had grasped what Hume really meant, he would probably have disagreed with that too. If B had agreed to s, if he had known what A really meant by it, although he verbally disagrees with s as he interprets it, we have pseudodisagreement between A and B concerning s in U and V.

Benedetto Croce in his *Historical Materialism and Marxist Economics* seems to think that Marx's opposition to Hegel's philosophy of history exemplifies pseudodisagreement. He doubts that Marx was really opposed to Hegel's conception of history. Croce thought Marx misunderstood Hegel's conception; hence, it was not really Hegel's views he rejected. Expressed agreements or disagreements are not, however, always sincere. One must therefore show that the (dis)agreements an author expresses, are his *real* opinions. Most regimes welcome consent to their doctrines, but are not so tolerant concerning dissent. Therefore many authors, especially under dictatorships, express insincere agreement with official views. In the same way an author's official disagreements with ideologies hostile to his government are sometimes contrary to his real views.

Insincerity sometimes occurs in connection with an ideology in little esteem. People who really agree with it state that they disagree. Many right-wing extremist groups thus often claim that they disagree with fascism, although one suspects that they really agree. To find out if an author is sincere is often difficult, yet it is sometimes possible to get results. The results are often based on private letters, diaries, and records from conversations between an author and close friends, where one has reason to believe that he was honest. Leibniz's real views on many matters exist in some of his private letters, which were not published until the nineteenth and twentieth centuries. The views he published while alive were intended to be approved of mainly by nobles.

Often authors want to have some of their real views published after their death. Hume thus kept his *Dialogues concerning Natural Religion* unpublished while he lived. They were instead published posthumously in 1779. Other examples are Spinoza's *Ethics* and Leibniz's *Nouveaux Essais.*

Subsumption Analysis.—To find out if two authors agree or not, one must validate at least one synonymity hypothesis, which is generally difficult, except when one can use questionnaires. In semantics other methods exist that can be used to verify such hypotheses. They are often of value to historians of ideas in connection with problems involving other semantical concepts. Especially important are subsumption and occurrence analysis, developed primarily by Arne Naess.

Problems of subsumption arise in finding out if some usage conforms to a given characterization. Subsumption analysis will here mean inquiry into whether given occurrences of a term in a text are in conformity, lack conformity, or are irrelevant to a known definition. A special case is an inquiry whether an author follows his own definitions. The goal is to find the arguments *pro et contra* subsumability and weigh them against each other.

The basic method in subsumption analysis is substitution. In a text with occurrences of some term, for which a definiens is suggested, one can substitute an occurrence with the definiens and look at the result. If the definiens "fits into" the context, the subsumption hypothesis is (weakly) confirmed. If the definiens seems malapropos in the text, ascribes to the author a meaning he did not hold, or makes the text incoherent, the hypothesis has been disconfirmed.

When we substitute and judge if some definiens fits in, we do not only use the given text for this estimation, but also a "constructed context." It may consist of propositions about the period when the text was written, about language habits prevalent at the time, propositions about the writer's psychology, about his friends, etc. Many such constructed propositions are uncertain, as are the conclusions in subsumption analysis.

A sufficient but not necessary criterion of disconfirmation is when a contradiction appears from the point of view of the author, which he would have seen, if a definiens replaced a definiendum. This contradiction may be in the text, so that after the substitution two contradicting propositions appear in it. But the contradiction may also be between a proposition in the text after the substitution and a proposition which one knows the author held, although it is not mentioned in the investigated text.

If this criterion is to be valid, we must assume that the author would not allow a contradiction, which is not always so. Sometimes an author may consciously allow contradictions, as when W. T. Stace defines pantheism as the philosophy asserting: "1. The world is identical with God. 2. The world is distinct from, that is to say, not identical with God."[18]

The validity of this criterion of disconfirmation presupposes that the author would have seen the resulting contradiction of a substitution. But often authors are unaware of contradictions in their texts, as when the contradictory propositions are not near each other. Other reasons for not seeing them may be rashness, or that the author has forgotten what he wrote some time ago. Contradictions unrecognized by the author probably exist in most philosophical works, even in the works of philosophers like Hume who emphasized analysis and clarity. Sometimes Hume denied that sensations have external causes, but sometimes he wrote as if they had. N. Kemp-Smith says that Kant contradicted himself in almost every chapter in his *Critique of Pure Reason.* Kant probably overlooked such contradictions partly because the book was written in haste. If, therefore, some definiens introduced in a text contradicts other propositions, this *need* not imply that the definiens does not cover the author's intentions, because he may have overlooked the fact that it leads to a contradiction. But a judgment that an author has overlooked a contradiction is generally uncertain.

Occurrence Analysis.—Subsumption analysis is always a part of occurrence analysis. The latter is therefore more comprehensive. In subsumption analysis we *start* with a definition and try to find out if certain occurrences of a term are subsumable under it. In occurrence analysis the definition of the investigated term is not given, but we try to find one that covers the occurrences of the term in some text. Generally one uses a trial and error method. Based on a few occurrences a definition is tentatively suggested, then tried on other occurrences by subsumption analysis. If it fits in, it is kept in its original form. If not, it is modified or rejected.

Occurrence analysts analyze use, not declarations about use. As stated, an author need not follow his own definitions. The result of an occurrence analysis can therefore be a definition never mentioned by the author. It is implicit in the author's text. Occurrence analysts also deal only with factual or cognitive meanings. They do not seek definiens-expressions, each of which in every respect is equivalent to a definiendum. When they thus try to find a definition for some occurrences in a poem, they do not seek a definiens-expression with the same artistic qualities as the definiendum. Usually the definiens expression

[18] W. T. Stace, *Mysticism and Philosophy* (London, 1972), 212.

not only breaks the rhythm but does not have the same emotional overtones as the definiendum. If it has the same cognitive meaning, then occurrence analysts are satisfied.

Occurrence analysis has four steps. The first consists in an orderly arrangement of the occurrences to be analyzed. Occurrence analysis is a rather thorough method, so the reference to the occurrences must be exact. It is not sufficient to give only the author, text, and edition, for each occurrence one must mention its exact place in a text.

The second step is to make occurrence inferences. That means that one takes each sentence with an occurrence of the investigated term and tries to find out what can be inferred about the cognitive meaning of the term in a simple way and with a fairly high degree of certainty, without differing significantly from the wording of the author. The inferences should be such that the author would have agreed to them. Occurrence inferences often seem trivial, yet they are a valuable first step toward a definition. As an example of such a list of inferences, I shall make some inferences concerning "nature" from the first occurrence sentence in Lovejoy's essay: " 'Nature' as Norm in Tertullian." He writes: "Well versed in the writings of Cicero and the Stoics and (as Eusebius records) accurately acquainted with the Roman Law, Tertullian carried over from these pagan sources into his teaching as Christian apologist and theologian a settled presumption that in 'nature,' in some sense or senses of the term, are to be found valid norms of belief and conduct." [19] I suggest the following inferences that Lovejoy would probably have agreed to:

I_1: Tertullian's conception of "nature" was at least partly formed by his pagan readings. I_2: "Nature" for Tertullian may have one or several meanings. I_3: "Nature" may be an ambiguous word for Tertullian. I_4: "Nature" is for Tertullian, at least partly, an ethical concept.

The second step of an occurrence analysis is completed when all occurrences of the term have been considered and their occurrence inferences listed.

In step three one interprets the occurrence inferences, draws other inferences from the occurrences, and makes inferences from sentences other than occurrence-sentences. The latter need not belong to the investigated text. It is not always easy to distinguish between occurrence inferences at step 2 and "other inferences from the occurrences" at step 3, but occurrence-inferences at step 2 should be more obvious, reliable, and certain than these other inferences.

The inferences and interpretations at step three must be made with due consideration to the text as a whole, to the list of inferences at step 2 and other relevant propositions. The goal is to make inferences as precise as possible, but not transintentional to the author. When making the inferences, the analyst generally uses auxiliary hypotheses. As an example of inferences from occurrences under step 3, I suggest the following, based on Lovejoy's text quoted above: "The valid ethical norms of conduct that Tertullian thought are inherent in 'Nature' are consistent with Christian ethics." Relevant sentences for drawing important inferences for this occurrence can be found in those parts of the

[19]Lovejoy, *Essays in the History of Ideas, op. cit.,* 308.

writings of Cicero, the Stoics, and Roman Law, that mention "Nature." When all interpretations and inferences at step 3 have been made, one should in review ask if they are consistent. If two propositions contradict each other, this may imply that: (1) some auxiliary hypotheses are untenable; (2) the author is inconsistent; or (3) the author uses the investigated term in at least two ways. If the evidence supports (1), one has to change some inferences and eliminate or modify one or more auxiliary hypotheses. If (3) is most probable, one must make at least two definiens-expressions for the investigated definiendum. If (2) is true, one has just to acknowledge that the author is inconsistent.

Step 4 consists in making and testing hypotheses about usage in the form of Ds-definitions. Generally the goal is to prove that occurrences of a term can be subsumed under a certain suggested Ds-definition. The Ds-definitions one arrives at are not logically deduced hypotheses. They are in principle probable guesses, relative to the evidence at hand, like the inferences from occurrence-sentences and other relevant information.

A simplified form of occurrence analysis is called limited-choice analysis. It starts with the assumption that the definiens of some definiendum exists among a limited number of Ds-definitions. Which of them it is, must be decided by subsumption analysis. A limited-choice analysis could, for instance, proceed from Lovejoy's assumption that "pride" in eighteenth-century thought had the two Ds-definitions or interpretations he mentions in the quotation cited above. Given a text from that period with occurrences of "pride," one could assume that the definiens of the term was one of Lovejoy's two interpretations. To find out which was used, on this assumption, one could use subsumption analysis.

Subsumption, occurrence, and limited-choice analysis have an important, yet limited significance in the history of ideas. Such arduous procedures, in which every occurrence of a term in a text is investigated, cannot be used on all texts studied by historians of ideas; yet they are valuable in the study of important key texts, especially controversial ones. These methods are probably the most reliable that exist when one wants to investigate the meanings of terms in texts. They make the historian of ideas more like a scientist than like a seer or prophet. This does not mean that they always yield the truth about some controversial matter. I don't think conclusions can be very certain in this field, because they in general depend on uncertain auxiliary hypotheses about psychological, aesthetic, and stylistic matters. Often the available evidence is insufficient to justify any conclusions, and the kinds of confirmation of hypotheses one obtains are usually weak.

In spite of their shortcomings, these methods are an important asset in making the reasoning more discernible and systematic. The methods enable a scholar A to follow the arguments of another scholar B more closely and point out just where B makes mistakes, when A disagrees with B, but with the more conventional methods in the history of ideas this is usually not possible. One is often only confronted with some sweeping statement and has no idea how it has been reached.

Inductive Methods.—Which methods should one use to find the meanings of terms, when the procedures described above, especially occurrence-analysis, will be to arduous? I think one should use inductive methods, i.e., inferences from a limited set of occurrences to a much larger number. This has to be done when one wants to say something in general about an idea in a whole period, as

Lovejoy often does, or if one wants to characterize a whole epoch, as those historians of ideas do who discuss the so-called *Zeitgeist.* In fact some sort of inductive methods are generally used by historians of ideas. A scholar may not have read all occurrences of an idea that he investigates as it appears in some period. No one can do much more than read many texts containing instances of the idea, and from them and his general knowledge of the period and various auxiliary hypotheses make some kind of inductive inferences from what he knows about the idea to its general use in the period under investigation.

Although such methods are used in practice, I don't think there exists any explicit theory on inductive methods in the history of ideas. Such a theory should state what the relation must be between some texts U containing occurrences of an expression "a," and a larger number of texts V, in which "a" also occurs, if conclusions concerning "a" in U shall be the basis for inductive inferences about "a" in V. I would think that if U and V consist of homogeneous material, such inferences will be more reliable than if the material is heterogeneous. And if U and V are written in the same period, such inferences are generally more justifiable than if they were written in different periods. No detailed methodological research, however, has been done on these problems, but such theories of induction must be central in the development of the methodology of the history of ideas.

On the whole, the methodology of the history of ideas is in its infancy. The field is in this respect behind general history, of which it is a part. One may therefore suggest that the interest of historians of ideas should be more directed towards the methodological problems of their field than has hitherto been the case. The reason is that when the foundation of a house is shaky, it does not make much sense continuously to add new stories to it.

University of Oslo.

Chapter XIII

"CREATIVITY" AND "TRADITION"

By Paul Oskar Kristeller

The term "creativity" has been much used and misused in recent literary and popular discussion, but it is vague and ill defined, and has poor philosophical and historical credentials. As a professional philosopher I should feel prompted to define such a word or term as creativity, and as a historian I am interested in its history. Although I am not an "ordinary language" philosopher, I am often inclined to start from a definition supplied by a standard dictionary. When I tried to do that in this case, I was greatly surprised to discover that the word "creativity" does not appear in the *Oxford English Dictionary*[1] or in the fifth edition of *Webster's Collegiate Dictionary*.[2] If I were a linguistic analyst, especially of the British school, I should have stopped after I failed to find the word in the first dictionaries I consulted, and concluded my discourse with the remark that since the word does not exist it must be dismissed as meaningless. Fortunately, I am not a linguistic analyst but an intellectual historian, and hence quite willing to admit that ordinary language is subject to continuing change, and that thinkers and writers as well as other people are perfectly free to coin new words and phrases to express new objects and thoughts. It is a relief, however, to find our word at least in the *Seventh New Collegiate Dictionary*.[3] Here "creativity" is defined as the ability to create. The definition is satisfactory, but we are led to infer that the word became an accepted part of the standard English vocabulary only between 1934 and 1961. We may even go back a few more years. The great philosopher, Alfred North Whitehead used "creativity" in his *Religion in the Making* (1927) and in his major work, *Process and Reality* (1929), and in view of the great influence of this last work, we may very well conjecture that he either coined the term or at least gave it wide currency.

Whereas the word "creativity" is apparently of recent vintage, it is derived from other words such as "creative" and "to create" that have a much earlier origin and history and that enable us to trace with much greater precision the origin and history of the ideas expressed or implied in these terms. In trying to indicate the main features of this important development, I shall make much use of a recent book by a leading historian of aesthetics, the late Wladyslaw Tatarkiewicz.[4]

---

[1] Compact edition, 1971.

[2] Springfield, Mass., 1939, based on the second edition of the *New International Dictionary* (1934).

[3] Springfield, Mass. 1972, based on the *Third New International Dictionary* of 1961.

[4] W. Tatarkiewicz, *A History of Six Ideas* (Warsaw and the Hague, 1980), chap. 8, 244-65. See also Milton C. Nahm, "Creativity in Art," *Dictionary of the History of Ideas*, ed. Philip P. Wiener (New York, 1972), I,577-89, and Nahm, *The Artist as Creator* (Baltimore, 1956). It should be noted that Tatarkiewicz and Nahm use "creativity" as a heading of their recent articles, but that the term does not occur in the sources they quote except for the most recent ones.

The word "to create" and its equivalents and derivatives have been used in Western thought in three different contexts which we might roughly describe as theological, artistic, and broadly human. For most of the history of Western thought, the ability to create was attributed exclusively or primarily to God, and to human makers or artists only in a restricted or metaphorical sense. Only after the latter part of the eighteenth century, that is, with the first stirrings of the Romantic movement, did poets and artists come to be considered as creators *par excellence*, and this notion has run strong through the entire nineteenth century down to the twentieth. A further change occurred in the present century when it has become a widespread belief that the ability to create is not limited to artists or writers but extends to many more, and perhaps to all, areas of human activity and endeavor: we speak of the scientist, of the statesman, and of many others as creative, and I for one should wish to defend the view that the philosopher and the scholar also are or may be creative in the pursuit of their work.

Before inquiring into the conceptual problems involved in our understanding of creativity, we need to pursue the history of the terms "to create" and "creative" somewhat further. As always in such investigations, we have to begin with the Greek language and with ancient Greek philosophy which is certainly the ultimate source of our philosophical method and terminology, although we do not deny the fact that later and modern trends of thought have in many ways transformed and outgrown the limits of ancient thought. The Greek language has only a single word for making and creating (poiein), and since the Greek word for poet (poietes), which is still our word, means maker, it is no wonder that the poets were often considered "creative" and inspired. On the other hand, the divine powers that Plato and other later philosophers considered as creators of the world were not thought to have created the world out of nothing, but rather to have given shape to a formless matter that preceded their action, and for this very reason the divine creators or makers were often compared to human artisans, architects, or sculptors. The analogy was sometimes reversed, and the human artist was thought to have shaped his work out of his material just as the divine artisan shaped the universe out of matter. Since for Plato and his Neoplatonic successors the divine artist conveyed form to matter by taking immaterial and intelligible forms for his models, it was sometimes claimed, or at least implied, that the perfect human work of art was also a material copy of some immaterial model to which the artist in his mind had direct access.

When we pass from Greek pagan philosophy to Latin Christian and medieval thought, two noteworthy changes took place. The Latin language, unlike Greek, had two separate words for creating and making, *creare* and *facere*, which suggested a significant difference between the divine and the human maker. Moreover, on the basis of the account of divine creation in the Old Testament, St. Augustine developed the doctrine, followed by all later Christian theologians, that God created the world not out of a preexisting matter but out of nothing. Creation out of nothing was the exclusive prerogative of God, and a human artist who produced a work out of material given to him could not be remotely compared with the divine creator, even less so than in Greek antiquity. The outlook began to change with the Renaissance when the achievement of the artist and the poet began to be more widely admired and when the attribute "divine" was associated with Dante and

Michelangelo. But the cases where a poet (let alone an artist) was said to create remained rare and exceptional. I take it that it is in the aftermath of the theological tradition, though in a naturalistic context and less rigid sense, that Bergson speaks of "creative evolution" in the world of living organisms, and that Whitehead uses creativity as the universal principle of cosmic innovation which belongs to God (who not only precedes the world but also pervades and follows it) and to all astronomical, biological, and social units within the world (I hope I correctly understand the thought of this great but obscure thinker).

The real turning point in Western thinking on what we now call "creativity" came in the eighteenth century. Poetry, music, and the visual arts were for the first time grouped together as fine arts[5] which became the subject of a new separate discipline, aesthetics or the philosophy of art, and the Romantic movement exalted the artist above all other human beings. For the first time, the term "creative" was applied not only to God but also to the human artist, and a whole new vocabulary was developed to characterize the artist and his activity although there were some partial or scattered precedents to be found in ancient and Renaissance thought. The artist was guided no longer by reason or by rules but by feeling and sentiment, intuition and imagination; he produced what was novel and original, and at the point of his highest achievement he was a genius. In the nineteenth century, this attitude became pervasive, and we might note with surprise that an age that found it difficult to believe that God created the world out of nothing apparently had no difficulty in believing that the human artist would create his work out of nothing. It is a part of the broader movement to free modern man (and woman) completely from all rules, restrictions, and traditions. In the arts it led in many cases to the disappearance of traditional forms and contents, and led either to other entirely new forms and contents or to complete anarchy.

If we wish to add a social factor (as it nowadays seems mandatory to many people, even where it is quite irrelevant to the problem under discussion), we may say that the social position of the artist underwent a profound change after the middle of the eighteenth century. He gradually lost the patronage of the Church and the state, of the aristocracy and patriciate that had sustained him for centuries, and found himself confronted with an anonymous, amorphous, and frequently uneducated public which he often despised and which he would either flatter with a bad conscience or openly defy, claiming that it was the public's duty to approve and support the artist even when it could not understand or appreciate the products of the artist's unbridled self expression. The examples of geniuses unrecognized in their time (something rarely heard of before the nineteenth century) finally gave the public and the critics such a bad conscience that by now almost anything has become acceptable. The artist no longer has to face or to fear any outside criticism, and only if he is serious his self-criticism and that of his friends may suffice to guide him. The excessive cult of the genius was exposed and

---

[5] P.O. Kristeller, "The Modern System of the Arts, "*JHI*, XII (1951), 496-527; XIII (1953), 17-46; last reprinted in P.O. Kristeller, *Renaissance Thought and the Arts* (Princeton, 1980), 163-227.

ridiculed by the late Edgar Zilsel half a century ago in two incisive books,[6] but this telling critique of Neo-romantic excesses has had no lasting effect. Perhaps the concept of genius has been less widely used in recent decades since it is definitely an "elitist" notion, whereas in an egalitarian age such as ours it is claimed and believed that everybody, not only some gifted and talented artists, is original and creative.

Egalitarianism, if not outright envy, is also the source of the more recent tendency, increasingly common during the last few decades, to apply the concepts of originality and creativity to other human activities besides the arts. Any person who is original in his field and who produces something novel has a right to be called creative. The term has been applied especially to scientists and to statesmen and reformers who obviously try to bring about something that is novel, but it is sporadically also extended to technicians, managers, editors, gourmet cooks, and fashion designers. I do not intend to deny the claims of these useful and respectable activities and professions, and merely wish to add the humble plea that not only philosophers and scholars but also humorists and punners should be admitted as stockholders in this flourishing creativity business. If present trends continue, and creativity will take the place of competence and intelligence as an educational and professional standard, we may look forward to methods of measuring and testing creativity, and if the term continues to defy precise definition, we may end up with the profound claim advanced some time ago by the testers of intelligence, namely, that creativity is what is tested by a creativity test.

To approach our problem in a more serious vein, we may start from the definition of creativity as the ability to produce something "novel."[7] The most obvious way in which this ability may be attributed to a human being is usually not mentioned in recent discussions, although Aristotle often refers to it: the ability to beget another human being. The current discussion of creativity is still largely dominated by the romantic notion of artistic creativity in spite of the recent tendency to apply the term to other areas of human activity. Creativity in this sense is a legitimate subject of psychological inquiry, and although there are evidently great differences in the extent and quality of artistic and other human products, it is quite possible to admit that every human being is creative to a greater or lesser extent, at least potentially. It is also plausible, so far as education is concerned, that creativity may be encouraged and developed mainly by removing such obstacles as timidity, rigidity, or inertia. Yet it definitely cannot be taught, and the occasional tendency to use creativity as an excuse for not teaching anything at all is sheer nonsense.

It is often believed that the test of creativity and originality is the feeling which the artist himself experiences before or in producing his work. This feeling is hard for an external observer to ascertain, and it may even be doubted that the intensity of this subjective feeling corresponds precisely to the originality and novelty, let alone to the artistic quality, of the work of art

---

[6] Edgar Zilsel, *Die Geniereligion* (Vienna and Leipzig, 1918); *Die Entstehung des Geniebegriffs* (Tuebingen, 1926).

[7] It is amusing to remember that Erasmus in his *Encomium Moriae* introduced Folly as the daughter of Wealth and Novelty (*Neotes*).

produced by the artist. There are instances in which artists who spoke with great emphasis of their originality and vocation did not have much to show for their effort, and vice versa, many authors of widely admired works have been rather reticent or humble about their feelings and efforts. We might even say that in the detached judgment of posterity the periods in which critics spoke most loudly about the artist and his creativity were not always those that produced the greatest works of art, and vice versa. It is evidently not very original or creative to speak about originality and creativity (just as the talk about an important subject is not always important[8]), nor does the talk about a thing necessarily produce the thing. Perhaps we are inclined to talk most emphatically about the very things which we should like to have but do not have, at least not to the extent to which we should wish to have them.

The best way to judge the creativity and originality of artists is to examine the novelty and originality of their works and to infer from them the creativity of their authors, just as in the old days the perfection of the universe was used as one of the arguments to prove the existence and perfection of its divine creator. A close survey of the large treasures of art, music, and literature that have been preserved for us from many different times and places suggests that irrespective of quality there is not a single work of art that is completely novel or original, and hardly a single product that is altogether unoriginal. What we have are different degrees of novelty and originality, and we are, of course, inclined to give a higher rating to those works and artists which show a higher degree of originality. Even the most original work of art is likely to be a new attempt within a well established genre—a novel, a play, a poem, a building, a painting, a composition for the piano or orchestra—and will have a greater or smaller number of traits in common with other specimens of the same genre. It is likely to retain at least residual traces of the patterns and vocabularies associated with its respective genre. Conversely, a copy of an original work will always be distinct from the model and its other copies, intentionally or not, and if one master makes a copy of the work of another master, Rubens of Titian, Manet of Goya, Van Gogh of Hiroshige, the copy will have its own originality and value without ceasing to be a copy. The same master may paint several works that have the same style or general content or that are outright replicas of the same composition, but each of them is an original work that any gallery will be happy to own since it cannot have all the others at the same time. Their subtle differences will be recognized only when they can be displayed side by side in an exhibition. The interpretation of a work of art also has this double aspect. A musical or theatrical performance is not original in relation to the work of the composer or writer, but it may also be considered original insofar as it transforms the work into another more complete reality and is an interpretation different from other interpretations of the same work. The

[8] We are reminded of Galileo's statement that the nobility of a science depends on the certainty of its method and not on the dignity of its subject matter; see *Opere, Edizione Nazionale,* ed. A. Favoro, VI (1896), 237 and VII (1897), 246. For the historical context of this statement, see P.O. Kristeller, *Renaissance Thought and Its Sources* (New York, 1979), 286, n. 76.

same is true of a critic or scholar who tries to understand a work of literature or of abstract thought; it is true also of a translator who tries to render a work of literature or of abstract thought in another language and may succeed in giving to it a new and impressive appearance. Even a verbatim quotation of one author by another may show the subtle transformation of an insight from one context to another.

In other words, originality and novelty, if we take them as descriptive terms, are never completely present or absent in any work of art but are always mixed with different degrees of unoriginality and of imitation. If we wish to set up originality as the main criterion of artistic quality and excellence, we must accept the consequence that a higher degree of originality will indicate a higher degree of excellence, unless we wish to reject as "elitism" all degrees of excellence (and of originality) and prefer to recognize even a product of minimum originality as a welcome expression of human creativity. This latter tendency is apparent in the applause that has been given to "action painting" and to the work of children and the insane.

Within the tradition of creativity (I do not hesitate to use this apparently paradoxical phrase) originality, as we have seen, is not only a descriptive term but also a highly praised value. I do not deny that a work of art may owe some of its excellence to its originality, but even if it were granted that originality is a *necessary* condition for artistic excellence (which I think it is not), I should argue very strongly that it is not a *sufficient* condition (a distinction that is all too often forgotten in many current discussions of this and similar problems). Originality as such does not assure the excellence of a work of art, or for that matter, of any human product. In the field of the arts, there are many works that are quite original but not especially good, and there are works of limited originality that attain a high degree of artistic quality. There are other criteria than originality that may be used to judge the excellence of a work of art, and in the critical and philosophical literature on the arts prior to Romanticism, these criteria were often set forth and emphasized: we may mention beauty, form, style, imitation of nature and of previous works of art, or of intelligible essences, good taste, human relevance, emotional power, truthfulness, moral and social consciousness, playfulness, usefulness, entertainment, craftsmanship, and many other features. I cannot now go into the precise meaning or validity of these criteria or into the question of whether and how they may be combined with each other or with originality. Yet I hope it has become apparent that on philosophical and historical grounds we are forced to admit that originality is not the only or even the main factor in determining artistic quality. The matter becomes even worse when we enter the areas of theoretical or moral creativity. In the fields of the sciences, scholarship, and philosophy no original idea is of any worth that does not also claim to be true. Velikowski's theory of worlds in collision may be original, but it is in conflict with the available astronomical, archaeological, and historical evidence, and hence it belongs to the realm of science fiction. Hitler's theory of National Socialism was certainly original, but hardly anybody would take that as an excuse for its violation of moral, legal, and political principles which are widely if not universally recognized.

I also do not think that the artist creates out of nothing. He obviously must have talent, from God or nature or chance, and the amount of talent is unequally, and if you wish, unjustly distributed among human beings. The artist must be trained in those skills and techniques that can be taught and that are pertinent to his craft. He should be exposed to those rules that have been considered useful by his predecessors, without being obliged to follow them blindly and uncritically, and to some of the masterpieces of the recent and distant past from which he may derive a standard of artistic quality, without trying to imitate the details that no longer fit his time and his own character. We do not know exactly how he works, although we have learned from drawings and sketchbooks how a painter arrived at his final work. He will draw on his memory and on the store of his knowledge, and must make an effort and take a risk that cannot be anticipated by planning. Mere intentions are not enough if the completed work does not embody them, and no artist should be judged by his intentions rather than by his actual work. The empty sheet or canvas breeds a *horror vacui*, and not a good idea. I like the story of the Japanese artist who promised a painting to the emperor. When the emperor became impatient, visited the artist in his study, and found no sketches or drawings, he blamed the painter for not having done any work. The painter grew angry, explained that he had been thinking about the work for months, went to his easel and started and completed his painting in a few minutes before the eyes of the emperor. I find this story more plausible than most other things I have heard or read about artistic creativity.

In other words, originality is not the main factor in a work of art, and it should not be the major goal of the artist. His goal should be to do a good piece of work, and if he succeeds, he will also turn out to be original.

In facing now the second part of our topic, tradition (and its relation to creativity), we are confronted with even greater difficulties and complexities. In an obvious sense, tradition does not form a simple contrast with creativity; it is only the advocates of creativity who have set tradition up as a straw man and claim that in their pursuit of novelty they free themselves and their contemporaries from the dead weight of tradition. It is clear that tradition means the preservation of extant ideas and possessions that are considered valuable, but when we talk about tradition it is not clear what the content of this tradition is, and whether there is, even in any given instance, one single tradition, or rather a multiplicity of traditions. Moreover, there have not been, at least in the areas that interest us and in recent times, any vocal or influential defenders of tradition, as there have been of novelty and creativity. When people talk about traditional scholarship or traditional philosophy, they usually do so with a negative and derogatory overtone, and one has to be rather careful and defensive in expressing even a qualified approval of both. The highly respected periodical *Traditio* represents traditional scholarship in the fields of ancient and medieval studies, but it has hardly been noticed by any except specialists of the subject. I must try briefly to clarify and to correct some of the current views on tradition. Since the defenders of creativity have been so much opposed to tradition, the temptation will be great to counter one exaggeration with another and to overemphasize the value of tradition. I shall try to avoid this temptation, to give a qualified defense of tradition, and to maintain that the excellence of works of art and of other human endeavors is usually not due to creativity alone but to a combination of originality and tradition.

We should realize from the beginning that a completely stable or rigid tradition that never admits change is humanly impossible and has never existed. Even those primitive societies that are most traditional and that oddly enough are held up as models by many anthropologists are stable only in a relative sense and subject to more or less subtle changes. The view often assumed by social scientists that human societies are stable by nature and that we must introduce special categories, ideological or otherwise, in order to account for change, strikes me as naive, because it is contradicted by the fact that these societies are made up of individuals that are constantly being born, grow up, engage in various activities, and finally die, to be replaced by others. The problem should be formulated the other way around: change is the general condition of nature, of societies, and even of individuals, and it requires a special effort to preserve continuity and, if you wish, tradition in the midst of change. A human individual does not easily maintain his style and identity from youth to old age when hardly a single part of the body and mind remain the same, and a family, a social group, a tribe, or a nation would constantly change and even disintegrate unless it created special institutions and traditions in order to maintain at least some of its identity. For any young member of a society it is necessary to learn and acquire the knowledge and skills needed for the functioning of that society. This has been known and practiced in all primitive societies, and if a highly complex society such as ours, that believes itself to be very advanced, neglects to teach its young the basic knowledge and skills needed for even a modest role in that society, it prepares its own destruction whatever the high sounding slogans used to justify or excuse this neglect. A writer has to know his language and its literature, if not other languages and literatures, before he can adequately begin to write; he must be familiar with the patterns and rules of the genres he wishes to employ, whether he wants to write novels or plays, poems or essays; and he must know some of the best specimens of previous literature in order to emulate their quality if not to imitate their external features. The same is true of the musician, the painter, and other artists, and an analogous rule applies to all areas of human activity. An architect must also learn the mechanical rules that will prevent his building from collapsing, and know the practical functions for which his building is intended, whether it is a home or office building, a factory, a museum, or a church. He may also have original ideas and express himself, but originality and self-expression will not excuse him when his building collapses or proves unsuitable for the purpose for which it was built.

Within each branch of the arts there are also traditions concerning the subject matter as well as the form of the work of art. Greek tragedy treated the same old myths for generations, and medieval and Renaissance painting treated the same religious subjects for centuries, yet we do not think that Euripides in his *Electra* lacks originality because the theme had been treated by Aeschylus and Sophocles before him, or that a particular Madonna or Adoration lacks originality or distinctive merit because the same subjects were treated by many painters of the same time or other times. The same is true of landscapes and still lives that allow of a great variety in detail and quality among numerous works of similar content. The artist evidently does not lose his originality when he adopts a theme previously treated by others, and the fact that the theme is generally known to his public and understood by it provides a challenge to treat the same subject in a novel way and to concentrate on fine details and nuances while the rough outline of the theme is given beforehand and cannot be changed. Variations on a theme are among the best compositions in music and also in other arts, whereas the invention of a new plot does not assure excellence or even originality because in many cases the plot is old and only the names of the characters have been altered.

However, in stressing the value of tradition in the arts and elsewhere, we must also emphasize that tradition as such is not always valuable. Within the multiplicity of traditions and traditional elements that have been handed down to us, there are many which are not valuable, or which have lost their value with changing conditions, and which hence do not deserve to be retained or revived. The appeal to tradition is valid only for those elements of a tradition which are considered to be valuable. Thus a tradition can be kept alive only by retaining what is valuable in it, by discarding what is bad or antiquated, and by replacing the discarded elements with novel features derived from other sources or from the originality of new carriers of the tradition. I have found this to be the only way to understand and interpret Platonism, one of the most respectable traditions in Western philosophy. However, traditional elements are also important in another way. Ideas, styles, and motifs of the past may lose their appeal in a certain period or climate of opinion, but this must not be final, for they may regain their validity at another time and under different conditions. It is therefore important to preserve in libraries and museums the monuments of past thought and productive activity. They should always be studied by specialists, for antiquarian purposes, if you wish, but they may also regain their life and relevance, as it were, at any time, and what was dead or unknown to one generation may suddenly and unexpectedly become important for the next. I may be permitted to cite the example of the period to which I have devoted much work for many years, the Italian Renaissance. In that period, the remnants of classical civilization, its literature, philosopy, and art, though not completely forgotten during the Middle Ages, suddenly regained an actuality and importance they had not had before, and the study, reinterpretation, and sometimes misinterpretation of classical models led to a period in the arts, literature, the sciences, and philosophy that impresses us, if for any reason, by its productivity and originality. I cite the Renaissance as evidence that creativity is not always stifled by tradition and must not always assert itself by denying the value of all tradition, but may very well combine with a selective use of valuable traditional elements to bring about quite excellent works of art, of literature, and of abstract thought. In the world of the intellect, that is, of the sciences, of philosophy, and of scholarship, new ideas and insights will constantly come forth but will have to be examined and tested for their compatibility with available empirical and rational evidence, whereas in private and public life, all actions, taken with or without precedents, should be tested and judged according to their conformity with valid and accepted principles and standards of ethics, law, and politics. In all these domains any laudable achievement requires originality and talent, but it must also conform to the rules of the game as well as to the standards of the past which we may or may not wish to call "tradition."[9]

Columbia University.

[9] I am indebted to Paul Kuntz for suggestions and information.

Chapter XIV

INTERPRETING THE ENLIGHTENMENT: A POLITICAL APPROACH

By Lester G. Crocker

A number of scholars in the twentieth century have undertaken the rather awesome project of writing a general or synthetic interpretation of the French Enlightenment.[1] The incongruity of these interpretations poses acutely the basic problem of historical interpretation. My purpose is to display this problem by concentrating on treatment of the Enlightenment's political thought, which all interpreters, to a greater or lesser extent, necessarily include, and to probe into it as far as I can by determining how it is integrated into their general reconstruction.

The two aspects of intellectual activity that a full account of Enlightenment political thought would have to encompass may be designated by the adjectives "critical" and "constructive." By "critical" I mean the uncovering of abuses and proposals for reform; by "constructive" I refer to more general political theories and schemes for a better society. Such an integrated study of both aspects has not been written. I shall, then, follow the bifurcation encountered into the interpretative studies themselves, and begin with the "critical." Here the problem of interpretation may be specifically designated. Were the *philosophes* realists, or were they on the contrary, locked up in their abstract systems and idealistic plans? This problem, whose importance is attested by its perseverance, is not easily solved. One would have to try to evaluate proposals on a case by case basis, by subjective judgment, by what did happen at the time, by what happened later. Moreover, one is impelled to ask, what does "realistic" mean? Even if we were to judge most of the proposals to be realistic *qua* projects, the question remains: Were they "realistic" in terms of the actual context of institutions and forces? It is not surprising that no satisfactory or universally accepted answer has yet been given—nor is it likely to be.

[1] The studies I have selected are the following: Ernst Cassirer, *Die Philosophie der Aufklärung* (Tübingen, 1932), English translation by J. P. Pettegrove (Princeton, 1955); Daniel Mornet, *Les Origins intellectuelles de la Révolution française* (Paris, 1933); Paul Hazard, *La Crise de la conscience européenne* (Paris, 1935); *La Pensée européenne au XVIIIe siècle* (Paris, 1946); Charles Frankel, *The Faith of Reason* (New York, 1948); Lester G. Crocker, *An Age of Crisis* (Baltimore, 1959); *Nature and Culture* (Baltimore, 1963); Jean Ehrard, *L'Idée de nature en France dans la première moitié du XVIIIe siècle* (Paris, 1963); Peter Gay, *The Enlightenment, an Interpretation,* vol. I, *The Rise of Modern Paganism* (New York, 1966), vol. II, *The Science of Freedom,* New York, 1969 (only the second volume treats of politics). The discussion will be in approximate but not exact chronological order. The inclusion of my own work may pose the problem of objectivity. The reader will judge whether I have overcome it.

Daniel Mornet's richly informed investigation will not help us very much. Important as it is in its own way, and as a precursor of the "Annales" school, it is short on interpretation. "La lutte contre l'autorité" is the theme he treats in rapid references in interspersed chapters. The diffusion of ideas interests him, rather than analysis of ideas themselves. He does however, sketch a picture of the struggles in which the *philosophes* engaged in their opposition to authority. He presents the evidence to show that the bases of divine right and the practices of oppression were challenged in widely circulated media. But the main thrust of critics of the régime, as we read Mornet, was reform: the uncovering of specific abuses and (sometimes) suggestions for their correction.

Mornet's method and his results were determined, I believe, primarily by two factors: (1) the upsurge of careful academic research that flowed from the influence of German universities; (2) the desire to counteract nineteenth-century critics, such as Taine, who had condemned the philosophes for their lack of realism. His work does not solve the problem because it is fragmentary and does not face the issue directly by a broad discussion of the pros and cons. Nor is he interested in political theory. Since his project and his perspective were governed by a reaction to his inheritance of nineteenth-century hostility to the Enlightenment, and since that hostility was highly prejudiced by religious and political preferences and was poorly grounded in the facts, Mornet's method is documentary. Not surprisingly, he finds that the facts justify his unspoken purpose: the *philosophes* were realistic reformers, rather than the abstract ideologues portrayed by their nineteenth-century enemies. In effect, this was a disservice to the movement he was trying to vindicate. There was political philosophy in it, as well as political "science."

The question on which Taine and Mornet were thus divided did not trouble Paul Hazard. He does touch on proposals for reform, principally in regard to the campaigns against slavery and the iniquities of the penal code and practices.[2] But Hazard's interest is mainly in the consequences of the theory of *droit naturel.* His remarks aim to show that the drives for reform were among the results of that theory. When it comes to judgment, Hazard is on the side of the Enlightenment's critics. He considers these campaigns to be another phase of the abstract rationalism and the optimism of the age, inasmuch as they were based on natural law theories which, he declares, had no effect on legislation anywhere. The reform aspect of Enlightenment political activity, Hazard concludes, was one of the great illusions of the time. The best that can be said for it is that it did create a will to justice and an atmosphere of humanitarianism.

Gay's interpretation of the critical phase stands in sharp opposition to Hazard's. In the chapters "The Politics of Decency" and "The Politics

____

[2] *La Pensée européene* I, 214-216.

of Experience," Gay does admit that the *philosophes* were "desperately satisfied with superficial solutions that were no solutions at all." Nevertheless, he argues, they were ahead of their time because they relied on public opinion to bring about changes that would install rational government and good administration. They did not seek fundamental change, only reform through existing institutions. Their campaign for toleration was "pragmatic," based on "the scientific method" and "a single view of man and of politics," of man as an autonomous being, responsible to himself—a view that follows "with inescapable logic from their general way of thinking" of man as good or neutral. The campaign against war was also realistic (since war is evil); this aspect of life led the *philosophes,* however, to pessimism. Their campaign against slavery, though often vague, helped to change men's way of thinking, and it did have a realistic basis in its argument for "the economic disutility of slavery." Their crusade for legal reform also had the hallmark of their empiricism, in their urge to exploit incidents. When, in the battle over the Maupeou *parlements,* Voltaire embraced the *thèse royale,* he did this on the basis of utility. In sum, "Enlightened politics is modern liberal politics" (400), and this is demonstrated again in Voltaire's and Rousseau's role in the "Genevan affair," the debate over the right of protest and legal procedure under the Genevan Constitution (1763-64).

A sharp and continuing opposition of views on this question thus continues from the nineteenth century to the present. As is usual in such cases, there is some right on each side. The *philosophes* did help to change men's minds (at least those of thinking men) in regard to legal reform and slavery as well as religious toleration. They focused attention on abuses that were, in western countries, to be alleviated later. But what of the effectiveness of all these efforts on the ambient reality? Furio Diaz's *Filosofia e politica nel settecento francese* (Torino, 1962) is the only serious and thorough exploration of the "practical" side of the *philosophes'* activity. It is a work that deserves to be more widely known outside of Italy. Since it is not, like the other studies we are considering, a general interpretation of the Enlightenment, we shall not go into the detail of its sweeping investigation; however, it has an important bearing on interpreting the political phase of the eighteenth century because in it the ideas and activities of the French Enlightenment are consistently embedded in the historical reality of the struggles within which they evolved. Still more pertinently, they are displayed as being tested by that reality, as responding or failing to respond. Diaz's conclusions are antithetical to Gay's. The facts, as he relates them, show the *philosophes* repeatedly failing the tests. The structure of the book reveals a series of crises in the fabric of the *Ancien Régime,* each of which was simultaneously a crisis for them. Each presented difficulties, challenges, and opportunities. They were all missed, with the single exception of miscarriages of justice (e.g., Calas); but the Establishment easily absorbed these setbacks. The

philosophes did not succeed in their objectives of reforming the structure
and functioning of French society and institutions, of creating a more
just and open society.

The ambiguity of positions in regard to this phase of Enlightenment
politics is readily accounted for by two factors. One is the prejudice—
in the sense of pre-judgment—of the historians who conceive, or choose
to conceive, of the Enlightenment differently, in itself and in its historical
import. The other factor lies in objective fact and deserves a brief comment
in the light of Diaz's study. The Enlightenment's political action was,
on the one hand, covered with honor and had a lasting influence on
men's ways of thinking; on the other hand, it was doomed to defeat in
its time. One reason for this outcome was the strength and resoluteness
of the opposition, whose unity, fundamentally flawed by dissensions, was
consistently recovered when threatened from without. A second reason
was the irresoluteness and disunity of the *philosophes,* their difficulty in
going beyond diverse and often vague proposals and abstract theories,
inchoate in their multiplicity, to a clearly formulated, practical program
around which they might have effectively organized. A third hindrance
was their obsession with attacks on religion and bigotry, which was
counterproductive with a wide span of popular opinion as well as with
the authorities.

If the politics of the Englightenment was destined to have lasting
effects, much of its influence came not from the cry against abuses, but
from the theoretical side of its political philosophy. Notwithstanding
Mornet's opinion on the matter, what interests readers of our own time
is less the *philosophes'* projects for reform than their imaginative theorizing. Not that the struggles against intolerance, cruelty, and torture
have lost their contemporaneity, but a result of eighteenth-century theorizing is our awareness of the ineradicable impulses in human nature
that foster inhumanity; and one of its historical sequels is that régimes
which practice such abuses propose a view of societies in some ways
announced by eighteenth-century political speculators and prophets. In
the various abstract political systems engendered at the time, there was
a conflict of principles and goals which is still of relevance to the twentieth
century.

Natural law theory plays an important part in interpretations of
Enlightenment politics. It deserves to be treated separately since it lies
between the critical and the constructive with connections to each. While
the idea of natural law was capable of serving reactionary or conservative
tendencies (by appealing to the universal and timeless), it could also be
used for contrary liberal, progressive purposes. Interpreters of the Enlightenment, like Paul Hazard, have seen it largely in the latter light.

The key point was made by Cassirer in his sixth chapter, "Law, State,
and Society." The opposition of the Enlightenment to tradition and
custom, he argued, was basically not destructive in intent but sprang

from its wish to strip away what was not viable or outmoded, in order to reach the bedrock of human nature on which a more solid social structure could be built. Natural law thus became the central point: the problem was to demonstrate its autonomy and its prior claims to those of theological or civil law. The philosophy of the Enlightenment, Cassirer contended, demanded "absolutely, universally valid and unalterable legal norms" (243). Even empiricists like Voltaire and Diderot strove, in this regard, to avoid the consequences of a strict empiricism—that is, relativity in law and morals—and to uphold the proposition that natural law is necessary and immutable. In Diderot's theory of natural law Cassirer found the crucial shift from the traditional *a priori* conception to a thoroughly empirical basis of "pure experience," based on men's universal inclinations, instincts, and appetites. The result was a utilitarian foundation for ethics.

Cassirer's perception of a relation that existed between natural law and nascent utilitarianism is a valuable contribution. (He could have found it in Voltaire, as well.) This relation is generally ignored by modern scholars; in fact, the two are often thought of as having been completely opposed to each other, as in Peter Gay's study. On the other hand, analogy with the laws of nature did not imply, as Cassirer contends, a conformity with the laws of the physical world. Voltaire's belief, contrary to the impression given by Cassirer, was that there must *also* be moral laws which relate to human beings alone. Furthermore, although Cassirer is justified in finding the origin of natural or inalienable rights in natural law theory, he does not show as clearly as one would like how the concept of natural law developed into that of natural rights.

Cassirer recognized that one cannot consider natural law divorced from social contract theory. Here the *philosophes* chose to follow Grotius' rather than Hobbes. The Hobbesian social contract, Cassirer held, gave the ruler an absolute power that annulled the concept of natural law (and so, one would assume, of natural rights). But Locke, arguing that there had to be a prior ground for legality, had included in natural law the rights of personal freedom and property. The *philosophes*—especially Voltaire—introduced this idea "into real political life," according to Cassirer, and gave it the power that bore fruit in the French Revolution, a power that derived from natural law theory and not from the Virginia and other American bills of rights. (This claim may be argued, and at least needs greater nuance.)

Cassirer found Rousseau's social contract to be the culmination of this trend in political thinking. He realized that under Rousseau's social contract the individual citizen no longer possesses inalienable rights, which belong only to the general will and find expression in its relations with the government. He does not object, however, to the seeds of totalitarianism in Rousseau's position; rather, he accepts as cogent Rousseau's contention that inasmuch as the citizen *is* the general will and the true sovereign (or a portion of it, in any case), it would be absurd to suppose that he has inalienable rights vis-à-vis himself. In short, the citizen does not require protection against the State so long as by virtue of the social contract he had a voice in its determinations. Although Rousseau broke with the Enlightenment over the values of culture, modernism, and reform, his political (and ethical) legacy, according to Cassirer, by its firm reliance on natural law remained in the mainstream of eighteenth-century thought. Now it is difficult to see, on the face of it, how natural-law theory could lead both to the affirmation of inalienable natural rights and to Rousseau's denial of such rights or, if the first assertion is true, how Rousseau can be said to belong to the mainstream of eighteenth-century political thought.

Cassirer, finally, also rejected Taine's verdict that "the Encyclopedists were utopian doctrinaires who constructed purely synthetic political and social systems which they proclaimed dogmatically without regard to concrete historical reality" (267).

Cassirer's aim and method were philosophical. He wanted to counter neglect rather than hostility, to show that the *philosophes* were philosophers, and that the movement played a significant role in the course of modern philosophy. The results were fruitful, and his work remains a classic. Nevertheless, from the historical viewpoint—which, precisely, was not his, even though he writes philosophically about historiography— his *Philosophy of the Enlightenment* is the narrowest of general interpretations in regard to political and ethical thought. The latter he completely neglects. The former appeals to him only in its natural law aspect. With the exception of Rousseau, the multiple facets of speculation that lie outside its orbit did not concern him.[3]

Jean Ehrard's starting point (ch. VIII, "Nature et Société") is that of most writers of the eighteenth century, the passage from natural to organized societies. He recognizes that the positions they took diverged widely. Some thought that if society violates nature, men must choose between despotism and anarchy. Others argued that obligation has its

---

[3] Cassirer's paradigmatic view, moreover, is far from being as valid as he makes it appear. Hobbes never tried to abolish the principle of natural law or natural rights. He believed that there are only separate self-interests, not a general welfare; and these, in the context of a society, require the sacrifices he demands. The utilitarianism Cassirer attributes to Diderot is closer to Hobbes than to traditional natural law theory. In fact, natural law plays no role for all practical purposes, in Rousseau's plan of a true society. Rather than being in the mainstream of Enlightenment political thought, as Cassirer affirms, he stands out as one with radically different ways of conceiving new political and social directions. It is difficult to think of Rousseau as "realistic," at least (as he admitted) in relation to contemporary régimes. And when one considers the abstract writings of d'Holbach, Mably, Chastellux and others, one sees the relation between their type of thinking and the unrealism of practice that Diaz has brought out. Cassirer has Voltaire principally in mind. In sum, he does not reconcile natural law as theory and empiricism.

sanction in self-interest (providentially arranged). To this some critics replied that a utilitarian explanation does not take into account the obligation to sacrifice one's self-interest, which requires a natural principle other than egoism. Thus a euphoric appeal to sentiment, to humanitarian feeling also comes to the fore. Contrary to Hobbes, Montesquieu and others maintained that the state of war began only in society when natural law and right reason lost their limiting power and sympathy was overcome by natural passions. Positive laws are therefore necessary to insure the rule of natural law, indeed, this is their purpose.

Such reasoning leads to another step. If the social order is to accord with natural law, it must unite virtue and happiness in order to fulfill its purpose, the happiness of its members. This, Ehrard argues, was the chief contribution of natural-law theory. One contract formed society, another was made between rulers and ruled. The rights of subjects, by virtue of the latter, become a claim. But while nature, for the innovators, was egalitarian, for traditionalists it was hierarchical, based on the family model—an idea that the innovators refuted as a model for royal power. Natural law theory thus turned into a theory of political liberalism. Ehrard, in this analysis, gives us a clearer view of the relation between natural-law theory and political theory than we find in other interpretations.

The foregoing analyses justify several comments. Natural law and natural rights are abstract concepts. Whether or not one accepts them, it remains that they postulate either a transcendental harmony or basic, stable uniformities in human nature and experience. If one chooses to emphasize the "rights" aspect of *droit naturel,* as the Enlightenment did, it may lead to other abstractions, such as the social contract theory and the theory of residual sovereignty, or to proposals relating to real situations (slavery, penal reform, bills of rights). The practical insertion of such demands into political reality—the reality of power—depends on means which, as Diaz shows repeatedly throughout his study, the reformers either did not possess or were unable to mobilize. Furthermore, there is no necessary relation between *droit naturel* and any particular form of government, as the concurrent acceptance of enlightened despotism, limited monarchy, and representative democracy (or aristocracy) testifies. Nevertheless, the crisis of the *Ancien Régime* was precisely and fundamentally one of outworn institutions whose inertial power was the force impeding the reforms that were eagerly sought both by *philosophes* and by those who were experiencing the realities of a changing economic life. Consequently, we must not look mainly to the many pages written about *droit naturel* for an understanding and evaluation of the Enlightenment's political thought. In the final analysis, its character and value are functions of its proposals for the future direction in which France, and Europe, should be heading, and of the assumptions on which those proposals were made. Some of these assumptions were, to be sure, those imposed by the ideas flowing from *droit naturel,* but we must see them in the light of such a connection.

Even those who see the *philosophes* as realists admit that political theorizing was popular. What were its aims? This is surely the crucial question. For Paul Hazard it was to make politics moral, to introduce into it the principle of virtue.[4] A virtuous republic would prosper. The chaos of politics would become a simple science in accord with natural law. Liberty was the watchword, meaning obedience only to law. Equality, outside of utopias, was generally rejected, except as equality before the law, or as abstract moral equality inhering in the commonality of human attributes. Inequality was held to be not only natural but socially necessary. Society must have classes, property is a sacred right: inequality ensues. A few extremists like Mably and Morelly challenged these ideas, but for most, the ideas of civil liberty and laissez-faire were developing together. The form of government seemed less important, provided there was separation of powers and rule of law. Thanks to Montesquieu, England became the ideal. With the stimulus of the American Revolution, all these ideas were to lead to the *Déclaration des droits de l'homme et du citoyen.*

Hazard undoubtedly traces a major trend; however, his hasty generalizations from selected writers oversimplify a complex reality and lack the needed depth of analysis. Separation of powers excludes the enlightened despotism that was popular among the Physiocrats and others. England was not the ideal model for all, and there was a strong anglophobic reaction during and after the Seven Years War, even among the Holbachian circle.[5] The major *philosophes,* except possibly Rousseau, were not exactly utopians, as Hazard seems to think. On the other hand, many utopias were written, and it would not be difficult to point out utopian elements in various works of political speculation, such as those of Helvétius, d'Holbach, and Diderot. As for works that were strictly utopias, they generally denounced and abolished property; socialistic thinking was not insignificant.[6] Hazard ignores the real role of utopianism in the intellectual dialectics of the age — its conflict with reformism, its relation to authoritarian modes of thought, its own inner structure.

In the second of his chapters devoted to political thought, Hazard emphasizes elements that differ considerably from those he presents at first. He notes an increasing pessimism, a realization that power is what counts, that political liberty might not be a panacea. He notes, too, the *philosophes'* neglect of the miserable conditions of the lowest classes, and the contradiction between their denunciation of tyrants and their attraction to the enlightened despots of Europe. This contradiction, he affirms,

---

[4] *Op. cit.,* Deuxiéme Partie, Ch. V, Troisième Partie, Ch. IV.
[5] See Frances Acomb, *Anglophobia in France, 1763-1789* (Durham, N.C., 1950).
[6] See André Lichtenberger, *Le Socialisme au XVIIIᵉ siècle* (Paris, 1895).

was a betrayal of their political philosophy. They should either have opted cleanly for "forcing nature" (the absolute State) or letting nature take its course (the liberal State).

To speak, as Hazard does, of "betrayal" is to give a clue to his own thought processes. Betrayal presupposes a standard and a commitment. In this instance, it implies an assumption, a prior option, by the historian, namely, that it is possible to speak of "a" political philosophy of the Enlightenment. Hazard knew better than to make such a claim. On the contrary, despite this rash accusation, his presentation leaves the reader with a rather chaotic impression, one that is doubtless more faithful, however incomplete in these pages, to the historical reality than more schematic accounts. Therefore the betrayal can refer only to a few figures, especially to Voltaire and Diderot.

Hazard's purpose was to compose a grand tableau, built around the thesis of a crisis in western civilization. With majestic sweep and gracious style, he studies its causes, growth, and radiation. It follows from his panoramic method that he surveys rapidly the political ideas he considers to have been important, with laudable objectivity, but (consequently?) without evaluating their interrelationship or assessing the ultimate directions in which they were heading. No doubt he is generally favorable to the Enlightenment. Yet, he is inclined to see the *philosophes'* efforts for reform as unrealistic, though conducive to a healthier atmosphere of justice and humanitarianism. He recognizes the extremists on the margins of the Enlightenment and faces its contradictions and "betrayals."

Objectivity seems, then, to rule on the whole, and no bias or impulse stemming from his *milieu* and his *moment* is displayed. Thus Hazard gives us no clue that he was writing these chapters while his country was under the heel of Nazism, the paroxysm of anti-Enlightenment and anti-rationalism. Such serenity may evoke admiration. Nevertheless, his unspoken choices and evaluations are implicit. Occasionally they are explicit, as when Voltaire arouses his ire or when his dislike of atheism appears through the objective stance. The implicit value message is enclosed in his evocation of a cosmopolitan Europe, with common civilized values rooted in rationality, the ideal of progress, human rights, toleration, humanitarianism, and the free pursuit of intellectual adventure. The tacit antithesis to the brutal nihilism of inhumane power is there for us to read in, rather than into, his panorama.

Charles Frankel took a quite different tack. His major concern was the idea of progress, and he went about it by examining the consequences of Condillac's philosophy on the work of Helvétius, Chastellux, and d'Holbach. Helvétius based his hopes for progress on the malleability of man, a supposition that rested on another idea: character is wholly a product of external circumstances. This being so, the educator (hence the politician) can use the universal motives of pleasure and avoidance of pain to manipulate behavior. Institutions thus recede to a minor position, and education becomes the main business of the lawmaker. We infer that when Helvétius declares that "laws do all," he meant that legislation is a mode of education. By one means or another, every individual can be made to find it in his interest to be virtuous. In this way, Frankel asserts, Helvétius used one part of Locke's philosophy to destroy the other, that is, self-evident natural rights. Helvétius wanted to show that physical science and the science of human affairs were continuous. Frankel sees the weakness of his utilitarianism in the fact that it was developed within the Cartesian notion of the nature and goal of science. It was based not on the empirical, self-critical method of science but on an antecedent and metaphysically established notion. By failing to take account of the qualitative differences between physical and moral man, and the diversity of human happiness, Helvétius wrote a parody, one which turned science into the external manipulation of behavior according to fixed and indubitable principles. This philosophy fitted the *philosophes'* program of enlightened despotism.

Frankel's analysis is valid by and large, although objection must be again taken to his reductive notion of "a political program," and to his finding it in enlightened despotism (not, it may be noted, in "modern liberal politics"—one would be hard put to find that in Helvétius). It was not the proponents of a liberal style of government who were most attracted to the control of behavior by "scientific methods." The linkage of such methods to theories of government was, it should be emphasized, a key element; and it is one that interpreters of the Enlightenment have more often than not ignored.[7]

In d'Holbach, Frankel finds further evidence for the thesis his book expounds, that French political and historical thought went astray by falling *à la* Descartes, into a rigorously deductive system of "social physics." D'Holbach asserted that by "going back to the nature of man, one can deduce from it a political system . . . as sure as in any of the other branches of human knowledge."[8] Since this method of thinking is what interests Frankel, he tells us nothing about d'Holbach's own political program. He again finds confirmation for this thesis (which is, within limits, valid) in Rousseau whose method and formal structure remain Cartesian. The sentiments Rousseau valued (Frankel means conscience, fraternity, community) have the same axiomatic status as the simplistic utilitarian notion of pleasure. He, too, took values out of the reach of analysis. But Frankel misses his main chance in his treatment of Rousseau. With some contradiction, he emphasizes that Rousseau's conception of

---

[7] It should be remarked that Frankel overlooks Hartley's influential theory of association of ideas—the background of Helvetius'. The real "parody" based on Helvétius was written by Godwin. Frankel proceeds to Chastellux (*De la félicité publique,* 1772), who developed Helvétius' method.

[8] P. 70, quoted from *La Politique naturelle* (London, 1773, I, v).

progress differs from that of "the rationalists." He is unaccountably oblivious to the relation between the theory of the malleability of man and Rousseau's own program. He does not mention Rousseau's initial project of a "*morale sensitive*" designed to control behavior and its partial implementation in *La Nouvelle Héloïse, Emile,* and the minor political tracts. To his credit, he does understand that for Rousseau nature is not merely the original material with which we are endowed, but the fulfilling of the potentialities of which "primitive" nature was the beginning. He recognizes that these can be made to lead to the making of a different person—the citizen.

Frankel attributes to the *philosophes* an ideal goal, a hope that human society will become like physical nature; specifically, that each individual will seek his own interest and at the same time promote the general happiness (59). It is difficult to see how such characteristics can be attributed to physical nature, or to admit that the *philosophes* neglected the psychological aspect of human nature. Moreover, that goal contained two possible implications that Frankel does not perceive: 1) the identification of private and public interest might be so construed as to lead to the extinction of individual rights; 2) conversely, it might lead to the realistic—or rebellious—denial of any such identity.[9]

Like Cassirer, Frankel was a philosopher. Although he contributes valid insights into the method of thinking of eighteenth-century writers, his shortcomings as a historian seriously flaw his philosophical analysis. In the political realm, he explores several of the vital *idées-force* characteristic of the new thinking: progress, the malleability of man, the power of education in the broad sense the word then had. He does not trace a connection between these and what he holds to be the prevailing option, enlightened despotism, or the ideals of the Enlightenment which, like Hazard, he cherishes. Nor does he give a glimpse of the many options proposed and their relation to those ideals.

What, then, is Frankel's perspective, and how does it determine his thesis? His view of the Enlightenment as the development of the liberal faith—*The Faith of Reason* is his title—mirrors American liberalism. That is the standpoint from which he writes. His predecessor, Carl Becker (1873-1945), in *The Heavenly City of the Philosophers* (1932), had been troubled by the failure of rationalist liberalism, and found its cause in an unperceived and disguised Christianity of the Enlightenment—a thesis which led to considerable distortions. Frankel, writing in 1942 (publication of his book was delayed), in the midst of the madness of World War II and the terrifying menace to civilization posed by the apparent triumph of Nazism—though he lacked as yet full knowledge of its crimes against humanity—was acutely troubled by these events. Without his

[9] Frankel does not reconcile two phrases occurring on the same page (p. 62): "the extraordinary malleability of human nature," and "human nature does not change."

mentioning them, they lie in the background. The Enlightenment was
the great fount of rational and liberal ideologies. How could faith in
reason and progress have produced, or allowed to develop, such aborted
and hideous offspring? These questions are the tacit directives of Frankel's
inquiry. Quite properly, he looked back to the eighteenth century in
search of clues. His search led to an incomplete and skewed picture of
its political thought, although it has the great merit of bringing out the
profound misconception of history, which we find in the authors he treats,
as a pathological deviation from a supposedly normative course.

In treating the aims of Enlightenment political thought, Jean Ehrard
again takes a broad view. One aim is located in the opposition to despotism. On this score, Ehrard finds no open conflict between bourgeois
mentality and the prejudices of the nobility in the first half of the century.
The one used the arguments of reason, the other those of history. Neither
challenged the bases of the social order; both agreed that inequality is
necessary to harmony, in the universe and in the social microcosm. They
feared *le bas peuple* and mob despotism or anarchy. The people are entitled
to civil rights but not to political rights; the upper layers of the Third
Estate are entitled to both. In this context, Montesquieu's idea of a
harmony among the classes was "philosophic" and liberal. It was self-
evident that civil equality is as different from natural equality as political
liberty is different from independence in the state of nature and can refer
only to a proper measure of legal protection.

There was also the class that could not speak for itself, but for whom
a few spoke. Protests against inequality were rare in the first half of the
century. The curé Meslier's manuscript work was an angry protest, but
the social class he stood for could not yet formulate an ideology and his
communisme de paroisse was a dream. The bourgeoisie, on the other
hand, eagerly accepted Locke's thesis that the right of property, founded
on the natural right to ownership of the fruits of one's work, was absolute.
They welcomed his joining of natural equality and social inequality.
Wealth is the sign of merit. The indigent are lazy, social parasites, deserving of their fate. Besides, the poor need not be unhappy since happiness is unrelated to one's social status. With Montesquieu we witness
the formation of an alliance between the old seigneurial order and com-
mercial capitalism, between social conformity and economic dynamism.
After this, the fundamental antagonism was between the Physiocrats,
partisans of an agrarian economy and the mercantilists, partisans of an
industrial economy. Montesquieu made another important contribution
to political theory by evaluating luxury in relation to types of government.
The paradox of republican asceticism is that it was represented as more
"natural" than the passions it suppressed; but democratic frugality, in
Montesquieu, turns into approval of wealth based on labor: he was im-
pressed by English prosperity, by a system of political institutions that
left the social hierarchy intact and encouraged the well-to-do business

man to stay in his place. Economic realities also led to the discovery of
novel economic principles, that the value of an object is proportional to
the quantity of work needed in its production, leading to the primacy of
industry over agriculture, and to the theories of Ricardo and Marx.

Ehrard is clear-sighted in his interpretation of Rousseau. The Genevan
saw society and nature in a dialectical relationship, not, like liberal
thinkers, as one in which society merely develops nature's potentialities.
Nature (i.e., nature as given) and society cannot be reconciled. While
Ehrard does not tell us of Rousseau's solution to this impasse, he shows
that Morelly (*Code de la nature,* 1755) avoided the dilemma by acknowledging natural sociability and interdependency. Society, reason,
nature—all, working together, demand the passage to civilized com-
munism.

Ehrard also points out that instead of the rivalry of custom and
nature, a new pair of opposites, education and nature, took their place.
"Education" came to include the whole social and historical context of
experience. It was conceived as acting independently of natural determinism. It intertwines and enters into conflict with the natural determinism of the individual's inherited "organization" (La Mettrie, Diderot,
Helvétius). This notion opened new possibilities in the minds of Helvétius
and Condorcet: society and its works can modify the human species.

This idea leads in the direction of utopianism. Among diverse interpreters of the Enlightenment, Ehrard alone pays adequate attention to
its utopian literature. The increase in utopias flowed from the widely
held belief in progress and in the power of laws and "education" to
change men. In a word, utopians had a faith that humans collectively
could achieve their happiness. Utopian works, being confined to imaginary worlds, separated them from the works of reformers, who hoped
to change the real world about them more directly and in a limited
measure. The world of utopias was most often one of regimentation and
authoritarianism. Ehrard only touches on the basic tension between the
utopian (that is, anti-historical, *de novo*) thrust and reformist (historical,
anti-utopian) projects.

Ehrard's political telescope, though limited to a segment of the panorama of eighteenth-century political thought and refecting his methodological and theoretical commitments, presents a well balanced view
of its complexities and diversity.[10] He brings out basic attitudes, hopes,
and failures. Avoiding an overt thesis, he does not limit us to one idea
of the Enlightenment, nor does he argue that its political speculations
headed in a specific direction. However, if one probes beneath the surface,
one finds again that the desired objectivity escapes his grasp. He, too,
has started out with a bias, a set of verities which influence his method

---

[10] Unfortunately, the chronological limit he imposed on his study short-circuits the
important later developments in political theory.

and his judgments. Although muted, a Marxist commitment and a subterranean nationalism inflect his presentation. It is obvious that the ideas
of "class' and "class struggle" are for him axiomatic guidelines in selection
and evaluation, although other options are surely available. One sees this
in his repeated attribution of ideas to a class origin or appeal—namely,
the bourgeoisie. There is undoubtedly a good measure of truth in such
a viewpoint, but the bourgeoisie as such remains a shadowy notion in
this work, and it is apparently assumed that the *Ancien Régime* class
structure matches the post-industrial revolution or Marxist class structure. The influence of this bourgeoisie on ideas is exaggerated. What is
meant by "bourgeois individualism" (307)? Could one not also speak of
an "aristocratic individualism"? Other questions of this kind arise. It
may well be that the conscience of the bourgeois (540) was not troubled
by intellectual protests; but was it otherwise with the conscience of the
aristocrats? Ehrard implicitly defines "l'homme nouveau" as a bourgeois
(544)—arguably a cramped view. It follows (in Ehrard's perspective) that
the bourgeois found happiness in activity and in social virtues and that
the bourgeoisie as a class was the great enemy of the Church and of
Christian morality, the great proponent of natural morality—again a
dubious assertion. In brief, it is as if ideas were determined in terms of
class and of only one class, at that.

My own two volumes (see note 1 above) are concerned with ethical
thought and its metaphysical and psychological foundations. In a final
chapter, I follow the ethical investigation with what I consider to be the
extension of all these aspects into the realm of political speculation. To
grasp its direction, we must look to the basic attitude of the *philosophes,*
who merged politics and ethics, but were unwilling or unable to recognize
that in the long run, to do so is to subordinate ethics to politics. Therefore,
they hoped to legislate solutions for moral problems, which were actually
social problems. But how was this to be accomplished? Opinions diverged
sharply. While some envisaged harmony as ensuing from such supposed
natural factors as the balance of private interest and more general public
interest, others equated the empirical with disorder and demanded the
creation of an artificial and enforced harmony. These tendencies corresponded to two parallel ethical currents: the transformation of natural
law into a theory of inalienable rights, and the drift to utilitarian social
control, which transferred moral judgment and its application from the
individual to the community.

Consequently, eighteenth-century thinkers proposed solutions along
these two general lines (omitting the fringe of anarchists or nihilists,
whom no one took seriously), and two types of society were envisaged.
Those we would today term liberals, for whom self-interest and the general
were in a good measure reconcilable, though never completely, called for
a minimum of regulation by the state. Their thinking was predominantly
empirical at least in this sense: they held the efficacy and desirability of

indoctrination and behavioral conditioning to be limited, and recognized the sway of historical and natural factors beyond the power of rational control by governments. Some of this group favored enlightened despotism; others demanded participation in government by selected elements of society and also demanded wide scope for individual freedom, promoted by a broad enlightenment of the citizenry.

On the other side, thinkers I have described as "proto-totalitarian" believed that individual wills could be coerced to coincide with the general interest, but only by indoctrination and wide-ranging control by government; they were (as Burke charged) rationalistic idealists. Discovery of the "scientific laws" of behavior (e.g., Rousseau's *morale sensitive*) provided rational rulers with the possibility of such redirection of behavior. Morelly, Helvétius, Mably, sometimes even d'Holbach wanted political restraints and mental conditioning which, in effect, reduced morals to a matter of public policy. Rousseau would mobilize all the resources of society—laws, education, rewards and punishments, censorship, religion, festivals and demonstrations, the arts, and even encourage informers—to create the "citizen" out of naturally unsocial man. These thinkers were ready to make short shrift of history (cf. Frankel's "deviation").

The first group was the more numerous one. It included Montesquieu and Burke, Voltaire, Diderot, d'Alembert, and the Physiocrats. While their plans and prescriptions varied widely in content and character, they all opposed change based on abstract, rationalistic schemes for a *de novo* society. They agreed that the powers of government should be limited, that citizens had certain inalienable rights, and thus they favored a partial separation of ethics from politics and provided the individual with a large measure of self-direction. Utilitarianism did not in their minds hinder the primacy of the individual. They agreed, then, on a pluralistic society.

Part of my argument is that the current that emphasized coercive or "molding" tactics, in accord with strict utilitarianism, originated in a strong pessimistic outlook on human nature and in the weakness of the current nostrums of enlightened self-interest and the identity of virtue and happiness. A stronger defense of culture against nature was required. Rights, on this view, have no status except as granted by laws, directed by the concept of general welfare; and traditional natural law, if maintained at all, is only a system of moral principles external to the political solution. For such thinkers, the social problem really escapes from the moral into the realm of power; in other words, the merging of ethics with politics has the aforementioned effect of reducing ethics to politics. Thus it was hoped to obtain a human harmony which is not the natural one, though it was constantly proclaimed to be in accord with natural laws since it was a way of obliging the members of a society to live morally and as good citizens, and thus reach their natural goal of happiness. Happiness comes from virtue, and virtue can be had by creating an imposed harmony between private and public interest.

I believe that the antithetical germs of nihilism and totalitarianism derive their antithesis from their initial assumptions: the first denies the primacy of the general interest or even the validity of such a concept; the second disparages private interest or denies its social validity. Individualistic revolt and repression of egoistic drives are both means to put an end to the war between natural man and social man, and to the liberal's illusions of their coexistence through compromise.

Like Frankel, I have assumed an underlying, unperceived perspective. It has directed my thinking and project. While trying to understand the Enlightenment on its own terms, I could not avoid responding to the cultural shock of what Hermann Rauschning, a repentant Nazi, had called "the revolution of nihilism." While investigating what I considered to be a moral crisis in Western culture that had germinated in eighteenth-century thought, in the perspective of its interrelatedness with metaphysical, psychological, and political speculation, I was led by this pursuit to emphasize the Enlightenment's complexity and inner tensions, and to stress the "dark side" perhaps more than the "bright side." This stress on the rise of the spectre of moral nihilism that ensued from the collapse of mythic structures and illusions and of ecclesiastical intellectual hegemony has been criticized as exaggerated. My search for the character and tendencies of political thought, which are consequent to the psychological and ethical aspects, also emphasizes the view that the conceptual origins of totalitarianism as well as of liberal democracy were developed by Enlightenment thinkers. Thus the political interpretation is guided by the initial perspective of an Enlightenment torn by polar tensions which are to be viewed not only in their own historical context but in relation to later developments. This method of viewing the past has also met with vigorous criticism.

Peter Gay's treatment of the subject is more extensive. After a preliminary chapter ("The Politics of Decency"), in which he gives a vivid account of the campaigns for toleration, peace, abolition of slavery, and legal reform—the main thrusts of the reformist impulse—a second chapter, "The Politics of Experience," begins with a general evaluation of the Enlightenment's political stance. Whereas Gay usually speaks of "a program" of the Enlightenment, he declares here that the *philosophes* were often baffled by contradictory prescriptions and were "desperately satisfied with superficial solutions that were no solutions at all." They sought reform through existing institutions rather than fundamental change. Nevertheless, their politics deserves to be characterized as "modern liberal politics." They abandoned the notion of a state of nature and gradually turned from natural law to utilitarianism. They retained their respect for universal values but were relativists in regard to differing political realities.

Gay centers much of his analysis on the division between those who upheld the *thèse nobiliaire* and their adversaries who stood for the *thèse royale,* especially in regard to the affair of the Maupeou *parlements.* Despite his assessment of "modern liberal politics," he affirms that ab-

solutism was "the most prominent political system for theorists," a position he finds justifiable because it was the most modern, efficient, and
enlightened form of government in the eighteenth century. (One wonders
about Britain and Holland.) Closing with a good summary of the Physiocrats' theory of "legal despotism," Gay argues that this theory was
really libertarian. The Physiocrats were authoritarians, but they opposed
privileged castes and capricious despotism, desiring minimal regulation
by laws formulated under the influence of public opinion enlightened by
universal education and a free press, together with unfettered property
rights—a "constitutional absolutism, which was an incomplete form of
liberalism."

In a third chapter, "The Politics of Education," Gay admits that the
philosophes did not trust the illiterate masses. They stood for reform and
for freedom; but reform, they thought, could best be realized through
royal paternalism—"a mockery of the world they hoped to bring into
being"; Diderot and Rousseau, however, insisted that reform without
freedom was no reform at all. The solution was education which could
have a greater effect than the character of political institutions. This view
was backed by what Gay calls the *philosophes'* doctrine of original in-
nocence; but no one fully faced the problem of the masses who were
despised (except, at times, by Voltaire and Diderot) as being beyond
reason and education. Finally, Gay presents his view of Rousseau, "a
libertarian who could not get compulsion out of his mind." Education,
Rousseau believed, could make men citizens out of necessity. At the same
time, by following the general will as expressed in law they would remain
individuals, models of the free citizen who is completely submissive to
the general will of which he is a part. Since Rousseau was not a liberal
he "eliminated the boundaries" between public authority and private
freedom. Nevertheless, Gay concludes, Rousseau, more than any other
philosopher, advanced "the science of freedom."

Gay is obviously hard put to maintain both his thesis of "modern
liberal politics" and "the science of freedom" which is the a priori directing assumption of his study. It leads him to paradoxes and contradictory descriptions, which his keen sense for historical fact does not
allow him to deny even in the material he has selectively chosen to
include. The spectrum of this complex field is shrunk to two tendencies,
liberal democracy and enlightened despotism; though they are conflicting,
his support of his thesis does not falter. Yet, what are we to think when
he calls Condorcet a "caricature of the Enlightenment" because of his
utopianism?

Gay clearly feels called upon to write as a kind of attorney for the
defense of the Enlightenment. He does not fail to point out weaknesses
and shortcomings, but the admissions may strike some readers as part
of a strategy of defense as well as an accurate presentation of historical
facts. His thesis is twofold: the Enlightenment can be defined, on the one
hand, as the revival of paganism; on the other hand, as the creative

principle of modern liberal politics ("the science of freedom"). In this way he carries out his purpose, explicitly stated in the preface to his second volume, of "defining the Enlightenment." It leads him to a restricted view. Not only are important phases of the Enlightment (the questioning of the basis of moral values, the totalitarian drift) excluded from the Enlightenment, but many important writers (La Mettrie, Morelly, Mably, etc.), and unwelcome aspects of other writers (Diderot, d'Holbach, etc.) are also excluded. Its mission is defined as one of subversion and demythologizing, based on neo-paganism. Its program hailed freedom, humanitarianism, and liberalism, but demythologizers who went too far are excluded from "Enlightenment," as are political countercurrents to liberalism and even to humanitarianism, which were very real. As a consequence, the non-liberal is non-Enlightenment.

Gay's treatment of political thought is directed and necessitated by the initial premise, which is carried out to the end: the Enlightenment should then be defined as an essentially unified movement, carrying out an essentially coherent mission and program, according to a no less coherent basic philosophy; but the facts go beyond Gay's definition. An inconsistent and multifarious historical reality will not be forced into the procrustean bed of a definition without serious mutilation.[11] The phrase, "Enlightenment politics is modern liberal politics" contains an unhistorical "is." Furthermore, one of Gay's principal theses is that the Enlightenment was the beginning of "modernity"; but I have argued that some of the developments he excludes—challenges to moral values, denial of preeminence to individuals, programs for social control of behavior, etc.—are some of the main elements of the modern world. Gay embraces the procedure Gustave Lanson (following the example of Buffon and d'Alembert) warned against in his seminal articles, "Origines et premières manifestations de l'esprit philosophique" (*Revue des cours et conférences,* 1907-1910, vols. 16, 17, 18 *passim*). Lanson warned that an axiomatic definition would reduce the Enlightenment to a preferred segment of the new movement of ideas.

Gay, writing in the late 1960's, is not affected by the historical events that influenced the outlook of the previously discussed scholars. He writes nonetheless within the same context. Americans, in a more unadulterated way than Europeans, are heirs of the Enlightenment. In it, their liberal ideas and institutions have their very origins. Judgment of the Enlightenment appears to imply, unconsciously perhaps, a judgment on their own past and present. This context manifestly provides the underlying lines of force which fix Gay's perspective and direct his value judgments. That later history and the contemporary world are not really far from his mind is evidenced in his concluding statement, that although the

---

[11] Cf. Hegel: "definitions should be stated in universal terms, while to use these immediately exposes in all its nakedness what contradicts them." *Hegel's Philosophy of Right,* transl. T. M. Knox (Oxford, 1967), 14-15.

world has not turned out the way the *philosophes* wished, their vision remains of permanent value—thus again assuming a singleness or unity of vision. It can be argued that Gay's own vision was determined by some of the Enlightenment's own "myths." These happen to be those he cherishes, and so they impose a certain limited perspective.

As we review the preceding interpretations, it becomes clear that each is the reflection of an elected general position toward the historic episode conventionally termed the Enlightenment. Each differs from all the others because its author conceptualizes that episode differently and sets out with discrepant assumptions, both substantive and methodological. Perhaps it can be said that a limited area of agreement exists concerning what we have termed its critical phase. Even here, agreement is only about what "happened"; moreover, differing perspectives show their face in the selection of facts that are emphasized and in the account of such episodes as the conflict around the *parlements.* There is a major disagreement about the character, motives, and the contemporaneous value of the efforts expended. There is agreement, too, that these focused attention on problems, helped to change men's minds, that they left a beneficial heritage to the future. But were these efforts politically effective? Were they realistic?

When we turn to the "positive" constructions of the *philosophes,* to their ideas for political and social reconstruction, to the ultimate directions in which their thinking was carrying them, we find a discord of voices that exhibits the crucial problem of historical interpretation. I have tried to explain how and why each interpreter takes the position he does, and what are some of their strengths and weaknesses.

Nineteenth-century French historians were engrossed by the spectre of the French Revolution. In the twentieth century, three Americans scholars, Carl Becker (here omitted), Charles Frankel and myself, and a Frenchman, Paul Hazard, appear to have been more or less unconsciously preoccupied with the plight of rationalistic liberalism and the cultural shock of Nazism. Both groups were asking and answering similar questions in relation to a different event. How could it have happened? What went wrong? Does the malady of their time have some roots in the eighteenth century? These may be called two moments of critical searching. Mornet, after the first moment, Gay after the second, were impelled, in entirely different ways, to counter criticism and to defend a view of the Enlightenment which they cherished. Each of the above-mentioned writers sees a different Enlightenment, and the images they project to the reader do not coincide. Each may be and will be judged on its intrinsic merits; but every judgment of such "intrinsic" merits will in turn depend to a significant degree on the picture of the Enlightenment which the maker of judgments has in his mind and prefers.

Cassirer and Ehrard seem to be unconcerned by the sequels of the Enlightenment and the problems of their own historical moment. Cassirer perceives a philosopher's Enlightenment. It was there, and he had the great merit of establishing it firmly; but many facets of Enlightenment thinking fall outside of his view. Ehrard, guided by his own political faith, consequently does introduce sequels and interprets the movement in a way different from all the others.

No general, historically important account and interpretation of Enlightenment political thought, integrating the critical and constructive aspects, covering not only the political philosophy but the political science of the period, the institutions proposed for the organization of a polity, and the conceptions motivating those proposals, has as yet been written. Such a study would have to include the organs and uses of power, the modes of participation in decision-making, the roles and relations of individuals and the State. Nor can it be forgotten that the word "institutions" designated not only social organisms but the great civic rules: mores and institutions were inseparable, and remained so in the eyes of the Revolutionaries of 1791-1794. The place of utopian thinking and utopias would have to be included in such an integral study, as would the attempts of the American Revolution and the French Revolution to realize the diverse aims of Enlightenment political activity—surely a revealing and fruitful contrast. Meaning and interrelationships, causes and effects, intentions, results and sequels—the stuff of historiography— should not be sacrificed to mere compilation of facts and texts.

One comes to wonder whether it is possible to speak, except as a vague label, of *the* Enlightenment rather than of some historian's Enlightenment. If we were to suggest a thesis for each of the studies we have discussed, it would be easy to epitomize them as sub-titles: Mornet, "The Enlightenment vindicated"; Becker (whose book has little about politics other than natural law theory), "Christianity disguised": Frankel, "Pseudo-science leads rationalism astray"; Cassirer, "The Enlightenment as Pure Philosophy"; Hazard, "Crisis and Change"; Crocker, "Man's ship unmoored"; Gay, "Paganism *redivivus*"; Ehrard, "Nature, the Grand Adventure of the bourgeoisie."

From what has preceded we can see another difficulty in writing a history of eighteenth-century political thought. It lies in the subject, politics. The debates and divisions of the time, which reached down into the deepest roots of social organization and the place of the individual in it, are in essence the debates and divisions of our own time. This problem does not exist with such sharpness in regard to certain other aspects of the Enlightenment—economics, linguistics, aesthetics, science itself, the campaigns for reforms. Nor do we find such a close and pregnant relation between ourselves and earlier centuries. Here indeed lies the "modernity" of the Enlightenment.

The University of Virginia.

Chapter XV

THE ART OF MEMORY RECONCEIVED: FROM RHETORIC TO PSYCHOANALYSIS

By Patrick H. Hutton

Mnemonics, or the art of memory, is today regarded as an arcane intellectual interest. It functions on the periphery of popular culture, largely through a literature of self-help designed to bolster the confidence of people insecure about their powers of recollection. If it is a useful skill, it is not an essential one in a civilization whose collective memory is stored securely in the printed word. Today's archive for reliable reference is the library or the computer, not the depths of a well-ordered mind. Yet there was a time in the not too distant past when the art of memory held pride of place in the councils of learning, for it enhanced one's power to lecture or preach in a world that trusted in the authority of the spoken word. From the wandering rhapsodes of ancient Greece who enthralled listeners with the epic tales of Homer to the philosophers of the Renaissance who constructed imaginary memory palaces to present their intricate designs of the cosmos, the development of the powers of memory was perceived to be an essential intellectual skill.

The art of memory as it was traditionally conceived was based upon associations between a structure of images easily remembered and a body of knowledge in need of organization. The mnemonist's task was to attach the facts he wished to recall to images that were so visually striking or emotionally evocative that they could be recalled at will. He then classified these images in an architectural design of places with which he was readily familiar. The memoryscape so constructed was an imaginary tableau in which a world of knowledge might be contained for ready reference. It was in effect a borrowed paradigm, the logic of whose imaginary structure gave shape to the otherwise formless knowledge he wished to retain.[1]

Most professional psychologists today dismiss mnemonics as irrelevant to the concerns of their discipline. Some are puzzled by the elaborate and seemingly cumbersome systems of recall employed by mnemonists through the ages, and question whether the systems themselves might not be more difficult to remember than the facts to be committed to memory. Others, while conceding the efficacy of schemes that help us to retrieve facts in serial order, regard mnemonics as a skill with relatively

---

[1] For a good example of how the art of memory was applied, see Jonathan D. Spence, *The Memory Palace of Matteo Ricci* (New York, 1984), 1-23.

few contemporary applications.[2] The study of the mind of an unusually gifted mnemonist by the distinguished Russian neuropsychologist Aleksandr Luria is a case in point.[3] The subject of his study, Shereshevskii, entertained audiences across Russia during the 1930s with his capacity to commit to memory any data with which they wished to test his talent, including long lists of random monosyllables or the elements of complex, sometimes incorrect, mathematical equations. He could still recall such information without prompting a decade later. Shereshevskii possessed what Luria characterized as a "marked degree of synesthesia," i.e., acute sensory perception that heightened his capacity to remember ideas by virtue of the vivid imagery that he could attach to them.[4] Yet Shereshevskii lacked the capacity for abstraction and the agility of mind essential for success in the modern world. Tormented by a clutter of facts that he could forget only through an enormous effort of will, he found his gift a burden. Unable to hold an ordinary job, he plied the trade of a showman for want of something better to do.[5] It is as if Shereshevskii were for Luria a clinical psychological find, akin to an anthropologist's discovery of a stone-age tribe in some remote jungle. One might admire the mnemonist's genius while recognizing its obsolescence. If the art of memory was an essential technique of learning for yesterday's rhetoricians, it has become for today's psychologists the stuff of sideshows.

In focusing upon the practical techniques of mnemonics, however, the psychologists have overlooked its theoretical foundations. The art of memory as it was understood in its classical formulation provided not only a useful skill but also a way of understanding the world. For some mnemonists the design of the structure of their mnemonic system corresponded to their conception of the structure of knowledge and so implied a vision of the world. The power of the mnemonist lay in his ability to interpret the world through a paradigm that would provide its initiates with a *clavis universalis*, a master key to the workings of the universe.[6] From this perspective the art of memory was not only a pedagogical device but also a method of interpretation. It is this link between the art of memory and the making of paradigms of cultural understanding that suggests the larger significance of this topic. If the art of memory as it was employed from classical antiquity until the Renaissance seems

[2] The psychologist's disdain for mnemonics is discussed by B. Richard Bugelski, "Mnemonics," in the *International Encyclopedia of Psychiatry, Psychology, Psychoanalysis, and Neurology*, ed. Benjamin B. Wolman (New York, 1977), VII, 245-50.

[3] Aleksandr R. Luria, *The Mind of a Mnemonist*, trans. Lynn Solotaroff (Chicago, 1968).

[4] *Ibid.*, 21-38.

[5] *Ibid.*, 66-73, 111-36, 149-60; cf. Michel Beaujour, *Miroirs d'encre* (Paris, 1980), 93-105.

[6] Paolo Rossi, *Clavis universalis: Arti mnemoniche e logica combinatoria da Lullo a Leibniz* (Milan, 1960).

cumbersome in comparison with our present mental operations and remote from our current needs, we may ask whether the art's intimate
association with model-building has not enabled it to survive in the
modern world in a different guise.

This essay will inquire into this revisioning of the art of memory since
the eighteenth century. It will search for correspondences between the
art of memory as it was practiced in the rhetorical tradition that culminated in the Renaissance and the use of memory as a technique of
soul-searching in the Romantic tradition of psychology that culminates
in psychoanalysis. Two figures especially are prominent in explaining
this transition: the eighteenth-century Neapolitan philosopher Giambattista Vico, who relates the power of memory to the poetic consciousness
in which civilization began, and the Austrian physician Sigmund Freud,
who pressed the search for memory's sources into the recesses of the
unconscious mind. Just as the mnemonists of the Renaissance sought to
convey to their initiates a hidden knowledge of the world, so this essay
seeks to show how the art of memory itself is hidden in the rhetoric of
more recent forms of intellectual discourse.

For an understanding of what the art of memory was in the distant
past, the work of the English historian Frances Yates is essential.[7] Yates
was a student of the intellectual underground of the Renaissance and her
study of mnemonics was an offshoot of her inquiry into the thought of
Giordano Bruno, a sixteenth-century Neapolitan philosopher whose fascination with systems of memory had roots in the ancient hermetic
tradition of gnostic thought.[8] Yates was intrigued with the Renaissance
revival of the art of memory at a time when one might suppose the advent
of printing would have rendered it obsolete. In the course of her investigations she traced mnemonics as a system of artificial memory to its
origins in Greece in the fifth century B.C. From its simple beginnings
in the rhetoric of sophistry to its sophisticated refinement in the hermetic
cosmology of the Renaissance, Yates explains, the art of memory was
employed in the service of diverse philosophies. In Greco-Roman times
it enhanced the rhetorician's eloquence. During the High Middle Ages
it was used to classify an increasingly complex scheme of ethics. By the
Renaissance it had become intertwined with Neoplatonic metaphysics.
Yet through all of these cultural transformations, Yates stresses, the
techniques of the art of memory remained essentially the same.[9] Indeed,
across these 2000 years a sense of a classical mnemonic tradition developed, as each restatement of the art alluded to earlier formulations,

[7] Frances A. Yates, *The Art of Memory* (Chicago, 1966).

[8] Frances A. Yates, *Giordano Bruno and the Hermetic Tradition* (Chicago, 1964),
and "The Hermetic Tradition in Renaissance Science," in *Art, Science and History in
the Renaissance*, ed. Charles S. Singleton (Baltimore, 1967), 255-74.

[9] Yates, *Art of Memory*, xi-xii, 145, 151.

notably to the *Ad Herennium*, an anonymous Roman tract written about 82 B.C., and even to that of its legendary Greek founder, the poet Simonides of Ceos, who was the first to reflect upon the emotional power of a system of images as an aid to memory.[10]

The techniques of artificial memory that Yates identifies with the classical tradition of mnemonics were essentially the same as those that the modern mnemonist Shereshevskii devised intuitively. They consisted of arrangements of places and images. The places provided an architectonic design in which the knowledge to be remembered was to be situated. These were places so deeply embedded in the mind of the mnemonist that they could not be forgotten. The architecture of place, often conceived as a palace or a theater, might be likened to a sacred space with which the mnemonist possessed intuitive familiarity. This deep structure of memory, in turn, was given its particular character by the images with which it was adorned. A good memory was a function of a resilient imagination, and images were chosen for their aesthetic appeal. Vivid pictorial imagery that inspired awe was judged to be the most effective.[11]

If the techniques of the art of memory remained essentially the same, change was interpreted in terms of the purposes for which the art was used. Yates explains that these oscillated between two theories of knowledge, one derived from Aristotle and the other from Plato. In the Aristotelian tradition the art of memory was merely instrumental. Aristotle taught that knowledge is derived from sense experience and that a mnemonic system is to be judged by its practical capacity to fix knowledge in images that heighten sense perception. Whether mnemonic images possessed any correspondence of meaning to the ideas to be conveyed was irrelevant. This conception was especially popular during the High Middle Ages, when scholastic philosophers valued memory systems for their utility in communicating moral lessons, yet held them in suspicion because of their derivation from the pagan learning of classical civilization. Mnemonics was a profane art, always subordinate to the sacred message it carried.[12] In the Platonic tradition, however, the powers of memory were judged to be more substantive. Plato taught that mnemic images were directly expressive of a transcendental reality. For the mnemonist who shared these views, the value of a mnemic image was directly

---

[10] Simonides (ca. 556-468 B.C.), according to legend, discovered the mnemonic power of pictorial images when he, a guest at a palace banquet, fortuitously exited just before the palace collapsed. Awestruck at his good fortune, he found that his emotional reaction to the experience enabled him to conjure up a vivid and detailed picture of the banquet's participants in their assigned places just before the crash. Thus he discovered that ideas difficult to remember can be systematically committed to memory by associating them with unforgettable images. *Ibid.*, 1-2, 22. See also Herwig Blum, *Die antike Mnemotechnik* (Hildesheim, 1969), 41-46.

[11] Yates, *Art of Memory*, 2-26.

[12] *Ibid.*, 31-36, 230.

tied to the ideal reality that it was empowered to represent. The art of memory, therefore, was a way of establishing correspondences between the microcosm of the mind's images and the macrocosm of the ideal universe, which were believed to be congruent structures. In such a conception, the role of the mnemonist took on added importance. Not only did he practice a skill, but he also assumed a priestly status as an interpreter of the nature of reality.[13]

This Platonic conception of the art of memory, Yates explains, received its fullest expression during the Italian Renaissance of the sixteenth century. In that era Neoplatonic philosophers employed the art of memory in an ambitious quest for a unified paradigm of knowledge. Among many ingenious designs, Yates singles out for special attention the mnemonic systems of Giulio Camillo and of Giordano Bruno, both of whom were in search of the key to the hidden structure of the universe in the hermetic teachings of the ancient Egyptian divine, Hermes Trismegistus. Camillo designed a memory theater in which the drama of all human experience was played out on an imaginary stage.[14] Bruno's model was more intricate still. Devising a memory wheel that incorporated geometrical designs borrowed from the best mnemonic systems of the day, he conceived of himself as the architect of a synthetic paradigm of the universe that would provide its practitioners with insight into the deep structural unity of all knowledge of heaven and earth.[15]

It is not surprising that these Neoplatonic paradigms were presented in images of wheels, palaces, theaters, and other geometrical configurations. The structure of knowledge envisioned by the Neoplatonic philosopher was spacial. It was based upon an unchanging reality, as all of these mnemonic images implied. Journeys into the memory moved along fixed trajectories to be travelled again and again. The wheel, the palace, and the theater were mementos of repetition. Working from a conception of a timeless cosmos, the Neoplatonic mnemonist possessed no sense of development. He was in search of knowledge that was eternal yet presently hidden. Discovered by the gnostic philosophers of antiquity yet forgotten in the intervening millennium, this hermetic knowledge was waiting to be revealed once more. As the purveyor of secrets at once ancient and powerful, the mnemonist viewed himself as a magus, dealing in an esoteric knowledge that made him privy to the workings of the universe, with all of the powers that such omniscience implied.[16]

[13] *Ibid.*, 36-39.

[14] *Ibid.*, 129-59.

[15] *Ibid.*, 199-230, and Yates, *Collected Essays* (London, 1983), II, 101-11.

[16] Yates, *Art of Memory*, 251-60, 293-99, 339-41; cf. Robert S. Westman, "Magical Reform and Astronomical Reform: The Yates Thesis Reconsidered," in *Hermeticism and the Scientific Revolution*, ed. Robert S. Westman and J. E. McGuire (Los Angeles, 1977), 5-72, challenging Yates's thesis about the magical implications of Bruno's cosmological design.

As a paradigmatic expression of the world-view of the idealist philosophers of the Renaissance, mnemonics survived into the seventeenth
century because it served a line of intellectual inquiry that continued to
display vitality. Mnemonics would begin to lose its honored status only
as Neoplatonic idealism was successfully challenged by scientific empiricism in the course of that century. The new science, Yates suggests,
would continue to employ the art of memory but in a less exalted role.
In a world in which reliable knowledge was identified with a systematic
understanding of sense experience, mnemonics was destined to return to
an Artistotelian formulation. Herein lies the importance of the English
philosopher Francis Bacon. Rejecting the notion of magical correspondences between mnemic images and the powers governing the heavens,
Bacon spurned the prideful role of magus for the more modest one of
scientific investigator.[17] Having contributed to the rise of science in its
stress upon systematic classification, Yates contends, mnemonics lost this
distinguishing characteristic as the scientific method acquired an autonomous identity.[18] Having outlived its usefulness, the art of memory as a
recognizable intellectual tradition came to an end.[19]

Yates persuasively explains the eclipse of the art of memory. But if
the art had contributed so powerfully to the paradigmatic expression of
such a variety of world-views popular in earlier periods of Western
civilization, would not its imaging resources be appropriated to advance
new schemes of knowledge in the modern age? The science into which
the classical art of memory was absorbed was a science of nature. By
the eighteenth century, however, a new science of humanity was in the
making, and it was in this context that the art of memory was to be
reconceived. The central figure in this revisioning of the role of memory
in culture was the Neapolitan philosopher Giambattista Vico. Vico's
conception of memory, as it had been for the Renaissance Neoplatonists,
was tied to a search for deep structures of knowledge hidden from contemporary humankind.[20] But for Vico such knowledge was hidden in the

[17] *Ibid.*, 370-73, and Yates, *Collected Essays*, III, 60-66. See also Paolo Rossi, *Francis
Bacon: From Magic to Science*, tr. Sacha Rabinovitch (London, 1968), 207-14.

[18] Yates, *Art of Memory*, 368-69, 378-89.

[19] Anachronistic applications of the art of memory nonetheless survived into the
nineteenth and twentieth centuries. Representative approaches include: Gregor von Fei-
naigle, *The New Art of Memory* (London, 1813); Aimé Paris, *Principes et applications
diverses de la mnémonique* (7th ed.; Paris, 1833); A. E. Middleton, *Memory Systems,
Old and New* (3rd rev. ed.; New York, 1888); Laird S. Cermak, *Improving Your Memory*
(New York, 1975); and Harry Lorayne, *Harry Lorayne's Page-a-Minute Memory Book*
(New York, 1985).

[20] On Vico's relationship to Renaissance Neoplatonic mnemonics, cf. Paolo Rossi,
"Schede Vichiane," *La Rassegna della letteratura italiana*, 62 (1958), 375-83, and *Francis
Bacon*, 77-79, 133-34; Emile Namer, "G. B. Vico et Giordano Bruno," *Archives de
philosophie*, 40 (1977), 107-14; and Donald Phillip Verene, "L'Originalità filosofica di
Vico," in *Vico oggi*, ed. Andrea Battistini (Rome, 1979), 114-17. On the roots of Vico's

origins of civilization, a lost history of human creation, not in the heavens as an expression of God's design. The Renaissance Neoplatonists had taught that the magi of antiquity were in possession of an occult wisdom that put them in touch with the divine plan. The ancients, Vico explains, did possess wisdom, but it was a wisdom of poetry not philosophy. The ancient poets were magi of sorts, seeking to divine the mysteries of the universe. What they discovered in the process were their own human powers of understanding and acting. What the art of memory in Vico's *New Science* (1744) promised to provide was a key to this poetic knowledge.[21]

Vico's vision of the world was historical rather than cosmological, and his work is significant for this study because he was the first philosopher to explain the historical origins of the art of memory. If the art had hitherto been understood in spatial imagery, he would recast it in a temporal design. For Vico the art of memory was more than a technique invented by Simonides. Simonides and the classical rhetoricians who embellished his teachings were only restating the principles of an art that had been intuitively understood since the dawn of civilization. The artificial memory systems employed by rhetoricians since the classical age were but studied variations on the poetic structure of language employed spontaneously by primitive peoples. Mnemonics, therefore, is no more than a refinement of the poetic logic of memory, grounded in the primordial structures of poetic expression.[22]

The key to understanding the nature of memory, Vico contends, is derived from the direct correspondence between image and idea in primitive poetic language. In the beginnings of civilization, image and idea were one. Primitive peoples possessed robust memories because of the inseparable association they made between images and ideas in their comprehension of the world. They thought metaphorically, and the metaphors that they uttered were easily mimicked and remembered because they were richly expressive, grandiose, and full of wonder at the world. The link between human imagination and the universe that the Renaissance Neoplatonists had sought to discover magically, Vico revealed to have been born historically in the development of human consciousness.[23]

The source of the mnemonist's method is visible in the poetic logic

---

"tree of knowledge" in mnemonic imagery, see Giorgio Tagliacozzo, "General Education as Unity of Knowledge: A Theory Based on Vichian Principles," *Social Research*, 43 (1976), 772, 774 n.30.

[21] *The New Science of Giambattista Vico* (3rd ed.; 1744), tr. and ed. Thomas G. Bergin and Max H. Fisch (Ithaca, 1970), 331, 342, 349, 374-83, 391, 494, 846; hereafter *NS*, (reference to numbered paragraph).

[22] *NS*, 201, 211, 699, 811, 819, 833, 855, 878, 896 contain Vico's principal references to memory.

[23] *NS*, 221, 700, 814, 816, 819, 833, 933. On the role of memory in Vico's theory of mind, see Donald Phillip Verene, *Vico's Science of Imagination* (Ithaca, 1981), 96-126.

of Vico's theory of the emergence of human consciousness. That theory, too, involves the relationship between places and images, which Vico labels topics and tropes. Topics were the poetic formulae through which primitive people identified the phenomena of the world.[24] As imaginative representations of particular aspects of reality, they provided common-places or fixed points of reference amidst the flux of sense experience. As topics multiplied, they came to constitute a structure of the perception of reality. Topics were in effect the groundwork of an emerging field of knowledge. For Vico consciousness develops out of the formulation of topics in imaginary expressions known as tropes. Originally, all topics were interpreted metaphorically. But the use of metaphor was itself a selection of a particular image in which to represent a topic, and the human capacity to be selective was gradually refined. As their knowledge of topics became more extensive, humans learned to express themselves in an imaginative shorthand that modified metaphor: first in terms of metonymy (an eidetic image of a detail that stands for a complete met-aphorical topic); then of synecdoche (an image that conveys the character or quality of a topic); and finally of irony (an image that has acquired a generalized meaning of its own, without reference to the particular topic to which it originally had been attached).[25] The development of consciousness, therefore, is for Vico a process of abstraction in which the distance between topics (places) and tropes (images) widens until the metaphorical origins of a topic are forgotten in the ironical imagery of modern discourse. The process of abstraction that inheres in the de-velopment of consciousness, therefore, is one of forgetting the connection between our present vocabularies and the poetic process through which they were originally formed. As Vico expressed it in a poetic image of his own, "metonymy drew a cloak of learning over the prevailing ig-norance of these origins of human institutions, which have remained buried until now."[26]

Considered in this context, Vico's new art of memory becomes a retrospective search for the connection between our present conceptions and the lost poetic images out of which they were born. In the logic of Vichian poetics, the new art of memory is a reconstruction of the imag-inative process by which the poets of antiquity gave shape to their per-ception of the world. Therein the imaginative sources of our present ideas are to be found. The original topic might be likened to a palimpsest, repeatedly covered over with more abstract imagery as the human mind historically ascended the tropological gradient of linguistic expression.

---

[24] *NS*, 297-98, 699, 768. Cf. Yates, *Art of Memory*, 31.

[25] *NS*, 236, 331, 404-11. See also Hayden V. White, "The Tropics of History: The Deep Structure of the *New Science*," in *Giambattista Vico's Science of Humanity*, ed. Giorgio Tagliacozzo and Donald Phillip Verene (Baltimore, 1976,) 65-85.

[26] *NS*, 402.

Vico's art of memory was to decipher each tropological layer along the way until the original metaphorical topic, long forgotten, was recalled to mind.[27]

We might say that what Vico offers is a model of the life-cycle of memory. Memory originates in the ontological act of creating images in order to give form and meaning to the phenomena of the world. But as civilization advances, memory comes to be identified with mimesis, i.e., mimicking or repeating the creative act in order to discover its original meaning.[28] Such meanings elude the modern philosopher, who does not understand the historical circumstances in which topics originated or the way in which the mind has been altered in the interim.[29] Vico's theory of memory as an act of interpretation that enables us to establish connections between the familiar images of the present and the unfamiliar ones of the past anticipates the modern science of hermeneutics.[30] Vico describes the hermeneutical process as it was understood metaphorically by the ancients in their image of the god Hermes. Hermes was the messenger of the gods, and he taught humankind the art of communication. He did so by travelling from familiar into strange places and back again. Hermes taught humans to understand the unfamiliar by relating it to the familiar. The ancient poet interpreted the world creatively by explaining strange phenomena in terms of images that he knew well, initially images of his own body. He created new images to explain new experiences but always related these to his extant structure of knowledge. The contemporary philosopher, Vico argued, must use his memory to reverse the process. He must return from the rational discourse in which he is presently at home into the alien poetic idiom of the past whose meaning he will rediscover as he establishes connections with its imagery. In descending the tropological gradient of linguistic expression, the new art of memory completes the hermeneutical circle, the circle of Hermes' flight and his return.[31]

Implicitly, Vico explained why the art of memory as practiced from classical antiquity until the Renaissance worked. In its association of a mnemic image and an unrelated idea, it borrowed primordial poetic techniques to convey modern prosaic knowledge. Amidst the flux of abstractions of modern discourse, it reached back to the poetic forms of an earlier age to aid in the classification of modern knowledge and to

[27] *NS*, 331, 338, 846.

[28] *NS*, 211, 217, 375-77, 381, 447, 520, 692, 849, 855, 878, 896. See also Patrick H. Hutton, "The *New Science* of Giambattista Vico: Historicism in its Relation to Poetics," *Journal of Aesthetics and Art Criticism*, 30 (1972), 362-64.

[29] *NS*, 220, 429, 444, 518.

[30] On Vico and hermeneutics, see Hans-Georg Gadamer, *Truth and Method* (New York, 1975), 19-26, 30-31; and Donald R. Kelley, "Vico's Road: From Philology to Jurisprudence and Back," in *Giambattista Vico's Science of Humanity*, 20.

[31] *NS*, 122, 604-6, 713, 741.

provide the emotional power needed to evoke that knowledge at will.[32] So wide had the distance between image and idea become for mnemonists who practiced the classical art in the modern age that they had lost touch with the structure of the poetic code. This structure was important because it provided a coherence which the ideas to be remembered did not in themselves symbolically convey. In other words mnemonics as a skill to be acquired was a response to the loss of a linguistic frame of reference. It was the need for such a frame of reference that prompted the search for a mnemonic model that might serve as a practical substitute. By the age of the Renaissance this need had set Neoplatonic mnemonists on a course of seeking to establish the connection between images and ideas in magical ways because they lacked the historical understanding necessary to uncover such connections in the past.

Vico's *New Science* pointed toward a fundamental reorientation of thought about the uses of memory. Henceforth memory would be employed as a technique to uncover forgotten origins understood as lost poetic powers. The quest to touch the original, imaginative powers that make us creative would become the primary quest of the Romantic poets and philosophers of the early nineteenth century. It pointed as well toward the new interest in autobiography, in which the notion of continuous development from infancy to adulthood would provide the sense of unity that could no longer be discovered in the heavens. As metaphysics yielded to psychology, memory as a key to magic was displaced by memory as a key to soul-searching. The distance that the art of memory had travelled in the journey from sixteenth-century rhetoric to nineteenth-century psychology is revealed in the revisioning of the image of memory itself. The image of memory as a brightly-lit theater of the world was replaced by one better attuned to the kind of inquiry with which the art of memory was henceforth to be allied—that of memory as a mirror of the dark abyss of the mind.[33]

As a practitioner of the ancient art of rhetoric, Vico had in the modern age come to appreciate not only the poetic resources but also the evolution of language. In Vichian terms the art of memory drew upon metaphor to further an ironical mode of understanding. The irony was that for all of the originality of his "new science," the discipline of rhetoric from

---

[32] Luria's study of the mind of the mnemonist Shereshevskii confirms Vico's explanation of the poetics of memory. When demonstrating his skill before audiences, Shereshevskii developed techniques to speed his commitment of facts to memory. When the facts were extremely difficult, he relied on detailed metaphorical associations. But to recall less complicated data, he intuitively turned to metonymic or synecdochic images. The easier the facts, the further he ascended the tropological gradient of abstraction in his search for images that might be incorporated more rapidly into his memory. Luria, *Mind of a Mnemonist*, 38-61.

[33] Georges Gusdorf, "Conditions and Limits of Autobiography," in *Autobiography: Essays Theoretical and Critical*, ed. James Olney (Princeton, 1980), 32-33, 40.

which he had derived his insights was losing its intellectual status. The age of Enlightenment in whose early days Vico lived marked an intellectual divide between manuscript and print culture. By the end of the eighteenth century the printing press, extant for three centuries, had fundamentally altered the way in which knowledge was transmitted and preserved.[34] The need for an art of memory to verify the integrity of knowledge through recourse to memorized oral formulae was rendered obsolete by the dramatic expansion of the publishing business and the rapid growth of the reading public. Encyclopedias and dictionaries transposed the task of indexing information for ready recall from the mind to the archive.[35] In the process the printed word displaced the oral maxim as the source of learned authority among literate people.[36]

At the same time the advent of print culture, however revolutionary its implications, had been made possible by the long developmental process through which communication was transformed in early modern European culture. The printed word was introduced into a society that had been literate for many centuries. That literacy, in turn, remained highly dependent upon oral tradition. Until printing became the primary mode of human communication during the course of the eighteenth century, oral interpretation continued to provide the basic topical codes for the organization of literate expression. In manuscript culture documents were still composed as if they were to be read aloud.[37] The transformation of the human mind that Vico describes in terms of the evolution of tropes, therefore, may also be understood in terms of the long-range shift from orality to literacy to print culture. Literacy was dependent upon orality in much the same way that reason was dependent upon poetry in Vico's scheme. The oral tradition in which Vico discovered "the true Homer" is the same one to which modern classicists return to explain the origins of literacy. From the Homeric epics (eighth century B.C.) to Greek tragedy (fifth century B.C.), they argue, oral modes of interpretation exercised an immense residual power over literary expression.[38]

[34] Robert Darnton, *The Literary Underground of the Old Regime* (Cambridge, Mass., 1982), 167-208, and *The Business of the Enlightenment* (Cambridge, Mass., 1979), 428-34; Elizabeth L. Eisenstein, *The Printing Press as an Agent of Change* (Cambridge, England, 1979), I, 3-159; François Furet and Jacques Ozouf, *Reading and Writing: Literacy in France from Calvin to Jules Ferry* (Cambridge, England, 1982), 5-47.

[35] André Leroi-Gourhan, *Le Geste et la parole* (Paris, 1965), II, 9-34; Robert Darnton, *The Great Cat Massacre and Other Episodes in French History* (New York, 1984), 191-213; Walter J. Ong, *Rhetoric, Romance, and Technology* (Ithaca, 1971), 278.

[36] Walter J. Ong, *Orality and Literacy* (London, 1982), 124.

[37] *Ibid.*, 5-10, 78-116, 119; Jack Goody, *The Domestication of the Savage Mind* (Cambridge, England, 1977), 112-18.

[38] Eric A. Havelock, *Preface to Plato* (Cambridge, Mass., 1963), 100-103, 115-28, and *The Literate Revolution in Greece and its Cultural Consequences* (Princeton, 1982), 143-49.

To this transition the art of memory is an essential guide, for its development was coeval with the rise of literacy. In the days when Homer's epics were first recited, a prodigious memory was still the intuitive talent of bards who stitched together formulaic verses in a different design each time they performed.[39] But by the time that Greek culture entered its classical age three centuries later, mnemonics had become the studied skill of the rhetorician. It is worth noting that the legend of Simonides' invention of the art of memory dates from the early fifth century B.C., precisely the time when literacy was becoming the dominant cultural mode. Moreover, the major theoretical expositions of the art in the ancient world, those devised by Roman rhetoricians in the first century B.C., were contributed during Rome's most illustrious age of literary expression. The revival of the art of memory in the Renaissance of the sixteenth century and its growing refinement over the following one hundred years might be characterized as a Vichian *ricorso* in that this era, too, was one in which a highly literate culture still organized learning according to the canons of oral conceptualization. Mnemonic formulae provided the deep structures for the classification of knowledge until the full impact of the print revolution was felt toward the end of the eighteenth century. Born of intuitive mnemonic powers common in the pre-literate cultures of antiquity, the art of memory as an acquired technique retained its importance as long as oral interpretation influenced the manuscript culture of early modern Europe. Not only was mnemonics a skill derived from oral culture; it was a mode of understanding essential to the organization of literate expression prior to the print revolution.[40] Only when movable alphabetic type had completely replaced oral formulae as the basis for indexing knowledge would mnemonics be perceived to be a marginal skill.[41]

The advent of print culture revolutionized human perception in learning. Print transformed words from sounds to be heard into surfaces to be seen.[42] As places permanently fixed on the printed page, words acquired an autonomy they had not previously possessed. Oral communication is dependent upon living memory, and an argument voiced in conversation must be repeated to be reported anew. But written communication is transacted through texts and thereby acquires a specific identity of time and place. With the coming of print culture, the dissemination of knowledge was thought of less often as the reporting of maxims drawn from a reservoir of timeless common sense, and more often as the recognition

---

[39] Havelock, *Preface*, 89-121; Ong, *Orality*, 57-68; Berkley Peabody, *The Winged Word* (Albany, 1975), 214-18.

[40] Ong, *Orality*, 26, 33-36, 115-16.

[41] *Ibid.*, 108-12, 125.

[42] *Ibid.*, 12, 71-74, 100, 117.

of ideas readily identifiable with individual authors writing at specific moments in history.[43]

As for the reader, the print revolution contributed to a change in his self-perception. Reading was a solitary act. As a conversation with an absent author, it encouraged the reader to think more about his own thoughts and feelings. As a mirror for his reflections, the printed page promoted introspection. In this way reading contributed to the discovery of personality, which so preoccupied Romantic writers and readers at the turn of the nineteenth century.[44] The psychological reorientation promoted by reading also permitted a new way of understanding the use of memory. The art of memory, previously identified with rote learning for a society whose knowledge depended upon living memory, was reconceived for one more secure about the permanence of its intellectual acquisitions. Less constrained by demands for assiduous memorization, the citizen of print culture was disposed to use his memory for a more inquisitive kind of learning.[45] If the art of memory appeared to many to have lost favor in the declining prestige of rhetoric, it was destined to rise once more in the guise of autobiography.

Autobiography, understood as a form of meditation (Augustine of Hippo) or as an exposition of personal accomplishment (Benvenuto Cellini), was a genre of long-standing.[46] Only in the late eighteenth century did it become closely identified with a more personal exploration of the psyche.[47] Best known among the practitioners of this new form of soul-searching was the French philosopher Jean-Jacques Rousseau, who thought of his *Confessions* (1770) as a distinctly original literary enterprise.[48] Rousseau's autobiography does display a marked departure from its immediate antecedents. Vico's life chronicle, for example, although written only fifty years before, is a tale of his intellectual formation.[49]

[43] *Ibid.*, 44, 101-4, 131-32.

[44] *Ibid.*, 54-57, 102, 105, 130-31, 153-54; see also the interesting discussion of the way in which Jean-Jacques Rousseau's novel, *La Nouvelle Héloïse*, promoted such introspection in Darnton, *Great Cat Massacre*, 215-52.

[45] Ong, *Rhetoric, Romance*, 277-79, and *Orality*, 133-34.

[46] A great deal has recently been written about the role of memory in autobiography. Some of the best articles on the topic are reproduced in the anthology edited by James Olney (cited above in n. 33). Indispensable on conceptions of memory in this context is the sprawling essay by Georges Gusdorf, *Mémoire et personne* (Paris, 1951). The only literary critic to examine the relationship between the classical art of memory and the rhetoric of autobiography, however, is Beaujour, *Miroirs d'encre*, esp. 81-112, who shows how the fields are joined by memory's constructive role in each.

[47] William L. Howarth, "Some Principles of Autobiography," and Michael Sprinker, "The End of Autobiography," in Olney (ed.), *Autobiography*, 113, 325-26.

[48] Jean-Jacques Rousseau, *The Confessions*, tr. J. M. Cohen (Baltimore, 1953), 17.

[49] *The Autobiography of Giambattista Vico*, tr. Max Harold Fisch and Thomas Goddard Bergin (Ithaca, 1963). Only posthumously was Vico's life narrative labeled an autobiography.

Rousseau's, by contrast, is a saga of emotional discovery. Rousseau professed to lay bare his interior life since childhood. His intent was to search
out the hidden feelings of the child within his soul. In much the same
way that Vico had identified emotional expression with the poetic perceptions of primitive peoples, Rousseau culled his memory for images
that had shaped his feelings about himself.[50]

One might contend, however, that Rousseau's *Confessions* display not
an art of memory but a memory without artful design. His professed use
of memory to recall spontaneously the significant events of his life implied
a kind of Vichian recourse to those sources of poetic logic in which
memory and metaphor are in transparent correspondence. Critics have
since pointed out the degree to which Rousseau's rummaging amidst his
memories to discover the sustaining thread of his personal formation was
disingenuous. The recollection of the past, they argue, is by nature constructive. One selects images out of the past on the basis of what one
deems significant from one's present vantage point, and weaves them
tendentiously into a narrative design of the life process.[51] The recollection
of the past is therefore a process of emplotting the landmarks of one's
life history as it is presently perceived. The search for mnemic images
that mark life's significant turning points (i.e., its commonplaces) is
reminiscent of the mnemonist's scheme, even if its structure has been
transformed from a spacial into a temporal model.[52] Life's continuity is
to be found in this imagined structure of images of one's life journey,
not in the objective recovery of the continuous chain of life's events.
Rousseau subjectively selected what he believed were the salient events
of his life when he composed his *Confessions*, and later in life admitted
to confabulations in its narrative in places where his memory failed him.[53]

If Rousseau's *Confessions* do not convey an obvious sense of the
mnemonic design of the developing self, the rough shape of such a design
was already in the making. By the early nineteenth century the life process
was being interpreted in terms of distinct developmental stages. The
growing awareness of childhood as a period of life distinct from yet
preparatory for adulthood, and of youth as a transitional age of passage
between these stages, adumbrated a theory of growth through stages

---

[50] Jean Starobinski, "The Style of Autobiography," in Olney (ed.), *Autobiography*,
80-82; Samuel S. B. Taylor, "Rousseau's Romanticism," in *Reappraisals of Rousseau*,
ed. Simon Harvey et al. (Totowa, N.J., 1980), 16-17; Ann Hartle, *The Modern Self in
Rousseau's Confessions* (Notre Dame, Indiana, 1983), 115-17.

[51] Stephen Spender, "Confessions and Autobiography," James Olney, "The Ontology
of Autobiography," and Louis A. Renza, "A Theory of Autobiography" in Olney (ed.),
Autobiography, 120-22, 254-55, 288-95; see also Huntington Williams, *Rousseau and
Romantic Autobiography* (Oxford, 1983), 218-23.

[52] Gusdorf, *Mémoire et personne*, II, 554; Beaujour, *Miroirs d'encre*, 65-69.

[53] Jean-Jacques Rousseau, *Les Rêveries du promeneur solitaire* (Geneva, 1967), 69-
73; see also Gusdorf, *Mémoire et personne*, I, 212-15.

along life's way.[54] The notion of the life process as a structured sequence of discrete units demarcated by crises of transition would provide the architectonics for a new art of memory devoted to self-analysis. In the following century, the conception of the life cycle would be further refined into a model of growing complexity, culminating in the eight-stage paradigm designed by Erik Erikson in the mid-twentieth century. It is significant that Erikson presents his model as an easily visualized "epigenetic chart," and that the same chart serves as the centerpiece of no less than four of his books.[55] This schematic diagram may not serve literally as an aid to memory in the classical sense of indexing an imaginary archive for the retrieval of ideas. But it does facilitate the interpretation of the meaning of mnemic images by providing a clearcut memoryscape on which they may be easily placed.[56] This suggests why Erikson, in his psychobiographies of Martin Luther and Mohandas Gandhi, concentrated upon mnemic images that signalled significant turning points ("historical moments") in their life histories rather than upon the detailed description that characterizes conventional biography.[57] The meaning of a life is epitomized in what Erikson calls the "moments and sequences" that give structure to one's life history.[58]

The use of memory to further self-understanding, of course, operated within an orbit far wider than autobiography or psychobiography. Nineteenth-century European society was reflective not only about personal recollection but also about collective remembrance. Cults of memory emerged in a myriad of manifestations. Philippe Ariès has pointed out the way in which exaggerated rites of mourning and monumental grave statuary were employed to reinforce the remembrance of departed loved ones. The cemetery was consciously redesigned as a field of memory for kin to visit and wherein they could reminisce.[59] More conspicuous was the way in which rites of commemoration were used to reinforce an emerging vision of cultural nationalism. The nineteenth century witnessed the revival and growing popularity of folk traditions about the mythological founders of nations, of the heroes and heroines of national liberation, of the deeds of revolutionary martyrs, and of soldiers fallen in battle. All of these emblems of the nationalist ideal were given concrete

[54] Philippe Ariès, *Centuries of Childhood: A Social History of Family Life*, tr. Robert Baldick (New York, 1962), 29-32.

[55] Erik H. Erikson: *Childhood and Society* (2nd ed.; New York, 1963), 273; *Identity, Youth and Crisis* (New York, 1968), 94; *Identity and the Life Cycle* (New York, 1980), 178; *The Life Cycle Completed* (New York, 1982), 32-33, 56-57.

[56] *Identity and the Life Cycle*, 150-58; *The Life Cycle Completed*, 61.

[57] Erik H. Erikson, *Life History and the Historical Moment* (New York, 1975), 36-37, 123-24.

[58] *Ibid.*, 113-68.

[59] Philippe Ariès, *Western Attitudes toward Death from the Middle Ages to the Present*, tr. Patricia M. Ranum (Baltimore, 1974), 72-82, and *The Hour of Our Death*, tr. Helen Weaver (New York, 1981), 474-75, 500-593, 508-13, 518, 524-46.

expression in national shrines, which served as places of pilgrimage and as sites for festivals on days of national remembrance. In effect such shrines were actual memory palaces, constructed of imposing architecture and adorned with aesthetically pleasing icons and artifacts designed to evoke memories of a heroic or glorious past and to imprint them vividly on the minds of visitors.[60] This association of images with places to further the nationalist ideal drew upon classic mnemonic techniques. As in the case of autobiographical reminiscence, the exponents of nationalist ideology believed that if people could recover lost memories of their common origins and heritage, they could make contact with emotions that would enliven their sense of a common identity. Invariably the memories they had in mind came clothed in enchantment.

If mnemonic techniques lay at the source of Romantic soul-searching, both personal and collective, they were only rarely the subject of comment. It was left to Sigmund Freud at the turn of the twentieth century to explain the role of memory in introspection in terms of a mnemonic code. Freud's search for a method with which to recall lost memories of the self is best appreciated in terms of its Romantic antecedents.[61] Like the autobiographers and the apologists for nationalism, Freud identified the search for the self with the recollection of past experiences. But he was suspicious of the enchanted imagery in which childhood memories or, for that matter, conceptions of national origins, were presented. His quest was to dispel that enchantment in order to expose realities hidden beneath. There was something akin to the method of the Renaissance magus in Freud's endeavor. Like Bruno, he was in search of a model that would enable him to uncover a secret universe. Freud was fascinated with the notion of a deep structure of the mind that shaped the workings of the unconscious. His search for a method with which to analyze the psyche was a search for a *clavis universalis*, a master key to this cosmos within.[62] Like Vico, Freud attached enormous importance to the formative influence of origins. What Vico had discovered about the mind in the beginnings of civilization, Freud believed was recapitulated in the present mind (ontogeny recapitulates phylogeny), and he hoped that the probe might proceed deeper into prehistory. Vico had explored new vistas upon

[60] George L. Mosse, *The Nationalization of the Masses* (New York, 1975), 73-99; Maurice Agulhon, *Marianne au combat: L'imagerie et la symbolique républicaines de 1789 à 1880* (Paris, 1979); Patrick H. Hutton, *The Cult of the Revolutionary Tradition* (Berkeley, 1981), 119-42; Charles Rearick, *Pleasures of the Belle Epoque* (New Haven, 1985), 3-24.

[61] Lancelot Law Whyte, *The Unconscious Before Freud* (New York, 1960), 167-70, 177-90; Henri F. Ellenberger, *The Discovery of the Unconscious* (New York, 1970), 204-10, 222-23; Arthur K. Berliner, *Psychoanalysis and Society* (Washington, D.C., 1983), 21-25.

[62] On this approach to Freud's work see Carlo Ginzburg, "Clues: Morelli, Freud, and Sherlock Holmes," in *The Sign of Three*, ed. Umberto Eco and Thomas A. Sebeok (Bloomington, Indiana, 1983), 84-87; Beaujour, *Miroirs d'encre*, 210, 213-16.

memory by virtue of his historical journey into remote regions of human origins. What permitted Freud to move beyond into original terrain was his desire to travel into a realm of which Vico could not have conceived— that of the unconscious mind. For Vico, this would have been a passage across the mythological river Lethe into a realm of oblivion beyond forgetfulness.[63] But what Freud discovered there by making the passage might be characterized as a mnemonics of the unconscious mind.

It was Freud's faith that, barring biological impairment, the unconscious mind retains all of life's memories. The problem of forgetting— of gaps in memory—is due to repression, the relegation of painful or unpleasant memories to the unconscious mind where they are stored intact. The loss of memory, therefore, is not a function of time's erosion, for the unconscious mind has no sense of time. Memory loss is rather a consequence of barriers erected by the unconscious. The analyst's task is to recall these memories from the limbo of repression where they await recollection.[64]

Freud was struck by the fact that childhood, the period of life most formative of our adult personalities, is the one about which we remember the least.[65] The more that we can recollect from this period of our lives, the more likely we are to understand ourselves. But Freud viewed with circumspection those childhood memories that did surface from the unconscious mind, for they were generally benign and sometimes bathed in nostalgia. Whereas the Romantics trusted that there was a direct correspondence between such mnemic images and the experiences through which they had actually lived, Freud denied that transparency of association. For him such memories were innocuous substitutes for more important ones that remained repressed and hidden from view.[66] If the Romantic project of establishing the connection between past and present identities was to be realized, then the fantasies in which the unconscious psyche clothes its past must be uncovered.[67] The task of Freud's art of memory was to decode these substitute, or screen, memories.

The substitution of an image for an idea, the key to the classical mnemonic code, is also the central proposition of Freud's theory of screen

---

[63] NS, 346, 717. For the relationship between Vico's and Freud's theories of mind, see Silvano Arieti, "Vico and Modern Psychiatry," Social Research, 43 (1976), 739-44, 746-50.

[64] Sigmund Freud, The Interpretation of Dreams (1900), tr. James Strachey (New York, 1965), 54.

[65] Sigmund Freud, "Screen Memories," (1899), in The Standard Edition of the Complete Psychological Works of Sigmund Freud, tr. and ed. James Strachey (London, 1962), III, 303-4, and The Psychopathology of Everyday Life (1901), tr. Alan Tyson (New York, 1965), 46.

[66] Freud, Psychopathology of Everyday Life, 47-48.

[67] Sigmund Freud, Totem and Taboo (1913), tr. James Strachey (New York, 1950), 91-95, and Interpretation of Dreams, 530, 539.

memories.[68] Screen memories are mnemic images that displace deeper, hidden memories. By comparison with the memories they shield, screen memories are of lesser consequence, arouse fewer emotions, and relate to more recent experience. They are projected backward in time to fill the gap created by the repression of the memory of actual experience, and thereby to fulfill the conscious mind's need for a coherent sense of life's development. As in the associations of the mnemonic systems of the Aristotelian tradition, the link between the screen memory and the repressed one is an attachment of place rather than of content. The screen memory fits the pattern of the past envisioned in our present fantasies, yet marks the place where the repressed memory of our actual experience may be retrieved.[69] As Freud explains, screen memories "are not made of gold themselves but have lain beside something that *is* made of gold."[70] Elsewhere he likens the connection to that of the hermit crab with its shell.[71]

But in contrast to the classical art of memory, the purpose of the screen memory is to enable us to forget. Screen memories are defenses employed by the unconscious mind to ward off the recollection of intense, painful, or traumatic experiences, especially those of childhood. Whereas the mnemonist employed vivid images to stimulate his recall of ideas, the unconscious mind uses inconsequential ones to spare the conscious mind the recollection of distressing memories.[72] Freud's theory might be characterized as a reverse mnemonics. Forgetting rather than remembering is what we wish to do because it is easier to live with a screen of fantasies about what our lives have been than with the reality. In his theory of screen memories Freud asserts the constructive power of the unconscious mind to shape recollection. To use his terminology, memory is tendentious in that it reflects unconscious psychic intent.[73] In this respect the unconscious mind is the guardian of memory. It legislates the selection of what is to be remembered and hides the rest away. As an art of memory, therefore, Freud's psychoanalysis is a technique for deciphering the psychic intent encoded in screen memories.

For Freud the analysis of dreams was also a fruitful source for drawing memories from the unconscious mind. Dreams are full of memories that the psyche more willingly gives up as it relaxes its watch during sleep. But the memories of dreams surface in random fragments and so, even if they are successfully interpreted, only provide clues to the code of

[68] Freud, "Screen Memories," 303-22, and *Psychopathology of Everyday Life*, 43-52. See also Paul Ricoeur, *Freud and Philosophy*, tr. Denis Savage (New Haven, 1970), 91, 97 n., 105.
[69] Freud, "Screen Memories," 307, and *Psychopathology of Everyday Life*, 43-45, 50.
[70] "Screen Memories," 307.
[71] *Psychopathology of Everyday Life*, 49 n.2.
[72] "Screen Memories," 308-9.
[73] *Ibid.*, 322; *Psychopathology of Everyday Life*, 43, 45.

unconscious psychic intent. These memory remnants must still be decoded to discover their connection to forgotten experiences yet to be disclosed.[74] Using the art of memory to interpret mnemic images, therefore, is far more difficult for the Freudian analyst than it was for the Neoplatonic mnemonist. The mnemonist was able to scan the complete array of images housed in the brightly-lit rooms of his memory palace, whereas the analyst is obliged to scrutinize the haphazard images cast up in shadowy dreams. The mnemonist worked from an index of clearly delineated architectural design, whereas the analyst must decode memory fragments in the hope that they contain pieces of the mosaic of unconscious psychic intent.

Freud's psychobiography of Leonardo da Vinci is his most famous case study of the analysis of a screen memory. It is based upon da Vinci's account of his recollection as an adult of a childhood memory of a vulture placing its tail in his mouth. Freud concluded that it was a fantasy transposed upon his early childhood from adolescence. This screen memory shielded him from the painful memory of his separation from his father during infancy, when he lived alone with his mother. During latency, when he had repressed his love for his mother, he took himself as a model for emulation to fill the void left by his absent father, and so came to love his own childish self. The screen memory of the vulture was a homosexual fantasy of this narcissistic self-love, projected into infancy to displace the painful memory of his lost father. But repressed memories continue to work their power upon the unconscious mind, and da Vinci's repressed memory of his love for his mother was eventually to be transfigured in the creative images that he painted in his adult years, notably that of the beguiling smile of Mona Lisa.[75]

Freud's work on the psychological development of individuals eventually led him to inquire into the psychological development of the species. Herein Freud wrestled with the problem of collective consciousness raised by the nineteenth-century Romantic nationalists. To deal with it, he returned to the approach first suggested by Vico—the analysis of our memories of human origins. Like Vico, he believed that the development of the consciousness of each individual recapitulates the development of the consciousness of all humankind.[76] He reasoned that if the analysis of a screen memory can disclose the lost experiences of childhood, then the analysis of the myths of primitive peoples should enable us to recover lost memories of human origins. But Freud sought to extract from these myths memories of experiences prior to the conscious beginnings of

---

[74] *Interpretation of Dreams*, 44-55.

[75] Sigmund Freud, *Leonardo da Vinci: A Study in Psychosexuality* (1910), tr. A. A. Brill (New York, 1947), esp. 33-49.

[76] Sigmund Freud: *Civilization and its Discontents* (1930), tr. James Strachey (New York, 1961), 86-89; *An Autobiographical Study* (1925), tr. James Strachey (New York, 1952), 138; *Moses and Monotheism* (1937), tr. Katherine Jones (New York, 1967), 90-101, 125-29, 153.

civilization that Vico had identified with the creation of poetic myths. For Freud, these myths were not transparent representations of the age in which they were created, as Vico believed them to be, but screen memories covering earlier events from which humankind wished to shield itself. The memory of civilization's beginnings was reconstructed after an historical period of latency, whereas the actual beginnings remained hidden in repressed memories that we collectively retain in our unconscious minds.[77]

To unblock these memories Freud turned to the analysis of religious myths of origins. Struck by the ongoing power of religion to mold people's minds from antiquity to the present, Freud sought to demythologize religious imagery to uncover the secrets about human origins that he believed they contained. Through his analysis of the myths of totemic religions, the earliest faiths of civilized people, Freud concluded that they screened acts of tribal parricide in which warrior sons murdered the omnipotent tribal father and reluctantly apportioned his power among themselves in a collective covenant. The totem, usually an animal, symbolized the displaced father even as it obliterated him from conscious memory. The totem feast, in turn, was a symbolic act of worshipping while devouring this father whom they had once held in awe yet had been willing to destroy.[78] The father and son imagery of monotheistic religions such as Judaism and Christianity merely reiterated the screening of this primal truth.[79] Religious myth transfigured the primordial conflict of love and aggression into a sacred memory that rendered tolerable a profane truth that remained repressed. The power of religious myth in the present age, Freud concludes, testifies to the power of the repressed memory it screens. Born historically in the first social contract, the religious myth of origins has become timeless as it is unconsciously recapitulated by each generation in the psychological revolt of sons against their fathers.[80]

To conclude we may return to the beginnings of the art of memory in the legend of Simonides, who reconstructed from memory the palace from which he had escaped as it was about to collapse into ruins. Each of the practitioners of the art of memory that we have discussed believed that he could reconstruct such an imaginary palace out of the intellectual ruins of his day because each had faith in his imaginative power to recreate the design of the human world. Each was a builder of paradigms, and each paradigm implied an art of memory. Whether in the guise of Bruno's magic, Vico's poetics, or Freud's psychoanalysis, mnemonics was based

[77] *Totem and Taboo*, 155; *Moses and Monotheism*, 101-2, 164-69.
[78] *Totem and Taboo*, 142-53; *Civilization and its Discontents*, 47-54; *Moses and Monotheism*, 102-8, 152-53.
[79] *Totem and Taboo*, 153-55; *Moses and Monotheism*, 108-14, 174-76.
[80] *Totem and Taboo*, 157; *Civilization and its Discontents*, 79; *Moses and Monotheism*, 157-60, 170.

upon the premise that imagination is born of memory. In the teachings of ancient Greek mythology, Mnemosyne, the goddess of memory, is honored as the mother of all of the arts and sciences of human creation. Through her ministry, all knowledge is continually being rebound into new configurations that express the harmony of understanding that humans seek. If Freud's depiction of the human condition is a grim one in comparison with the Romantic ones it challenged, it still provides the consolation of a coherent conception of the human condition. Freud is one of the last exemplars of a tradition of learning based upon the faith that humans have the capacity to recover all human experiences that have been forgotten and thereby to make the record of human history whole.

Since Freud's death that tradition has come under more frequent criticism. Our age possesses considerably less faith in the proposition that the development of civilization, or for that matter the development of the individual psyche, possesses a continuous thread of meaning. In this respect, recent work by cultural historians has tended to place the accent upon the discontinuities between historical epochs, and even among the mentalities of different social groups living beside one another in the same historical era.[81] Michel Foucault's notion of "counter-memory," which denies the ability of collective memory to bind meanings across dissimilar historical epochs, is a provocative statement of this point of view.[82] Foucault's questioning of the intrinsic value of remembering the thought of ages past reveals the degree to which our present perception of the art of memory has shifted from the problem of forgetfulness to that of oblivion. The current popular obsession with maladies of amnesia may well be a legitimate medical worry. But it is also a metaphor for the cultural malaise of our time. As Oliver Sacks, a neurologist with a philosopher's bent, suggests in his recent analysis of the consciousness of a victim of Korsakov's syndrome, amnesia is especially terrifying in our culture because our sense of identity is profoundly tied to specific experiences in our past with which we believe it is crucial to maintain present connections.[83] But the decline of mnemonics itself is perhaps a better example of our forgetfulness of the cultural sense of memory's

[81] Among historians who put the accent upon discontinuity, see esp. Fernand Braudel, *The Mediterranean and the Mediterranean World in the Age of Philip II*, tr. Siân Reynolds (New York, 1972), I, 20-21; Carlo Ginzburg, *The Cheese and the Worms*, tr. John and Anne Tedeschi (New York, 1982), xi-xxvi. On the challenge to the notion of the integral self in autobiography, see Sprinker, "Fictions of the Self," in Olney (ed.), *Autobiography*, 321-42.

[82] Michel Foucault, "Nietzsche, Genealogy, History," in *Language, Counter-Memory, Practice: Selected Essays and Interviews*, ed. Donald F. Bouchard (Ithaca, 1977), 139-64.

[83] Oliver Sacks, "The Lost Mariner," *The New York Review of Books* (16 February 1984), 18-19.

meaning. Those psychologists who today dismiss the art of memory as irrelevant to their professional interests may think that they have sound reasons for doing so. But they are missing the historical connection it has always maintained with the human capacity to explain human experience in terms of a vision that unifies knowledge in coherent ways.

The University of Vermont.

Chapter XVI

HORIZONS OF INTELLECTUAL HISTORY: RETROSPECT, CIRCUMSPECT, PROSPECT

By Donald R. Kelley

> . . .nos esse quasi nanos gigantium
> humeris insidentes, ut possimus plura
> eis et remotiora videre. . .
> —John of Salisbury, *Metalogicon*

> Man vergilt einem Lehrer Schlecht,
> wenn man immer nur der Schüler bleibt.
> —Nietzsche, *Ecce Homo*

"Make it new!" Ezra Pound demanded, and many scholars and critics are still following this call to modernization. Not only "new criticism," "new history," "new science," and "new humanism" but also, revealingly, "post-modernism," "post-structuralism," "post-western" history, and even "post-historicism" (marvellously ironic term which affirms what it affects to deny) suggest that what Wyndham Lewis called the "Demon of Progress" haunts intellectual discourse as well as the fine arts.[1] As so often before, winds of doctrine coming from Paris (though mainly originating, as so often before, in Germany) have brought many conceptual novelties, or at least neologisms; and it seems unwise for intellectual historians to ignore these new waves of scholarly opinion, however superficial.[2] Even the history of "ideas," though it reaches out for the enduring, must in practical terms trade in the currency of the transient— must start from and finally return to the cave of human discourse.

Battles between ancients and moderns never cease. The prototype is Socrates, who completed the first conceptual "turn" against convention;

---

[1] *The Demon of Progress in the Arts* (New York, 1926). See most recently Ricardo Quinones, *Mapping Literary Modernism, Time and Development* (Princeton, 1985), the issues of *New German Critique*, no. 33 (Fall 1984) devoted to this topic; also Peter Burger, *Theory of the Avant-Garde*, tr. M. Shaw (Minneapolis, 1984), Paul de Man, "Literary History and Literary Modernity," in *Blindness and Insight* (2nd ed.; London, 1982), J.-F. Lyotard, *La Condition postmoderne* (Paris, 1979), not to forget Robert K. Merton, *On the Shoulders of Giants* (New York, 1965). Cf. Lynn Thorndike, "Newness and Craving for Novelty in 17th Century Science and Medicine," *JHI*, 6 (1951), 584-98.

[2] Literary introductions abound; and for English language studies I should refer in particular to *The Structuralist Controversy, The Languages of Criticism and the Sciences of Man*, ed. R. Macksey and Eugenio Donato (Baltimore, 1979); Frederic Jameson, *The Prison-House of Language* (Princeton, 1972); Frank Lentricchia, *After the New Criticism* (Chicago, 1980); Terry Eagleton, *Literary Theory* (Minneapolis, 1983); Jonathan Culler, *The Pursuit of Signs* (Ithaca, 1981); David Couzens Hoy, *The Critical Circle* (Berkeley, 1978); and Howard Felperin, *Beyond Deconstruction* (Oxford, 1985).

and other philosophical sects followed suit. In modern European thought it was Aristotle who, posthumously, revived the generational patterns of the ancient academy and who became, in the eyes of the intellectual establishment of the thirteenth century, the new corrupter of youth. But though "modernized," Aristotle soon became an *antiquus* again, and new battles with the *moderni* broke out in the universities. In the sixteenth century it was the anti-Aristotelian Peter Ramus who, in the name of rhetorical "invention," affected to become the voice of (the new) modernism, the scourge of intellectual tradition.[3] Like Aristotle before him, Ramus provoked outcries from more conventional scholars. "Good God!" exclaimed one English author,

What an age do wee now lyve in? A sophister in tymes past was a tytle of credite, and a woord of commendation; now what more odious? Aristotle then the father of Philosophy; now who lesse favoured? Ramus rules a broade, Ramus at home, and who but Ramus? Antiquity is nothing but Dunsicality, and our fore fathers inventions unprofitable trumpery. New-fangled young headed hare-brayne boys will needes bee Maysters that were never Scholars; prate of method, who never knew order; rayle against Aristotle assoone as they are crept out of the shell.[4]

The words change but the music sounds familiar. In the Renaissance as in our day, mainstream philosophy was threatened by foreign fashions. Then Ramus was the Parisian menace, the new Abelard (the new Socrates). Aristotle was all wrong, Ramus charged; and for a correct "method" one had to adopt a new, more human, and less abstract view of language. At his death in 1572 Ramus was Levi-Strauss, Barthes, Foucault, and Derrida all rolled into one (with Calvinism providing a sort of sub-text comparable to Averroism in the thirteenth century and to Marxism, or perhaps Nietzscheanism, in this century). In that age, as in ours, there was a deeper layer of "new learning" (*nova doctrina*), and again it was in large part German, with the "new logic" of Rudolf Agricola and Philip Melanchthon (which underlay Ramism) performing functions similar to the anti-metaphysical arguments of Martin Heideg-

---

[3] See especially *Ramus, Method, and the Decay of Dialogue* (Cambridge, Mass., 1958) by Walter J. Ong, who has pursued the modernizing of the Word into more recent times; also James H. Overfield, *Humanism and Scholasticism in Late Medieval Germany* (Princeton, 1984). Cf. Ramus, *Advertissements sur la reformation de l'université*, in *Archives curieuses de l'histoire de France*, ed. L. Cimber and F. Danjou (Paris, 1834), V, 118: "Comme naturellement la viellesse est avare et rechigné, ainsi la jeunesse est dereglée et abandoné a son plaisir." And see, e.g., Tina Stiefel, *The Intellectual Revolution in Twelfth-Century Europe* (New York, 1985); Joseph Levine, "Ancients and Moderns Reconsidered," *Eighteenth Century Studies*, 15 (1981-82); and Michael Ermath, "The Transformation of Hermeneutics: 19th Century Ancients and 20th Century Moderns," *Monist*, 64 (1981), 175-94; also the symposium on the *via antiqua* and *via moderna* by William Courtenay, Neal Gilbert, Heiko Oberman, and Charles Trinkaus, above pp. 3-50.

[4] Abraham Fraunce, *The Lawiers Logike* (London, 1588), dedication to Gray's Inn.

ger, Hans-Georg Gadamer, Paul Ricoeur, and their hermeneutical colleagues over the past generation.

Nor was the problem merely prating over "method," as Ramus's rhetoric and Fraunce's polemic might suggest; in fact it concerned the interpretation of and control over the philosophical (hence the religious) canon, over the minds of contemporaries and youth (hence posterity), and so, ultimately, over a major form of social and political power, at least within the educational and intellectual institutions of Europe. Rabelais poked fun at the ridiculous *quam-quam* ("can-can") debate within the university, but he realized that the stakes of academic controversy went far beyond the pronouncing of words. If it began with terms, it ended with ideas; if it began in rhetoric, it ended in philosophy and even (as we might say) in ideology.[5]

Such historical parallels are never exact, but the generational and interdisciplinary patterns are similar and longstanding enough to suggest that current controversies—it is really too trite, sensationalist, and unhistorical to say "crisis"[6]— over philosophical methods are novel neither in extent nor in intensity. The parallel becomes more striking when one reflects that the contemporary "transformation of philosophy" (as Karl O. Apel has called it)[7] is likewise rooted in fundamental questions about the role of language and communication in understanding and interpretation.

Philosophers often seem to imagine themselves standing, uniquely and crucially, at the center of the world and perhaps at the end of time (not only Luther and Marx but also Heidegger and Jacques Derrida have written in this apocalytic and unhistorical mode). Indeed their conceptual "projects" may demand a stance of perpetual novelty. Yet from a more mundane perspective it may seem preferable to regard the current intellectual predicament as another stage in the interminable conflict between philosophical "sects," or rather between philosophers and rhetoricians,

---

[5] D. R. Kelley, *The Beginning of Ideology* (Cambridge, 1981), ch. 4; also "Civil Science in the Renaissance: The Problem of Interpretation," forthcoming in Anthony Pagden (ed.), *The Languages of Political Theory in Early Modern Europe*, and "Homo Politicus: The Jurist as Renaissance Man," forthcoming in *The Journal of the Warburg and Courtauld Institutes*.

[6] There has been an extraordinary proliferation of alleged "crises" in this century, especially in the wake of Husserl's "crisis of the European sciences"—almost exclusively human sciences—as, e.g. (P. N. Medvedev and) M. M. Bakhtin, *The Formal Method in Literary Scholarship*, tr. A. Wehrle (Baltimore, 1978), tracing "six crises" in idealism and positivism, which characterizes the bourgeois "ideological environment." Such literature has been commented on, though hardly stemmed, by Randolf Starn, "Historians and 'Crisis,' " *Past and Present*, no. 52 (1971), 3-22, and various later contributions to what has been called, more or less facetiously, *Krisisforschung*.

[7] Apel, *Transformation der Philosophie* (Frankfurt, 1973), especially vol. 2, "Sprachanalytik, Semiotik, Hermeneutik"; and also Joseph Bleicher, *Contemporary Hermeneutics* (London, 1980).

another effort of modern "sophisters," perhaps, to restore their good name—or of latter-day Ramists to make a new one.[8] The history of thought, if not of formal philosophy, might be seen as a series of footnotes not only to Plato but also to Protagoras; and historians of ideas should perhaps attend to the likes of Ramus as well as Aristotle. They should consider the views of Gadamer (if not Derrida) as well as, let us venture to say, Arthur O. Lovejoy.

Retrospect. A view of the current condition of the history of ideas (more broadly intellectual history, or the history of thought) may properly begin with a glance at the temporal horizons. We cannot hope to escape what has been called the "burden of history," nor perhaps the "anxiety of influence," and the "crisis of historicism" may still be upon us; but we can hardly ignore these disturbances either, whether modern or post-modern in provenance.[9] Philosophers often take license to reconstruct their tradition in accordance with doctrinal preferences, but historians need not be so selective and self-serving in their reviews. Historically, the intellectual pedigree of the history of ideas may be traced back along several disciplinary and doctrinal lines, and we may begin by reminding ourselves of a few of the most relevant of these antecedents.[10]

The history of philosophy goes back at least to Aristotle's and Plato's reviews of their predecessors, but for intellectual history a more immediate ancestry may be sought in various conceptual traditions produced by (or by reaction to) the continental Enlightenment, most notably the critical (or "neo-critical") philosophy emerging in the wake of Kant and developed especially by Windelband, Dilthey, and Cassirer; in a number of

[8] A *locus modernus* is the work of Kenneth Burke, but the systematic study is Ch. Perelman and L. Olbrechts-Tytec, *The New Rhetoric,* tr. J. Wilkinson and P. Weaver (Notre Dame, 1969); see also, e.g., Brian Vickers (ed.), *Rhetoric Revalued* (Binghamton, 1982) and Paul Veyne, *Comment on écrit l'histoire* (Paris, 1971).

[9] White, *Tropics of Discourse, Essays in Cultural Criticism* (Baltimore, 1978); Bloom, *The Anxiety of Influence* (Oxford, 1973); and for a more "traditional" view cf. Edward Shils, *Tradition* (Chicago, 1981).

[10] Among important discussions I should mention William J. Bouwsma, "Intellectual History in the 1980s," *Journal of Interdisciplinary History,* XII (1981), 279-91; Robert Darnton, "Intellectual and Cultural History," in *The Past Before Us,* ed. M. Kammen (Ithaca, N.Y., 1980), with further bibliography; Felix Gilbert, "Intellectual History: Its Aims and Methods," in *Historical Studies Today,* ed. Gilbert and S. Graubard (New York, 1972); John Dunn, "The Identity of the History of Ideas," *Philosophy,* XLIII (1968), 64ff.; and various articles in the *JHI,* also in *History Today* (1985) on "What is Intellectual History?"; and two new periodicals, *History of European Ideas* (1980) and *Intersezioni* (1981); Gene Wise, "The Contemporary Crisis in Contemporary Intellectual History Studies [sic]," *Clio,* 5 (1875), 55-71; and see also Jeremy L. Tobey, *The History of Ideas: A Bibliographical Introduction,* vol. 2, *Medieval and Early Modern Europe* (Santa Barbara, 1977), with my review in *American Historical Review,* 82 (1977), 921. The collection by Preston King (ed.), *The History of Ideas* (London, 1983) is useful only for bibliography.

French schools, including Positivism (from Condorcet to Taine), Ideology (Degérando), and Eclecticism (Cousin, who again provided the vital German link); and in a variety of Anglophone authors, such as Dugald Stewart, W. E. Lecky, A. D. White, and John Draper.[11] Telling the "story" and tracing the "career" of philosophy have become more complex operations over the past generation or two, with the new, or renewed, appreciation of post-scholastic, pre-Cartesian thought by Renaissance scholars like Ernst Cassirer, Eugenio Garin, and P. O. Kristeller, and with attention given to humanistic and scientific subjects neglected in recent generations but formerly part of "philosophy" and so of its history. Nevertheless, the general lines of descent, which is to say the canon, have remained much the same. Nor has short-sighted, post-modernist talk about the "end of metaphysics" or even the "end of philosophy" liberated us from tradition and its attendant burdens and anxieties.[12]

The history of science, originally a compartment of the history of philosophy, has expanded vastly in the past generation or two, admitting into its domain not only a variety of sub-fields beyond the hard—the "theoretical"—sciences but also mysterious areas of magic and the occult, and of course many special topics ranging from institutions to ideas, from the plenum to the vacuum. In effect the history of science has become a separate discipline and in some respects has moved beyond the grasp of older-style history of ideas.[13] Yet for intellectual historians it has become even more significant because of its fundamental concerns with the complex processes of the discovery and criticism, the reception and rejection of ideas. Indeed because of its appreciation for what Thomas Kuhn has called "a role for history," this field has become a methodological model for the history of many other disciplines, including social

---

[11] As elsewhere I must omit a vast bibliography, especially older materials; suffice it to mention the listings by L. W. Beck in *Monist*, LX (1969), no. 4, and various authors in *Philosophy and History*, ed. R. Rorty, J. Schneewind, and Q. Skinner (Cambridge, 1984), and in A. J. Holland (ed.), *Philosophy, Its History and Historiography* (Dordrecht, 1985); also Francesco Bottin, et al. (ed.), *Dalle origini rinascimentali alla "historia philosophica"* (2 vols.; Brescia, 1979-81), eventually 5 vols. Degérando's seminal book is *Histoire comparée des systèmes de philosophie relativement aux principes des connaissances humaines* (Paris, 1804). Victor Cousin, *Introduction to the History of Philosophy*, tr. H. Linberg (Boston, 1832), 105, went so far—and long before Croce—as to identify philosophy and history. Cf. Gianna Gigliotti (ed.), *Il Neocriticismo tedesco* (Turin, 1983).

[12] The history of philosophy suffers not only from the "anxiety of influence" but also and more specifically from "Cartesian anxiety," according to Richard J. Bernstein, *Beyond Objectivism and Relativism* (Philadelphia, 1983). On the "end of philosophy" see, e.g., Hugh J. Silverman and Don Ihde (eds.), *Hermeneutics and Deconstruction* (Albany, N.Y., 1985), 2-32.

[13] Arnold Thackray, "History of Science in the 1980s," *Journal of Interdisciplinary History*, XII (1981), 299-314; Georges Gusdorf, *De l'Histoire des sciences à l'histoire de la pensée* (Paris, 1966); Thomas Kuhn, *The Essential Tension* (Chicago, 1977), 127-61, "The Relations between History and the History of Science," and 3-20, "The Relations between the History and the Philosophy of Science."

science, linguistics, the fine arts, and even archeology and literary criticism.[14]

The history of political and social science, also normally subsumed
under philosophy (and concomitantly, I believe, under law), has been
enriched by various parallel traditions, including moral philosophy, political economy, sociology, and ethnology; but on the whole these areas
have not been cultivated as intensively or as critically as the history of
natural science; and (recent political thought excepted) they seem to be
still in a largely hagiographical stage. As the editor of a sociological
journal once wrote about his colleagues, "Their histories are simply
mechanisms for the canonization of different paradigms."[15] This is obviously not what Kuhn meant by "a role for history"; rather, it is the
"whig fallacy" with a vengeance—and it suggests one reason why Ernst
Becker mourned over American sociology as "the lost science of man."
In such cases it is the history of ideas that may have something to offer
"disciplinary histories," rather than the reverse.

Literary history, represented by the work of such scholars as Taine
and De Sanctis, has been less significant than the modern tradition of
philology, represented by Vossler, Auerbach, Curtius, and Spitzer. This
field, or set of national fields, though likewise rooted in Renaissance
scholarship, is indebted to and indeed long dependent upon classical and
Biblical studies and the *ars critica*; and it has been one of the strongholds
of "historicism" since the eighteenth—or may we say the fifteenth?—
century. The history of literature has also been reinforced by the history
of criticism, for instance in the magisterial work of René Wellek, and in

[14] Let me note, in the wake of Kuhn's *Structure of Scientific Revolutions*, Gary Cutting
(ed.), *Paradigms and Revolutions* (Notre Dame, Ind., 1980), with further bibliography
of Kuhniana, and Loren Graham, Wolf Lepenies, and Peter Weingart (eds.), *Functions
and Uses of Disciplinary Histories* (Boston, 1983); also Robert W. Friedrichs, *A Sociology
of Sociology* (New York, 1970); Remi Clignet, *The Structure of Artistic Revolutions*
(Philadelphia, 1985); E. F. K. Koerner, *Toward A Historiography of Linguistics* (Amsterdam, 1978); Bruce C. Trigger, "Writing the History of Archeology," *Objects and
Others*, ed. G. Stocking (Madison, 1985); and Robert C. Holub, *Reception Theory, A
Critical Introduction* (London, 1984).

[15] Referring to a letter rejecting my "Prehistory of Sociology: Montesquieu, Vico, and
the Legal Tradition" (later published in *Journal of the History of the Behavioral Sciences*,
XVI [1980], 133-44, and repr. *History, Law and the Human Sciences* [London, 1984])
and received from a journal, the founder of which, Albion Small, is the subject of Ernst
Becker, *The Lost Science of Man* (New York, 1971). Another such letter added, "Montesquieu and Vico may be historically important, in some sense, but they are not figures
around whom 'paradigms,' or whatever you want to call them, are built." And more
legislatively: "Montesquieu does not figure in our present reconstructions of the history
of sociology and, until it is shown that they are in that sense significant, there is no
justification for publishing the paper in a sociological journal." Recent periodicals of
interest to the history of ideas include *History of Political Thought, History of Political
Economy, Journal of the History of Sociology, History and Anthropology*, and the annual
History of Anthropology, ed. George Stocking.

a renewed interest in the history of rhetoric, which has established ties between literary criticism and philosophy of great importance for intellectual history.[16]

As for the professional study of history, the most relevant developments have been certain new waves in twentieth-century historiography, including German *Geistes-* or *Ideengeschichte*, the *histoire synthétique* of Henri Berr, and the "new history" in this country, which tried to pioneer—or rather, in a longer perspective, to resettle—areas of cultural and intellectual history deserted by the professional "science" of history. It cannot be claimed, however, that any of these movements has been of lasting significance for the history of ideas.[17]

This list could of course be extended to include the history of various perhaps more peripheral fields, such as the history of art (including music and theater), religion (including mythology and the occult), and other disciplines with complex or problematic genealogies, such as anthropological (philosophical or empirical?), psychology (natural or social science?), and linguistics (natural or social science or literature?)—not to speak of newer fields, such as the sociology of literature and the anthropology of law, and such abstract or arcane topics as cultural space and time, perception and sentiment, symbol and gesture, sexuality and madness.[18] Such inter-, para-, and super-disciplinary problems bear directly (as Lovejoy would probably have agreed) on the study of intellectual history, its conceptual, scholarly, and ideological environment.

In general, then, the history of ideas has had, if not a coherent tradition, at least a rich heritage; and, initially at least, its American practitioners tried to preserve a suitably broad vision as well as a commitment to precise scholarship. More specifically, the "history of ideas" American style owes its genesis, character, and persistence to the work of Lovejoy, his colleagues and his epigones, and has developed more or less independently. Despite the early contributions of European émigré scholars, there is nothing quite comparable in the European academic world, though there have been occasional professors of the "history of ideas" (e.g., Jean Starobinski).[19] *Begriffsgeschichte* has been mainly an

[16] *A History of Modern Criticism* (New Haven, 1955-85), the last two volumes of which, on English and American criticism, will be reviewed by Jonathan Culler in *JHI* (1987). Cf. Dominick La Capra, "Writing the History of Criticism Now?" in *History and Criticism* (Ithaca, N.Y., 1985), 94-114.

[17] For example, Georg Iggers, *New Directions in History* (New York, 1984; 2nd ed.) is devoted largely (and no doubt justifiably) to novelties arising from the social sciences.

[18] Again it is impossible here to offer bibliographical suggestions for such works falling into the interstices between conventional disciplines, nor will be found in conventional reference works such as Tobey's (cited above, n. 10).

[19] Among relevant French notice Jacques Chevalier, *Histoire de la pensée* (Paris, 1955-66), really a history of philosophy; as are Roger Duval, *Histoire des idées en France* (Paris, 1953), following the line of Etienne Gilson, *Les Idées et les lettres*, and François

adjunct of German philosophy (or philosophical lexicography), and the history of *mentalités* of French social history; and neither has paid much attention to American scholarship.

The strength of the American school, by contrast, derives from its original international and interdisciplinary range, as well as well as from Lovejoy's original encyclopedic agenda, which included not only the history of philosophy, science, language and (as he comments) "what is unfortunately called comparative literature," but also, in a more qualified way, folklore, economics, political and social history, the "climate of opinion" (in the phrase which Lovejoy derived from Joseph Glanville via Whitehead and Carl Becker), and even the "sociology of knowledge."[20] A noble dream indeed—and a fitting program to launch the *Journal of the History of Ideas,* which has served as a critical and interdisciplinary forum for almost half a century.

The original problem facing Lovejoy—and still facing us—was best posed by his friend George Boas: "Just what am I writing the history of?"[21] Since the history of thought exists at the confluence of several disciplines, the answers, when formulated at all, were often naive and contradictory. For historians it might be "consciousness" ("the greatest fact in history," wrote J. H. Robinson) or the cultural past in some larger sense (Berr's "l'histoire de tout"), but accessible only on the level of the most uncritical generalizations. For literary critics it might be "literature" in some equally unexamined sense (the "great tradition" of Leavis, or whomever else). Lovejoy's answer, drawn from his own discipline, seemed to offer common ground, and his recognition of "endemic assumptions" or "unconscious mental habits" and broad social concerns seem to open up vistas of a major synthesis. Yet for some scholars, perhaps most notably Spitzer, the focus of "ideas" seemed equally uncritical and unhistorical; and recent commentators have continued this line of criticism.[22]

Chevalier's Marxist *Histoire des Idéologies* (Paris, 1978-). On *Begriffsgeschichte* see below, n. 54.

[20] *Essays in the History of Ideas* (Baltimore, 1945), 1ff., *JHI*, 1 (1940), 1ff.; and *The Great Chain of Being* (Cambridge, Mass., 1936). See also Daniel J. Wilson, *Arthur O. Lovejoy and the Quest for Intelligibility* (Chapel Hill, N.C., 1980), Philip P. Wiener, "Centenary of A. O. Lovejoy's Birthday (October 10, 1873)," *JHI*, 34 (1973), 591-98, and Francis Oakley, *Omnipotence, Covenant, & Order* (Ithaca, 1984), ch. I, "Against the Stream: In Praise of Lovejoy," and P. and M. Kuntz (eds.), *The Great Chain of Being after Fifty Years* (New York, 1986). There is a recent French thesis by Gladys Gordon-Bournique, *Arthur O. Lovejoy et l'histoire des idées* (Paris-IV), kindly shown me by Philip Wiener. See also Columbia University, Dept. of Philosophy (ed.), *Studies in the History of Ideas,* 3 vols. (New York, 1918, 1925, 1935). Quinones (*Mapping Literary Modernism,* 15) calls Glanville's "climate of opinion" a Modernist phrase. Lovejoy and the "great chain" will be reconsidered by various scholars, including Daniel Wilson, Francis Oakley, and Edward Mahoney in the *JHI* (April 1987).

[21] *The History of Ideas* (New York, 1969), 3.

[22] Spitzer, "Geistesgeschichte vs the History of Ideas as Applied to Hitlerism," *JHI,*

For whatever reason, Lovejoy's original vision seems to have faded in recent decades, and it seems useless to deny that the "history of ideas" has cut channels rather narrower and less venturesome than those mapped out by Lovejoy. Certainly and conspicuously, it has become increasingly estranged from those three original fields of cultivation and colonization—history, literature, and philosophy—which Lovejoy called "the common seed-plot" of the history of ideas. Even in Lovejoy's day there was disciplinary opposition to his interdisciplinary program—historians who saw ideas (and especially "unit-ideas") as vaporous byproducts of an antecedent "material" reality, "new critics" who found history (and perhaps ideas, too) a threat to pure aesthetic judgment, and analytical philosophers who found it a threat to pure reason or various technical advances.[23] Over the past generation, however, such criticisms have become more subtle and perhaps more relevant. Vulgar Marxist conceptions of "superstructure" have been replaced by efforts at a "social history of ideas" (not to speak of speculative "psychohistorical" interpretations); the "new criticism" has been superseded by historically (even quantitatively) grounded textual and contextual methods and an awareness of the relativity of literary canons; and a rather naive scholastic view of the history of philosophy has been at least supplemented by perspectives that are at once more historical, more human, and more critical than, say, the approach of Etienne Gilson (not to speak of Bertrand Russell). Indeed questions essential to the history of ideas—and to the more general question of how we confront, make use of, or protect ourselves from our cultural heritage—have been posed by an emergent sub-sub-discipline called "the philosophy of the history of philosophy."

Once again a younger generation seems to be responding to the cry, "Make it new!" Much of the attendant criticism, of course, may be regarded as the noise of a new sophistry, again emanating from Paris— Abelard or Ramus redivivus—but historians of ideas may well attend to some of the implications, if not the conclusions, of this discourse. They should certainly have something to say about "the future of intellectual history," which was the title of a conference held at Cornell in 1980, and "new directions in American intellectual history," another conference at Wingspread in 1977.[24] At the Cornell conference in particular there

---

5 (1944), 191, not too far removed in spirit, perhaps, from more recent criticisms of Foucault and Derrida. Cf. Harry Levin's review of Lovejoy's *Essays* in *Grounds for Criticism* (Cambridge, Mass., 1972), 131.

[23] See, e.g., Charles Trinkaus and others in *Science and Society*, 1 (1936), 410ff.

[24] Dominick LaCapra and Stephen Kaplan (eds.), *Modern European Intellectual History, Reappraisals and New Perspectives* (Ithaca, 1982), and see the reviews by William Bouwsma in *History and Theory*, 23 (1984), 229-36, and Michael Ermath, "Mindful Matters: The Empire's New Codes and the Plight of Modern European Intellectual History," *Journal of Modern History*, 57 (1985), 506-27; also LaCapra, *Rethinking Intellectual History* (Ithaca, 1983), and the review-essay of Anthony Pagden forthcoming

was much prating of "method," new-fangled ways of reading texts, and some "rayling" against the fathers of intellectual history; but however "hare brayne" this youthful dialogue might be judged, it has served at least to disturb the dogmatic slumber into which some historians of ideas have fallen.

With this in mind, I turn from a retrospective to a circumspective view of intellectual history and some of the new waves (if not old backwashes) which have appeared on its horizons. My intention is not to venture into philosophical criticism but only to suggest productive strategies for the theory and more especially the practice of intellectual history. My hope is not in any startling way to "make it new" but only (recalling the words attributed by John of Salisbury to Bernard of Clairvaux) to try, in small ways, "to see more and further" than our teachers.

Circumspect. "Hermes ... is an interpreter [*hermēneus*] and a messenger," Plato has Socrates say in the *Cratylus*; "[he] is wily and deceptive in speech and in oratorical."[25] This etymological canard stands for all of the contempt with which, over the centuries, philosophical idealism (and medieval realism) has shown for rhetoric and often philology. But interpretation, as Harold Bloom says, must on principle be a "misreading," translation must be inadequate, and human expression must usually be content with mere opinion. Any attempt to "rethink intellectual history" must begin with this sort of Socratic doubt—and hermeneutical caution—in mind.

One of the central features of twentieth-century thought (shades of Ramus!) has been the famous "linguistic turn," which in effect aims at the recovery of the rhetorical dimension of ideas. "To think everything through once again in terms of linguistics!" marvelled Frederic Jameson.[26] Yet this sort of "turn" is hardly novel in a general sense, and indeed it has attracted many critics of conventional "philosophy" over the centuries, from Ockham to Valla and from Ramus to Vico. It has also been virtually axiomatic in recent efforts to reevaluate intellectual history; and here it is that literary criticism has had a shaping effect, especially through

---

in *JHI*. Less venturesome are the discussions in J. Higham and P. Conkin (eds.), *New Directions in American Intellectual History* (Baltimore, 1979).

[25] *Cratylus*, 408. Harold Bloom, *A Map of Misreading* (Oxford, 1975).

[26] *The Prison-House of Language*, vii. Cf. Richard Rorty (ed.), *The Linguistic Turn* (Oxford, 1967); cf. Ian Hacking, *Why Does Language Matter to Philosophy?* (Cambridge, 1975), and Manfred Frank, *Was Ist Neostrukturalismus?* (Frankfurt, 1984). Most influential here, perhaps, have been the views of Benjamin Whorf, as, e.g., in *Language, Thought, and Reality* (New York, 1959), and Emile Benveniste, e.g., *Le Vocabulaire des institutions indo-européennes* (Paris, 1969). The "linguistic turn" has even reached *History Workshop*, 10 (1980), 1-5, "Language and History," as well as British Marxism, as in Raymond Williams, *Keywords* (London, 1983), and G. Stedman Jones, *Language and Class Studies in English Working Class History, 1832-1982* (Cambridge, 1983).

its promotion of what, without differentiation, I call "textualism," a modern and radicalized form of the old literal or "historical" interpretation which in effect sets concrete "discourse" above transcendent "ideas."

In recent years textualism has burst its literary bonds. Through the efforts of Ricoeur and Derrida in particular, it has been imported, or smuggled, into philosophy itself; and (along with its even less elegant companion "narratology") it has been championed by a number of unorthodox intellectual historians, most notably Hayden White, the consubstantial presence at the Cornell conference.[27] In some ways the "metahistorical" reach, as well as the historical grasp, of White and such like-minded younger scholars as Dominick La Capra and Martin Jay may seem tangential to the history of ideas; and yet some of their critical and methodological views, and more especially their foreign sources of inspiration, may deserve more attention than they have received from historians of ideas.

What is the significance of the "linguistic turn" for the history of ideas? In important ways, as Gadamer suggests at the outset of his *Wahrheit und Methode*, this *Kehre* reflects a return to the tradition of Renaissance humanism (for him, if not for his former teacher Heidegger). In this connection we might recall not only Ramus's complaints about the *mentitia* of Aristotelians but also Vico's attack on Cartesianism and Herder's "Metacritique of Kant's critique of pure reason," which argued that the proper object of criticism is human and not abstract reason and that the mind operates through words (*die menschliche Seele denkt mit Wörten*).[28] We might think of the philological studies of Auerbach, Curtius, and Spitzer—whose "philological circle," in its aim of recapturing "meaning," resembles the more famous "hermeneutical circle" of Heidegger and Gadamer.[29] Perhaps the most determined conventional effort of language-centered intellectual history is the omnivorous survey of the "human sciences" by Georges Gusdorf, who is still in the process of telling the epic story of the modern "encyclopedia" of arts and sciences.[30]

---

[27] *Metahistory* (Baltimore, 1973), and see the comments of LaCapra, *Rethinking Intellectual History*, 72ff.

[28] Herder, *Metakritik*, in *Samtliche Werke*, XXXVII (Stuttgart, 1853), 17. Hamann also wrote a "Metakritik," published later, on which see James H. Stam, "Perspectives on 'Linguistic relativity,' " in *Psychology of Language and Thought*, ed. R. W. Rieber (New York, 1980), 254. For the background of this view in Condillac and others see Hans Aarsleff, *From Locke to Saussure* (Minneapolis, 1982).

[29] Spitzer, *Linguistics and Literary History* (Princeton, 1948), 28. For Cassirer, *The Philosophy of Symbolic Forms*, tr. R. Manheim (New Haven, 1953) I (*Language*), 80, "the critique of reason becomes the critique of culture."

[30] *Les Sciences humaines et la pensée occidentale* (Paris, 1966-), a work that arose from Gusdorf's own linguistic turn, as suggested in his earlier manifesto, criticizing Levi-Strauss and Foucault, *Introduction aux sciences humaines* (Paris, 1960; 2nd ed. 1972), vi: "L'homme ne peut etre compris qu'en langage humain." Remarks Friedrich Heer,

In any case the road "on the way to language" (in Heidegger's phrase) passes through scenes largely unfamiliar to classical philosophy. Its point of departure is not natural science but rather history and hermeneutics, not the universalizing language philosophy of Russell and the early Wittgenstein (now discredited even within the tradition of logic, at least implicitly, by Kurt Gödel's incompleteness theorems) but from the renewal of philosophical interest in the human sciences by the likes of Cassirer, with his philosophy of symbolic forms, and of Dilthey, with his proposed "critique of historical reason."[31] More remotely, it may be traced back not to the heritage of Cartesian metaphysics or Leibniz's "universal characteristic" but rather to that of Vico's "new science," itself rooted in philology, rhetoric, and law, and devoted, in one of its aspects, precisely to "the history of human ideas" (*storia dell'umane idee*). Indeed, this phrase was probably first coined by Vico, who adapted it from a work by J. Brucker, though the latter had applied it more strictly to Platonic "ideas." But already in Vico there was a sort of deliberate "turn" away from the Platonic tradition back to the practical wisdom and social concerns associated with sophism.

Philosophical hermeneutics, especially in the wake of Heidegger, has radicalized this inclination—has completed this *Kehre*—by arguing that, not forms of reason or a world of phenomenology (not, that is, "ideas") but linguisticality (*Sprachlichkeit*) constitutes the fundamental condition of thought and existence, language the very "house of being." To express the logocentric, even mythopoeic, character of existence, Heidegger quotes the last lines of Stefan George's poem *Das Wort*:

> So lernt ich traurig den verzicht:
> Kein ding sei wo das wort gebricht.[32]
> (And so I sadly came to see:
> Without the word no thing can be.)

Or as Gadamer has put it, "Being that can be understood is language." If existence precedes essence, neither has "meaning" outside the human condition as defined by the medium of language.

These are some of the considerations underlying the intriguing question recently posed by Martin Jay: "Should intellectual history take a linguistic turn?"[33] The question is not trivial (except in an etymological

---

The Intellectual History of Europe, tr. J. Steinberg (London, 1966), 474: "All intellectual discussions in our time are struggles for language."

[31] See Michael Ermath, *Wilhelm Dilthey: The Critique of Historical Reason* (Chicago, 1978), Rudolf Makkreel, *Dilthey: Philosopher of the Human Studies* (Princeton, 1975), and Michael J. Mooney, *Vico in the Tradition of Rhetoric* (Princeton, 1984). Cf. Vico, *Scienza nuova*, #347, citing Brucker, *Historia doctrinae de ideis* (1723).

[32] Heidegger, *On the Way to Language*, tr. Peter D. Hertz (New York, 1982), 139-56; and cf. Gadamer, *Philosophical Hermeneutics*, tr. D. Linge (Berkeley, 1976), 31.

[33] In LaCapra and Kaplan, *Modern European Intellectual History*, 86-110.

sense). Important as the old philological tradition was for Lovejoy, the history of ideas in his formulation was tied to a kind of philosophical realism—ideas being the ghost in the machine of language—and from the point of view of hermeneutics it has remained in this precritical position.

Here a bit of historical perspective may again be in order. Ever since Kant the aim of philosophers has been to find a truly "critical" position, an Archimedean point, from which to view, to judge, and perhaps to move the world; and following Dilthey's lead, philosophical hermeneutics has tried in effect to take this enterprise one step further (a neo-neo-Kantian critique?). This time the target of criticism has been "consciousness" itself, especially as preserved in "neo-critical" (neo-Kantian and neo-Hegelian) and phenomenological thought, including the sort of realism expressed by Lovejoy ("critical realism" was his term).[34] What confronts us, in other words, is a new "Copernican revolution": not only the *Ding an sich* but also the *Geist an sich* is put in question and made forever inaccessible to critical examination, even through psychoanalysis (which may be seen, as in the work of Ricoeur, as a kind of neo-Romantic or neo-idealist hermeneutics which has not quite completed the "linguistic turn"). The lesson is, as Gadamer puts it, that we can never "get behind the back of language."[35]

One of the first and most crucial issues—the thin edge of the textualist wedge—is that of intentionality (in a literary not a phenomenological sense). For over half a century literary critics have been discussing the "intentional [or intentionalist] fallacy," which proposes to fix precisely the original meaning of an author and which insists that this is the primary task of the critic.[36] Classically, this is expressed in the hermeneutical aim of determining the *mens auctoris* (in the parallel legal tradition, the *mens legum*, identified with the will of the legislator)—not the mind but the meaning, and in this sense the *Geist*, of the author or authority. More recently, this critical convention has appeared (for example) in Quentin Skinner's conception of social explanation and in the "recognitive interpretation" which E. D. Hirsch has opposed to relativism, historicism, and other reprehensible manifestations of what he has called "cognitive atheism."[37] By contrast literary critics seem, by and large, to have accepted the implications of Harold Bloom's view of interpretation as a "map of misreading" (rather than a retrospective act of mind-reading). Although modern critics have done this for their own imperialistic pur-

[34] Wilson, *Arthur O. Lovejoy*, 94.

[35] Gadamer, *Philosophical Hermeneutics*, 35. Ricoeur, *Freud and Philosophy: An Essay on Interpretation*, tr. D. Savage (New Haven, 1970).

[36] W. K. Wimsatt, Jr., *The Verbal Icon* (Louisville, Ky., 1954), 37, and many later commentaries.

[37] E. D. Hirsch, *The Aims of Interpretation* (Chicago, 1976), 13; and Skinner, "Meaning and Understanding in the History of Ideas," *History and Theory*, 8 (1969), 3-53.

poses (to challenge the sovereignty of the author), the philosophical arguments for what Ricoeur has called the "semantic autonomy of the text" are persuasive, especially for historians of ideas; and they constitute both a limitation on and a challenge to the writing of intellectual history.[38]

If we cannot "get behind the back of language," what can we get from its surface? Gadamer begins by assuming the primacy of *Sprachlichkeit* as the inescapable medium of historical understanding as well as communication; and of textual interpretation in particular he requires a double focus—that is, an appreciation of at least two different cultural contexts. In order to understand—to find meaning or give meaning to— the expression of ideas over an expanse of time (and/or cultural boundaries), there must be, in Gadamer's term, a "fusion of horizons" (*Horizontverschmelzung*), a metaphorical meeting of minds through the changing (but interconnecting rather than interfering) medium of language, if not, to compound the problem, through translation.[39] The Italian proverb to the contrary notwithstanding (*traduttore traditore*), translation—the *interpretatio* of classical and scholastic tradition—is not betrayal or "intentional" misreading (for this too can be a fallacy); it is, or it should be, the very paradigm of historical interpretation and extricating bygone thoughts and cultural remains from texts.

What are the conditions of this meeting of minds (or possibility of translation)? To suggest one of them Gadamer, again following Heidegger, has tried to rehabilitate the concept of "prejudice," in the sense—not of partisanship, which was the Enlightenment's "prejudiced" misreading of "prejudice" but—of a shared or "fore-structure of knowledge" that forms the basis of an intellectual and linguistic continuum or tradition.[40] Cartesian doubt affected in the most fundamental way to cut off not only this tradition but also (if it was to be consistent) human language as well (as Vico for one well understood and protested). Yet language can and must accommodate a meaningful dialogue with the past (as Gadamer argues and Descartes surreptitiously admits), and only a naive and precritical intentionalism will deplore such dialogue as a series of unfortunate "mis-

---

[38] Ricoeur, *Interpretation Theory* (Ft. Worth, 1976), 25.

[39] Gadamer, *Truth and Method*, tr. G. Barden and J. Cumming (New York, 1975), 273ff. The relevance of Gadamer here is not his philosophical claims about the "universality of the hermeneutical problem" but rather the inference that hermeneutics as he views it affords the most comprehensive theory of the history of ideas—of "what we are writing the history of"—or at least access to such a theory. No less significant, though less appreciated, is Emilio Betti, on whom see my "Hermes, Clio, Themis," in *Journal of Modern History*, 55, (1983), 644-68, repr. in *History, Law, and the Human Sciences* (London, 1984).

[40] Gadamer, *Truth and Method*, 235, and Heidegger, *Being and Time*, tr. J. Macquarrie and E. Robinson (New York, 1962), 191. And cf. Ernst Behler, "What It Means to Understand an Author Better than He Understands Himself," in Joseph P. Strelka (ed.), *Literary Theory and Criticism, Festschrift in Honor of René Wellek* (New York, 1985), I, 69-92.

readings" or will hope to rise above all "anachronism" (a concept which is also perhaps in need of a certain reevaluation). Existentially, there can be no "intersubjectivity" beyond language in some sense—or if there is, we must be silent about it. What is left is interpretation: the practical and localized effort to gain that measure of understanding circumscribed by the "hermeneutical circle."

The case of Ramus reminds us that such a potentially humanistic and historical orientation may itself become de-"humanized"—universalized, schematized, scholasticized—and such indeed has been the tendency of Derrida and especially certain American "Derrideans," who, in quest of a higher (and a newer) "criticism," have created a new fetishism of texts, and potentially a new mandarinate or rabbinate of criticism.[41] Irreversibly, Derrida has shifted emphasis from linguisticality to scripticality (from *Sprachlichkeit* to *Schriftlichkeit*), making writing or inscription the last battleground, or intelligible field of study, of the human sciences. For Gadamer's "nothing behind the back of language" Derrida substitutes his "nothing outside the text" (*il n'y a pas de hors-texte*). As Ramus had tried to replace a philosophical with a rhetorical method, so Derrida extracts from a still lower level of the trivium a method which he calls "grammatology," which aims a death blow to the writing as well as the thinking subject. So the Cartesian *Cogito*, which is deprived of memory, is supplanted by the Derridean *Scriptum*, which is deprived of its author. Cut off both from reality and from itself, consciousness is condemned not only to the "prison-house of language" (in Jameson's phrase) but even to the cemetery of the written, and especially the printed, text—which will be guarded over, of course, by the Grammatologist and the Deconstructor.

Philosophically, to put the best construction on it, "deconstruction" may be seen as the last "decentering" of humanity: what Copernicus did in terms of astronomy, Darwin of biology, and Freud of psychology, Derrida claims to do, paradoxically, in terms of language. To paraphrase Marx, we might conclude that man (with woman) makes language—but not in the way that he (she) intends. So it may be, too, with "ideas."

A parallel and overlapping line of criticism over the past century has been the series of "obituaries" which have appeared since the time of Nietzsche—the "death" first of God, then of "thinking subject," so of course of the author, and for Foucault "Man" himself—in short all of the underpinnings of "ideas" as classically understood. And this line of

---

[41] Derrida, *Of Grammatology*, tr. G. Spivak (Baltimore, 1974); cf. Susan Handelman, *The Slayers of Moses* (Albany, N.Y., 1982). LaCapra, an American "Derridean," also distinguishes writings treated as "documents" from those treated as "works" (by definition aesthetically superior), and his focus on the latter has in effect carried him into what used to be thought of as the history of literature, or of criticism, and has tended to make him a victim of the jargon and confusion of tongues (as it may seem to philosophers as well as historians) characteristic of some practitioners of post-structuralist criticism.

criticism can be understood, in turn, as part of another series of attacks on the "self," including those of Hegel against Kant, and Marx against Hegel. It has been continued in a rather different way by structuralism, for as Paul De Man puts it, "Levi-Strauss had to give up the notion of subject to safe-guard reason."[42] Yet if the "I" and the "ego" may be banished from thought, they—"we"—can hardly be extricated from language and dialogue, despite such efforts of (dei- and) sui-cide. Language, western language anyway, is bound irreversibly to subjectivity and intentionality, and so must set limits on skepticism, which is itself a form of subjective discourse that may provoke doubts.

Inevitably, there is a political dimension of this French extension of what, since Nietzsche, has been a basically German line of criticism.[43] For what Foucault has called the "sovereign subject" not only establishes a conventional source of predication but also conceals a form of "social domination"; and it—classically "he"—is an expression of authority, or unconscious conformity to authority, as well as authorship. To return to the parallel with the earlier "prophet of Paris," just as Ramus's attack on Aristotelian authority concealed an attack on Roman Catholic orthodoxy, so Foucault's opposition to rational, "logo-centric" discourse carries with it an assault on the ideological interests underlying this discourse. For him language is not merely a structure transcending the individual, it is a social construct imposing control on the thinking (and especially writing) subject, signifying patterns even more of power than of "ideas."[44] For Foucault one of the casualties of this Marxoid (and Nietzschean) critique is the comforting notion of the continuity and persistence of ideas—conventional "historicism"—which the self-conscious and self-controlling subject has seemed to guarantee at least since Kant, if not since Descartes.

It is easy to criticize such criticism (for how can there be "power," or indeed communication, without freedom and subjectivity?—all of which, as Charles Taylor has remarked, belong to the same "semantic

[42] *Blindness and Insight, Essays in the Rhetoric of Contemporary Criticism* (New York, 1983; 2nd ed.), 18. See also David Quint, *Origin and Originality in Renaissance Literature* (New Haven, 1983), and Thomas M. Greene, *The Light in Troy* (New Haven, 1982). A recent illustration of the application of literary criticism to historical scholarship is Sande Cohen's semiotic critique, *Historical Culture* (Berkeley, 1986).

[43] See especially Allan Megill, *Prophets of Extremity: Nietzsche, Heidegger, Foucault, Derrida* (Berkeley, 1985).

[44] A good recent exposition is Mark Cousins and Athar Hussein, *Michel Foucault* (London, 1984); see also Mark Poster, *Foucault, Marxism, and History* (Cambridge, 1984), and Hubert Dreyfus, "Beyond Hermeneutics: Interpretation in the late Heidegger and the Recent Foucault," *Hermeneutics: Questions and Prospects*, ed. G. Shapiro and A. Sica (Amherst, 1984), 66-83, among many. On the reception of Foucault in this country see Allan Megill, above pp. 117-41.

field").[45] But in any case the primary aim of these deconstructive and "archeological" strategies is no doubt to shift the control over meaning from the original author to the theoretically better equipped interpreter, and certainly the acquisition of such critical license (and authorial power) must appeal to aspiring young intellectual historians as well as literary critics. In pursuit of deeper and deeper meaning there is obviously a problem of infinite regress, since the "semantic autonomy of the text" and the ideological forces of language obviously apply to the interpreter as well as to the author, to the historian as well as to his source.

Construction, reconstruction, deconstruction: such is the logic of textualism—and so, we may infer, intellectual sovereignty (the ultimate critical stance) passes from author to text to historian to critic (to revisionist historian and to "new critic" . . . etc)—and so from ancient to modern to "post-modern." For intellectual historians the aim is, by suppressing or bypassing the (thinking, writing) subject, including the voice of authorial will, to gain access to the metalinguistic and metahistorical patterns of social intercourse and conflict—to find the critical, Archimedean point which philosophers have sought for centuries. What Foucault has called the "will to knowledge" (though ultimately this is not Nietzschean or even Baconian but Aristotelian) has always hoped to "demystify" the products of human consciousness—to tear away the last mask with which culture, ideology, and language cover the naked truth of nature, or of power.

This is more than a noble dream; it is an impossible dream. Gadamer would perhaps reject the effort as another attempt to "circumvent language," McLuhan regard it as a classic example (after Ramus) of the permeation of print culture, Vico see it as another "learned conceit," Valla scorn it as one more scholastic fiction, Fraunce deplore it as more vain prating of method and rayling against the forefathers, and Lovejoy would no doubt dismiss it as another attempt to suppress the dualist condition of human knowledge. For there is no point "beyond criticism." Like consciousness itself (the *Geist an sich*) the "meaning" of a text, beyond particular constructions (or reconstructions or deconstructions) must remain inaccessible, or at least unutterable. It is like the Spitzer's "philological circle," or perhaps like the Nicolas of Cusa's infinite-sided polygon, always short of perfection and always beyond any exhaustive human formulation—and indeed are the "ideas" of which we aspire to write "the history."

How, under these conditions, can the "history of ideas" American style move—indeed, how is it moving—into the last years of the twentieth century and, one hopes, beyond? With this question I turn from this

---

[45] Charles Taylor, *Philosophy and the Human Sciences* (Cambridge, 1985), 175-84, and cf. Emile Benveniste, "De la subjectivité dans le langage," *Problèmes de linguistique générale* (Paris, 1966), 258-66.

brief and selective circumspectus of contemporary thinkers and rethink-
ers, dwarfs though they may be, to an equally brief and still more selective
prospectus of the field and its conceptual limitations and possibilities in
the 1980s.

Prospect. In the past generation or more the horizons of intellectual
history have been opened up in several directions. Attention has shifted
not only from thought to "discourse" but also, in a number of ways,
from the conscious to the unconscious, from creation to imitation, from
intention to meaning, from authorship to readership, from the history of
ideas to the "social history of ideas," from science to the occult, from
tradition to "canon formation," and from the sociology of knowledge
(included in Lovejoy's original prospectus) to what Apel has called the
"anthropology of knowledge."[46] The novelty of such shifts may be debated, but the issues do suggest possible advances in critical understanding
(the Demon of Progress still haunts us). In any case, if we are at all
interested in "rethinking" intellectual history, we ought to be at least as
open to the horizons of the future as Lovejoy was a half-century and
more ago in his own interdisciplinary agenda. In order to suggest some
of the current prospects for intellectual history, let us return to the
complex of traditional fields out of which the history of ideas emerged
in the first place.

Recently, philosophers have taken a renewed and critical interest in
the past of their discipline and have posed a number of significant questions for intellectual history. Should historians of philosophy be mere
doxographers or hagiographers, asks Richard Rorty, or should they be
intellectual historians and critics? These questions are tied to the Kuhnian
proposal for a "role for history." Perennially, philosophy needs what
Charles Taylor calls a "creative redescription"—even if only, perhaps,
to wipe the conceptual slate clean and "make it new."[47] Borrowing from
literary criticism, Rorty examines philosophical "canon-formation,"
which aims at self-justification and excluding this or that text from the
apostolic succession of authorities, and consigning it to what Habermas
has called "abandoned stages of reflection."[48] Yet the effort of historical
understanding must also be pursued, and in "rethinking" the history of
thought, we need to confront again the old dilemma posed in a new form
by hermeneutics—how to reconcile efforts of purely historical reconstruction with current "projects" of philosophy, literature, criticism, and
the human and natural sciences. (And we are surely deluding ourselves
if we think the two can be separated.)

[46] Apel, *Transformation der Philosophie*, I, 35.
[47] *Philosophy and History*, ed. Rorty, et al., 19.
[48] *Ibid.*, 56. Thomas McCarthy, *The Critical Theory of Jurgen Habermas* (Cambridge,
Mass., 1982), 55. The classic treatment of "canon-formation" is Ernst Curtius, *European
Literature and the Latin Middle Ages*, tr. W. Trask (Princeton, 1953), 256.

Among the most impressive recent efforts to rethink intellectual history has been the project of Hans Blumenberg, who has devoted himself to the critique of what is perhaps the central "prejudice" of modernism— that is, the thesis of "secularism," or secularizing Progress through the replacement of myth by enlightenment.[49] As Gadamer confronted the persistence of "prejudice" in the human linguistic condition, so Blumenberg has tried to demonstrate the persistence of myth, including the myth of the "end of myth," which modern historians accept, or write as if they accept; and he goes on to question the idea that myth is somehow a product of "tradition," arguing rather that it is the product of unintended historical selection—a "Darwinism of words," which like language itself is beyond human control. In general Blumenberg himself has avoided the linguistic turn and writes in a theological mode. Yet he has offered provocative insights into the problem of conceptual change and suggestions for the "project" of the history of ideas.

Within the history of science there is still a lively debate over questions of conceptual change (though not necessarily in the "revolutionary" terms of Kuhn's "paradigm"), of "internalist" versus "externalist" approaches, and of the significance of what we must retrospectively judge to be pseudoscience and blind alleys of naturalistic as well as supernaturalistic investigation. Beyond these perennial issues, what has been called "post-empiricist philosophy and history of science" has opened up questions not only of individual originality, influence, and the "logic of scientific discovery," but also of styles of research, the function of "prejudice," intellectual consensus, and the nature of scientific communities; in some cases it has made its own "linguistic turn" by examining the "rhetoric" of scientific explanation and legitimation; and in a variety of ways it has come to provide the model for the historical interpretation of many other disciplines, humanistic as well as scientific.[50]

In the history of political and social science the lines of investigation have come increasingly to converge on the question of language and various issues shared with literary criticism, especially intentionality and canon-formation. According to Quentin Skinner, some notion of intentionalism or authorial responsibility is essential to any interpretation of texts that aspires to be historical. J. G. A. Pocock has projected the problem of political languages over a larger sweep, and in particular he follows, and celebrates, what he calls the "paradigmatic language" of

[49] *The Legitimacy of the Modern Age*, tr. Robert M. Wallace (Cambridge, 1983), and *Work on Myth*, tr. Wallace (Cambridge, 1985), and William Bouwsma, "Work on Blumenberg," forthcoming in *JHI* (Apr. 1987), and see also the discussion of the "new mythology" by Manfred Frank, *Der kommende Gott* (Frankfurt, 1982), 59ff.

[50] Bernstein, *Beyond Objectivism and Relativism*, 22, citing Mary Hess; also Timothy Reiss, *The Discourse of Modernism* (Ithaca, 1982). An example of recent "rethinking" of this field is Nicolas Jardine, *The Birth of History and Philosophy of Science* (Cambridge, 1984).

"civic humanism" over a span of centuries and an itinerary trans-Atlantic, or planetary, in geographic scope.[51] Together they provide a useful commentary on the old question of whether *man spricht* or *Sprache spricht*. To put it briefly and for present purposes, authorial intention connects text with historical context, while language, or a more particular political idiom, ties text to tradition, or canon. It is the interpretive task of the intellectual historian to read texts, if not to divine eternal "ideas," from both of these points of view—neither of which, we should add, is necessarily compatible with, or at least exhausted by, purely logical analysis.

In many ways "new literary history" has been carrying on re- and trans-valuations in terms of textualist methods, "imitation," canon-formation, "reception" of texts, strategies of persuasion, and other implicitly historical modes and manifestations of what has been called the "new historicism." The field of *Rezeptionsgeschichte*, which is an offshoot of modern philosophical hermeneutics, derives mainly from problems of aesthetics and the history of taste. If deconstruction marked the death of the author in literary criticism, reception theory marked the birth of the reader. Going beyond Gadamer's view of the "fusion of horizons" (too far beyond, Gadamer believes), Hans Robert Jauss and Wolfgang Iser have launched and sponsored inquiries into meanings provoked by works in readerships occupying various environments—and in effect to the role of "prejudice" in tradition. There are diachronic as well as synchronic features in textual meanings. "The repertory of a literary text does not consist solely of social and cultural norms," according to Iser; "it also incorporates elements and, indeed, whole traditions of literature that are mixed together with these norms"—and potentially shared, we might add, by the readership and *its* tradition.[52] This line of inquiry into "reader-response" obviously compounds problems of interpretation, his-

---

[51] Richard Bernstein, *The Restructuring of Social and Political Theory* (Philadelphia, 1978), and see Skinner's review in *New York Review of Books* (1979); also David Boucher, *Texts in Context: Revisionist Methods for Studying the History of Ideas* (Dordrecht, 1985), treating Greenleaf, Pocock, and Skinner; more generally Paul Rabinow and William Sullivan (eds.), *Interpretive Social Science* (Berkeley, 1979); also Keith Baker, "On the Problem of the Ideological Origins of the French Revolution," in La Capra and Kaplan (eds.), *Modern European Intellectual History*, 197ff. For indication of a "linguistic turn" in economics see Donald N. McCloskey, *The Rhetoric of Economics* (Madison, 1985). J. G. A. Pocock (whose own linguistic turn is evident especially in his *Politics, Language, and Time* [New York, 1973], reacting in part to Peter Laslett's famous obituary notice of political philosophy) will review some recent criticisms of his work in *JHI* in 1987.

[52] Jauss, *Aesthetic Experience and Literary Hermeneutics*, tr. M. Shaw and W. Godzich (Minneapolis, 1982), and *Toward an Aesthetic of Reception*, tr. T. Bahti (Minneapolis, 1982), and Iser, *The Act of Reading* (Baltimore, 1978); cf. Robert C. Holub, *Reception Theory*, and Robert Weimann, " 'Reception Aesthetics' and the Crisis in Literary History," *Clio*, 5 (1975), 3-35, and J. Bleicher, *The Hermeneutical Imagination* (London, 1982). Among the relevant and significant journals in English one should mention *Critical Inquiry, New German Critique, New Literary History, Representations,* and *Philosophy Today.*

torical as well as aesthetic, but it also contributes to the historian's aim of joining text and context and of determining cultural meaning.

As for history, the older "new histories" have themselves been generally superseded by methodological *gardes* still more *avants*. Recently, the "new social history" has addressed itself to various questions pertaining to the history of ideas, including oral, scribal, and print media, literacy, popular and elite cultures.[53] Quantitative historical methods have also been applied successfully to the study of texts, especially by determining word frequency, associations, gender preference, literary context, and other features of writing formerly treated by stylistics. This sort of lexicographical investigation lies at the foundations of two recent enterprises closely related to the history of ideas—and indeed to the "social history of ideas"—the Italian *Lexicon Philosophicum* and the German *Archiv für Begriffsgeschichte*, both with a variety of supplementary theoretical, monographic, and reference publications.[54]

Much of this scholarship has no doubt arisen from impulses outside the sphere of history proper, but (recalling Martin Jay's question) it might be inferred that intellectual history has in fact been taking a linguistic turn. The same may be said, perhaps, of the recent commotion around "the new historicism" (and its British counterpart, "cultural materialism"), which has rediscovered the historical nature of mankind and the ideological aspects of its literary activity.[55] In quantity at least, the production of this movement has been impressive. Yet, ironically, it

[53] On oral and pre-literate culture see (besides various works by Walter Ong) Eric A. Havelock, *The Muse Learns to Write* (New Haven, 1986), Brian Stock, *The Implications of Literacy* (Princeton, 1983), and *New Literary History*, 16 (1984), "Oral and Written Tradition in the Middle Ages"; also M. T. Clanchy, *From Memory to Written Record* (London, 1979).

[54] See especially Reinhart Koselleck, *Futures Past*, tr. Keith Tribe (Cambridge, 1985), and Koselleck (ed.), *Historische Semantik* (Stuttgart, 1979), publications correlative to *Archiv für Begriffsgeschichte* and the handbooks of political and social language, *Geschichtliche Grundbegriffe. Historisches Lexikon zur politisch-sozialen Sprache in Deutschland* (5 vols.; Stuttgart, 1972-) and *Handbuch politisch-socialer Grundbegriffe in Frankreich, 1660-1820* (Munich, 1985-); also Gadamer, *Die Begriffsgeschichte und die Sprache der Philosophie* (Opladen, 1971); Erwin Holzle, *Idee und Ideologie* (Berlin, 1969); I. Veit-Brause, "A Note on *Begriffsgeschichte*," *History and Theory*, 20 (1981), 61-67. The work of Koselleck will be reviewed by Melvin Richter in *JHI* (Apr. 1987).

The *Lexicon Philosophicum*, I (1985-) is related to an important series of publications entitled *Lessico Intellectuale Europeo*, which includes colloquies on such terms as *res* and *spiritus*, vols. 26 (1982) and 32 (1984), as well as a concordance to Vico's *Scienza nuova* and other valuable monographs.

[55] Reviews of this phenomenon include Jonathan Goldberg in *English Literary History*, 49 (1982), 514-82, and *Studies in English Literature*, 24 (1984), 57-91; Louis Montrose and Jean E. Howard in *English Literary Renaissance*, 16 (1986), 5-12, 13-43; Kevin Sharpe in *History*, 71 (1986); and David Sacks, forthcoming in *Journal of British Studies* (1987). The phrase "new historicism" is commonly credited to Stephen Greenblatt, *Power of Forms in the English Renaissance* (New York, 1980), 5, but this unfairly—and unhistorically!—slights Wesley Morris, *Toward a New Historicism* (Princeton, 1972).

appears to be curiously lacking in historical perspective in its self-advertizing insistence on its "newness," in its fascination with only the latest historiographical and literary fashions, and in its preservation, in many cases, of what may be regarded as a "correspondence theory" of relations between literature and social context, in which one more or less directly "reflects" the other.

What of other interdisciplinary prospects? "Psychohistory," which is perhaps the ultimate attempt to understand the genesis of ideas, has won little respect among intellectual (or any other sort of) historians. Yet the goals of such an approach are not necessarily irreconcilable with more conventional kinds of intellectual history and textual criticism. For Peter Gay (though he seems to have missed the linguistic turn that Lacan, for example, has made within the Freudian school), psychohistory is more than the imposition of a dogma; it is an "informed style of inquiry" seeking access to the private world, though it reaches out to society and to "group behavior" as well.[56] A number of western intellectuals—Augustine, Petrarch, Erasmus, Luther, Bodin, Campanella, Newton, Descartes, Vico, Rousseau, Goethe, Mill, Emerson, Nietzsche, Wittgenstein, Collingwood—have cried out, posthumously, for psychological analysis; and indeed a few have received such treatment, to the (at least marginal) benefit of historical understanding. Posthumous therapy may be impossible and behaviorist reductionism undesirable, but psycholinguistic analysis of texts may tell us much that authors perhaps never "intended" to reveal, including those "endemic assumptions" referred to by Lovejoy. In general historians may profitably look to the sort of psychohistory which aims not at reduction or "demystification" (according to Ricoeur's distinction) but at the recovery of meaning—not only at unmasking but also, or perhaps rather, at restoring ancient or alien masks.

To turn from the individual to the collective—from *parole* to *langue*, in structuralist terms—is to recall that "social history of ideas" which historians as diverse as Peter Gay and Robert Darnton have been talking about for over a decade and which has long represented a standing rebuke to Lovejoy's approach (as commonly read—or misread) to the history of ideas.[57] In this effort Marxism, chameleon-like as ever, continues to be significant, as in the eclectic work of Fredric Jameson, who calls for a return to historicism, and Terry Eagleton, who wants to restore ties between literary criticism and political consciousness. Feminism and "gender studies" have also tried to add a critical dimension, most notably by reevaluating the "patriarchical canon," the essentially male conception

[56] Gay, *Freud and the Historians* (New York, 1985); and see Gerald Izenberg, "Psychohistory and Intellectual History," *History and Theory*, 14 (1975), 139-55.

[57] Gay, "The Social History of Ideas: Ernst Cassirer and After," *The Critical Spirit: Essays in Honor of Herbert Marcuse* (Boston, 1967), 106-20, and Darnton, "In Search of Enlightenment," *Journal of Modern History*, 43 (1971), 113-32; but these scholars have moved on to other novelties.

of authorship prevailing in most disciplines, and more generally the relations between discourse and power.[58]

Social criticism has also tried to make a "linguistic turn," perhaps most conspicuously in the work of Apel and Habermas, who combine post-Marxist social analysis with hermeneutical philosophy. For Habermas discourse is viewed as a phenomenon of production and exchange, and it is analyzed through a critique of ideology and an "unmasking" of "interests." Habermas's *Knowledge and Human Interest* has been called "a history of ideas with systematic intent."[59] For historians, however, his contributions to "critical theory" seem increasingly more theoretical and less critical; and his objections to Gadamer suggest that he still aspires to a universalist system of social metaphysics, or metalinguistics, designed rather to answer old questions than to pose new ones, to close rather than to open windows. As Geertz has remarked, "The only thing that links Freud, Piaget, von Neumann and Chomsky (to say nothing of Jung and B. F. Skinner) is the conviction that the mechanics of human thinking is invariable across time, space, culture, and circumstance, and that they know what it is."[60] Habermas also thinks he knows what it is, or at least that he will soon come upon it, that he has found the Archimedean point in a "theory of communicative action."

Another recently influential deviation from Marxism appears in the recently retrieved work of Mikhail Bakhtin. The major premise of Bakhtin, too, is the intractably social nature of language, which in fact he views as fundamentally "dialogical" in the sense that it is always implicitly a response to a previous statement and always presumes a listener as well as a speaker, an audience as well as an author, a social context as well as an intellectual tradition.[61] In contrast to Habermas, Bakhtin has taken care to tie language to the study of specific social and cultural forms, in particular the extra-literary (*volkisch*?) sources of literature, scanning as it were the sub- (rather than the super-) structure of society as reflected in popular language and culture. If Petrarch led the "chorus of muses," according to Bakhtin's "carnavalesque" updating of the old classical

---

[58] Examples include L. Clarke and S. Harding (eds.), *Discovering Reality: Feminist Perspectives on Epistemology, Metaphor, and Philosophy* (Boston, 1983); Elaine Marks and Isabelle de Courtivron (eds.), *New French Feminisms* (Amherst, 1980); Sandra M. Gilbert and Susan Gubar, *The Madwoman in the Attic* (New Haven, 1979); and *Rewriting the Renaissance*, ed. M. Ferguson, et al. (Chicago, 1986).

[59] McCarthy, *op. cit.*, 110; and see Habermas's most recent systematic effort, *The Theory of Communicative Action*, tr. T. McCarthy, I (Boston, 1981). Cf. Ricoeur, *Hermeneutics and the Human Sciences*, tr. J. Thompson (Cambridge, 1981), 63.

[60] *Local Knowledge* (New York, 1983), 150.

[61] *The Dialogical Imagination*, tr. C. Emerson and M. Holquist (Austin, 1981), *Rabelais and his World*, tr. H. Iswolsky (Cambridge, 1968), and *The Formal Method in Literary Scholarship*; see also Tzvetan Todorov, *Mikhail Bakhtin and the Dialogical Principle*, tr. W. Godzich (Minneapolis, 1984), and the exposition by Samuel Kinser in *Journal of Modern History*, 56 (1984), 301-10.

topos, it was Rabelais who led the "popular chorus" of the Renaissance. In his own way Bakhtin, too, has aimed at a "philosophical anthropology" as the basis for interpreting literary, and implicitly intellectual, history.

What this prospectus suggests seems hardly less eclectic than Love-joy's original agenda; and despite talk of "rethinking," I should not want to exaggerate claims to novelty or departures from that seminal vision. On the contrary, I have been emphasizing the traditionalism of many of these apparent novelties. Perhaps the best way to summarize these observations is to invoke (I hope not too fancifully) the old notion of "levels of meaning," adapted from the medieval conception of four-fold readings (literal, allegorical, moral and anagogical).[62] Literal interpretation (*gestas docet*), according to the old mnemonic verse, turns our eyes toward the past and concentrates on historical reconstruction, with due respect for authorial "intention" (unconscious as well as conscious), "climate of opinion," and the resources and limits of language as determined by contemporary sources. Allegorical interpretation (*quid credas*) would place texts in a longer intellectual continuum, through the common language and "prejudices" which permit historical understanding of changing meanings. Moral interpretation (*quid agas*) brings in the "ideological" dimensions of discourse, which suggests not reduction of ideas to another form of behavior but rather such features of "local knowledge" as appreciation of social context, the nature of intellectual communication, and the power relationships which this entails. Anagogical interpretation (*quid tendas*) finally, to have done with this conceit turns our attention toward the future and questions of general "significance," suggesting in various ways a "role for history" in the human sciences. But we must leave this question—as well as the future itself—open for further examination.

In general, to conclude this brief prospectus with a proper balance between the old and the new, let me suggest a number of conceptual conditions, premises or predilections, which historians of ideas are bound these days at least to notice. One is the relentless critique of metaphysics begun by Nietzsche and carried on by various readers and mis-readers, interpreters and traducers, of this bitterly critical, overreaching and undercutting view of philosophical tradition (which likewise had its roots in literary and indeed a sort of psychohistorical criticism).[63] Whether or

---

[62] Cf. Jameson, *The Political Unconscious*, 31; Abraham Edel, "Levels of Meaning and the History of Ideas," *JHI*, 7 (1946), 355-60; Henri Lubac, *Exégèse médiévale* (Paris, 1959-64); cf. LaCapra, *Rethinking Intellectual History*, 36ff., and especially Ricoeur, *Interpretation Theory*.

[63] Starting with David B. Allison (ed.), *The New Nietzsche* (New York, 1977); also Daniel J. O'Hara (ed.), *Why Nietzsche Now?* (Bloomington, Ind., 1985), on textualist and aesthetic aspects of Nietzsche and his current "uses." Contrast the effort of Patrick Madigan, *The Modern Project to Rigor* (Lanham, Md., 1986), to restore Nietzsche to the canon of critical philosophy.

not this threatens "the end of philosophy," for intellectual history it has encouraged a shift from the presumed life, or immortality, of ideas to the demonstrable persistence of texts, from spiritual and speculative traditions to concrete and humanly formulated canons. Not (to put it in more conventional terms) that philosophy would be subordinated to, but rather that it should be grounded in modern philology, and that the double focus of critical, hermeneutical, historical interpretation should be respected. What has been called "horizon-structure of experience" seems especially appropriate for the history of ideas.[64]

Another premise has to do with the challenges to natural-science models of interpretation—what Hans Blumenberg has called the "retraction of the Socratic turning" toward self-knowledge—which philosophers have brought forward, or resurrected, in recent years.[65] Charles Taylor, Richard Rorty, and Richard Bernstein have all endorsed a hermeneutical mode of understanding for the human sciences, and this seems even more essential for intellectual history. In conventional terms this implies that history—that is, memory—should be allied not merely with reason but also with imagination, that third faculty of mind so long eclipsed by the vulgar scientism often associated with Baconian as well as Cartesian method. This was the message of Vico, who joined memory and imagination not only, as was his wont, etymologically (*memorare = imaginare*)[66] but also methodologically, since it was the union of history and poetry that produced his "new science." This was the view also of Emilio Betti, for whom historical interpretation was simply the reverse of the creative process. Carried to extremes this may imply something like a "poetic for sociology" (in the phrase of Richard Brown) or (as in the vision of Heidegger) the tendency "to replace the scientist with the poet and the literary critic as the new cultural heroes."[67] For the history of ideas it simply suggests the sorts of imaginative reconstruction, creative anachronism, and "fusion of horizons" which, through the medium of language, produce not only "misreading" but also historical understanding.

Parallel and perhaps overlapping in its implications is another sort of "refiguration of social thought," which Geertz (the *genius loci* at Wingspread) calls "local knowledge." What Geertz defines as "cultural hermeneutics rather than conceptual mechanics," is also based on a kind of translation or text-analogy and an internal analysis of symbol systems, or rather how one system translates into another; and like hermeneutics

[64] Gunther Buck, "The Structure of Hermeneutical Experience and the Problem of Tradition," *New Literary History*, 10 (1978), 31-47.

[65] Blumenberg, *The Legitimacy of the Modern Age*, 243.

[66] Vico, "On the Ancient Wisdom of the Italians," *Selected Writings*, tr. Leon Pompa (Cambridge, 1982), 69.

[67] Brown, *A Poetic for Sociology* (Cambridge, 1977); and especially Heidegger, *Poetry, Language, Thought*, tr. A. Hofstadter (New York, 1971).

it follows a "horizon-structure" of experience, though of course it proposes to expand the horizon through explorations of the most alien of
cultural fields. The question posed by this "ethnography of thought"
include "how a Copernican understands a Ptolemaian, a fifth republic
Frenchman an *ancien régime* one," or perhaps (in a recent textualist view
of the scientific revolution) how modern scholars, trapped in the "discourse of modernism" with all the rationalist "prejudices" this entails,
can understand the pre-Copernican world we have lost.[68] What is needed
for such understanding is not a rigid *theoria* but a flexible *phronesis*—
not a universalizing yet reductionist sociology of knowledge but a local-
izing yet venturesome "anthropology of knowledge," which is at once a
more critical and culturally specific strategy, if not a method, for retriev-
ing "meaning" in its own (and our own) terms.

None of this, though it may suggest the end of "Modernism," bespeaks
"the decline of the new."[69] As in the sixteenth century the winds of
doctrine seem to be blowing furiously in several directions, toward several
horizons. Reactions vary. Some philosophers, literary critics, and historians turn away from older ways, achievements as well as errors, embrace continental fashions with enthusiasm; some seem fearful, resistant,
or merely scornful. Others set about reinventing the wheel, though as
usual under the banner of novelty. Historical experience suggests that all
these reactions may be exaggerated. Aristotle survived the challenge of
Ramus, after all, as Kant survived that of Herder; and so philosophy
itself seems likely to survive the assault of the neo-Nietzschean obituary-
writers, proclaiming the death of modernism as well as ancientism. And
the half-life of literary theories is surely less than an intellectual "generation."

As for "historicism," it has never really disappeared from the scene,
though like "naturalism" it has indeed passed through many stages. In
most quarters historicism has long since put aside the old values and
habits which had drawn the scorn of Nietzsche and brought about the
much publicized "crisis of historicism" of the earlier past of this century;
and it seems too soon to place it (along with consciousness and the self)
among the unliving or make it a candidate for disinterment.[70] In the

---

[68] Geertz, *Local Knowledge*, 150, and Reiss, *The Discourse of Modernism*.

[69] Irving Howe, *The Decline of the New* (New York, 1978), and above, n. 1.

[70] The literature is almost unmanageably vast; most recently, see Franco Bianco (ed.),
Il Dibatto sullo storicismo (Bologna, 1978), and *Storia e ermeneutica* (Rome, 1974). Years
ago I tried to suggest the importance of the literary view of "historicism" (*Foundations
of Modern Historical Scholarship* [New York, 1970], 4, 301), illustrated by the usage of
Auerbach, for example, instead of the doctrinaire conception derived from Meinecke and
unrecognizably distorted by Popper; and I still believe there is need for a general rubric
for attempts at historical investigation, interpretation, and conceptualization, a companion
term to "naturalism," shorn of ideological or methodological specificities and suggesting
the sort of practical impulse that leads the Marxist, or post-Marxist, critic Frederic

various turnings in the human sciences, in Cassirer's "philosophy of symbolic forms," in the awareness of what Heidegger calls the "underwayness" of human existence and the "horizon structure of experience," in the anthropological search for "local knowledge," and perhaps in the works of "new historicists" (the rhetoric of novelty is the one legacy of the past which seems absolutely inescapable), historicism may find new life and perhaps, in intellectual history, new possibilities of growth, though within the conditions of ancient scholarship and modern "criticism."

I do not want to end with a prescription for writing intellectual history or a "philosophy" of the history of ideas—especially since, strictly speaking, the "horizons" surveyed here are really just my own. The main thing for the history of ideas, nearing the century's end, is not to lose its moorings, in either its backward or its forward view. If we can criticize criticism, we can hardly undo it. We may lament but we can hardly escape the current climate of scholarly opinion and conceptual predicament produced by the "linguistic turn" and the critical perspectives it has brought. Intellectual history is the one area in which we may be permitted a long view. As Gadamer has observed, it is only "in the light of our futurity" that we can read the "great dark book" of history, "the collected work of the human spirit, written in the languages of the past."[71] What the history of ideas needs, it seems to me, is another hermeneutical "fusion of horizons"—in this case between the "great horizon of the past," which historians continue to scan, and that of the future, which a younger generation regards as its own. Not that we can hope to avoid the incessant quarrels between ancients and moderns, or between moderns and "post-moderns," but at least we might pursue the dialogue, the logomachy, on the same field of battle.

Better yet (to revert to the epigrams at the head of this essay) we might try to restore the old academic relationship between giants and dwarfs. Every generation has its own horizons, and defines them with claims of "newness" or "post-" previous stages; but this perspective may be extended, and claims to novelty moderated, by making use of previous wisdom (or avoiding previous unwisdom). Thereby, perhaps, we too may be able "to see more and farther" than our teachers, and so repay them, whom we would indeed serve badly, as Nietzsche taught, by being forever disciples.[72]

University of Rochester.

Jameson, to begin a recent book with the demand—not "Make it New!" but rather—"Always historicize!"

[71] Gadamer, *Truth and Method*, 156.

[72] For all sorts of advice and warnings I should thank, among others, Lewis Beck, Anthony Grafton, Quentin Skinner, Hans Aarsleff, Harry Levin, Melvin Richter, Michael Mooney, Anthony Padgen, Samuel Kinser, David Sacks, Bonnie Smith, the late Charles Schmitt, and especially Allan Megill.